CHARITY ENTREPRENEURSHIP

How to launch a
HIGH-IMPACT
NONPROFIT

Second edition

Published 2021

CHARITY ENTREPRENEURSHIP

How to launch a
HIGH-IMPACT
NONPROFIT

Second edition | Published 2021

www.charityentrepreneurship.com

Foreword by Peter Singer

"In books like *Animal Liberation*, *The Life You Can Save*, and *The Most Good You Can Do*, I have argued that we should aim to reduce avoidable suffering for every sentient being, and as far possible enable them to live the best life possible for them. Over the past decade I have been greatly encouraged by the many people who have made this one of their life-goals and decided to focus their donations, or planned their entire careers, so as to provide the most effective possible assistance to those most in need.

Charity Entrepreneurship was created by a group of young individuals who were inspired by my writings and those of others thinking along similar lines. They are eager to make the world better and to give others an opportunity to do the same. This book provides thoughtful, engaging, and very useful practical advice for aspiring entrepreneurs who want to start high-impact charities. All of this with one goal in mind: to do the most good we can."

- Peter Singer, Professor of Bioethics, Princeton University, author of *Animal Liberation* and *The Life You Can Save*.

Acknowledgments

If it takes a village to raise a child, it takes a community to write a book. We'd like to thank some of the numerous contributors who offered their time.

Everyone on the Charity Entrepreneurship team contributed directly or indirectly to making this vision a reality. In particular, we'd like to thank:

- Andrew Player, for authoring the bulk of our operations section and keeping our organization structured day to day.
- Ishaan Guptasarma, for major written contributions to many chapters, including the bulk of the cost-effectiveness and hiring sections.
- Ula Zarosa, for illustrations, cover design, and the visual communications section.
- Antonia Personette, Steve Thompson, and Mike Vance, for the final edits and attention to detail.
- Karolina Sarek, for contributions to our decision-making tools, co-founding the organization, and leading the research team that made CE possible.
- Vicky Cox, Sam Hilton, and Ashwin Mandakolathur Balu for their research to identify the great charity ideas that will be founded through CE.

Many interns, volunteers, former staff, and broader members of the CE community also made significant contributions.

- Peter Wildeford, Erik Hausen, Juliette Finetti, and Kat Woods, for written contributions.
- Peter Brietbart, Aaron Hamlin, Varsha Venugopal, Judith Rensing, Andres Jimenez Zorrilla, Cillian Crosson, and Dan Wahl, for comments, suggested improvements, and input on key concepts.
- Taylor Jones, Laura Tresch, John Fogle, Beatrice Erkers, and Katete Jackson Jones, for helping with the content and graphics.

Many of our incubated charities contributed comments and feedback, as well as their own "putting it into practice" stories. Thank you, Amy Odene, Anna Christina Thorsheim, Anne Wanlund, Clare Donaldson, Fiona Conlon, George Bridgwater, Haven King-Nobles, Jack Rafferty, Katriel Friedman, Kenneth Scheffler, Lucia Coulter, Michael Plant, Nikita Patel, and Thomas Billington, for your contributions.

Thank you all for your help and for the positive impact you have created for the world!

Preface: Saving a life

Arthur felt the smoke first; it stung his eyes and filled his lungs. As he turned the corner, a house on fire lit up the night. He saw bright flames through the windows and black smoke billowing from cracks in the walls. Hearing a scream from inside the house, Arthur didn't think twice. No one else was around and he knew he had to help.

Few people have saved someone's life. Those who have say it's a profound and surreal experience to know that a person would not be alive if not for your actions. And the impact doesn't stop there: from their friends and family to passing acquaintances, dozens of lives are affected.

You might get a single opportunity in your lifetime to save another individual, often at great personal risk, such as running into a burning building. Or you might take a job that gives more opportunities to help others, such as becoming a paramedic. However, few jobs give the opportunity to affect someone's life so drastically.

What about saving a life every day? This is a tier reserved for only the most talented scientists, the most well-known political activists… and the most successful charity founders. Just as many of the richest people on the planet are entrepreneurs in the for-profit world, many of the most impactful people are entrepreneurs in the nonprofit world. Successful business founders such as Elon Musk, Jeff Bezos, and Mark Zuckerberg are household names, but less well known are charity entrepreneurs Rob Mather, Elie Hassenfeld, and Esther Duflo, who have saved a life for every day they have lived.

Helping this many people is a task normally reserved for superhero movies. Yet this feat can be achieved with luck and a lot of hard work. This is the main reason to consider charity entrepreneurship as a career path. Charity entrepreneurs have made a massive difference to countless lives and tackled incredibly important problems that otherwise would have been forgotten.

If your idea is backed by strong research and a good set of decision-making tools, starting a high-impact nonprofit can be an achievable goal. For the right person, becoming the founder of a field-leading charity can be the greatest good you could achieve with your time.

This handbook is about how to become that founder.

Building a rocketship

Think of your organization as a rocketship. Each section of this book is modeled on a part of the ship, and all are essential for completing your journey. So you get to do a little rocket science on your way to founding a charity!

Launchpad: Introduction

The launchpad is the platform that supports a rocket before takeoff. Similarly, learning more about charity entrepreneurship as a career path forms the foundation from which you launch your new nonprofit.

Guidance system: Decision-making

Having a highly sophisticated guidance system is crucial: being off even the tiniest amount leads to huge differences down the road. Consistent good or bad decisions add up and will take you to your destination or leave you hundreds of miles off course.

Payload system: Key decisions

The payload system carries what you want to bring to your destination. Our payload when founding a charity depends on the macro (our ethical views) and the micro (four key decisions). What counts as "good" and "impact"? And more concretely, how do we then choose our Career path, Charity idea, Co-founder, and Country?

Propulsion system: Support

The propulsion system is the fuel that gives your rocket speed. This corresponds to your ability to gather support and communicate. Without fuel, it will be hard to gain funding or staff, and your accomplishments will slow. Even if you're heading in the right direction, you won't get there fast.

Structural system: Operations

The structural system is the metal skeleton that holds everything together. This is our section on building a charity, covering everything from budgeting to day-to-day project management. Without a strong, well-planned structure, your rocket will fall apart when it experiences tough shocks.

Together these systems create the foundation for launching a new impactful charity.

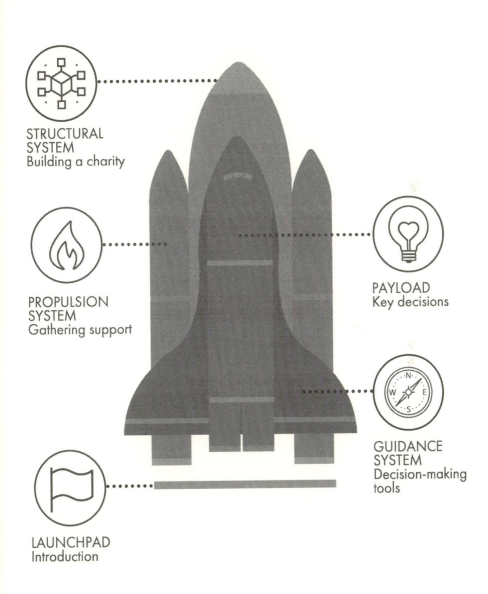

STRUCTURAL SYSTEM
Building a charity

PROPULSION SYSTEM
Gathering support

LAUNCHPAD
Introduction

PAYLOAD
Key decisions

GUIDANCE SYSTEM
Decision-making tools

Contents

Part I. Introduction

The launchpad is the platform that supports a rocket before takeoff. Similarly, learning more about charity entrepreneurship as a career path forms the foundation from which you launch your new nonprofit.

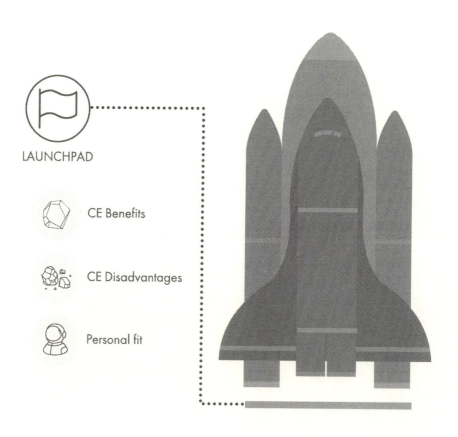

LAUNCHPAD

CE Benefits

CE Disadvantages

Personal fit

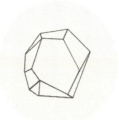

1. Benefits

Sometimes the best way to help the world is to quit your job.

In the 1990s, the World Health Organization (WHO) had an important function. They had to calculate, estimate, and publish the number of deaths caused by different diseases. These numbers influenced important details, from government spending on treatment programs to the public perception of progress being made on different issues. However, as Jeremy Smith's *Epic Measures* reports, even though the people doing the calculations were well-meaning and generally competent, there were some big problems. There was little oversight and the process lacked consistency, meaning that each individually talented WHO group used different methods, calculations, and assumptions. This resulted in estimates sometimes double- and even triple-counting a single death.

This misestimation was potentially fatal, with funding and intellectual resources being devoted toward certain diseases over other, more important areas. One insightful staff member at the WHO noticed the problem after discovering that the four biggest killers (malaria, diarrhea, TB, and measles) in a lower-income country added up to more than 100% of the total number of deaths in that country, and that was without even counting all other causes of death. When the employee brought up the concern with coworkers and management, it was largely dismissed. It would have looked bad, both for the individual groups and the WHO as a whole, to admit or address such a large mistake. Even after the staff member triple-checked his work and strengthened it through deeper research, his concerns went unheard.[1]

---

1 Jeremy N. Smith, *Epic Measures: One Doctor. Seven Billion Patients* (New York, NY: Harper Wave, 2015).

The end result was the founding of a completely new project outside of the WHO – the Global Burden of Disease Study – which measured impact correctly, did not double- or triple-count deaths, and is, in fact, used to this day by organizations like GiveWell, the Gates Foundation, and many others.[2] These updated and crucially important data have led to organizations prioritizing the most important issues, saving and improving countless lives. **If not for a brave founder who noticed a problem and created the solution, these data might never have come into being.** The biggest benefit of charity entrepreneurship is the positive impact a founder can have on the world. We can break impact down into two parts: direct and indirect (which considers your long-term impact, the impact on your team, and your impact on the NGO sector as a whole).

1.1. Direct impact

Some jobs save more lives than others, and some career paths have more impact than others. However, impact can be fickle. For example, if you save someone's life as a doctor, whomever you replaced in medical school would probably have saved that same life in the same way: you might not have created the impact you would initially assume. This consideration can equally apply for money fundraised (where would that donor have donated otherwise?) and most jobs (would a charity you work for have hired a different staff, but with similar skills?).

It's easy to imagine that you might miss out on a highly impactful job due to a gap in credentials or skills. However, one of the biggest ways people fail to have a long-term impact is by **working on something that is not that impactful without realizing it**.

Success in the nonprofit world is hard to quantify, as we'll see below. Knowing how much good you have done is much more difficult than measuring how much profit you have made. Evaluating a charitable organization is a major challenge, often requiring a large external team such as GiveWell to consider all the details and data. Calculating personal impact is often even more challenging, as it requires a sense both of your organizational impact and of your personal impact on the organization.

When calculating the impact of charity entrepreneurship, **you can simply**

---

2 Smith, *Epic Measures*, as cited by Joey Savoie, "Triple Counting Impact in EA," Effective Altruism Forum, May 26, 2018, https://forum.effectivealtruism.org/posts/fnBnEiwged7y5vQFf/triple-counting-impact-in-ea.

assess the impact of the organization as a whole, avoiding some of these concerns. Often, the limiting factor for the establishment of an effective organization is a single co-founder. Having these kinds of attributable results means that an individual can more clearly evaluate their career path to maximize their direct impact.

So how can we determine the direct impact of charity entrepreneurship? Let's look at some different possible approaches to this problem, including track record, cost-effectiveness estimates, expert views, and neglectedness.

Track record

Have charity founders made an impact? If we could not be sure of how charity entrepreneurship has so far affected the world, there would be much less of a reason to keep going. And calculating the impact of every charity in the world, past and present, would be a near impossible task. So, we have to find a way to shrink the number of charities we consider to a smaller group. One big differentiator is the reason they get founded. Many nonprofits begin due to personal interest or passion, but some are started using a more evidence-based approach that carefully examines areas where intervention is both sorely needed and decidedly possible. This latter group is more reflective of the approach to charity entrepreneurship discussed in this handbook. Charity work that falls into this category has a clear goal: save or improve the lives of as many people as possible, as effectively as possible. And that, we can calculate – or at least get close.

When we look at the direct impact that even just a few highly effective charities have made, we start to get a clearer picture of the power of charity entrepreneurship as we see it. For instance, take a few of the GiveWell[3] top-rated charities: GiveDirectly, after extensively researching the positive effects of unconditional cash transfers to the global poor, began a successful program that has given over $300 million in cash to over 170,000 families living in extreme poverty or affected by disasters; the Against Malaria Foundation has currently distributed 152,223,263 insecticide-treated bed nets across the globe to prevent malaria; New Incentives, a newer organization, has so far enrolled over 400,000 infants in their vaccination programs, using cash incentives to encourage families to get their children vaccinated from deadly preventable

---

3 GiveWell is an independent charity evaluator organization.

diseases.[4] These charities did not choose their interventions based on "what feels like the right thing to do." Their decisions have been driven by cost-effectiveness and a dedication to saving lives, and their work is certainly achieving that goal.

So what about us? We, at Charity Entrepreneurship (CE), work on finding founders and starting new charities using evidence-based reasoning and a focus on impact above all else. The nonprofits we've helped launch through our Incubation Program have been given all the tools that we hope to explain throughout this book, and they have exceeded our expectations as they have gone out into the world of doing good. We have incubated well over a dozen effective charities so far, and in just a few short years, several of them have become field leaders with the potential to become GiveWell-recommended themselves.[5]

Cost-effectiveness analysis

Past examples offer a soft sense of the direct impact of CE, but to take a more concrete angle, we can next look at cost-effectiveness analysis. A cost-effectiveness analysis outlines how much impact you get for each dollar spent. A more advanced impact evaluation takes into account where the money and talent used in order to accomplish something might have gone instead, factoring in the losses that result from redirecting those resources toward something else. For example, what if the money that someone gave to the Against Malaria Foundation were to go to another bed net charity instead? In that case, the same sum would have saved half as many lives or fewer.

Cost-effectiveness estimates can be highly complex and are done in different ways by different organizations, making it hard to do an apples-to-apples comparison. However, one approach compares a career's impact to a dollar amount donated to a charity. For example, working for a charity that spends $0.5 million and making it 10% more effective (no small feat, considering that the whole organization would have to be 10% better) could have about the same impact as donating ~$50k to that same charity. This "donation baseline" can be used to compare careers in more numerical terms.

---

4 See GiveDirectly, "Financials," last modified Sept. 20, 2021, https://www.givedirectly.org/financials/; Against Malaria Foundation, "Net distributions - World," https://www.againstmalaria.com/Distributions.aspx; and New Incentives' home page, https://www.newincentives.org/, respectively, for these numbers and intervention details. Accessed Nov. 10, 2021.

5 See Giving What We Can, "What are the best charities to donate to in 2021?" accessed Nov. 10, 2021, https://www.givingwhatwecan.org/best-charities-to-donate-to-2021/ on Happier Lives Institute, Fish Welfare Initiative, and ourselves, Charity Entrepreneurship; and GiveWell, "Fortify Health - General Support (2019)," Jan. 2020, https://www.givewell.org/research/incubation-grants/fortify-health/august-2019-grant on Fortify Health.

A few estimates have been done to assess the impact of starting a new charity (through an incubation program specifically) compared to donating to an existing charity:

- One estimate by Peter Wildeford suggests that founding a GiveWell top charity could be as impactful as donating $400,000 per year.[6]

- An estimate done by our team on our incubated charities concluded that founding a charity through CE has an expected value equivalent to donating ~$190,000 per year to the most effective charities in the world (as ranked by GiveWell).[7]

These sums suggest a very high impact can be had following this career path, as few have the ability to earn these sums of money, not to mention donate that amount every year. Even careers with the ability to influence very large sums (such as policy or foundations) rarely have this level of impact. This is because the impact of influencing a given dollar from a low-impact area to a medium-impact area can be a hundred times less than getting a dollar from no charity to the most impactful charity in the world.

Expert views

Many organizations in the space of doing the most good have historically been positive about founding effective charities as being a highly impactful career path. These include evaluators like GiveWell and impact-focused career organizations like 80,000 Hours, Animal Advocacy Careers, and Probably Good. However, each one notes that this can also be very challenging, with a high chance of failure even for talented founders. Our conversations with experts in the field (e.g., leaders of top charities in the global poverty and animal welfare spaces as determined by external reviewers) have also echoed this sentiment.

Neglectedness

When faced with the idea of starting a new charitable organization, many people ask, "But aren't there already lots of effective organizations out there?" In reality, the nonprofit world is relatively small. There are ~169,000 registered

---

6 Peter Wildeford, "What is the Expected Value of Creating a GiveWell Top Charity?" Effective Altruism Forum, Dec. 17, 2016, https://forum.effectivealtruism.org/posts/drRsWTctSqNRveK56/what-is-the-expected-value-of-creating-a-givewell-top.

7 CE Team, internal "Early 2021 CEA," Google Sheets, accessed Nov. 10, 2021. This model should not be compared against others. The way it accounts for counterfactuals means that even a small net positive score would imply that CE is the most impactful use of those resources and time.

charities in the UK.[8] This may seem like a lot, but only 5% of them are large enough to employ any paid staff, and most of these charities are devoted to local issues. Even within the category of international charities, most run interventions that are significantly less cost-effective than the ones effectiveness-minded donors are interested in. Out of the hundreds of charities that GiveWell has considered, they've only recommended about ten as top charities[9] – and bear in mind that GiveWell generally only considers those with some degree of promise in the first place.

The truth is, effective organizations are rarer than you might think. David Anderson, Assistant Director at the Coalition for Evidence-Based Policy, writes:

"…what's not often recognized is how rare – and therefore, valuable – such examples of proven effectiveness are. Their scarcity stems from two main factors: 1) the vast majority of social programs and services have not yet been rigorously evaluated, and 2) of those that have been rigorously evaluated, most (perhaps 75% or more), including those backed by expert opinion and less-rigorous studies, turn out to produce small or no effects, and, in some cases negative effects."[10]

In the current state of the field, there is a lot of good work to be done, and unfortunately no real incentive structure in place to push people to do it.

Taking all these factors into account, it seems likely that the direct impact of starting a charity that implements an intervention chosen via a thorough research process to maximize good done presents a potentially extremely valuable and cost-effective career option.

Indirect impact

The direct impact of eating your favorite fruit is a short-term delicious taste; the indirect and longer-term health benefits are, arguably, even more positive. Direct impact is highly important. But it's far from the only channel of change. By founding a new charity, you can guide your and your team's future ability to do good and influence the charitable movement you support. We consider

---

8 D. Clark, "Charities in the UK - Statistics & Facts," Sept. 13, 2021, https://www.statista.com/topics/3781/charities-in-the-uk/.

9 GiveWell, "Our Top Charities," last modified Nov. 2020, https://www.givewell.org/charities/top-charities.

10 David Anderson, "Guest post: Proven programs are the exception, not the rule." The GiveWell Blog, last modified March 21, 2019, https://blog.givewell.org/2008/12/18/guest-post-proven-programs-are-the-exception-not-the-rule/.

this collection of benefits to be the **indirect impact** (also called flow-through effects[11]) of charity entrepreneurship as a career.

Your future impact

Doing good year to year is important, but many are concerned with making sure they can continue to have a large impact throughout their whole life. When considering this factor in a career context, take into account not just the direct impact of a job, but also its impact on your future. Charity entrepreneurship as a career path builds skills, credentials, background, and knowledge, and puts you in a strong position to do good later on down the road.

Striving for impact is fundamental to pursuing a highly effective career, but what we value can change over time. This can lead to value drift – a gradual loss in motivation to behave altruistically. Thankfully, there are steps you can take to mitigate this risk,[12] such as surrounding yourself with impact-focused individuals. Having a job in the charity sector keeps you engaged with doing good, and charity entrepreneurship is no exception. Maintaining a great workplace culture with a supportive, impact-focused peer group can be a way to increase greatly the chance that you stay the course in the future.

Charity entrepreneurship helps you stay focused on the goal of impact and gives you the qualifications you need to attain it. Many employers like to see entrepreneurship on a résumé, as it suggests an ability to work without a high level of management. Founders often take CEO or managerial roles, and the greater responsibilities that come with them, much earlier in their career than had they joined an established organization. This allows them to build the skills and credentials needed to take on more senior positions at larger organizations in the future. In such roles, they are able to steer established NGOs and donors on a path of evidence-based development, touching many lives.

As well as advancing specific abilities, such as management, charity entrepreneurship enables you to develop skills in building skills. Due to the wide range of challenging tasks, entrepreneurs learn a lot every day. By the time you've mastered a skill, you often end up hiring an employee to do that aspect of the job while you go on to learn about a different area. Picking up and mastering

---

11 See the Effective Altruism Forum, "Indirect Long-Term Effects" tag, accessed Dec. 8, 2021, https://forum.effectivealtruism.org/tag/indirect-long-term-effects.

12 Joey Savoie, "Empirical data on value drift," Effective Altruism Forum, April 22, 2018, https://forum.effectivealtruism.org/posts/mZWFEFpyDs3R6hD3r/empirical-data-on-value-drift.

new skills quickly is a highly valued ability – one that is developed through charity entrepreneurship.

Some founders stay on a successful project for the rest of their lives, but many move on to other high-impact pursuits. A key benefit of starting an organization compared to, say, earning to give, is that **you can step back and the organization can keep creating impact**. In the for-profit world, this would be called a passive income. A company could continue to generate revenue with relatively little input from its founder. In the nonprofit world, the same concept can apply. A founder can pass the reins to an equally capable replacement and move on to a new undertaking, while having passive impact from the previous one. Handing over a project in this way opens up new pathways for your future impact. For those bitten by the entrepreneurship bug, serial charity founding can lead to multiple high-impact projects running, all thanks to one persistent co-founder.

Your impact on the broader community

Our default when considering impact is to examine our individual output – our personal work hours, money moved, and results achieved. However, we also need to look at the outward flow-through effects, such as enabling others to achieve impact and improving the charitable sector as a whole.

Fostering talent

Many impact-focused individuals want to work in an effectiveness-minded organization. It's easy to see why: these jobs provide a strong opportunity to build skills while having a direct impact. They also provide a like-minded community, which is one of the biggest predictors of job satisfaction. However, these jobs are very limited and difficult to get. Founding new organizations in promising areas with an effectiveness mindset is one way to create more impactful positions that job seekers can apply for and use to build their own skills, career, and impact.

Many charity workers who later went on to do highly impactful activities talk about their earlier jobs building their capacity for these roles. Impact-focused organizations often realize a portion of their overall impact from fostering talented people within their operation, even if they do not stay indefinitely. With strong staff training, several employees can take on far more ambitious projects later in their careers than they would have been able to otherwise.

Spreading concepts

Sometimes the biggest influence an organization has is in its concepts, not in its direct impact. Numerous concepts and ideas from the effective altruism (EA) universe are not yet widespread, or remain limited to a particular cause area even within EA. When a new charity brings a focus on cost-effectiveness or randomized controlled trial (RCT) evidence into a space, these concepts can spread to nonprofit partners that otherwise would never have heard of them.

Likewise, strong charities can affect donors. A donor might like your transparency and make it a requirement for other charities they fund. Frequently, funders and other stakeholders are affected by concepts they learned in one field and may apply them in others. For example, over time, the Gates Foundation became a supporter of open science, and now all research they fund is published openly.[13] This change is arguably more impactful than any grant the foundation gave in the open science field, but was likely caused by their initial interest and investment in the space.

Community building

Sometimes, a charity or individual goes further than just learning a few concepts, and becomes a member of the growing EA movement, a movement still largely populated by science, math, and philosophy majors in the USA and UK.[14] With the introduction of more EA-minded organizations and jobs, it can expand, stabilize, and diversify.

Though smaller in scale than the EA movement, the community that forms around your organization has an important impact. Often, when a new charity is founded in an area, there is a boom of interest. Volunteers are keen to contribute, donors to support it, and other projects to link up. Having a central point of contact for a specific issue or concern, or a default place that someone with an interest in that area can go (a Schelling point[15]), can make the difference between key members of a community connecting or not.

---

13 See Bill & Melinda Gates Foundation, "Open Access Policy FAQ," accessed Dec. 8, 2021, https://www.gatesfoundation.org/about/policies-and-resources/open-access-policy-faq.

14 Lauren Whetstone, "EA Survey 2018: Community Demographics & Characteristics," Rethink Priorities, Sept. 20, 2018, https://rethinkpriorities.org/publications/eas2018-community-demographics-and-characteristics.

15 Scott Alexander, "Nash Equilibria and Schelling Points," LessWrong, June 28, 2012, https://www.lesswrong.com/posts/yJfBzcDL9fBHJfZ6P/nash-equilibria-and-schelling-points.

Channeling resources

Starting a strong charity can benefit the broader cause area your organization is focused on through generating interest and influencing funders. By raising a cause area's profile, you can draw resources into underfunded spaces; by modeling effectiveness, you can shift resources toward more effective organizations.

The presence of an effectiveness-focused charity can raise the bar for an entire cause area. It allows donors and staff to have higher, but still realistic, expectations for other charities. In areas that are less effectiveness-focused, donors will often not even know what an impact-focused charity would look like. Yet after they see one, they can become a strong advocate for similar principles.

Charities can often serve as proof of concept for larger-scale actors, like governments, and they can also create some norms and methodologies for implementation that can later be used by those actors. Of course, often the charity will work directly with the government and apply for a program after it has been run on a smaller scale. This process can allow a cause area to receive a huge amount of resources that governments would otherwise have spent elsewhere.

1.2. Benefits beyond impact

Why are some entrepreneurs happier than they ever would be in a standard job?

Helping hundreds of thousands of beneficiaries with an evidence-based and cost-effective program: that's your ultimate goal as a charity entrepreneur. It's not a coincidence that many benefits of taking this path are related to impact. Yet, the advantages of starting your effective nonprofit go beyond impact alone. As a founder, you will grow in various ways. This section covers three of the many additional advantages of becoming a charity entrepreneur.

Satisfaction: find excitement in autonomy

Working on a variety of tasks not only increases your skills, it is also exciting and fun. Yes, it can be fulfilling to obtain expert knowledge in a particular subfield. For the typical entrepreneur, however, it quickly becomes dull. A variety of tasks and challenges stimulates a curious mind and contributes to job satisfaction.

By nature, the job of an entrepreneur comes with a high degree of autonomy, which is another key ingredient of satisfaction.[16] Autonomy increases motivation while reducing mental strain at work. Decision-making autonomy has a particularly large effect in the literature. There is no shortage of decisions for a charity entrepreneur: from high-level questions regarding which region to operate in, down to the specifics of a particular recruitment process. You have the final say and, therefore, the highest level of autonomy.

Autonomy translates to flexibility. As a co-founder, you decide when and where you work. Good luck explaining your 11 a.m. to 11 p.m. work routine to your supervisor in your country's public service! The same applies to your work location. While you want to be based as close to your beneficiaries as possible, you are generally free to decide where you work. Type away as you sit on your apartment's couch, and nobody will bother you. Similarly, you might be able to travel and work remotely. Depending on your location, you may benefit from low living expenses. It is not unheard of to take work calls over the internet next to a beach in Southeast Asia and be fully productive.

Meaning is a key pillar of life, and going beyond the self and helping others is a profound path toward it. Both ancient belief systems and modern psychology come to this conclusion.[17] The mission and impact of your charity are strong contributors to meaning, which will be reflected in your job and life satisfaction. The effects can be felt in the present and in hindsight. When you look back at your life at age 85, you will be happy about the time spent as a charity entrepreneur, while you might regret waiting so long to pursue your path to personal fulfillment.

Personal growth: become a master of challenges

Beyond career capital and satisfaction, entrepreneurship triggers personal growth whether you have asked for it or not. Running a start-up charity, you face numerous challenges that push you beyond your comfort zone. Your intervention fails in a randomized controlled trial, your key partner is not delivering, a major donor pulls back – these are just some of the roadblocks you could face.

---

16   Simeon Muecke and Anja Iseke, "How Does Job Autonomy Influence Job Performance? A Meta-Analytic Test of Theoretical Mechanisms," *Academy of Management Proceedings*, no. 1 (2019). https://doi.org/10.5465/ambpp.2019.145.

17   Elizabeth Hopper, "Can Helping Others Help You Find Meaning in Life?" The Greater Good Science Center at UC Berkeley, Feb. 16, 2016, https://greatergood.berkeley.edu/article/item/can_helping_others_help_you_find_meaning_in_life.

Yet navigating them is a surefire way to learn more about your personality and weaknesses. As a result, you will grow not only in the narrow sense of your career but also as a human being.

As you can imagine, this process can be difficult, so be sure not to push yourself too hard. There's a fine balance between challenging yourself to grow and setting yourself up for a breakdown. Reach out for help from your co-founders, coaches, and trained professionals. Recognize that basically everyone feels similarly in your position. This is normal, although you might not see it, as there is a bias for celebrating success stories over realistically reporting the ups and downs of a start-up. As insiders of highly successful ventures can tell you, the inside picture always looks messier than the outside perception might imply.

As you master increasingly bigger challenges, you will notice how you feel more confident with high-stakes situations, public speeches, and general uncertainty. You will also build a more realistic self-image as you better understand your strengths and weaknesses.

You might curse your choice of entrepreneurship at times, but you will grow.

Exposure: collaborate with your heroes

When running a start-up, you collaborate with your heroes in two ways. First, as you run the show, you get to pick colleagues who share your values and work ethic. You have the privilege of working with committed individuals from whom you can constantly learn, given that their talents will surpass yours in many areas.

Secondly, as a leader of an organization, you interact with the highest levels of established organizations and governments. How many young recent graduates sign a deal with a Ministry of Health or get to speak at a global conference? As a charity entrepreneur, you will gain exposure, build strong networks, and, most importantly, be able to work with super-smart and nice people inside and outside of your start-up.

In summary, opt for charity entrepreneurship if you would like to have an impact, and you will get a full package of goodies that goes beyond it: satisfaction through autonomy, personal growth in mastering challenges, and the ability to collaborate with your heroes.

2. Disadvantages

Three years of hard work, long nights, stressful decisions, and emotional investment. The result of that work would all come down to this.

John and Alice had been working on a new charity start-up for years and had done a good job. Their idea had been picked via an intensive research process. They had piloted a small-scale version of their program, which showed promising results. Their execution was best in the field. But now they were waiting nervously for an email.

This was not their first time waiting for an email that would decide the fate of their charity. From funder updates to critical advisor feedback, they had dealt with many tough messages – but none quite like this one. The email they were waiting for contained the results of the high-quality randomized controlled trial run on their project. They had some promising evidence from their pilot and other studies in different contexts, but there was still a solid chance that this RCT would show minimal or negative effects. This would mean their project would not be seen as impactful, requiring a large pivot or shutdown. Good or bad, the results would determine the fate of their charity and suggest the historical impact of their work.

They both were startled by the sound of an email arriving in their inbox. It was unpoetically named "RCT – results." Alice clicked the subject line and quickly read the contents. Her heart dropped. The results were bad – quite bad if the summary at the top of the email was correct. The study had found the program to have no significant effect.

It was hard to believe, given all the hard work they had put in. They had done everything right and still lost. She looked up at John, who was reading the results himself in disbelief, trying to process that their charity was a failure.

Charity entrepreneurship is a high-risk career. Even if you do everything right, new data can come in that shows your intervention is not effective. A government can change and the doors that were once promising can all immediately shut. A seemingly small argument with a co-founder can build until both people resent each other. Even for the best charities, there is an over 50% chance they end up having minor or no impact.

This harsh reality is hard to grasp in the abstract. Imagine flipping a coin at the start of your charity, and that if the coin comes up tails, your charity shuts down as a failed project. Information can be gained from failed projects and skills can still be built; however, the psychological experience of failure is only somewhat mitigated by these benefits.

2.1. Five challenges (and how to manage them)

"Why take this risk?" Mentioning at a family gathering that you would like to become a charity entrepreneur might trigger looks of concern and opposition. What about the high failure rate of start-ups, the low entry salaries, the need to work around the clock? There are potential personal challenges related to charity entrepreneurship. Neglecting them would be dishonest. Yet often, these challenges are either exaggerated or can be dealt with successfully.

Uncertainty and a high risk of failure

The cliche is correct: a high percentage of start-ups fail. In the case of charity start-ups, an impact evaluation might show negative results, your funders might move on to other cause areas, or your team might no longer be sufficiently motivated by the organization's mission. Even successful start-ups involve a lot of uncertainty. It is often hard to predict how the organization will look just 6-12 months in the future. The risk of failure and the general sense of uncertainty have an effect on both a psychological and financial level.

While financial concerns often come up first, the underlying challenge in uncertainty is likely psychological. As human beings – even more adventurous ones – we strive for a certain degree of stability in our relationships and tasks.

A start-up provides anything but. Yet these concerns are manageable with a few simple strategies. For instance, **acknowledge the worst-case scenario of failure** in a visualization exercise inspired by stoicism. Even in this scenario, your efforts will not be in vain on a personal or societal level. The lessons learned will contribute to shared knowledge, while you will have personally benefited from the journey since you worked on a meaningful project and gained valuable career capital.

The pressure generated by your venture will also trigger personal growth that you might not have achieved otherwise. Other simple activities, such as sports and meditation, can help you take a step back when you feel overwhelmed by the uncertain outlook of your charity.

Financial limitations

The financial challenges related to a charity start-up are twofold. First, you might worry about what happens financially in the case of failure. Second, you might be anxious about lower salaries in the nonprofit space and limited financial freedom.

In dealing with the financial risk of failure, it might help to **perceive charity entrepreneurship as an investment** similar to a university education. You will benefit in the long term – and, as a charity entrepreneur, you get paid a salary instead of being confronted with school fees. Further ways to alleviate your financial concerns include building a 6- to 12-month **financial buffer before starting** and checking out the social security benefits of your country of origin (as a last resort). And don't forget that, having chosen this path, you are likely highly skilled, so it is realistic that you could find another well-paid job in the worst-case scenario.

In terms of financial freedom, starting your charity will restrict you more than working for an established company. Maybe you will have to reduce your budget for vacations, the latest gadgets, or eating out. However, **becoming a charity entrepreneur does not equate to joining a monastery**. Your donors understand that you can only be productive if your living costs are covered. So you will not have to switch from smart to feature phone, stop going out with friends, or spend holidays on your balcony. Finally, as an entrepreneur running an early-stage organization, you are likely already cost-conscious, so cutting back a bit will feel natural to you.

Separation from friends and family

Your happiness depends, to a large degree, on your social network. Being away from friends and family can be challenging. Charity entrepreneurship will mean time away from your loved ones. You might have to set up a program in a rural Indian state or attend multiple donor conferences in a faraway global capital.

However, job mobility is not unique to this career. It has become a common feature of modern working life. The autonomy you enjoy as an entrepreneur can even help you stay close to your social circles. Many tasks can be accomplished remotely. For deep concentration, a quiet remote setting is even better than a hectic field setting. Moreover, if you have a co-founder, you can split up the time spent in faraway locations between multiple people.

Work-life balance

The first years as a charity entrepreneur might not be the best to start time-consuming new hobbies or plan extended holidays. Your work-life balance is likely to suffer as you start your venture from scratch, test it in the field, and recruit the first employees. Forty hours per week will likely not be sufficient. At the same time, the workload should also be put into perspective. For many charity entrepreneurs, the counterfactual would be climbing the career ladder in a highly demanding job such as management consulting. The work-life balance there is arguably worse.

As an entrepreneur, the distinction between work and life will become less clear. After all, you have started something you truly believe in, that you pursue with a high degree of autonomy. This is a different path than working for a conglomerate in an anonymous office building.

As your organization grows, delegation processes will also become more established, and you will not have to extinguish fires constantly on top of your leadership duties. Staff will take care of operations, and you will be able to focus on strategic questions. All of this reduces your workload and stress levels.

Finally, while working more than 40 hours per week is clearly beneficial in the beginning, the science of productivity[1] shows that more is not always better.

---

1 Lonnie Golden, "The Effects of Working Time on Productivity and Firm Performance, Research Synthesis Paper," *International Labor Organization (ILO) Conditions of Work and Employment Series,* no. 33, Conditions of Work and Employment Branch (2012). SSRN: https://ssrn.com/abstract=2149325.

Resist the urge to work constantly, and **consciously set windows for uninterrupted rest and recuperation**.

Unglamorous work

The movie version of your life as a charity entrepreneur might involve speaking at a prestigious conference and drafting research reports in a shiny coworking space in a global capital. The reality is often less glamorous. You might be sweating in a tiny hotel room in a foreign country as you try to fix your internet connection to update your organization's website.

Initially, your organization only has you and your co-founder(s) as employees. By definition, you will have to carry out all or most of the tasks. Moreover, the large majority of duties at an NGO are operational: revising budgets, talking to lawyers, drafting work contracts, and so on. This is particularly important to consider if you come from a research background and expect charity entrepreneurship to be an applied research fellowship, which it is not in most cases.

The upside of this breadth of tasks is **broad skill-building** and **career capital**. You also get to understand every process from scratch, a good remedy against the detached decision-making that hampers many larger organizations. Of course, you will be able to hire staff eventually so you can focus your time on more strategic responsibilities. In the meantime, you could **outsource** repetitive or IT-related tasks to freelancers available through platforms such as Upwork.

3. Personal fit

Robert was an unlikely candidate to cause a famine. He had an infinitely sunny demeanor and a passion for helping others. After working in the nonprofit sector for a number of years, he had a brilliant idea for a new charity: microloans for low-income farmers, to stabilize their income.

There were already some loan services in the area, but they charged prohibitively high rates and Robert had a better plan for a payback system. They would only give loans to groups labeled "low risk" using a new algorithm. With a higher chance of repayments, they could charge lower rates and make their money go further. As he explained the idea to experts in his field, close friends, and family to positive responses, his excitement grew. He was a skilled communicator and was able to raise some initial funding for his idea. In a few short months, he was starting the first delivery of his product.

His excitement turned to frustration as the project stalled on roadblock after roadblock. One governmental agency had given him the go-ahead, but another said it was illegal to run any loan company in their district. Robert hired an expensive lawyer who confirmed it was legal, but it still stressed him out and kept him up at night. Soon afterward, he received an email from a recipient denied a loan due to being considered "high risk." Robert managed to set him up for another appointment and approved his loan manually. An angry phone call from an existing loan company that had to shut down sent him into a depression that lasted weeks. As soon as he came out of it, two of his employees were caught gaming the system and giving generous loans to their family members.

Every day, there was so much to do and so many things to stress about. Finally, Robert gave up. It was too hard to run this charity; he shut it down and moved on. Sadly, the community he pulled out of suffered greatly. With both the new NGO loan company shut down and previous loan markets closed due to competition, a lean year caused by weather conditions meant that the community faced one of the longest famines they had experienced in recent history. Unintentionally, unwittingly, and tragically, Robert had played a significant role in causing a village-wide famine, hurting the very people he had set out to help.

Unlike becoming a lawyer or an accountant, **there is no degree for charity entrepreneurship, and no certification you can get to confirm you are ready for it.** Just like every career, it's not a good fit for everyone, and would be a terrible fit for many. Starting a charity involves a lot more risk, open-ended tasks, and responsibility than most other jobs. The goal of this section is to make sure you do not go down the same path as Robert, and to give you the information you need to consider deeply whether charity entrepreneurship is the right career for you.

The quickest way to test? A simple question: "Can I get myself through an independent online class using my own motivation?" Not only will this be invaluable to help learn the dozens of skills you need to found a new charity, but also it reflects the open-ended nature of charity entrepreneurship. With no boss and few deadlines, motivation can be a major challenge for those pursuing this path. Of course, any one question is highly limited in its predictive power; however, it can still be one of many useful tools – with another being this handbook. As you read about the key elements required, think about whether it sounds like a path you might fit.

The surest way to test? Deep and honest advice from a number of people who have seen many projects begin and succeed. Do you fall into the reference class of those who succeed? What are the most common ways charities fail? If they did a pre-mortem of your project, at what stage would they expect it to come apart? Getting time from experts like this can be challenging, but incubation programs can cover the ground. Going through the application process and Incubation Program our organization (Charity Entrepreneurship) runs is the best test we know of for determining long-term fit. However, this is quite an undertaking, with a seven-stage application process and then the Incubation Program itself, which takes place over two months full-time.

3.1. Key elements

"The river of life affects everyone, but in different ways." Noticing his student's confusion, the old man gestured for him to follow and continued. "See that stone?" He pointed to a rock jutting out of the river. "Many people are like this stone – unmoving, regardless of what life presents them with. As the world changes around them, they wear down, but resist change as much as they can. Even the most powerful current only moves them temporarily, until they find rest in a new spot."

They walked in silence for a few more moments. Then the teacher again motioned at the water. "Others are like this stick. It flows with the water's currents. Moving along the easiest path, it may travel much farther than the rock, but still thinks about as much as the rock does. The stick and rock have no control over their destiny, no agency; their paths are highly predictable."

They walked in silence for a touch longer. The student was the next to speak: "So you don't want to be a rock or a stick – you must want to be a fish!" And no sooner than he had spoken, they could see a fish swimming through the water.

"Indeed," the old man replied, "the fish can think for himself. He can go up or down the river; he makes choices in a far different way than the rock or stick. The fish thinks himself wise, as he can swim anywhere he pleases, seeing many options in front of him. However, the fish does not recognize the water he is in. Look there –" Another animal had entered the water, a small otter who swam and bobbed along the surface. After finding a rock she seemed to like, she waddled out of the water to another river close by. "The fish thinks he sees the options, but there are worlds he cannot access. He is limited by his perspective, unable to see beyond the conventional choices set before him."

"So, the otter is the wisest animal?" The boy asked hesitantly. "Almost." The old man gave a wry smile and they continued along the river bank.

Finally, the boy saw what was coming. In front of them was a large wooden dam, blocking the river and sending it in another direction. "The beaver is wise enough to know not just the world of water and the world of air, but also that he can affect what others perceive as the whole world. The beaver both finds and creates new paths that others can share in. With the help of a beaver, a new world opens up before the rock, stick, fish, and otter. Beavers create the change others do not envision."

As an entrepreneur, you must become a beaver. You have to see what others cannot, and by forging new paths, you can affect not just your world but the worlds of many others.

Some people come into entrepreneurship with three skills, others with eight. But you need about a hundred to run a new project effectively, so it's far more important how fast and well you pick up skills than what you come in with. If not specific skills, then, what are the key elements that predict good personal fit for charity entrepreneurship?

Personality traits

Many personality traits can set you up for success as a charity entrepreneur. Below we talk about five. Each one of these traits is not 100% necessary, nor is it a guarantee of success to have all five. But the more of these boxes you check, the higher the odds that your personality is a good fit for charity entrepreneurship.

Some traits are hard to change, but many are dynamic. It's possible to cultivate certain traits if you want to, so an unchecked box may suggest an area to work on.

- Self-motivated

As an entrepreneur, you have to convince many people that your idea is a great one, but **the first person you must convince is yourself**. You have to be able to get yourself up in the morning without a boss breathing down your neck. You have to motivate yourself to do unpleasant but necessary tasks. It's difficult, and some people just can't get the work done without a push.

A good way to proxy this style of work is to take an online course. There are thousands that you can take for free at your own pace. With such a powerful resource publicly available, it may seem amazing that people pay such huge sums of money for a university degree, but much of it comes down to motivation. Most people cannot complete an online course by themselves without a teacher guiding them to the finish line. You can set up a board or peer group to help you with this, but when it comes down to it, being able to motivate yourself is crucial.

- Conscientious

One of the most popular personality tests in modern psychology is the Big Five. Although quite a few of these traits can be important (such as high emotional stability), none is more so than conscientiousness.

Conscientiousness is the personality trait of being careful, organized, or diligent. Behavior-wise, it tends to result in systematic and organizational thinking and a tendency to neatness. When you say you will do something, how often do you follow through? The neatness of your bedroom or how often you are on time can also be quick proxies for conscientiousness. If keeping on top of your own tasks and planning is a challenge, running a charity will be a huge step up.

- Irrepressible

In the past, we've talked a lot about grit as a top trait for entrepreneurs. It's undoubtedly important. All founders will face challenges, regardless of the strength of their project – even the best projects we've known were at points held together with duct tape and super glue. But persisting through hardship takes its toll. The visual image of a gritty person might be someone battle-worn and a bit haggard (think *Harry Potter*'s Mad-Eye Moody).

Irrepressibility overlaps with grit, but takes on a more positive framing – someone "full of energy and enthusiasm; impossible to stop" (think Hermione Granger). When we first came across this term in conversation with Kevin Starr, we felt immediately that it rang true for some of the strongest charity entrepreneurs in our program. Their energy and passion fueled them to move forward relentlessly, almost ceasing to notice hardship, at least relative to the more important endline goals. Where others would have to use willpower or grit their teeth to succeed, these entrepreneurs found motivation or even fun in the challenges. It's this unrelenting motivation to succeed that's so important for entrepreneurship.

- Open-minded

Good charity entrepreneurs always remain open to the possibility that any and all of their assumptions may be incorrect. If you don't consider new evidence and update your beliefs and actions accordingly, you're much more likely to fail. As a small condolence, you probably won't realize that you've failed because, as Kathryn Schulz explains, how you feel when you are wrong is identical to how you feel when you're correct.[1] Feedback loops and openness to criticism allow you to change your mind and grow your organization. This requires a rare willingness to admit mistakes. Cultivate a "scout mindset," trying to understand situations and concepts as honestly and accurately as possible, even when inconvenient.[2] Remember, changing your mind is the ultimate victory, because in those moments you are improving your model of the world and making your charity better.

- Creative

Almost every day, entrepreneurs need to devise and compare multiple solutions to any given problem. Great entrepreneurs aren't afraid to think outside the box, do things differently, and bend or break social norms. **Difficult problems require creative solutions**.

Can you think outside of the box? Have you irritated a teacher or two by going too far outside the bounds of expectation? Are you comfortable going against social norms? These might be good signs for entrepreneurship.

Goals

Your goals are even more important than your personality for determining your fit. Without the right targets, it is very hard to found a charity that has a large impact on the world. Three important goals are required to be a great charity entrepreneur: you need to be doing it for the right reasons, be results-oriented, and be ambitiously altruistic.

- The right reasons

You want to found a new nonprofit because you want to do good in the world as effectively as possible. There are countless reasons to start a charity, and not all of them are altruistic. Some people do it to impress others, to have adventures, or to feel good about themselves. If you let these kinds of motivations interfere with the ultimate goal of helping, people will be harmed. For example, say your primary motivation is the warm glow of assisting others. When you find out

---

1 See Kathryn Schulz, "On being wrong," TED talk, 2011, https://www.ted.com/talks/kathryn_schulz_on_being_wrong/transcript?language=en.

2 Julia Galef's term, discussed in depth in her book *The Scout Mindset: Why Some People See Things Clearly and Others Don't* (New York, NY: Portfolio, 2021).

that, instead of ministering to the ill, it's better to prevent the disease in the first place, you may choose to stick to ministering because prevention is not as emotionally rewarding as treatment. Many people will lose their lives because of your misguided motivations. Likewise with prestige, a desire to impress others may cloud your judgment. Often the best thing for a charity to do is give the credit to somebody else.

- Results-oriented

You worry that a lot of charities, while well-intentioned, are misguided. They often accomplish nothing, and sometimes even make situations worse. Your response to knowing that things can go wrong is not to say that making a positive difference is impossible, but instead that you have to learn as much as you can about the situation before making a decision. You want the analytical, critical, rigorous, and empirical thinking found in the scientific sector to be the norm in the nonprofit sector, too. **The stakes are too high for decision-makers to value emotional appeals over evidence and results.**

- Ambitious altruism

You want to help so many people over your lifetime that they wouldn't all be able to fit in a football stadium. You want to wake up knowing you are pushing the limits of what is possible. Most people want to make the world a better place, but the majority only go so far as to be nicer to those around them or put a little extra thought into a present. These gestures are laudable, but running a great organization needs more vision. Otherwise, you'll be too tempted by easier ways to change the world. You need the ambition of a Silicon Valley start-up, but with the goal of helping as many others as possible instead of getting as big as possible.

4. Meta tools

Once you start collecting tools, the first thing you'll notice is that you need some unified heuristics and techniques in terms of which to use when, and for how long. Some techniques cross apply to a wide range of decision-making tools, such as when to make a decision or how much time to give yourself to make it. This section covers some of these cross-cutting, more meta techniques. They are the toolbox that allows you to store and organize your tools for optimal use.

4.1. Explore vs. exploit

We live in a complex world with ever-changing variables. When it comes to doing the highest-impact activity or running the most optimal project, it can seem impossible to be confident in one plan over another. Additionally, new information from further research or even just time passing can make plan A seem better than plan B, only to have it switch back again the next day. This can cause some people to get caught in **analysis paralysis** or switch far too frequently between ideas, making little progress on each one. On the other hand, some people can pick a direction and never update again, constantly leaving impact on the table. So the question becomes how to find a balance between those two.

Sam Altman observes: "A pattern I've noticed in very impactful people: Spend ~1 year exploring broadly, ~4 years relentless focus executing on the most interesting direction, repeat."[1]

The specific numbers can be debated (perhaps it should be 6 months and 3 years), and for charity-focused founders, our focus is on the highest-impact thing instead of the most interesting direction. But the fundamental pattern of exploration followed by relentless focus rings true. A strategy like this allows you mentally to commit to and finish large, important projects. It also greatly increases the odds of a project coming to fruition.

4.2. Time capping

In the exploration phase, you want to be careful and fair-minded, researching a broad range of options to determine the top contenders. You do not want to commit to any idea psychologically, but instead remain impartial. This can be helpful when considering co-founders or project ideas. Not settling on the first idea or person you click with, but rather taking the time to explore and test, can result in far more progress long term.

When open to ideas, you will find many competing options that look promising. You then want to compare them carefully and get external views from respected peers. This is the best time to gather broad information, as you are not committed to the project and can directly show the comparison. You could ask trusted mentors if they think plan A or B is better, and explain the merits of both. A wise advisor will be able to answer honestly, knowing that you have not already made the decision. Supportive people often won't disagree with your plan if you're already committed, for fear of demotivating you or hurting your feelings.

The biggest enemies in the exploration phase will be getting lost in analysis or being too quick to commit to a plan. A solution to both these concerns is **setting a specific amount of time for making your decision.** This is called "time capping" and is useful for founders and researchers in many situations.[2] Take our Incubation Program as an example. The first month allows broad exploration of ideas and co-founders. The second month involves working more deeply and thoroughly with those co-founders and committing to testing out a team. One month is not enough time to evaluate every facet of every idea, nor to consider

---

1 Sam Altman, Twitter post, Jan. 23, 2018, https://twitter.com/sama/status/955900505875558400.

2 Joey Savoie, "The Importance of Time Capping," Charity Entrepreneurship, Dec. 16, 2018, https://www.charityentrepreneurship.com/blog/the-importance-of-time-capping.

every factor that could make a co-founder a good fit. However, these decisions can take an indefinite amount of time, and most of the progress can be made in a short "time capped" period spent considering the issue.

This situation also presents a fact of entrepreneurship: **there will always be far more to do than time to do it**. Moving forward on one topic will mean reducing time spent on another. The truth is, there will be very few occasions in entrepreneurship when you feel absolutely certain. Ultimately, what you can hope for is to make a well-informed guess at the best option. And it's important to learn not to eliminate all uncertainty, but rather to **develop the art of being confident that you made the best choice you could have in the time available**. On the other side of the coin, if you're predisposed to jump into the first good idea that comes along, seeing that you're only a fraction of a way through the time you set aside will remind you that you probably haven't carefully considered enough of the alternatives.

Story of an application	Example cross-applications
One of our charities had to make a challenging decision. After asking a mentor for advice, the mentor said: "Both options have merits. Considering the importance of the decision and the time you've put into it, you have narrowed down to the top two good options. It seems like any more time will do little to aid your answer. Picking either and moving forward would be a more correct choice than further debate."	• When deciding how long to explore before implementation, assign yourself time according to the value of information. • When doing a cost-effectiveness analysis, assign time to researching each parameter according to its weight in the final result. • When looking back at past choices, don't consider whether they were right in hindsight; consider whether they were right given the information you had at the time.

4.3. Iterative depth

When making a decision or evaluating options, often hundreds of possibilities stretch as far as the eye can see. However, we have limited time to explore these options. **Iterative depth** is a meta-process that can be used to narrow down a large list into a much smaller one. In this context, we can frame it as systematically time capping each stage of a research process. This ensures you don't end up spending a large amount of time on a less promising option.

For example, CE faces the challenge of narrowing down from all the charity ideas in an area (often several thousand) to a reasonable number for deeper research. Our solution is to conduct multiple rounds (iterations) of research, sometimes using different techniques, at different levels of depth. As the list slowly narrows, the level of depth goes up. With our 2020 charity research, that meant doing a quick 30-minute prioritization of hundreds of ideas, then a longer two-hour prioritization of dozens of ideas, and, finally, an 80-hour prioritization of the top five to 10. Each level of depth examines fewer ideas than the previous round, but invests considerably more time into each one.

This same process cross-applies to most decision-making situations. If you are considering career options, there are likely hundreds of possibilities. But as you do a bit of research into each, you will arrive at a shorter list. Maybe you consider volunteering or interning as the top five options, or applying for education programs in the top three. When hiring staff for your organization, you will go through a similar process, gathering more and more information on fewer and fewer candidates. Near the end, you have a final shortlist of a small number of candidates, with multiple interviews and test tasks for each one.

Iterative depth will not give you 100% confidence in the value of the ideas you ruled out. Yet it does give considerable transparency to your process. People can see how much time you spent on a given idea, or how many options were considered before selecting your final choice. It also tends to encourage brainstorming many different options, an invaluable meta-skill, and results in a systematically and thoughtfully made decision.

Story of an application	Example cross-applications
After considering a long list of hundreds of cities to base their HQ out of, the co-founder team picked ten to examine more deeply. They learned a few key things that eliminated some, and ended up visiting their top three cities. After they had in-depth information, they were able to make a highly informed choice.	• Methodologies your charity is considering using (e.g., cost-effectiveness analysis). • Research, including country-level research and determining what interventions to consider.

4.4. Narrow focus

Entrepreneurs can be passionate people, getting excited about many ideas at the same time. Your level of focus or number of projects to split time between has implications both personally and organizationally. Some individuals may put careful analysis into their budget, but not apply the same rigor to the way they spend their time on projects. This is particularly true for pursuits that are alluring and seem to have minimal time commitments. However, ten half-finished projects are not equivalent in value to a single finished project.

An important piece of evidence for keeping a narrow focus is the endline results of individuals who have been focused compared to those who have been less so. We have found that individuals who spread themselves across many projects tend to let things slip through the cracks. They end up spending time on projects that, after a comparative analysis, would not compete with the top thing they are working on. When we compare these people to others of seemingly similar abilities but a much tighter focus, we tend to find that those in the latter category end up having significantly greater success, without a proportionally lower number of accomplishments.

There are a few possible reasons this could happen. We think there is likely a heavy cognitive cost to switching your mind between very different projects, leading to less deep and creative thinking than you would expect given the split of hours. A second possibility is that smaller projects tend to be hit harder by the planning fallacy than large ones. We may expect it to take three years to start a high-impact charity, yet often, it has ended up taking five years. But many small high-impact projects presumed only to take 10 hours ended up requiring orders of magnitude more time.

Another possibility is that many of the most worthwhile pursuits are really difficult and require full-time attention. Many of the most impactful projects are sufficiently challenging that their odds of success are under 50%, even with multiple talented full-time co-founders.

Story of an application	Example cross-applications
Why do TV remotes have so many buttons? One reason is that each department has an incentive to add a button to the remote. The contrast team feels a contrast button is important, as does the brightness team. No one really has an incentive to reduce the number of buttons. As such, remote controls get bulky and difficult to use. Your charity will run much the same way if you do not have a sharp focus on your key mission.	• Whenever a new project is suggested, review it carefully and determine whether it would be as impactful as your primary mission if it took twice as long. If not, don't even consider switching focus for it. • When considering a small diversion from your organization's mission, remember that it can open the door for less focus across the board. • One well-written book is worth 10 poorly written ones; the same is true for project arms.

4.5. Feedback

Feedback sharpens your tools, allowing them to get better at their jobs. Every great piece of writing, successful project, or large public achievement has undergone several rounds of feedback, each one an improvement. It's fair to say that feedback – giving, receiving, and implementing it – is **one of the most important cross-cutting skills**.

Unlike at many jobs and at school, charity entrepreneurship does not have built-in feedback systems. But for a wise founder, building these networks is one of the first steps to take. Set up specific points to get feedback (e.g., during your plan reevaluation points) and find trusted people who can frequently give an external review of your progress and hard-to-come-by accountability.

Listen to feedback, but find it from many sources. It's easy to take one piece of feedback too strongly. As a charity entrepreneur, you will receive extremely negative and extremely positive feedback from different people. Many people will say things are impossible that you accomplish a few short years later. Listening to feedback does not always mean taking it to heart or applying it. To be a master of feedback, you have to know which to disregard.

- Consider the person's motivation in giving feedback. Your family might give great feedback for some areas, but weak feedback for charity entrepreneurship ideas – they might be more concerned about your stress levels than about the impact you have on the world.

- Think about whether the person offering feedback tried to come up with solutions, or only listed problems. Rarely is there a problem with no solution, so feedback can be an indication of where to put your time.

- Does this person have relevant experience in the areas in which they are giving feedback? A fundraiser will give strong fundraising advice, but don't let that fool you into thinking their advice on implementation is good. Try to find mentors and advisors who have had success doing projects similar to the one you want to do.

Good feedback has saved many projects from taking a wrong turn. Having diverse mentors and informed peers is the only way to master these other tool areas.

Story of an application	Example cross-applications
A charity had come up with a great name. It was short and catchy, and both co-founders loved it. However, when they shared it with their advisors, they noticed a significant flaw. When you looked it up, a bunch of 18+ search results came up, as it meant something quite different in another language. Thanks to the early feedback, the co-founding team was able to change their name.	• Getting feedback on public-facing material such as project proposals or announcement posts can help you catch mistakes that would otherwise be pointed out in comments. • Feedback on your long-term plans can allow you to avoid mistakes you would have otherwise made. • Getting feedback on your communication style can allow you to improve in ways that never would have come to mind.

4.6. Reevaluation points

Careful exploration and relentless focus seem like forces in opposition. The question becomes how to balance them in a way that maximizes impact and your project's success. This tricky issue is compounded by the fact that for most ambitious projects, some days your project will be going great and you will feel positive about it. On others, it will take all of your energy just to stay afloat, and everything will feel like it's falling apart. **Days like this will come and go for even the best projects.** And although it's great to think carefully about impact, if you are constantly reevaluating your project, it will be hard not to abandon it on a hard day/week/month.

A solution to this problem is to set "plan reevaluation points" where you review your project and plan with fresh eyes, looking over all the data you can to see if it is still worth doing. How often to do these varies a bit depending on how long you have been working already. It might start as once every 6 months but double in length every reevaluation until it's once every couple of years. You can set plan reevaluation points for a specific moment when you expect to be better informed – for example, at the end of a study or program. These points can allow you a deeper level of focus without sliding into questioning your whole project every week. It also still ensures you update appropriately based on long-term trends and evidence.

The real trick to being able to hold off between plan reevaluations is having strong confidence in your initial decision-making phase, so you know you made a good call. This system can save a lot of pain, and also increases your chances of staying on an impactful project long term, rather than pivoting when you hit the first speed bump.

Story of an application	Example cross-applications
The project was going terribly and both co-founders felt like quitting. However, they had set a plan reevaluation for two months from that date, so they resolutely decided to hit the mark. After two weeks, a few things had changed for the better. By the end of the two months, the project had hit a big milestone that had previously seemed miles away. With clear heads at the reevaluation point, they decided to continue the project.	• Setting a key time to reconsider can allow you to determine how much to fundraise, and where the money will go, while remapping your plan. • A manager frustrated with an employee set a reevaluation point to revisit the issue. After reconsidering a few weeks later, they felt confident that letting the employee go would be the right call. • The research team had gotten so caught up in their research that they had not improved or looked critically at their process. A plan reevaluation point gave them a chance to take a step back.

4.7. What makes a good tool?

A simple and intuitive breakdown involves three components: speed, cross applicability, and accuracy.

Speed measures how long it takes to use the tool. If two tools are otherwise equal but one is faster, using the faster one is better. In many situations, you will only have the time to use quick tools, such as when comparing hundreds of options or making a time-limited decision. Complex tools will tend to be slower than simple ones. Speed is easy to measure, as you can simply see how long it takes to use a specific tool on a given problem – for example, looking up the population of a country is far quicker than looking up how effective its government is at enforcing regulations. Of course, many tools do not specify how long to spend on them, and most could be done in a larger or smaller amount of time. For example, a five-hour cost-effectiveness analysis (CEA) might be very different in usefulness from a 50-hour CEA. So to get an accurate measure of the speed of a tool, it generally has to be both specific and time capped, for example, "A CEA created by an unbiased semi-experienced CEA creator in five hours." Tools at this level of specificity can much more easily be cross-compared to other tools and understood by a reader.

It seems likely that almost every individual tool can be put on an optimal time curve (how much time will yield the most effective results). For example, spending five minutes speaking to experts will yield almost no information (as you generally will not even be able to contact them in that time). Alternatively, talking to the 51st expert will likely not yield the same value as talking to the first three. Many tools will follow a similar trend: put too much time into a CEA, and the returns of a further hour are small; put in a sufficiently small amount of time, and marginal additional hours would make it more valuable.

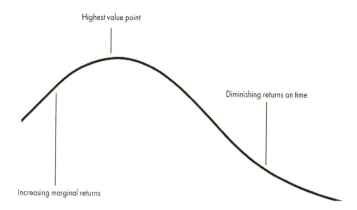

Highest value point

Diminishing returns on time

Increasing marginal returns

The highest-value point of tools is not easy to determine in the abstract and likely varies depending on the experience of the tool user and the complexity of the problem. A five-hour CEA might be overkill for comparing toasters, but insufficient for comparing cause areas.

Our second criterion, **cross applicability,** is also fairly simple to understand intuitively. A better tool can be efficiently used in multiple situations. For example, "neglectedness" applies to any cause area, while "number of human lives saved" applies more narrowly. Tools do not need to be universally cross applicable, e.g., when comparing two interventions with similar outcome metrics. Two charities that both aim to save lives could be effectively compared by asking how many lives each saves. But when comparing more broadly between many different options, tools need to be cross applicable enough to be relevant to all the options considered.

The third component is the most important, but also the most complex: **accuracy**. Does the tool's accuracy narrow down the option space in the way you want it to? For example, if we want to know if it will rain, looking to see if there are clouds is a fairly accurate tool. It's not enough to know for sure, but it does provide some data on the odds of it raining. A slightly accurate tool might be enough to update you a little bit – "Oh, there are clouds, rain might happen" – whereas a highly accurate tool might update you a lot – "Oh, the weatherman says there is a 95% chance of rain."

The more accurate a tool, the more decision-making weight it can be given. However, telling whether a tool is accurate is much harder than telling if it's fast or cross applicable, particularly for situations where the outcome is not known, has never happened before, or was never known. For example, we can know whether it rains, but we might never know the truly optimal career.

Even for unclear outcomes, accuracy can still be quantified and determined, such as when comparing a quick version of the tool to a much deeper one. If a 5-hour CEA correlates at 0.5 with a 500-hour CEA, and a 50-hour CEA correlates at 0.75 with the 500-hour version, it could be said that the 50-hour CEA is more accurate (at predicting the result of the deeper 500-hour CEA). Quicker tools can be correlated in this way with their deeper and more extensive counterparts to determine their predictive accuracy, even in different areas. For example, if a 5-hour CEA predicts what speaking to experts, creating a CEA, using a weighted factor model, and deep introspection for 500 hours would eventually show, then that 5-hour CEA could be said to be an accurate tool.

Trade-offs in tools

Often trade-offs have to be made between a very fast but semi-accurate tool and a slow but more accurate one. The specific trade-off will depend on the importance of the answer, how much time you have, and how many options you are comparing. However, this is not to say there is not an overall "strength of tool." There is an average line of speed (time taken) vs. accuracy (predictive ability) trade-off. This is shown in the figure below as a line of best fit.

Tools that fall close to the line (light grey) might be considered average. Those above the line (medium grey) are particularly accurate for how long they take and are highly useful. Tools below the line (dark grey) are below average – they might take a long time and still not be that accurate. For the time being, all tools are assumed to be equally cross applicable.

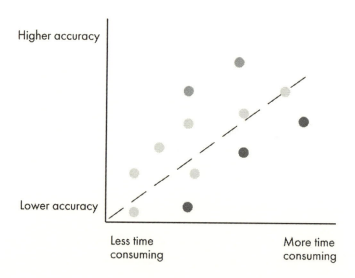

Determining the overall strength of a tool is impossible to do perfectly, but worth the time. Often, decision-makers rely on informal, unquantified, inconsistent, unconsidered tools. Even an imperfect prioritization based on a short amount of careful thought can yield a list of tools that perform better or worse in a given situation. Such a list can suggest which to value, when to use them, how to deal with conflicting results, and how much to update from a priori after getting data from a tool. It also gives a clearer, more descriptive sense of how you value different types of information when making a decision.

Using multiple tools

Indexes: If the goal is to get the most accurate answer, often multiple tools can be used to home in on the truth. An index of tools operates much like the index of elements evaluated during an IQ test, which aims to understand the near impossible to measure "g factor" perfectly.[3] In many cases, the use of three fast tools will give more overall accuracy than the use of a single better, but slower, tool. These indexes, in theory, could also be put on the speed vs. accuracy chart, combining the time cost of doing all of them and seeing what the resulting accuracy score is for the combined conclusion.

Convergence: One principle that can be helpful when considering indexes of tools (which are commonly used in traditional evidence weightings) is the concept of convergence or triangulation. The basic idea is that multiple pieces of evidence should converge on the same answer, which brings additional confidence to the conclusion. For example, if experts and a CEA both suggest the same charity to be high impact, more confidence could be placed in that conclusion than if a single strong argument were used. The value of convergent data is a part of why replication studies are done. Tool convergence occurs when using tools from very different sources leads to similar results; it can be seen as a positive sign that you are arriving closer to the truth.

Convergence curve: Similar to our time curve, there is likely a curve for the optimal number of tools to use. Each tool might offer a distinct way to gain evidence on the topic. For example, talking to experts has a different fundamental methodology than creating a CEA estimate. Taking more angles or using very different tools is a better methodology for finding the truth, but it's likely that at some point the benefit of convergence between different angles also hits diminishing returns.

---

3 The "g factor" here refers to the "general intelligence" factor, which influences performance on cognitive tasks. IQ and other psychometric tests attempt to pinpoint this variable, but it cannot be determined with 100% accuracy.

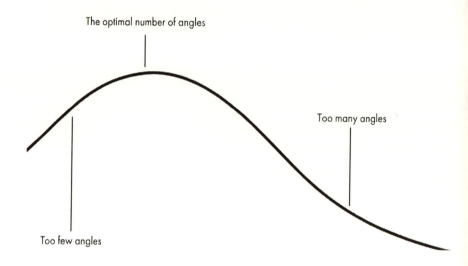

Putting it all together in the charity world

When Charity Entrepreneurship was first starting out, we had to make some key decisions that would affect our organization long-term. One of the first was how long to research before recommending ideas. The charity world is complex and we could easily spend dozens of years coming up with a single recommended charity. That charity might be fantastic, but how would it compare to the tens of charities that could have been started over that same time span?

We had to consider how long to spend exploring ideas vs. launching the best ideas that had come up. After consideration and many rounds of feedback from research and implementation-focused mentors, we determined that recommending a set of charities every year would allow the most impactful charities to be founded. One of our strongest research advisors gave us the key piece of feedback that if we spent too long on research, our previous work would get out of date. For example, in 10 years, the global health space would change sufficiently such that research that year would still have to be done.

Although this time capped our research to one year for a given area, it left us with another problem: how to narrow down a broad area in a single year. Thankfully, another mentor suggested that we use rounds of exploration to narrow down to progressively fewer ideas throughout the year, finally arriving at around ten that were highly researched out of an initial list of hundreds. Using this system allows us to narrow down in a single year from many ideas to the most impactful ones, which can get started quickly enough to make a real difference.

– Joey Savoie (co-founder of Charity Entrepreneurship)

5. Multi-factor decision-making

If you were only allowed one practical tool, the Swiss Army knife would likely be your choice. With multiple smaller tools attached, it can be useful in a large number of situations. However, although helpful, it would pale in comparison to using a more specialized tool or a full toolkit. The Swiss Army knife of decision-making is called multi-factor decision-making, and it involves combining multiple factors or variables into a single conclusion. Unlike the Swiss Army knife, this tool only gets stronger as you acquire other tools, as its combining process can get more informed and sophisticated.

One proponent of this sort of system was Charles Darwin. An analytic fellow, he loved practical lists and well-organized information. He was a user of systems in the extreme, famously making a pros-and-cons chart for whether to marry.[1] Although not much of a romantic, he was wise to realize that when making important decisions it can be extremely helpful to take the factors out of your head and put them to paper.

Models can range from the fairly simple, like a pros-and-cons chart, to the highly complex. Some pros-and-cons lists add a layer of complexity by weighting each factor by importance. For example, when considering which restaurant to eat at, weights will capture the idea that the food being amazing at one eatery is more important for the decision than the fact that it's two minutes farther

---

1 Charles Darwin, Frederick Burkhardt, and Sydney Smith, essay in *The Correspondence of Charles Darwin 2*, 1st ed., 2: 1837–43. (Cambridge: Cambridge University Press, 1986).

from home.

This handbook primarily looks at multi-factor decision-making using spreadsheets, a convenient (but far from the only) way to do it.

5.1. Weighted factor models

Creating a weighted factor model (WFM) involves generating a set of criteria – often between three and twelve – and assigning a weight to each. Possible options are then scored on each of the criteria. The final score incorporates the option's performance on each criterion and the weighting of each criterion, often by multiplying the two together.

Hard factors (such as population size in absolute numbers) and soft factors (such as a score out of ten for population size) can be used in WFMs. It is a particularly useful tool, as it allows decision-makers to combine a large number of objective and subjective factors and identify which ones drive the results. However, it has some weaknesses, such as its inability to adapt automatically to new research that comes in. Like any decision-making tool, it is best used in combination with other methods.

Example weighted factor model (Charity Entrepreneurship 2019):

Metric	Total welfare score (with evidence)	Range	Level of depth	Estimated population size	Odds of feeling pain	Death rate/ reason	Human preference from behind the veil of ignorance	Disease/injury y/functional impairment	Thirst/hunger malnutrition	Anxiety/fear pain/distress	Environment al challenge	Index of Biological markers of happiness	Behavioral interactive restriction
Max score	100 to -100	100 to -100	Hours	In millions			20	20	17	15	15	5	4	4
Human in a high-income country	81	63 : 90	1	36	99%		17	17	13	13	11	5	2	1
Wild Chimp	47	13 : 76	1	2.3	85%		6	8	9	11	7	3	0	2
Human in a low-middle-income country	32	23 : 61	1	1324	99%		13	9	6	0	2	1	2	0
Wild bird	2	-18 : 45	5	400,000	78%		10	0	4	0	2	1	2	0
FF Beef Cow	20	-53 : 7	3	1500	75%		2	7	4	4	1	1	0	3
Wild rat	-28	-48 : 2	3	7000	72%		-12	10	-16	3	-1	3	2	-3
Wild fish	-31	-51 : -3	5	3500000	60%		-6	4	-10	0	-6	1	6	-2
FF Cow milk	-34	-65 : -13	5	264	75%		-4	-12	-7	2	-7	1	-2	-2
Wild bug	-47	-63 : -4	3	10,000,000,000 +	18%		-16	-10	-6	-6	2	-3	6	9
FF Fish-traditional aquaculture	-44	-58 : -27	2	1000000	60%		-16	-14	4	4	-7	-3	-2	-3
EU FF laying hens (enriched cages)	-46	-75 : -31	6	500	70%		-11	-14	-3	4	-2	-2	-3
Wild fish for human use	-47	-69 : -22	3	0.97-2.7 million	60%		-16	-13	-12	0	4	-1	-2	-2
FF Broiler chicken	-48	-71 : -25	3	22000	70%		-17	-19	-16	8	9	-4	-2	-2
FF Turkey	-57	-71 : -26	6	244	70%		-13	-16	-12	1	-16	3	-1	-3
USA FF laying hens (battery cages)	-57	-72 : -46	6	266	70%		-17	-17	-12	4	-16	-3	-2	-4

Reasons this is a helpful tool (in rough order of strength):

Systematism in comparison: WFMs allow a much closer and more systematic comparison than other models (e.g., cost-effectiveness analysis or consulting experts), which generally have more variability. For example, when considering two charity ideas, comparing each of their bottlenecks in very similar terms can lead to a much stronger sense of how well each one performs in this aspect. Many models can be largely affected by unconsidered factors or gaps in information. If a single important factor were not included in a CEA, it would be hard to detect but could strongly affect the results. However, if the same factors are considered across all options and informed by a similar process as in a WFM, there is a lower chance of gaps affecting one idea but not another.

A WFM also excels at increasing the chance of equal rigor when evaluating the options, particularly if answering the questions that define the criteria in the same way. This can be aided further by spending the same amount of time on each option and evaluating them similarly.

Integrates multiple factors: Many models struggle to include multiple different factors in a single number. For example, CEAs do not handle limiting factor concerns very well unless multiple CEAs are done for many different possible levels of scale. Similarly, many CEAs do not include strength of evidence other than as a simple discount at the end of the calculation, which does not capture how to weight different types of uncertainty (e.g., Knightian vs. non-Knightian[2]).

Sandboxing: A large difference between CEAs and WFMs lies in the total weight that a single factor can hold. In a CEA, one very large number can swamp many small numbers. For example, if an intervention could potentially affect a huge number of beings but has a very low chance of working, this initial huge number can still make all the other numbers in the CEA trivial. In contrast, one single large factor can affect a WFM far less, as each factor has a maximum weight. The impact of that factor is thus "sandboxed."

Allows soft and hard inputs to be combined: Some important factors are easy to get a single hard number on (e.g., "total population affected by measles"); for others, it's impossible (e.g., "the tractability of founding a new charity in India"). In a WFM, these factors can be given a soft, but consistent and comparable, number. These soft numbers can be calculated with harder numbers' Z-scores[3] to determine which ideas are outliers in terms of many positive factors.

More angles for learning: One of the purposes of our research process overall is to generate better empirical information about how to rule charity ideas in or

---

2 This refers to the differences in "known unknowns" and "unknown unknowns," i.e., risky, vs. truly unpredictable. For a lengthier explanation, see Andrew Jaffe, "Knightian Uncertainty," *Andrew Jaffe: Leaves on the Line*, May 3, 2017, https://www.andrewjaffe.net/blog/2017/05/knightian-uncer.html.

3 A Z-score represents, roughly, a statistical measurement of how far from the mean a data point is.

out more quickly. WFM is the only system we use in which subcomponents can be correlated individually to our endline results. For example, we can determine if the score for a particular criterion (e.g., evidence base) strongly predicts which interventions are recommended after deep reports are conducted. Pulling out a single aspect like this from a CEA or expert interviews would not be easy.

Preregistration: In many ways, a WFM leaves the fewest areas open to interpretation, with preset questions and descriptions for how different items would score ahead of time. This means that researchers with fairly different starting points and intuitions will more often reach the same conclusions when using a WFM as compared to systems that are more open to researchers' interpretations. This concern most affects the softer elements of a decision-making process, but can also greatly affect CEAs.

Understandability: Intuitive systems can be built into a WFM, making it quick and easy to understand relative to other systems. Color coding is easily used to show areas of comparative strength and weakness across a large number of ideas; conditional formatting can be used on spreadsheets to color code automatically, quickly offering a visual sense of the variance. Methodologies like expert views lend themselves to written paragraphs, which are slower. It's faster to grasp the endline number of a CEA, but understanding the full logic and weightings behind the numbers takes longer than with any other system.

Encourages quantified consideration: Like CEAs, WFMs encourage the quantified and numerical consideration of factors. By default, many people (including experts) do not think in quantitative terms. For example, when asked if an event will happen, most people think of this as a binary question (yes/no) rather than thinking about the probability of the event happening. WFMs require quantitative inputs for each variable, which encourages quantitative thinking and calibration (e.g., an event being 20% vs. 80% likely).

Can lead to novel conclusions: Like CEAs, WFMs can lead to surprising conclusions. With preset methodology and calculations, it is common that after filling out the data, a WFM will suggest something to be high impact that would not have appeared so initially by taking a softer, higher-level look.

Makes it easier to communicate conclusions: Because all the factors are researched and scored separately, we can easily distill the advantages and disadvantages of each idea and explain why one is better than the other.

We think that although this model has considerable promise, it also has many weaknesses that can be counteracted by using multiple tools.

Flaws of WFM (from most to least problematic):

Not a commonly used methodology: WFMs are not a commonly used system, at least in the formal way we use them. Thus, there are few established norms and a lower level of initial understanding from team members and external readers alike (although they can be presented intuitively through tools like color-coding, allowing readers to gain familiarity with the system quickly). This also suggests there might be an unknown but good reason why this sort of methodology is not used more often.

Low flexibility: This system is the least flexible and adaptable across different options if the questions, full methodology, and criteria weightings are all preset. This reduces bias, but can also give a large amount of weighting to a factor that might be important overall, but far less important for a specific option.

Limited question cross applicability: A related concern to its low flexibility is that even if a specific question is not always important to cover, research hours will go into it anyway. Likewise, a question that is important but specific to a given charity is less likely to be covered by this methodology.

Can be hard to determine the source or reasoning of weighting criteria: Endline weights are often the only factor closely examined. Due to these endline weightings being used to represent a large number of questions and sources of evidence, it can be hard to track down what questions factored into this weighting and how heavily each one was factored.

Considerable upfront time required: A large amount of upfront methodological time is required when compared to other systems, because most of the methodology is designed ahead of time and closely followed throughout the process. This means that research is not produced for a long time at the start of a research year and also does not yield feedback loops as quickly.

Can make nonnumerical data look numerical: A concern with the WFM is that it assigns numerical ratings to nonnumerical data. This can confuse and mislead people as to the objectivity of the system if not explained clearly.

5.2. Using a spreadsheet to make decisions

Making a spreadsheet is a practical way to create a weighted factor model. Spreadsheet decision-making can be used on a huge number of problems.[4]

Here it is, as a ten-step process:

1. Come up with a well-defined goal.

2. Brainstorm many plausible solutions to achieve that goal.

3. Create criteria through which you will evaluate those solutions.

4. Create custom weights for the criteria.

5. Quickly use intuition to prioritize the solutions on the criteria so far.

6. Come up with research questions that would help you determine how well each solution fits the criteria.

7. Use these research questions to do shallow research into the top ideas.

8. Use research to rerate and rerank the solutions.

9. Pick the top ideas worth testing and do deeper research or MVP testing,[5] as is applicable.

10. Pick the final option based on the information gathered.

This ten-step process immediately uses iterative depth to narrow down options. Take as an example of this process Charity Entrepreneurship's first round of research, through which our team decided to launch Charity Science Health.

Come up with a well-defined goal: We wanted to start an effective global poverty charity, where effective is taken to mean a low cost per life saved comparable to current GiveWell top charities.

Brainstorm many plausible solutions to achieve that goal: For this, we decided to start by looking at the intervention level. Since there are thousands of potential interventions, we placed a lot of emphasis on those that were plausibly highly effective. We looked at GiveWell's priority programs plus a few that we thought were worthy additions.

---

4 The following process contributed by Peter Wildeford, "Using a Spreadsheet to Make Good Decisions: Five Examples," Effective Altruism Forum, Nov. 25, 2016, https://forum.effectivealtruism. org/posts/q7s8v7LjAdcYXAyAs/using-a-spreadsheet-to-make-good-decisions-five-examples.

5 MVP here refers to Minimum Viable Product, i.e., a minimalistic early prototype of your product or idea that has just enough features to be used for testing, feedback, and gathering information for improved future iterations.

Create criteria through which you will evaluate those solutions/create custom weights for the criteria: For this decision, we spent a full month of our six-month project thinking through the criteria. We weighted them based on both importance and the expected variance that would occur between our options. We strongly valued cost-effectiveness, flexibility,[6] and scalability, moderately valued strength of evidence, metric focus, and indirect effects, and weakly valued logistical possibility and other factors.

Come up with research questions that would help you determine how well each solution fits the criteria: We came up with a list of questions and a research process.[7]

Use the research questions to do shallow research into the top ideas, then use research to rerate and rerank the solutions: Since this decision was important and we were pretty uninformed about the different interventions, we did shallow research into all of the choices. We then produced the following spreadsheet:

Program		Overall	Flexibility	Cost effectiveness	Metric focus	Logistical possibility	Indirect effects	Evidence	Scalability	Other factors
Malnutrition	Iron supplementation	8	Mid	Mid	High	Easy	High	High	High	Mid
Cash	Conditional cash transfers	8	High	Low-High	Low-High	Mid	High	High	High	High
Malnutrition	Super salt charity/multimicronutrient	8	Mid	High	Mid	Easy-mid	High	Mid	High	High
Behavior change	Mass media to promote behavior change	8	High	Low-High	Low-High	Easy-mid	High	Mid-low	High	High
Immunization	immunizations	7	Mid-low	High	Mid-low	Hard	Mid	High	High	Mid
NCDs	NCD best buy	7	High	High	Low	Mid-Hard	High	Mid-low	High	Mid
Malnutrition	Treatment for severe acute malnutrition	7	Mid	Mid	Low	Easy	High	Mid-low	High	Mid
Malnutrition	Vitamin A supplementation	7	Mid	High	Mid-low	Easy	Low	High-mid	Low	Low
Data	Charities that collect or generate information and data relevant to GW	6	High	Unknown	Mid	Mid	Low	Low	Low	High
Malnutrition	Salt iodization	6	Mid	High	Lowest	Easy	High	High	Mid	Mid
Behavior change	Breastfeeding promotion	5.5	Mid	High	Low	Mid-Hard	Low	Mid	Mid-High	High
Malnutrition	Folic acid	5.5	Mid	Mid-low	High	Easy	Mid-low	High	Mid	Mid
Behavior change	Handwashing promotion	5	Mid	Mid-high	Mid-low	Mid-Hard	High	Mid-low	High	High
Targeted treatment	Pneumonia treatment	5	Mid-High	Mid	Low	Mid-Hard	High	Low	High	High
Diarrhea	Oral rehydration therapy	5	Mid-low	Mid-low	Low	Mid-Hard	Mid	High	High	Mid
Mass treatment	Deworming	4.25	Mid	High	Mid	Easy	High	Low	Mid-low	Mid
HIV	Provision of anti-retroviral therapy to treat HIV/AIDS	4	Low	Low-High	Low	Hard	Mid	Mid	High	Mid
Diarrhea	Therapeutic zinc supplementation	4	Mid-low	Mid-low	Low	Mid-Hard	High	Mid-low	High	Mid
HIV	Prevention of mother-to-child transmission of HIV	3	Mid-low	High	Low	Mid	Mid	Mid	Low	Mid
Targeted treatment	Trachoma control (mass drug blind)	3	Mid-low	High	High	Hard	Mid	High	Mid-low	Mid
Targeted treatment	Tuberculosis case finding and first-line treatment	3	Mid-low	Mid	Mid-low	Hardest	Mid	High	Low	Mid
Cash	Unconditional cash transfers (external)	3	Mid	Low	High	Easy	Mid	High	Mid	Mid
Malaria	Malaria treatment	3	Low	Mid-low	Low	Hard	Low	Mid	Mid	Low

Afterward, it was pretty easy to drop 22 out of the 30 possible choices[8] and go with the top eight, which ranked 7 or above on our scale.

Pick the top ideas worth testing and do deeper research or MVP testing, as is applicable/Repeat steps 8 and 9 until sufficiently confident in a decision:

---

6 See Charity Entrepreneurship, "The Value of Being Flexible," June 22, 2016, https://www.charityentrepreneurship.com/blog/the-value-of-being-flexible.

7 Charity Entrepreneurship, internal "Intervention level research questions and process poverty," Google Document, accessed Nov. 10, 2021.

8 See Charity Entrepreneurship, "Summaries on Areas we are No Longer Researching," March 14, 2016, https://www.charityentrepreneurship.com/blog/summaries-on-areas-we-are-no-longer-researching.

We then researched the top eight more deeply, aiming to turn them into concrete charity ideas rather than amorphous interventions. When reranking, we came up with a top five and wrote up more detailed reports – SMS immunization reminders, tobacco taxation, iron and folic acid fortification, conditional cash transfers, and a poverty research organization.

Pick the final option based on the information gathered: As we continued to research further, it became more clear that SMS immunization reminders performed best on the criteria. It was highly cost-effective, with strong evidence and easy testability.

5.3. Improving your models

There are many ways to learn and improve your modeling; here, we will briefly discuss three of the more meta. Each of these can help improve your WFM and make them come to better conclusions in the end.

- Selecting the right factors
- Weighting factors well
- Z-score

Selecting the right factors

Likely the hardest part of making a good WFM is picking the right factors to model. This is partly because the ideal factors will differ according to the exact problem you are aiming to solve, and partly due to the abstract nature of the factors themselves. Factors in the model can include anything from quite hard data like CEA results to very soft judgment calls such as a general sense of logistical difficulty. As you learn more tools throughout this book, many of them will become future columns in your weighted factor models.

Three criteria separate good factors from bad ones.

Relevance: The first and most obvious; the factor has to be relevant. If we are trying to determine what charity to start, the number of letters in the intervention name could, in theory, be a column, but it would not correlate with our endline goal. A much more relevant criterion might be how many studies have been conducted on the intervention.

Cross applicability: As discussed in the previous chapter, tools must cross apply. A column like "estimated lives saved from malaria" would work if you were only considering malaria interventions, but not if you were considering many different global health interventions as it would only apply to some of the options considered. Another thing to watch out for is columns that do not differentiate between options. If a factor is scored as "medium" for all options, it does not add value to the decision-making process.

Operationalizability: Can you get data on it? A column that would take ten years to fill out is not helpful for making a decision that you need to make in a month. Is it more objective or subjective? Can others understand what the column indicates? These sorts of factors can allow your model to be interpreted and criticized by outsiders.

For highly important decision spreadsheets, you can even make a weighted factor model for possible metrics, as we did for our animal welfare points system.[9] Our detailed metrics sheet outlined how different metrics performed on the various criteria, and the animal spreadsheet used our top metrics to compare the lives of different animals.

Weighting factors

A similar process to the way you select factors can be used to weight them. Certain factors will be better than others and more important to your endline conclusion. Having a "weights" column at the top of your spreadsheet can allow you to adjust weights quickly and easily based on how important they are. It also helps to order the factors by how heavily they are weighted so the most important factors are at the front of the sheet.

Z-score

Some columns will be objective; others will be subjective. Some will have wide ranges; others will have very tight ranges. A column like "population size" might be different by a factor of 100, while a factor like vaccination rate might only vary by a few percentage points. These differences mean that simply multiplying these sorts of factors together would lead to unhelpful conclusions; therefore, we turn to the Z-Score.

Put simply, a Z-Score is a statistical measurement of one data point's distance from the mean, or average, within a given dataset. Larger Z-Scores indicate that

---

9 Charity Entrepreneurship, "Is it Better to Be a Wild Rat or a Factory Farmed Cow? A Systematic Method for Comparing Animal Welfare," Sept. 17, 2018, https://www.charityentre-preneurship.com/blog/is-it-better-to-be-a-wild-rat-or-a-factory-farmed-cow-a-systematic-method-for-comparing-animal-welfare.

the data point is farther away from the mean (which always has a Z-Score of 0). Once a data point reaches a calculated and sufficiently high Z-Score, whether positive (above average) or negative (below average), it's considered an "outlier," as it's noticeably different from the average data points.

These scores are calculated using statistics, but you don't need to be a statistician to understand them. Technically, they measure "standard deviations," which is a term that explains the relative distribution of your data points as a whole. For example, if you had a dataset of 50 numbers, and half of them had a value of 1 and the rest a value of 2, there wouldn't be much "deviation from the norm" there. They're all concentrated right around 1.5. So, the standard deviation would be a pretty small value. If you then replaced a "1" with "37," that data point would increase the overall standard deviation pretty significantly. It would also still have a pretty high Z-score; it's way above all the rest, and the other 49 data points aren't very different from one another. It's so big, relative to your other points, that it might even be an outlier. To take this idea further: if you had 50 numbers ranging from 1 to 1 billion, the standard deviation would be huge. There's tons of variation there. It would take a wildly high or low number to show even one "standard deviation" from the mean – and remember, that's your Z-score – so most Z-scores for any given data points would probably be pretty low.

Don't worry too much about the nitty-gritty. All this means is that we now have a helpful way to compare different data points using a standard unit. Since the Z-score for each data point comes from its own dataset and is defined by distribution, not numerical value alone, it won't be affected by other, different types of factors. To give an example: a population of one million and a vaccination rate of 10% might end up with similar Z-scores, despite being hugely different in absolute terms. As a result, when we standardize using Z-scores, the numerically much higher population data point does not take over the data we have on vaccination rate.

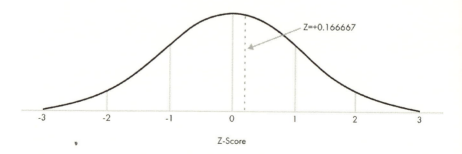

Image: Z-score indicating a value 0.16 standard deviations above the mean.

Z-scores can be used informally to:

- Standardize values measured across multiple different criteria, so they can be combined into an overall score and compared to other ideas. For example, we can have an overall Z-score for a given idea based on how it compares to the average in terms of CEA, expressed in $ per DALY;[10] population size affected, expressed in millions; and crowdedness, expressed in percentage of the problem addressed by other entities.

- Assess how a given idea scores compared to all the other ideas considered (including an average idea), for example, idea x is better than 70 percent of the ideas on our list.

- Spot anomalous values. For example, if one of the factors in the scale were an objective number such as population size, a Z-score value would show which countries are outliers relative to others even though population size can differ by orders of magnitude.

- Reduce risk of some biases. For example, in a situation where the score is not converted to a Z-score, we may happen to use a higher range of values for one criterion but not for another, effectively changing its weight. For example, suppose a given intervention is evaluated on each factor on an arbitrary scale of 1 to 10. However, one criterion, scale, varies significantly, and you tend to give out 7s and 8s frequently, while on the criterion of tractability, you tend to give very consistent scores of 4 or 5. The net effect is that even if you think tractability is more important, you end up weighting the scale higher. Converting to a Z-score takes care of this.

Z-scores are fairly simple to generate in all spreadsheet software and can solve many issues that can come up when comparing very different types of numbers.[11]

---

10 Disability-adjusted life-year.

11 More on Z-scores can be found in Dana Lee Ling's "Introduction to Statistics using Google Sheets," accessed Nov. 10, 2021, http://www.comfsm.fm/~dleeling/statistics/text6.html; and in Douglas Hubbard's *The Failure of Risk Management* (Hoboken, NJ: Wiley, 2009).

Putting it all together in the charity world

The Lead Exposure Elimination Project advocates for lead paint regulation to reduce childhood lead poisoning. When LEEP was looking to implement our initial pilot program, we wanted to make sure we targeted the ideal country. The wrong country choice could mean wasted money, wasted time, and worst of all, failure to achieve impact. Country selection is a complex decision with lots of variables. Because of that, multi-factor decision-making is the perfect tool. Spreadsheets helped us assess all of these factors at once.

We included every country in our spreadsheet, selected factors that would influence the impact of our intervention, and then compiled and color-coded the relevant data. We took into account factors affecting counterfactual impact, potential scale of impact, and likelihood of impact. To get a sense of counterfactual impact we created columns to collate data on whether there was already lead paint regulation in place, and whether there were already other organizations working on lead paint advocacy in each country. For the potential scale of the impact we created columns for population size and growth, and severity of the lead burden. For the likelihood of impact we looked at factors affecting tractability and feasibility, including the level of English spoken, safety, government stability, travel accessibility during the pandemic, and the level of COVID-19.

Weighting these different factors to establish an overall ranking of countries was challenging. Multi-factor decision-making allowed us to combine hard and soft inputs of different importance and reliability to select the most promising first target country, and also to identify a number of viable alternative target countries. The systematic comparison of countries has also allowed us to communicate our decision-making clearly to others and adjust prioritization easily as new information arises.

- Jack Rafferty and Lucia Coulter (co-founders of Lead Exposure Elimination Project)

6. Rationality

The humble hammer is a tool that most are familiar with and many will have used, although few are experts. It can be used to make progress quickly on something and is a key tool in building new things. However, a hammer can also make us overconfident. It is often overused due to its intuitive importance. Many people think they are an expert builder if they own a hammer, and hammers can cause a lot of damage if used improperly.

Similarly, rationality, i.e., using reason and logic, is a powerful instrument that can improve a huge number of decisions. Although knowledge of rationality runs far deeper than we are able to cover in this book, techniques can often be taught in a single blog post that rapidly lead to better choices and avoiding obvious mistakes.

6.1. Strengths and weaknesses

Rationality differs from many of our other tools in that it's often less formal, more philosophical and theoretical. It can take into account forms of evidence and considerations that may be neglected by other methodologies.

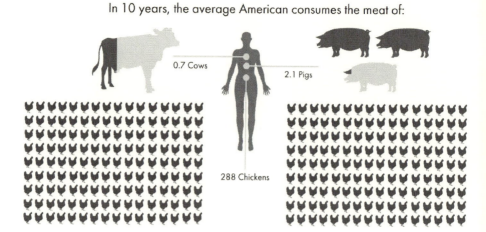

In 10 years, the average American consumes the meat of:

0.7 Cows

2.1 Pigs

288 Chickens

Rational model example: identifying the small animal replacement problem, which demonstrates how shifting consumption patterns from larger animals (e.g., cows) to smaller ones (e.g., chickens) can cause a greater number of animals to suffer, due to the increase in lives lost for the same number of calories. Source: www.BlitzResults.com.[1]

Strengths

Many weak arguments can often be stronger than a single strong argument.[2] Sometimes intuition can differ substantially from a calculated estimate, even when both are based on the same information at the outset. Some lines of reasoning are more theoretical or subjective in nature but still make for crucial considerations that make a charity idea worth pursuing or not.

Reasons this is a helpful tool (in order of strength):

Captures information that does not fit into other systems: The biggest advantage of rational consideration is that it takes into account large pieces of information not easily captured by other systems. For example, maybe we know that a nonexpert group has a very strong view on an intervention, or there are

---

1 BlitzResults, "Meat-Calculator to Evaluate the Environmental Impact of Meat Consumption," March 23, 2021, https://www.blitzresults.com/en/meat/. The image here has been altered and is licensed under the Creative Commons Attribution-ShareAlike 4.0 International License. To view a copy of the license, visit https://creativecommons.org/licenses/by-sa/4.0/.

2 Jonah S., "Many Weak Arguments vs. One Relatively Strong Argument," LessWrong, June 3, 2013, https://www.lesswrong.com/posts/9W9P2snxu5Px746LD/many-weak-arguments-vs-one-relatively-strong-argument.

some wisdom of the crowds or Chesterton's fence[3] arguments in favor of an intervention. Often, formal models do not offer a clear way to include this sort of information even to a small degree. Rational consideration gives both time and space to outline this sort of evidence.

Captures information that would otherwise be lost: Some information may fit into a different system but might not have been clearly captured. For example, if you have several quick conversations at a conference, you might get a sense of a given issue but not know exactly which individual or combination of individuals this sense came from. Information like this can easily get lost when creating deep formalized reports, but it is still important data and can lead to differences in researcher-intuition vs. model-based results.

Allows space for more divergent conclusions: Many of the most valuable research contributions have come from divergent or original thinking. Detailed models do not often encourage divergent conclusions or thinking when applied to an intervention or issue. For example, rational consideration would more easily spot if an intervention made sense only when paired with a different intervention instead of being performed in isolation.

Takes into account many perspectives: Because rational consideration includes both information that does not fit into other systems and information that would otherwise be lost, it ends up taking a large number of data points into account.

Takes into account multiple reference classes: One of the largest challenges in research is picking an appropriate reference class to compare the current intervention to. Often when comparing something it's easy to get stuck considering a single or limited number of reference classes, whereas softer comparisons often use a broader range of classes.

Is very quick: Rational consideration is a much faster system to use to go deeper on a specific issue. A researcher can more quickly read and synthesize information when there is not a prespecified question list or methodology than when seeking specific answers to specific questions. It is also one of the quickest ways to get a broad overview of a topic.

---

3 "Wisdom of the crowds" is the concept that large groups of people may have better sense than individual experts. "Chesterton's fence" refers to the saying, "Don't remove a fence until you know why it was put up in the first place." Essentially, there might be a good reason that things are done the way they are, you just don't know it yet.

Has a high degree of flexibility across ideas: Some ideas require more time to be put into certain aspects compared to others. For example, an area that affects the total human population might require more philosophical consideration than a simpler intervention that merely makes already existing people less sick. Thanks to rational consideration's lower level of structure, it can be used to direct more time toward idea-specific concerns.

Formalizes already existing intuitions/heuristics: One goal of writing out one's considerations is to make more transparent the intuitions and heuristics that are used. Almost every important evaluative decision relies on intuitions or best guesses at key points, but having these considerations discussed and elaborated on makes it clearer where they come from, compared to a system such as a CEA where the full explanation might be "best guess."

Cross-domain knowledge is generated: Many times, the hours spent in rational consideration are used for cross-applicable questions that might not be the most important for any single charity idea but are important for a wide range of charity ideas.

Weaknesses

Rational consideration has a lot of breadth-based advantages; however, it suffers from many of the same concerns as expert views, but on a larger scale. Rational models are generally formed by a single individual, making standard human biases a substantial concern.

Nonsystematicity: Given the huge amount of data, conflicting experts, and possible angles from which to consider a complex issue, it is often easy for a researcher to find a long list of citations broadly supporting their views, even if the views are wrong. Rational consideration is particularly susceptible to this concern.

Lack of precommitted methodology: The best studies conducted in science generally have a pre-analysis plan. There are many resources on why this is a good policy that improves research quality.[4] Some forms of research have clearer ways to precommit to certain methodologies or sources.

---

4 See Rachel Glennerster, "Module 8.3, Pre-analysis plans, Plain," under "Resources," accessed Nov. 10, 2021, https://rachel-glennerster.squarespace.com/lecture-notes, for a useful Powerpoint and further reading.

Nonnumerical: Rational consideration is generally soft and nonnumerical, which can easily lead to factors holding inappropriate weight based on salience and general human weaknesses with numbers. It also makes many of the assumptions less clear because terms such as "it seems probable" are softer, which does not give the reader a clear sense of the percentage-based confidence of the claim.

Cognitive bias: Some of these mental heuristics reflect useful knowledge that is hard to backtrace; however, it is well documented that biases can consistently negatively affect decision-making in a wide range of ways. Rational consideration is the most vulnerable system we use in this respect, with biases all but guaranteed.

Dependence on researcher strength: Rational consideration leaves the bulk of the time distribution and research decisions to the individual researcher. This could lead to considerable quality differences between reports and researchers, making comparative results less useful. For example, a generally skeptical researcher might use their time to focus on flaws, and a more optimistic one might focus on implementation strategies. This could lead a reader or researcher to have an unreflective conclusion of what would have happened if a different research lead had been running the project.

Overweighting personal experience: Overweighting personal experience is a cognitive bias that is likely more severe for rational consideration. If someone has tried an idea or methodology in the past and it did not work for them, this is extremely likely to affect their judgment of similar ideas in the future even when it should not. For example, imagine your odds of success at an activity are ten percent. If when you try you do not succeed, your update should be almost nothing, rationally, but in practice will generally be substantial intuition-wise.

Intractable issues: Given this methodology's focus on theoretical issues, it's easy to spend a considerable amount of time on a question that cannot be resolved. Some issues will be important for decision-making but very difficult to make progress on – for example, meta ethics.

Subjective individual judgment call: If a reader's values or epistemology are largely different from those of the lead researcher, the results will be less cross applicable than expert interviews or cost-effectiveness estimates would be. It is also not easy to, for example, change a single input and see the difference in results, as it is with the more numerical and quantitative models.

6.2. Making decisions more rationally

Biases

In theory: Most books or courses on rationality start first with a large section dedicated to the many biases and common mistakes the human brain makes. They are both numerous and damning for our ability to make good decisions. Some are well known, such as loss aversion (the tendency to prefer avoiding losses to acquiring equivalent gains) and confirmation bias (the tendency to look for evidence that favors the conclusion we already have). Others are less familiar, such as the illusory truth (the tendency to believe something if it's said multiple times).

In practice: Knowing about cognitive biases is a far cry from escaping them. For every choice, dozens of biases push in every direction, and it's often fruitless to try to determine which option is more biased.

The better path is to minimize biases by creating systems and cultivating attitudes that are less susceptible to them. For example, try to come into a decision with a truly open mind and as little invested into the outcome as possible. Or, spread out the conclusion over a long period of time so a temporary bias is less likely to affect you.

Some questions worth considering to reduce your bias include:

- Have I taken a step back and considered this at a later time?
- Are my emotions pulling me toward an answer before I've considered all the options?
- Am I coming in keen to find the truth whatever the outcome?

Example: A hard decision came up in a conversation between two charity co-founders. One thinks they should approach a potential partner now; the other thinks it's better to wait till they are more established. They decided to take 24 hours and sleep on the decision to see if they would change their minds about which course of action was the right call. They also both agreed to come back to it with fresh and open minds. Thanks to briefly hitting pause on the decision, they were able to make a much less biased choice.

Broad research

In theory: When making a decision, it is easy to rely on a few sources or types of sources for the bulk of your information. For example, it would be easy to read many studies and books written by academics but gather limited information from field workers, who often have a very different perspective. The point of broad research is to get a sense of the area from multiple angles.

In practice: This involves watching related documentaries, reading related books, going through overview sources such as Wikipedia, and trying to look at the issue from as many different introductory perspectives as possible. The exact way that hours are used in broad research will vary depending on the decision and where the most information can be found, but often involves many different methods and sources.

The main questions worth considering in the broad research phase include:

- Have I looked at all the related summary material available on evaluation websites and summary websites, or generated by cross-cutting organizations?
- Have I considered at least four distinctive clusters with different views on this issue and read some resources from each?
- Have I reviewed information from a number of different media (e.g., studies, news articles, Wikipedia, documentaries, interviews)?

Example: When conducting broad research on malaria-preventing bed nets, one might read a book on the historical progress of the fight against malaria; watch a short documentary on a specific village that is combating malaria; read the Wikipedia pages on malaria, bed nets, and other related interventions; read blog posts from half a dozen different authors writing on the topic; and listen to a podcast interviewing a bed net producer.

Crucial considerations

In theory: Crucial considerations are factors that could significantly affect an intervention. Often the most important use of rational thinking is in where to spend the majority of your time. In some cases, a consideration will be important and cut across many possible paths you are weighing. Thinking carefully about where to put your mental resources is an important and neglected skill.

In practice: When researching an intervention, a consideration that is very important to the conclusion and will require dedicated hours will often present itself, as will many other considerations that are much less important. Often, it will be worthwhile to brainstorm multiple possible crucial considerations and spend an hour split between them (according to their importance and the progress expected) before diving into one.

Questions to consider:

- What are the top crucial considerations in this area?
- How likely am I to make progress on this consideration given the hours I have?
- Does this affect enough charity ideas to be worth a supporting report?

Example: When considering an online cognitive behavioral therapy (CBT) application, one of the biggest questions might be whether online therapy has evidence of working and, if so, in what contexts. This issue is likely large enough to be worth spending a few days of research on, but not large enough to spend a full month on.

Steelmanning views

In theory: Two common terms used when considering arguments are the strawman and the steelman. Strawmanning an idea creates a weakened version of it that is easy to knock down. Steelmanning creates a stronger version. Steelmanning arguments can lead to much better conclusions, as how well the case is presented is less important than finding the truth.

In practice: Strawmanning can be commonly seen in debates. For example, one person might claim, "I think X country has more people who are clinically obese." A strawman of the argument might be, "So you think all people in X country are obese?" This version of the claim is weaker and therefore easier to argue with, but may not be what the original speaker intended. Conversely, a steelman of the above claim might be, "So you think country X has more people who are obese than other relevantly similar countries?" This framing, in fact, makes the argument stronger and is likely what the person meant had they expressed themselves more clearly.

Questions to consider:

- What is the strongest possible version of this argument?

- Can I paraphrase a person's argument to them so that they might respond, "That's even better than how I said it"?
- Am I confusing the strength of an argument with the strength of the arguer?

Example: A co-founder was speaking with an employee about ways to improve the organization. The employee mentioned that they did not understand the long-term vision of the organization and it was affecting their motivation. A strawman response to this argument might be: "So you struggle to stay motivated unless you have the ten-year plan laid out in all its minutiae?" A steelman of the argument might be: "Many employees will have trouble staying motivated without a good sense of the organization's long-term vision. At least one and potentially multiple people in our current organization feel this way. Co-founders often seem like the people best placed to make sure that vision is communicated and understood, and in this organization, this is an area with room for improvement." After really getting a sense of the strongest argument their employee was making, the co-founder changed their processes to include more updates about longer-term planning to less senior members of staff.

Epistemic modesty

In theory: It's hard to know when you are wrong or right about something – particularly in areas where there is less hard data. Epistemic modesty is the idea that you might be wrong. It connects to being self-skeptical and setting up your beliefs to be falsifiable. Basically, epistemic modesty means being humble about your own viewpoints, particularly when compared to those of someone equally or more knowledgeable on a topic.

In practice: Epistemic modesty is about really putting a solid chance on the possibility that someone else is right and you are wrong (no matter how correct you feel internally) and acting accordingly. This is common in some instances – if a doctor tells you what's causing your symptoms, you tend to defer to their judgment – but much less so in others. At times, someone's values might diverge from your own; for instance, your parents might have a different vision of what will make you happy. But sometimes, disagreements are about how to assess evidence and how to weigh different factors. If you assign an equal chance to your peer being correct as yourself, you should weight their view accordingly.

Questions to consider:

- Whom among my peers do I trust as much as myself for this decision?
- Do I not only speak but also act in a way that reflects uncertainty?
- When was the last time I went against my intuition and trusted someone else?

Example: A founder of a fantastic impactful charity once told me that to found a charity, you need to know more than is possible for any one person. Instead of thinking, "How do I learn all these things?" you instead need to ask, "Who might know the answer to this question already?" This founder was able to build up an expert advisory board of some of the best people in the field and use it to help guide their strategy – sometimes deferring to their judgment, and other times sticking the course after listening and reflecting.

Putting it all together in the charity world

"The map is not the territory," as famously remarked by the scientist Alfred Korzybski. We often confuse models of reality with reality itself. Every time you try to make sense of the world, keep in mind that ultimately your model is only a map. It might stop you from getting lost, but it will always be an imperfect representation.

When CE modeled the effectiveness of corporate cage-free campaigns, one of our biggest concerns was whether companies would follow through on their commitments. To chart a map of the true follow-through rate, I applied multiple tools from the rationality toolbox to come to a best guess given the information I had.

- Modeling with non-binary outcomes. Given the uncertainties, I should assign credence to my judgment according to how much evidence points in the same direction, and how strong the evidence is, etc. For example, I might accord a 77% credence to my belief that 80% of companies will follow through. As more data comes up, I gradually update my beliefs and credence.
- Evidence from radically different sources (e.g., animal advocates, farmers, and data). This can create robustness in the model and indicate where my map differs from others and why, uncovering crucial considerations.
- Imagining two worlds: world 1, where X is true (e.g., where companies will follow through on their commitments); and world 2, where it is not. Which world does reality most closely resemble? Look for confirming and disconfirming evidence.

All these techniques and more (Bayesian reasoning, cluster approach, Occam's razor, etc.) led me to consider 35 independent factors that together informed my thinking about the effectiveness of these campaigns. As I encounter new evidence, I can easily update my map and, hopefully, edge closer to understanding the territory.

– Karolina Sarek (co-founder of Charity Entrepreneurship)

7. Scientific method

Science loves taking things apart and understanding how they work. Often scientific progress is slow and incremental, like tightening a screw. Matching the hundreds of types of screwdrivers is a huge range of scientific techniques useful in a wide range of different situations. And sadly, in both cases, there is limited standardization in the methodological process.

The scientific method is likely the most established and proven of the tools that we cover here. While you will not be able to learn it at the same speed as rationality, it can be used to build a much stronger foundation of evidence and confidence in the way the world works.

7.1. Strengths and weaknesses of the scientific method

The scientific method is an incredibly powerful tool that propels entire fields forward. The amazing progress of medicine over the years is due in no small part to its utilization of scientific methodology. However, like every tool, it has strengths and weaknesses. When talking about science, we are broadly referring to the collection of tools used at the higher end of scientific data such as those used in randomized controlled trials (RCTs) or meta-analysis.

Reasons this is a helpful tool include:

Well understood and well developed: Of all the tools described in this book, scientific evidence and the scientific methodology are likely the most understood and developed. Scientific methodology has been a mainstay in key fields for years, and although it's less common in the charity world, it has rapidly been gaining traction, with the randomista movement[1] in global health leading the charge. Since scientific tools and methodologies have been used for so long, a wealth of information is available both on subcomponents such as randomization and on improving the field itself (meta science).

Rigorous and consistent: Due to the level of effort and time put into the methodology, it has relatively clear and consistent usages. Although there are entire books written about how items like statistical significance are misused, the consistency in the terms used and the ways to evaluate the outcome of studies is quite unique among the tools of decision-making.

Incredible track record: Scientific tools have the most demonstrated ability to improve the choices that are made. When scientific methodologies, particularly those at the top of the evidence pyramid, have been used in the past, they have consistently improved fields. Even complex fields like psychology and policy have been aided by the methodology's use.

Multifaceted: The tools of science are extremely numerous and could span several books. Science is designed more as hundreds of heuristics and method-ologies than as one grand overarching theme. Although this means it takes far longer to master, learning scientific methodology can continue to improve your decisions up to a very high level of expertise.

While science might be the most reliable tool, it does have weaknesses that mean it cannot be used in every situation.

Speed: One of the biggest flaws of science is that it can be a very slow meth-odology both to learn and to use. Typically, the best sorts of scientific evidence can take years to generate, and if it goes through formal publishing channels it can take years more to be peer reviewed. This can make many of science's best techniques best suited for a charity later in its life. Slow speed of application also often means that when testing a factor using, for example, a large-scale study, a charity cannot adapt or change its model partway through. As such, conducting a study is not only a significant time investment but also a significant

---

1 Proponents of randomized controlled trials in development cooperation. See the Nobel prize-winning work of Esther Duflo, Abhijit Banerjee, and Michael Kremer; starting point at Ewen Callaway, "'Randomistas' who used controlled trials to fight poverty win economics Nobel," Nature News, Oct. 14, 2019, https://www.nature.com/articles/d41586-019-03125-y.

commitment to the current model.

Cost: Many of the top techniques can be highly expensive compared to other methodologies. A weighted factor model can be done by a single staff member with a few months' training. The cost of running a full study can be hundreds of thousands of dollars, or even millions, depending on the context. Often, one study is not enough to make the full case for a given element, meaning this cost can be incurred multiple times.

Breadth: Due in part to factors like cost and speed, but also due to the specificity often needed to best apply its methodology, science can sometimes be limited in its scope. In low-evidence situations, it can be hard to make sense of the data using scientific tools. Scientific tools also have little to say about creating hypotheses or comparing the value of different options. They are designed far more to explore the "how" to test a given idea rather than the "what" of which idea should be tested.

7.2. The importance of evidence

Any money spent on an intervention that doesn't work is money wasted – money that could have saved lives. This is why evidence is so important. You've got to have a high level of confidence that the intervention is having the intended effect. Imagine two charities: Stop AIDS (a made-up charity for illustration's sake), and Homeopaths Without Borders (a real charity, unfortunately). Stop AIDS provides antiretroviral drugs, which are clinically proven to improve the quality and quantity of life of HIV positive patients dramatically. Homeopaths Without Borders provides "medicine" that has been proven ineffective.[2]

Now, we chose an obviously ineffective charity to prove our point, but there are many other charities that have no scientific evidence of their impact. In fact, it's the norm.[3] And there are a fair few charities out there that have been evaluated and deemed harmful, yet they're still actively seeking and accepting funding.

---

2 See an evidence review at NHMRC, "Homeopathy," last modified Oct. 14, 2021, https://www.nhmrc.gov.au/about-us/resources/homeopathy.

3 GiveWell, "Most Charities' Evidence," accessed Nov. 10, 2021, https://www.givewell.org/giving101/Most-Charities-Evidence.

Different types of scientific evidence

There are hundreds of different types of evidence, ranging from casual anecdotes to randomized controlled trials with tens of thousands of participants. How can you know which sources to trust when researching interventions? Below, we summarize some of the key pros and cons of the types of evidence charities use most commonly, in order from strongest to weakest.

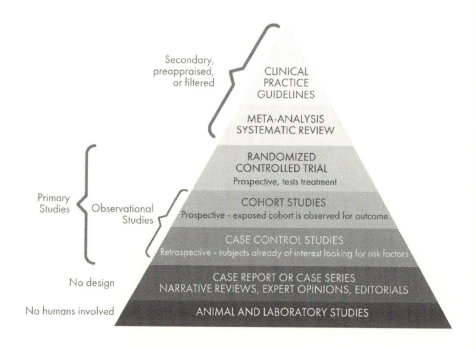

Image: illustration of study types adapted from the file "Research design and evidence.svg" from Wikimedia Commons, the free media repository.[4]

Meta-analyses and systematic reviews

Meta-analyses and systematic reviews are high in the evidence pyramid. These publications systematically identify all the studies that satisfy predefined

---

4 Adapted from the file CFCF, "Research design and evidence.svg," Sept. 2, 2015, https://commons.wikimedia.org/wiki/File:Research_design_and_evidence.svg. The image here has been altered and is licensed under the Creative Commons Attribution-ShareAlike 4.0 International License. To view a copy of the license, visit https://creativecommons.org/licenses/by-sa/4.0/legalcode.

criteria, such as strength of study or target population. They then analyze the dataset and determine which conclusion is best supported by all the currently available studies. General standards for meta-analyses and systematic reviews make them less prone to bias than simply perusing the existing literature according to interest and coming to a conclusion at an arbitrary point.

This is a huge part of the reason we like the work done by organizations like GiveWell, as they can look at large numbers of studies and put together important overviews that allow others easily and painlessly to come to an informed opinion.

Individual scientific studies

Generally, scientific studies are very reliable sources of information. In the medical sciences, studies are necessary to determine whether a new drug is working. For charities, studies are equally important to prove whether the charity is having a real positive impact. However, they can vary widely in strength, from randomized controlled trials to much weaker observational studies. Since they vary in quality, do not take the results at face value, but rather evaluate each one based on its own merits.

Expert opinions

The reliability of expert opinions is entirely dependent on who the expert is and which field they are in. At the most basic level, a recommendation from a prominent expert in a relevant field will usually be much more trustworthy than a recommendation from an academic who specializes in another subject.

You must also try to gauge whether the expert is biased. For example, academics tend to favor their own fields and their own work within them. A researcher who specializes in vitamin A supplements may think that their cause area is the most important and another researcher in education will think the same, though neither has much understanding of the other's field. While they may know within their area which is the best intervention, they will be hard pressed to compare between areas.

This natural bias can be used to your advantage, however. When considering whether to implement an intervention, try running your idea past several reasonable outsiders whose values and epistemologies you respect. If many of them give you negative feedback, you can be pretty sure that the idea isn't as good as you thought, as the vast majority of people tend toward over-optimism, or at least try to be positive to avoid hurting your feelings.

Additionally, expert advice is more useful for some subjects than others, according to how tractable they are. A mechanic, for instance, will likely know exactly what to do to fix a car. Cars have limited moving parts and each part is understood well, with clear and quick feedback loops. On the other hand, if you ask ten futurists what will happen in 50 years, you will get ten different answers. There are countless moving parts, each of which is poorly understood, and feedback loops are muddy and slow. While most of the charitable areas you will likely consider do not have the advantage of being as well understood as the mechanics of a car, some fields still do have more reliable experts than others. For example, health experts are more reliably correct than experts on social change, which is a much messier and less well-understood field.

Be aware that, while your source may have some valuable insights, it's also equally possible that their recommendation could be useless. Even if you think your recommender is genuinely reputable, you should be sure to question their original sources. Is their opinion based on personal stories and reasoning, or more solid evidence like studies and systematic overviews? If at all possible, rely on the primary sources that the expert is using rather than the opinion of the expert themselves. Expert opinion should generally be used as a jumping-off point or a resource for when you are not planning on putting much time into an area, rather than a primary source for choosing a charity to start.

Historical evidence

Some people use historical evidence to predict which interventions will work and which might require more thorough testing. Sadly, there are significant problems with most historical evidence. In practice, most charities' historical evidence is largely unreliable and cherry-picked to support a predetermined conclusion.

Some general characteristics of good and bad historical evidence:

Bad historical evidence	Good historical evidence
Theory before evidence	Evidence before theory
Non-systematic (researcher follows interest)	Systematic (researcher follows a predetermined process)

Anecdotal and cherry-picked	Large, representative sample
Strong causal attribution	Cautious causal attribution
Only looks at successes	Looks at successes and failures
Shallow research (examined few resources)	Deep research (examined many sources)
A bad example: "Protesting worked for the civil rights movement in the past, so it should work for our cause!"	A good example: Open Philanthropy's "History of Philanthropy"[5]

A priori reasoning

A priori reasoning is based on logic or common sense. For example, "Women in developing countries have to collect water at pumps, which is a long and difficult process. Children have a lot of pent-up energy but no playgrounds. If we make a merry-go-round that pumps water, the children will have a place to play and run around while simultaneously getting water, and the women will be free to follow other pursuits."

Logical or commonsense reasoning can feel more reliable than personal stories, but it suffers from many of the same problems. The reliability of a priori reasoning depends partly on the field of research. For example, this reasoning in mathematics is more useful than historical evidence, but historical evidence in sociology is more useful than a priori reasoning.

In the charity sector, the world is messy and rarely goes according to plan. For that reason, you should not rely on this kind of evidence alone to evaluate charities and interventions. With lives at stake, armchair reasoning is not enough.

Anecdotes and personal stories

Anecdotes and personal stories are the weakest forms of evidence and, sadly,

---

5 Open Philanthropy, "History of Philanthropy," accessed Nov. 10, 2021, https://www.openphilanthropy.org/research/history-of-philanthropy.

the most commonly used in the charity sector. They are almost always cherry-picked and unrepresentative of the norm. You should never rely on them as your sole form of evidence for an intervention's effectiveness. These are sometimes called case studies, but have similar issues with cherry-picking and sample size.

However, that's not to say that personal stories don't have a place in the charity sector. Good personal stories can be extremely compelling emotionally, and they can be a great way to attract donations for a cause that other evidence already supports. Often, this sort of evidence is best used to understand or explain the narrative of why something (as proven by stronger methods) is happening.

Getting the evidence yourself

It's often a good idea to run an RCT on your own intervention, even if there's already some strong evidence that it has been effective in the past. You might be running a slightly different intervention or working in a different context than previous experiments. You may also want to take into account metrics that other RCTs do not typically measure, such as subjective well-being, or look into any flow-through effects that may concern you.

Falsifiability

So, how can you assess the available evidence to identify the strongest? Your best bet is to look for controlled studies, with an emphasis on falsifiability.

A claim is "falsifiable" if evidence could prove it wrong. In other words, we can make a prediction and test it, and if the prediction is inaccurate, then the claim is proven to be false. However, if a claim is "unfalsifiable," that means it can never be proven or disproven. "Unfalsifiable" charities ignore any evidence against their effectiveness or explain it away with post hoc rationalizations.[6]

For example, many studies have shown that microloans don't increase income, and it's better to give impoverished people money with no strings attached.[7] However, microloan charities still exist, and either ignore this evidence or say that the real point of microloans is to empower women. When more evidence

---

6 "Post hoc rationalizations" claim that because X happened after Y, Y must have caused X.

7 Holden Karnofsky, "Cash transfers vs. microloans," The GiveWell Blog, last modified April 17, 2013, https://blog.givewell.org/2013/01/04/cash-transfers-vs-microloans/.

comes out casting doubt on whether they are even successful at that,[8] they say the point of their services is actually to smooth out income fluctuations. This claim might be true, but at this stage, you should be skeptical – you'd need to wait to find supporting evidence, and it's starting to look like microloans are not all they're cracked up to be.

Note that microloans are technically falsifiable, but psychologically not so. They did indeed make claims that were disproven. Nonetheless, the proponents either refused to see the evidence or moved the goalposts, making it essentially unfalsifiable.

Just as scientists had to accept that the world is round, charities must learn to admit when we realize our interventions aren't working. We can never improve the world if we refuse to acknowledge and learn from our mistakes.

How can you make sure your intervention is falsifiable? There are four main ways to hold yourself accountable to the evidence:

Make sure you can clearly define success and failure, so you cannot sidestep confronting failure later by saying you were trying to accomplish something different anyway.

Counter confirmation bias by actively trying to prove your intervention wrong.

Be prepared to abandon or change your intervention if it doesn't work. It helps to have a Plan B you're excited about so that you do not feel like the world will end if Plan A doesn't work out.

Get an external review. It's very hard to evaluate the evidence objectively, but an intelligent third party can be much more impartial than you. (GiveWell is a good example of this.)

An exemplary falsifiable charity: GiveDirectly

GiveDirectly is a charity that's as falsifiable as they come. They give money to the poorest people in Kenya and Uganda, no strings attached. Eleven randomized controlled trials have shown that this intervention improves long-term

8 Sam Donald, "Why We (Still) Don't Recommend Microfinance," Giving What We Can, last modified April 15, 2018, https://www.givingwhatwecan.org/post/2014/03/why-we-still-dont-recommend-microfinance/.

income, empowers women, and makes people happier,[9] which we believe is the ultimate metric for a charity's success.

Not only that, but several of the studies were run by GiveDirectly themselves. In advance, they publicly defined what they would regard as success or failure, explained how they would analyze the data, and precommitted to publishing the results regardless. This was a bold and admirable move. They could easily have found that the data did not confirm their intervention's success.

You can see their dedication to transparency even in their marketing. In one of their social media campaigns, they told stories about what people spent the money on. Unlike the vast majority of other charities, they did not cherry-pick the most compelling stories. They randomly selected them, so the examples were truly representative.

GiveDirectly is one of the very few falsifiable charities that go to great lengths to test themselves. That means you can trust them to actually do what they say they will.

Replicability and extraordinary claims

A recent crisis has happened in many scientific fields, shaking the confidence in studies and the scientific methodology as a whole. This is known as the replication crisis. Hundreds of studies, including some very important ones, were found not to replicate – meaning, the same effect was not found when they were tested again by a different scientist. Something being replicable is key to the scientific principles, and so many studies failing to replicate casts serious doubt on their results.

Interestingly, it's somewhat predictable which studies do not replicate, with even non-scientists being pretty good at guessing. A big part of how they were able to guess what data would replicate was based on how surprising it is. "Chocolate helps you lose weight" is a more shocking finding than "Chocolate slightly increases your BMI," and is also less likely to replicate.

This ties in with commonsense assessments of evidence and boils down to the idea that the more shocking or extraordinary the claim, the stronger the evidence you need behind it. If someone said they saw a red car outside their

---

9 See GiveDirectly, "Research at GiveDirectly," accessed Nov. 10, 2021, https://www.give-directly.org/research-at-give-directly/.

window, you would likely take them at their word. But if they said they had seen a red elephant, you would probably want to see a picture. This principle is key to considering how strongly to weight a piece of evidence. Two studies may look equally good, but if one makes a far more extraordinary claim you might still believe it far less.

Typically, replication is best done by someone external to the first piece of data. In the world of science, replication aims to mimic the first test as closely as possible, but the concept can be used far more widely. If you come across a piece of important evidence (scientific or not), looking at it from another angle can be a great way to confirm it.

Replication is a highly useful technique to sort out the mistakes from the true surprises. It's an important concept that should be considered across all sorts of evidence when getting data on whether something is a true effect or an error in the study, a random effect, or a biased description.

The case for testing new ideas without any evidence – yet

Under the right circumstances, testing new and innovative ideas can be very valuable. For example, testing allows you to share your results with other charities, which can then learn from your mistakes or replicate your successes. Without testing new unproven concepts, we may never find the most effective interventions. And in this circumstance, settling for less than the "best" intervention means accepting the fact that your target population will suffer more, or for a longer period of time.

Of course, not every idea is worth trying, and we wouldn't usually recommend taking a chance on an intervention with zero evidence to suggest it may work. We believe the most promising contenders for trial and error have some prior evidence suggesting they may be important, but not enough to answer all key questions. Looking into an intervention with a foundation of suggestive positive evidence lowers the chance that your research will turn out to be useless or irrelevant.

In addition to looking at what evidence already exists, other things to consider include time and expected value. Weigh the existing evidence for the innovation against the resources required to test it. For example, if an idea would take only a day to test, the threshold of strong positive evidence required to give it a try would be much lower than if the test were to take six months of work. If the intervention has extremely high expected value, then the risk will be more favorable. We can compromise on evidence because the potential payoff would be astronomical.

7.3. Ways people mislead with science

Scientific evidence, like most other systems, can be gamed and made misleading. Entire books have been written on how to lie with statistics.[10] These are worth reading, but in the interim, a few fast tips can save you a world of time when analyzing data.

Be wary of popular science summaries of research. Popular science has a different goal than normal science: its aim is more to be read than to be accurate. This tends to lead popular science to make much stronger claims than what a proper systematic evaluation would show. To return to a previous example, a study claiming that "Chocolate is healthy" is far more interesting than one that says "Some minor negative effects and some minor positive effects found in mice eating chocolate." Whenever something starts to seem a bit too polished or shocking, it often ends up entailing stronger claims than the original science. This sort of "pop science" is also extremely common on charities' websites.

Be wary of abstracts. An abstract is a handy tool for quickly understanding a study, but much like pop science, it can often overstate the claim. For studies that are really important to your charity's impact, you will have to dig a bit deeper.

Check effect sizes. "Statistically significant" is what many studies focus on, but unfortunately, this number is just not enough to make important claims. An effect size shows the magnitude or importance of the effect. For example, it could be statistically true that eating a certain food reduces cancer risk. However, if the effect size is extremely small, it would likely not be worth changing your diet. With respect to charitable interventions, it might be true that clean water reduces diseases, but the really important question is: by how much does it reduce them – i.e., what is the effect size?

Do a multiple analysis correction: A huge mistake many researchers make is to measure and analyze a large number of effects without taking this into account during statistical analysis. A simple example of how this could go wrong: if you are trying to determine the effect of jelly beans on cancer and you measure and

---

10 For example, see Darrell Huff, *How to Lie with Statistics* (California: Penguin Group, 2009).

analyze a single variable, you will find jelly beans have no effect. However, if you break the jelly beans down into groups by color and test each one individually, you will have a much larger chance of finding an effect by pure chance, even if no true effect exists. There are very simple ways to fix this problem, such as using a Bonferroni correction.[11] If a study measures a lot of factors, it's worth using something like this to see if the effect holds up.

Do a multiple study correction: The same problem described above can also happen when considering multiple studies. If you see a single study that makes a claim, for example, that chocolate is healthy, make sure to check the other similar studies. If there are 100 studies saying it's bad for you and one saying it's good, it's very likely that the single study is wrong.

Replicability: In general, be careful with how often you expect a study to replicate. Many people assume that if an effect is statistically significant at a 95% level of confidence, it will replicate 95% of the time in future studies. This is far from the truth. In fact, a p-value of 0.04 means that it'll only replicate, on average, 25% of the time.[12] This is part of the reason why having multiple studies that converge on the same answer is so important.

Regression to the mean: Extreme effects generally get weaker as they are studied more. This is a universal statistical phenomenon. Therefore, extreme or very surprising initial measurements tend to become closer to average the next time they are studied. This should make you very cautious of single pieces of evidence that show unbelievable effects.

---

11 See Wolfram MathWorld, "Bonferroni Correction," accessed Nov. 10, 2021, https://mathworld.wolfram.com/BonferroniCorrection.html for a more detailed explanation of the mechanics and further resources.

12 For a more in-depth explanation, see Jim Frost, "What is the Relationship Between the Reproducibility of Experimental Results and P Values?" *Statistics By Jim*, accessed Nov. 10, 2021, https://statisticsbyjim.com/hypothesis-testing/reproducibility-p-values/.

Putting it all together in the charity world

In the animal protection movement, there is often very little data to base decisions on. At Fish Welfare Initiative, much of the available data aims to increase fish health and productivity, not welfare. A strong temptation for us, therefore, is to fall back on a priori reasoning to guide our work: what seems the most effective intuitively. This is particularly dangerous for animal charities like us, as our intuition is even less applicable to the other species we work for. We have tried to keep ourselves to a higher standard of scientific evidence, and this necessitates effort and some creativity on our part.

When starting our project in India, we knew through our previous expert consultations and literature reviews that water quality was theoretically the most important aspect for fish welfare. There was some sparse literature on the issues fish farmers faced, but we essentially had no idea what conditions were like on farms. After visiting a few farms, we quickly started to feel that we could identify some of the welfare issues fish were facing, but we knew that this wasn't enough to reliably run a cost-effective intervention on. Since the information wasn't coming to us, we had to get creative with generating the information ourselves. We:

- hired local staff and surveyed 125 farmers in the region to tease out what welfare issues may be on their farms;
- bought water-quality monitoring devices and monitored the water of 40 ponds over a week;
- hired local experts and built relationships with people who know the Indian aquaculture industry;
- budgeted $50,000 for a study working with farmers to trial higher-welfare farming practices.

However, these channels of information are still not enough to really understand our impact. We have to account for the fact that the level of scientific data available to us will always be lower than that available in other cause areas.

– Haven King-Nobles and Thomas Billington (co-founders of Fish Welfare Initiative)

8. Effective altruism

A relative newcomer in the world of decision-making, the effective altruism movement combines insights from economics and philosophy to attempt to cause the most good with the smallest amount of resources. Like a wrench, effective altruism is about amplification and the maximum effect.

Effective altruism (EA) is specifically built around doing good and charitable output, so many of its decision-making frameworks are directly applicable to founding a new effective charity.

Two core concepts underpin effective altruism:

1) Some ways of doing good can do more good than others.

2) This difference can be meaningfully measured.

Most people in the charity world find it intuitively plausible that a poorly run charity could indeed be worse than a well-run one. But EA tends to take this idea further, saying that even a well-run charity could be far less effective than an equally well-run counterpart due to differences in cause area and impact strategies. This fits with the models people have about the for-profit world – one strategy might be far better, even if two entrepreneurs are equally hardworking.

However, that impact can be tracked does not mean it's easy to compare. In straightforward situations, you might be able to compare two charities that do the exact same action (e.g., giving out bed nets). But comparing interventions in very different areas (for example, improving someone's health vs. improving someone's wealth) is more complex. Thankfully, many sectors have been dealing with similar challenges for a long time. Medical science created the disability-adjusted life-year (DALY), economics uses measures of how many dollars of benefit are created per dollar spent, and charity evaluators such as GiveWell have created metrics like equivalent lives saved. All these measures can allow careful cross comparison between charities that are very different but each strive to cause good in the world.

Understanding that some ways of doing good are better than others does not get us very far in knowing which of those paths are the best. Ideally, we would proceed systematically, conducting in-depth research on an array of cause areas and paths to doing good. But far too many interventions, charities, and cause areas exist for us to conduct extensive research into each. Instead, we narrow down the field with heuristics – mental shortcuts that ease the cognitive load of making a decision. Misused, they lead to systematically wrong decision-making; used correctly, they can help prioritize where an issue is too difficult or complex to compare in full.

Some heuristics used in effective altruism include:

- ITN framework
- Track record
- Limiting factor
- Evidence base
- Expert recommendation
- Cost-effectiveness analysis
- GiveWell recommendation

8.1. ITN

The ITN framework is the most common set of heuristics used in the EA movement. These letters stand for three traits that effective altruists, or EAs, look for when rapidly assessing an area:

- Importance: how significant is the issue, and how many beings are affected?
- Tractability: how hard is it to make progress in an area?

• Neglectedness: how much attention is paid to the issue (where the most overlooked areas likely have more room for impactful ways of doing good)?

This framework is fairly intuitive and has been written about extensively by the EA community (for a starting point, head to the EA Concept map[1]). The bulk of this chapter focuses on some slightly less common heuristics, but you'll find that our discussion often connects back to these three concepts.

8.2. Limiting factor

Some cause areas and interventions are predicated on very strong scale arguments, such as far future or wild animal suffering. The idea is that problems affecting a very large number of beings might be more effective to work on (assuming these problems also score well on other criteria). There's no doubt that the magnitude of an issue can suggest how promising founding a charity would be, as a larger problem suggests potential for a large impact. But as a charity entrepreneur, watch out for claims that "we should work on intervention X due to its massive problem scale." We don't just want to consider how big the issue as a whole is, but how big a charity could practically get in that area – the limiting factor.

For some organizations, the limiting factor might be the scale of the issue. An organization working on a nearly eradicated disease might find its limiting factor to be just how much more of the problem there is left to deal with. However, there are many times when scale and limiting factor diverge. GiveWell has talked about surgeries being limited by the supply of surgeons.[2] A scale model might suggest that, since a ton of surgeries remain to be done, this is a worthwhile issue to focus on. A limiting factor model would suggest that an attempt to address this issue would be quickly capped by the number of surgeons. Below is a very simplified comparison of vaccinations and surgeries using a limiting factor model.[3]

---

1 You can peruse the "importance, tractability and neglectedness," or ITN, framework tag on the Effective Altruism Forum for a quick explanation and further reading.

2 GiveWell, "Developing-world corrective surgery," 2010, https://www.givewell.org/international/health/surgery#What_is_the_bottleneck_to_more_surgeries_money_or_skilled_labor.

3 These numbers are estimates based on our work and research in these areas. The magnitudes of the categories are set to be more cross-comparable (e.g., 1 million compared to 10 full-time staff).

A scale model would only take into account the leftmost column in the bar chart – the size of the problem. The limiting factor model shows that although the scale is similar, surgeries are limited by the talent pool far sooner than vaccinations hit their limiting factor. And both are limited several times before their problem size limit. In this case, scale does not matter if a new charity will be stopped by talent, logistics, and funding before they can help even a fraction of the people affected. The importance of a new charity getting founded in this area is not directly connected to the scale of the problem.

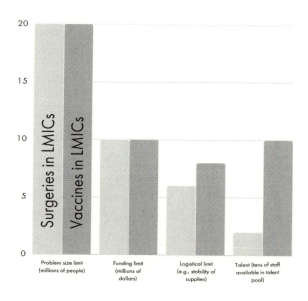

Image: examples of limiting factors in low- and middle-income country interventions.

A common concern for a nonprofit is funding limits. Funding isn't a hard limit in the way that problem size is; it can be improved upon through more fundraising and field-building efforts, for example. Even so, it shouldn't be underestimated as a limiting factor. We suggest estimating a reasonable bound for how much could be fundraised while taking into account the current donor space and a reasonable amount of time (e.g., 2-5 years). This can change over time, but so can the size of the problem; factory farming is a growing problem and global poverty is a shrinking one, but that does not change the importance of having a sense of their scale.

Of course, the perspective changes depending on what you are looking to do in a given area. For example, when considering donating to a charity, you want to look at room for funding – an intervention whose limiting factor that prevents them from doing more good is funding. As an employee at an NGO, you mostly have to consider how much of a limiting factor talent is for the organization. As a charity entrepreneur, what the funding space looks like for a given organization should play a big role in deciding what charity to found.

Some questions worth asking when considering the limiting factor and importance of an issue:

- Is there reason to think that this intervention will be difficult to market?
- What is the total amount of funding in this area?
- How many existing charities working in the same field are hiring for positions that are crucial for the success of this intervention?
- Are there any strong charities working in this area?
- Would this need to be evaluated with an RCT before scaling?

8.3. Counterfactual impact

A neglected issue has gaps that could be filled by a new organization or person working in that space. This is sometimes called your counterfactual impact. Counterfactual impact looks at what would happen if you did X compared to what would happen if you didn't do X to determine the most impactful course of action. For instance, if you brought chlorine to a village in rural Kenya with no safe water source, you would probably feel like you'd accomplished some good in the world. If, on the other hand, you gave the same gift to the average Swedish city, they'd probably give you a funny look – they already have chlorinated water.

Let's take a look at the counterfactual scenario (i.e., what would have happened if you hadn't donated the chlorine). The Kenyan villagers would have continued to drink contaminated water and die from waterborne diseases. The Swedes, however, would have continued to drink their clean water. In fact, even if a Swede drank straight from a contaminated river, they could likely go to a hospital, get the required treatment, and survive to tell the tale.

This section will explain how to make sure that your counterfactual impact is as high as possible.

Neglected spaces

When evaluating your counterfactual impact as a charity entrepreneur, the biggest factor to consider is other charities in the field. Bear in mind that when we talk about **neglectedness**, we mean **in comparison to other cause areas**. There are many unresolved problems in the world, but some receive disproportionate attention. For example, cancer is a huge problem, but it would not be categorized as a neglected cause area under the EA use of the term. This is because compared to similarly pressing issues, like malaria for example, more people are working on resolving cancer. The implication is that a comparatively less well-known or populated cause area may have more **low-hanging fruit** and, therefore, investing time or money in this more neglected problem will go further than investing the same amount in a more well-known one.

Each year, innumerable well-meaning people start new charities in spaces that are already crowded. One of the first things to do when considering an intervention is to check if someone else is already implementing it in that location and in an effective way.

Be careful not to overestimate the size of the other organizations in the space. Nonprofits often put very optimistic numbers for coverage rates. For example, if they say they have one million people in their program, it might be safe to assume they have efficiently and fully covered 100,000 people. Any claims that are hedged with "we expect" or "we plan on" should be taken with even more skepticism.

Another thing to bear in mind is **even though charities may exist in the field, many geographies may not be covered**. If one nonprofit is promoting fortified flour in Kenya, this doesn't mean there isn't room for another doing the same in India. In fact, even if there is already one in India, the size of the country means there could be states bigger than most nations that are still underserved.

And even if someone is already working on the same intervention in the same place, that doesn't necessarily mean they are successfully fulfilling the needs of the entire target population. The existence of one orphanage in Ukraine does not guarantee that all Ukrainian orphans are taken care of. It's very common in the charity sector to forget just how large the planet is, and lose heart if even just one charity out there is doing something similar to you.

If you've researched the other charities currently operating in the field and identified a gap you could fill, the next thing you should do is find out why that gap exists. Some potential reasons include:

- It's a new idea, so it's taking a while to catch on.
- It requires a particular value set or epistemic stance that is rare.
- The organizations that would like to fill the gap don't have the funds to do so.
- The unserved areas are difficult to help (e.g., cultural barriers, conflict zones, lack of infrastructure, etc.).
- An organization has actually already committed to filling the gap – it's just a matter of weeks or months until they do so.

If the gaps are there for reasons that you can overcome or reasons that do not apply to you, great! If you uncover a persuasive reason why you shouldn't go into the field, great! You have just saved yourself months or years of time.

Often, you won't find the answers to these sorts of questions online, so make sure to **reach out to experts working in the field and ask them directly**. You might assume they wouldn't want to talk to you and give away "trade secrets," but most charity workers are, well, nice people. They have the same goals as you and more often than not, they will be willing to answer any questions.

Speeding things up

The next thing to take into account is that if you come up with a really excellent intervention, people will eventually start copying it. This may be a very good thing for the world, but it does make it trickier to establish your counterfactual impact.

As an example, consider the 19th-century debate about who discovered the theory of evolution, Darwin or Wallace. Most likely, despite being separated by thousands of kilometers, both brilliant men came to the same conclusion at roughly the same time. If Darwin hadn't been the first to publish his theory, Wallace would have done so shortly afterward.[4] So, even for something as unintuitive and revolutionary as the idea of evolution, Darwin only sped up humanity's knowledge by a few years.

All else being equal, your counterfactual impact will usually be much higher if you focus on neglected cause areas and problems that are very far from solved.

---

4 Wikipedia, "Publication of Darwin's theory," last modified June 18, 2021, https://en.wikipedia.org/wiki/Publication_of_Darwin%27s_theory.

A note on motivation

You might be feeling discouraged after reading all about how someone someday will probably have the same brilliant idea as you. Try not to focus on the forest and instead zoom in to the individual trees. If you say to yourself, "I'm only moving this field forward by ten years," that doesn't sound so good. However, **look at the individuals you are helping**. Think of the mother whose child has just died of a vaccine-preventable disease. She's hurting right now, and telling her that others in ten years won't suffer the same does little to comfort her. You can also think of your own life. If somebody saved your life, would you dismiss it as "just helping one person," or would you be immensely grateful? **Behind statistics are real lives**. If you move a field forward ten years in expectation, you are likely making a huge positive impact on the lives of many individuals.

8.4. Equal application of rigor

Once you've chosen the right heuristics, the next challenge is to ensure equal application of rigor: that is, making sure that the same methodologies and level of skepticism are used when comparing different areas.

You might think that when choosing an intervention, you should account for as many positive and negative outcomes as possible so as to get the most accurate number. While it is good to practice this sort of thoroughness for the sake of improving your knowledge and identifying any crucial considerations that may dramatically influence your effectiveness, when making the final comparison between interventions, **you want to avoid a situation where the numbers you get are primarily an artifact of the methods you used to get them.**

Therefore, when making comparisons between interventions, you should try to make sure that your analyses are as parallel as possible. You might not ever be able to say definitively how many lives are saved per dollar, but you might be able to say that one intervention was three times as good as another when the two were evaluated side by side using as similar a method as possible. This doesn't solve everything, of course – if you switch to a different method, even one applied uniformly across both interventions, 3x better might rise to 10x better, or drop to only 0.5x as impactful. Applying equal rigor will unfortunately not remove all forms of model uncertainty. However, it is a good tool to keep in your arsenal, and it will help prevent one form of inaccuracy.

The case of the life-saving bus

A common bus ad says, "Save a life for $10," with a picture of a child. Now, this is a pretty exciting claim. GiveWell top charities currently save a life for $3,000-$5,000, so this charity on the bus is apparently many times more effective. But, of course, the difference here is not in impact but in measurement methodologies and rigor. With $10, the charity gives out a life-saving bed net. A bed net could save a life, but many nets need to be given out per life saved – and in fact, GiveWell's top charity AMF gives out nets for about $3.[5] This makes the bus charity less than half as effective.

The difference is that GiveWell takes into account a much wider range of factors, including how many nets need to be given out on average to save a life. If you took the raw numbers, saving a life for $10 seems like a far better deal than saving a life for $3,500. But on closer inspection, giving out a bed net for $3 seems better than the same net for $10. Many of the differences you see in charity estimates and impact evaluations come from differences in methodologies, not differences in the charity. This is part of why we should not get excited every time we see weak evidence (like a bus ad) of a new charity that is highly effective. It's most likely a weaker methodology rather than a hidden gem of effectiveness.

The case of mosquito nets

Imagine that an established charity evaluator estimates the degree to which mosquito nets protect against malaria, estimates the degree to which a net distribution scheme leads to the actual use of nets among the population, estimates the prevalence and lethality of malaria in the region, combines these numbers to estimate the amount of malaria prevented and the number of lives saved, and thereby comes up with a cost per life saved estimate for mosquito net distribution based on those numbers. Is this number accurate?

You can't be certain. Even if all of the above estimates are accurate, the true amount of good that is done might be greater than that. Not having malaria

---

5 GiveWell, "Our Top Charities."

could improve developmental outcomes for children by a quantifiable amount, grant parents greater capacity to earn income and take care of children, shield people from the mental health trauma of losing loved ones in a way that makes a measurable life satisfaction difference, and so on. Your original analysis may not have accounted for this, and if you add it in, your number might change.

The true amount of good that is done might also be less than that. You might discover that some fraction of the nets are used for less effective activities like making fishing nets or clothing, or end up being sold on a market where they do less good, decreasing the efficiency. You might discover that helping people earn more raises prices and hurts the neighboring villages, resulting in a small negative effect. Your original analysis may not have accounted for this, and if you add it in, your number might change.

The freedom to choose which secondary effects you choose to account for allows you a lot of control over the end result of a cost-effectiveness analysis, regardless of how thorough and accurate the analysis is.

The more positive secondary/side/flow-through effects you add to your analysis, the more good it will seem like you're doing. The more negative effects you add, the less good it will seem like you're doing.

Watch out when assessing your own ideas

One area where it is especially important to remember to apply equal rigor is when evaluating your own work and your own ideas. When you are directly working on something, you can often see with your own eyes the positive impact that it has and observe some extremely good flow-through effects that may not be captured by your cost-effectiveness analysis. The temptation may be then to adjust your analysis to take the evidence of your eyes into account, come to a high cost-effectiveness number, and trick yourself into thinking that your intervention is definitely the best use of resources on the margin. However, what's really happening is that you see all the good that your own project is doing in very high definition while you look at other projects in terms of only summary statistics that don't capture everything.

If you find yourself comparing your projects and ideas against others and notice that yours seem unusually good, **consider whether you're quantifying the good aspects of your own projects with greater rigor due to being able to see them better.**

A person who gives money to impoverished individuals whom they personally know can easily list all the positive effects on each and every one of them: "I gave $2,000 to John, and so he was able to rent an apartment and get his family medical care, and one of his children had a life-threatening disease that was caught early thanks to this medical care, so, therefore, my cost-per-life-saved is at least $2,000" may be an accurate statement. However, this is not a fair comparison, because this individual can see everything that happens to John. If a parent avoids malaria and has more parenting capacity to get her kids medical care which saves their lives, you wouldn't see that reflected on a GiveWell spreadsheet.

Of course, interventions are often very diverse, and evaluating them using the same methods is hard. If they are somewhat similar, you can try to make them comparable (e.g., both vaccinations and mosquito nets protect against disease by some quantifiable amount, and share many similar considerations such as base rate of the disease in the population, lethality, etc.). Another way might be to judge all interventions according to their one or two biggest and most straightforward effects (e.g., lives saved) and ignore all smaller indirect effects.

None of this is to suggest that indirect effects don't matter or should be ignored. You should try to quantify as many effects as seem useful to your decision. **The important thing is to make sure that comparisons between interventions are made with model equivalency in mind.**

Putting it all together in the charity world

The Happier Lives Institute got started because of something very technical but also very important: measuring impact.

Here's the familiar problem. As an aspirant effective altruist, you want to do the most good. But there are many ways of doing good. Stopping children dying from malaria, providing cash transfers to the poorest people in the world, reducing extinction risks for new technology, improving conditions in factory farms – how do you compare them?

Let's take a step back. What's ultimately important, I'd argue, is well-being. So, we need a way of measuring well-being. In economics and psychology, research using subjective well-being (SWB), self-reports of happiness and life satisfaction, has taken off in the last few decades. A common question is 0-10: "How satisfied are you with your life, nowadays?" Obviously, this only really helps for humans, who can provide these self-reports.

I looked into SWB in my philosophy PhD and it struck me as about the least bad way to measure well-being (for humans…). However, effective altruist organizations like GiveWell were using alternative, less 'direct' measures of well-being, such as incomes and Q/DALYs, then making educated guesses about how to trade these off against each other in terms of their impact on well-being.

The issue, the psychologist research shows, is that there are differences between what we expect makes us happy and what does. For instance, mental health problems are broadly worse than people expect, and physical health conditions less bad, because we adapt to the latter, but not readily to the former. This raised the worry that EA organizations could be systematically mis-prioritizing.

It struck me that someone really should do the research to work out if measuring impact using SWB would change priorities for EAs. I realized that, sadly, no one else was going to do this for me, so I worked to set up an organization that would do that – HLI. In essence, we're doing EA-style cause prioritization, just adding the lens of SWB to improve our methodological rigor.

– Michael Plant (founder of Happier Lives Institute)

9. Independent experts

No matter how talented you are, you will always need outside help. Like a carpentry expert would call a colleague for a second opinion, great decision-makers know how and when to get advice from others. External experts, wise advisors, and thoughtful outsiders can provide tools and perspectives that would otherwise be overlooked. As with using a cell phone, it is equally important to understand when to ignore certain notifications.

Experts can give a broad overview of a topic in layman's terms, allowing founders and others new to the field to gain a comprehensive understanding of an idea. They can offer a much easier entry to a topic than if you were to trawl through meta-analyses. However, consulting experts should never be the only method relied on in decision-making, because human judgment often suffers from cognitive biases.

We can break up experts into three groups.

Specialist experts will often be highly versed, but in a very specific situation or content area. For example, a fish disease expert would fall under specialist domain experts. They can provide a piece of the picture, but often not a broad comparison. If your goal is to start a charity that helps the most fish, they would not be able to compare disease to transportation issues, and often specialist experts would not even offer a guess on it. However, they would be able to provide highly specific information about disease rates in a given species and situation that you have identified as promising.

Domain experts have a sense of a single area. They might know about many different possible factors that affect a single type of fish, but would not be able to compare a fish-based intervention to a chicken-based one. The heads of nonprofits in a given area would be good examples of domain experts.

Broad experts can provide comparisons across different domains. For example, a funder who supports half a dozen different fish organizations might have a strong sense of how disease compares to transportation, even if she does not have as detailed a sense of specific diseases as the specialist.

All of these experts can be very helpful, but in very different situations. Consulting experts should almost always be one of the decision-making tools used, but rarely should it hold more than one-fifth to one-third weight in a final key choice. Given the considerable variation depending on the specific charity idea and cause area, we expect experts to play a greater role in decision-making in areas where it is harder to get solid numbers. In these cases, common-sense intuitions come in handy.

Taking notes on your conversations with experts will give you something to come back to and help you retain their insights. GiveWell has some of the best expert conversation notes in the charity field – it's worth taking a look at their archives.[1]

9.1. Why is consulting experts helpful?

Experts are in many ways the broadest source of information. They rarely give specific conclusions, but instead offer a valuable overview of a large field, covering a lot of ground. Their views may be easy to explain in terms of conclusion but hard to explain in terms of the factors that went into their formulation.

Reasons they are a helpful resource (in rough order of strength):

Utilize a large number, and a variety, of evidence sources: Experts have formed their views from a wide range of information sources, ranging from studies to conversations and personal experiences. Combining diverse sources into one has a number of advantages, including making conclusions more robust and grounded. You can also combine multiple expert perspectives into a synthesized piece of information, merging a huge number of views and evidence types:

---

1 GiveWell, "Notes from Research Conversations," last updated Oct. 2021, givewell.org/research/conversations.

Example of synthesized expert data (Charity Entrepreneurship 2018)[2]

Broad area	Intervention	Ordered Sub-interventions	Weighted average	Average	Range in views
Corporate Outreach	Broad area ranking	NA	2.8	2.7	Small
Research	Broad area ranking	NA	2.6	2.7	Large
Product Creation	Broad area ranking	NA	2.5	2.5	Large
Political Outreach	Broad area ranking	NA	2.2	2.3	Small
Welfare Condition Improvements	Broad area ranking	NA	2.5	2.2	Mid
Wild Animal Suffering (WAS) / Bugs	Broad area ranking	NA	2.3	2.2	Large
Improving Existing NGOs	Broad area ranking	NA	1.8	1.8	Mid
Events	Broad area ranking	NA	1.6	1.7	Small
Veg Outreach	Broad area ranking	NA	1.8	1.6	Small
Other	Broad area ranking	NA	2.0	2.0	Mid

Apply common-sense filters: When you are new to a field, you do not have a strong common-sense filter. Experts have often seen many projects come and go, and have a strong sense of what could be more successful or impactful, as well as what might go wrong in a project or lead it to failure. These filters can be helpful and informative in prioritizing among areas and making long-term plans.

Quickly assess weaknesses: When talking directly to an expert, you lay out specific situations and combinations of ideas in a way that makes it is easier to identify flaws in reasoning or failure points. This information would often be hard to find from informal research or even deeper, more systematic research.

Are insensitive to single-number model errors: One of the biggest concerns with many multiplication models such as cost-effectiveness analyses is that a single error (e.g., a mistyped number) can have a large effect on the model. Experts are rarely overly affected by a single model or a single number, and tend to be slow to update on shocking conclusions. They more intuitively and directly apply "extraordinary claims require extraordinary evidence" heuristics.

Use new sources of information: Experts often have connections and knowledge about what resources are worth considering for further research or which other experts are worth talking to. Consulting experts lends itself to finding more information and getting a clear path of whom to talk to next or what resources to read. They sometimes have access to studies or other research that is not yet available or easily accessible in the public domain. Well-positioned experts can often have access to information a full year before it is publicly available. They also often have details about what studies are being worked on and will be

---

2 Joey Savoie, "How to make an impact in animal advocacy, a survey." Effective Altruism Forum, Aug. 26, 2018, https://forum.effectivealtruism.org/posts/jR2LKoXoL4Aq9T2MQ/how-to-make-an-impact-in-animal-advocacy-a-survey.

completed in the near future.

Are a respected source of information: Consulting experts is a respected and even expected tool to use when researching an area. It is also common practice in many fields, including charity evaluation.

Offer multi-session engagement: Experts are one of the few sources of information that can directly engage in back-and-forth discussion. After discussing a more basic idea, you can later come back and update them on any changes or advances in your thinking.

Can directly compare possible strategies: You can present an expert with highly specific plans and have them compare different elements much more quickly than a more formal model like a CEA could. If you are considering three interventions in three different countries with three different partner organizations, the number of permutations quickly becomes overwhelming for a formal model. Experts can compare multiple iterations and suggest which combination seems to be highest impact or most promising for further research.

Provide field-level convergence: Experts can give a sense of whether many individuals within a field have a fairly unified view (i.e., if all three experts you speak to agree on a topic) or if there is a variety of views (i.e., three experts give three different answers). If an area has a high level of convergence, it is good to get these conclusions, and if it does not, that leaves open more areas that should be considered or researched.

9.2. Why you shouldn't over-rely on experts

Despite experts being a helpful source of information, they are not our only endline perspective. A number of weaknesses have been demonstrated to affect expert judgment negatively, and studies have shown that in some areas, such as predicting the future, "many of the experts did worse than random chance, and all of them did worse than simple algorithms."[3] These concerns limit experts' usefulness and make us confident that they should not be the only perspective used.

---

3 AI Impacts, "Evidence on good forecasting practices from the Good Judgment Project: an accompanying blog post," accessed Nov. 10, 2021, https://aiimpacts.org/evidence-on-good-forecasting-practices-from-the-good-judgment-project-an-accompanying-blog-post/.

Many of our biggest concerns with experts[4] are cognitive biases that cross apply to the vast majority of human judgments (as mentioned in our earlier chapter on Rationality). Not all the following concerns apply to every expert, but they are generalized and will apply to a large number.

Unequal application of rigor: A major concern with experts is equal application of rigor. Given all the information currently available, a motivated actor can find evidence supporting almost any viewpoint. Thus, a fairly weak argument could hold a lot of weight in an expert's view if they have not considered it skeptically or if it fits their prior worldview. Similarly, if an expert does not like an idea, they find it easy to be significantly more critical of it than would be justified compared to other ideas or viewpoints they hold. This rigor concern makes it highly challenging to take in expert conclusions without a deeper sense of how they react to any new idea.

Inconsistent and unclear epistemology: Experts often have views about how to weigh different types of evidence, but few have thought about this problem explicitly. Even fewer have publicly laid out how they would compare and integrate different pieces of evidence into their endline viewpoints.

Cognitive bias: A number of cognitive biases affect humans. Experts are, fundamentally, just more well-informed humans and so suffer from the same biases. One mitigating factor is that if multiple experts are spoken to, their biases will not necessarily overlap, and their average quality of judgment tends to be higher than that of a single expert. Hundreds of biases can affect judgment and decision-making, but some that seem particularly pertinent are:

- **Anchoring**: "When an individual depends too heavily on an initial piece of information offered (considered to be the "anchor") in making decisions."[5] Experts can often anchor on a specific idea for a charity early in a conversation or before the conversation has even started. Many experts will have projects they have already supported or invested time into. They will generally regard ideas that compete with their existing projects with a high level of skepticism.

---

4 Farnam Street, "Future Babble: Why expert predictions fail and why we believe them anyway," Farnam Street Media Inc., accessed Nov. 10, 2021, https://fs.blog/future-babble-why-expert-predictions-fail-and-why-we-believe-them-anyway/.

5 Charity Entrepreneurship, "Expert View," accessed Nov. 10, 2021, https://www.charityentrepreneurship.com/expert-view.html.

- **Groupthink**: "A psychological phenomenon that occurs within a group of people in which the desire for harmony or conformity in the group results in an irrational or dysfunctional decision-making outcome. Group members try to minimize conflict and reach a consensus decision without critical evaluation of alternative viewpoints by actively suppressing dissenting viewpoints and by isolating themselves from outside influences."[6] In the case of charity ideas, if an idea has not been previously tested or considered by other experts in the field, often they will be more inclined to dismiss the idea than they would if the same concept was presented by someone connected to their ingroup. Although this is a useful heuristic for experts to use, it can make them under-weight new ideas relative to more established ones.

- **Illusion of control**: "The tendency for people to overestimate their ability to control events."[7] This connects closely to experts having difficulty discerning effects from randomness or noise. Often, experts will put more weight on their personal experiences. If idea A has worked in the past, idea A will always work, and if idea B failed in the past, idea B is likely to fail. These assumptions are often held without careful consideration of the different environmental factors or non-results-focused factors (for example, a higher chance of failure might be worth it if the win could be several times larger).

Lack of transparency in argument generation: Experts have formed their views using a considerable number of sources and experiences. A byproduct of this is the great difficulty of tracking down the basis for a given viewpoint. This can make it very challenging to confirm or disprove a given idea, or even to know how much weight it should be given.

Memory concerns: Memory is a fallible tool, but generally when speaking to an expert there is a high level of reliance on their memory. A remembered version of a study or conversation could be significantly different than the original. It is also hard or impossible to detect these memory effects given the

---

6 Wikipedia, "Groupthink," last modified Nov. 2, 2021, https://en.wikipedia.org/wiki/Groupthink.

7 Wikipedia, "Illusion of Control," last modified March 20, 2021, https://en.wikipedia.org/wiki/Illusion_of_control.

unavoidable lack of transparency.

Limited specificity: Many experts are unwilling to give specific estimates such as a percentage-based chance of success. They are also often unwilling to make claims that could be used in other methodologies such as CEAs, particularly if those claims cannot be anonymized.

Lack of decisiveness: Similar to the specificity concerns, experts are often unwilling to make decisive claims, as even taking a neutral or unsure stance would have its own ramifications. This is often a taught practice in academia and can be a good habit when it comes to truth-seeking, although it can impair comparison among different options.

9.3. How to know which experts to trust

When you are wheeled into a hospital with a broken arm, you place your trust in multiple people and establishments. You trust that the nurses are giving you the right medication and that the doctor will make the right call on how to fix your arm. And yet, you personally know relatively little about the specific treatments that are going to be applied.

We defer to people all the time on different issues, whether it's the doctor at a hospital, the weatherman for the forecast, or the baker who tells us the bread is fresh. Even in our domains of expertise, many judgment calls are made by others, and we have either to trust or distrust their data.

Knowing whom to trust is a difficult and important skill. Trust the wrong person, and they can fill your head with the wrong information. But trust no one, and you have to fix every broken bone yourself. So how can we determine who is credible and who is not?

There are four key ways to determine whether a source or person is worth putting your trust in. In descending order of how good an indicator it is, you can:

- Check against reality
- Check against further research/reasoning
- Check the source's reliability in other areas
- Check for signs of credibility signaling

Each of these is more of a spot check than perfectly predictive, and not all can be done in every case. Over time, as sources become highly reliable, you can use them to check other sources. If you check Cochrane[8] a dozen times and it dovetails with further research, you can eventually start to use it as a reliable source to check others against.

Check against reality

The best way to test if you can trust a person or source is to check their statements against reality. Say there are two weathermen, and you are unsure whom to trust. In this case, a reality check is easy. You could compare each of their historical predictions with the historical weather to see which has been accurate more often. This does not guarantee who will be a better source in the future, but it's strongly suggestive. Similarly, if a source predicts a certain reality, particularly in a manner that is easily falsifiable, this evidence can be used to support or create skepticism for its credibility.

Reality checks can also be used for groups of sources. For example, lots of people go to the hospital with broken arms and generally come out with a cast and an improved state. Thus, we might generally trust hospitals to fix broken arms, even if we have not checked the specific doctor.

The key point here is that reality is the ultimate arbiter. It does not matter if one weatherman speaks more confidently, wears a better suit, or has a PhD – the one whose predictions more closely correlate with reality is the better source.

Check against further research/reasoning

Not all claims can be checked against reality, but a large number can be checked with further research. For example, the first time we heard from GiveWell that global poverty was reducing over time, our team was surprised. However, when we checked multiple other sources, it indeed looked like this was the case.[9] This made us trust GiveWell's research more. If it had turned out that global poverty was in fact on the rise, we would have been more skeptical of their research.

Enough spot checks, and slowly a source as a whole can become trustworthy. For example, we have checked over a dozen different sections of GiveWell's

---

8 A global independent network of researchers, professionals, patients, carers, and people interested in health.

9 GiveWell, "Standard of Living in the Developing World," accessed Nov. 10, 2021, https://www.givewell.org/international/technical/additional/Standard-of-Living.

work, often putting several dozen hours of research into a specific claim. Again and again, from our best assessment, it looks like they are correct. Over time, this builds trust, so now we can use GiveWell as a reliable source to check other claims against.

Check the source's reliability in other areas

Trustworthy in one domain does not always mean trustworthy in another. Despite the hospital fixing a broken arm, we would be wary of their ability to predict the weather. However, sources can often make claims in some areas that are testable and others that are not. In such cases, it can be useful to look into a source's reliability in a different area. For example, imagine you have a friend who, for fun, memorizes facts that your research shows consistently to be correct. Were this friend to share a new fact in a hard-to-check area, you would likely believe him. Likewise, if a source is highly trustworthy in one area, it's more likely to be trustworthy in others. If GiveWell started recommending animal charities, we would be inclined to trust them even if we had not yet checked them against reality or further research.

Check for signs of credibility signaling

The last way you can try to get a sense of whom to trust is by looking at generally accepted forms of credibility signaling (e.g., legitimacy of the source, or an individual's qualifications). This has the advantage of being quick, but it's also fairly unreliable compared to the other methodologies. A nice website is a strong signal that a source has funding, but a pretty weak signal in terms of them being trustworthy. Credibility signaling is often where people go wrong with trusting a source – by giving a certain signal far too much weight compared to its actual correlation with reality.

9.4. A process for speaking to experts

Selecting

How do we find experts to consult? Lists of experts are generally created opportunistically rather than systematically.

- **Via research.** When someone is conducting directed or undirected research, names of key people in the field often come up. These names are noted and can later be contacted.

- **By recommendation.** Often when speaking to experts it is possible to ask for others who would be helpful to talk to. Thus, many experts can be found from peer recommendations.

Always try to reach out to three times as many experts as you want to talk to in the end.

Contacting experts

When contacting an expert for the first time, we suggest using an email along these lines:

Dear _____,

I am a research associate at an organization that researches and funds new nonprofits to put the findings into action (your website here).

[person] recommended that I speak to you because of your background in _____ OR I am researching _____ and I read your paper on _____, which drew my attention because [detail]. Based on this, I thought you might know the answers to a few questions about the topic.

Some questions I have are: _____ and _____. Would you happen to have the time to jot down some quick answers to the above, or maybe discuss them via a quick Zoom call if that might be easier? We'd really love to have your input and research inform our funding and charity decisions.

Best regards,

_____

How to speak to experts

Experts are, ultimately, just people like anyone else, so most standard conversational rules apply to them. A few elements to highlight are:

- **Be humble** – At the point you are talking to experts, you are new to the field, so you should try to come across as someone who is surprisingly informed for a nonexpert. Ask for only a little bit of time, such as one Skype, instead of longer commitments. Say you are happy to keep any comment anonymous if they review the conversation notes or say it should be so during the conversation. Try to take a broad interest in the subject matter as a whole, even if it's not directly tied to the question you are asking.

- **Be prepared** – Being thoughtful with an expert's time is important. If they have written a whole book on a given topic, for example, you should at the least review a summary before talking to them about it. The same goes for website content they have created. In addition to reading content beforehand, you should think about which questions are most important and which could get cut if you run out of time. Have a backup system for contacting if the first one does not work (e.g., a Google phone credit you can use to call someone if Skype is not working).

- **Frame opposing views using a citation** – If you want to push on a point or perspective that an expert has claimed, do not describe it as ‚"I am skeptical of point A"; instead, tie it directly to your research ("A different expert I spoke to was skeptical of point A.").

- **Go deeper** – Try to cover the key questions on your agenda, but if something comes up that seems important, you can ask more questions relating to that area. Ask follow-up questions, such as, "You said that . . . Why do you think that is?"

- **Ask comparative questions** – Few experts will have a great sense of the percentage chance of something happening or a clear expected value for a given intervention, but they often give excellent answers to more comparative questions. Answering, "Does X seem like it would cost more per person than Y?" is easier than giving an exact number for either.

- **Ensure that they have answered your question** – If you ask questions such as, "What are the main strengths and weaknesses of X intervention?" it is quite easy for them to forget the initial question once they have been talking about the strengths for a few minutes. Follow up on this with something like, "Thanks for outlining the strengths of

X intervention. What do you think are the main weaknesses?"

- **Give them space to think** – Don't move on to the next question immediately after they finish answering the previous one. Ensure that there is a small pause so that they can add something else if they think of it.

- When speaking to experts, keep in mind that they might be a good fit for potential mentors, particularly if they are very excited about your project and gave great advice.

Example questions

- A little bit about the project: I am surveying <cause area> experts to get a sense of what the best way to run a charity start-up in the area would be. Our project is currently doing ABC.

- Give an outline of the interview (types of questions, length, etc.) – e.g., "I have about 10 questions I would love to ask you."

- What got you interested in <cause area>? (start with easy questions to warm them up).

- How long have you been working in <cause area>?

- All things considered (cost-effectiveness, execution difficulty, what existing organizations are already doing, etc.), what specific organizations would you love to see founded in the next five years?

- All things considered, what intervention or organization do most people think is effective but in your opinion is not? Why?

- Are there any areas you think are neglected by current actors in the field? Why do you think these areas are neglected?

- What do you think of work being done in X space, and what things should a new organization look out for?

- What are good resources (blogs, books, podcasts) for more information?

- Do you know anyone who would be great to speak to about these sorts of topics? Would it be possible for you to introduce me to them?

- Do you have any questions for me?

Note-taking and summarizing

Recording and notes – Although recording the interview might be ideal, most experts will be less open if they are being recorded. Unless you need to publish the information, the easiest method is to take notes that will only be shared internally. You can always ask if they are happy with you sharing them later.

For every conversation, try to jot down some notes as you are talking, and spend 10 minutes writing notes after the conversation is done. You can then summarize these messy notes into a single page to remind yourself of the key points.

We often offer to send them a copy of any notes we take so they can comment if they feel we misunderstood anything. We also offer to send them a copy of our full report if they are interested in seeing other experts' views or synthesized research we conduct on the topic, and highlight that we would welcome any feedback.

Synthesis

Although the bulk of the information gathered will be in single expert conversation notes, you can synthesize these thoughts into a one-page easy-to-read summary. This can include a narrative explanation of concepts that came up multiple times in conversation notes and table-based data with rough quantification on what experts thought.

Putting it all together in the charity world

Animal Ask conducts research on behalf of animal advocacy organizations to optimize and prioritize farmed animal welfare asks. An example of an ask could be asking a retailer to commit to only selling cage-free eggs or asking a government to ban cages for laying hens.

The scope of the research to identify the optimal ask can range across species and implementation methods. A multi-tool decision approach is required - one of which is high use of expert views.

Experts are selected based on criteria that include their experience, discipline, and credibility. We prioritize those with experience in the specific species (animal welfare specialist - specialist/domain), the implementation approach (corporate relations and campaigns staff - domain/broad), and those with the necessary country context (industry - domain/broad) to ensure that impractical asks do not progress to future rounds.

We use experts in various ways throughout our process. In the earliest rounds, we ask experts to cross compare (and if appropriate, rank) a broad spectrum of as many as fifty asks. Generally, we will ask the advice of broad and domain experts, such as researchers at other animal advocacy organizations and animal welfare specialists. In the later research rounds, we interview experts on the record as they cross compare the finite details of up to five asks or provide in-depth information about a single ask.

When interviewing any expert, it is important for us to acknowledge cognitive biases at play. We may flag any experts who seem to be prioritizing based on irrelevant factors or missing key considerations. If their judgments seem particularly questionable without providing strong reasoning, we may discount their opinion.

We benefit not only from expert offerings within our process, but also from an ever-increasing database of reliable experts we can turn to for advice.

– Amy Odene and George Bridgwater (co-founders of Animal Ask)

10. Task planning

In a workshop, often you just don't have enough hands. You might need two to secure a piece, one to measure, and one to make a cut. Most of us only have two, so we need to use tools to help us. Clamps provide the solution, holding your work in place so that your attention can be directed elsewhere. Likewise, good task planning holds your tasks organized and consistently allows you to direct your attention to specific aspects of a project without things falling through the cracks.

The art of task management can seem elusive, with monk-like adherents following complex sets of belief systems to arrive at the holy grail of maximum productivity. While advanced users of task management and productivity techniques might indeed beat the average entrepreneur by far, the Pareto principle[1] applies: 20% of your effort may give you 80% of the benefits. Pareto Productivity (trademark request pending as a medium-priority task in Asana...[2]) presents simple task management guidelines that go a long way. So feel free to cancel your 21-day productivity retreat and return the fancy sleep tracking ring. This will get you covered in much less than one Pomodoro slot.[3]

---

1 The Pareto principle states that for many outcomes, roughly 80% of consequences derive from 20% of the causes.

2 Asana is our project management software of choice.

3 The Pomodoro technique involves completing work in multiple intervals, often 25 minutes in length, with short breaks in between.

10.1. Focus on high-impact tasks only

"Besides the noble art of getting things done, there is the noble art of leaving things undone. The wisdom of life consists in the elimination of non-essentials."[4]

Before jumping into managing tasks, select only those with high priority – and leave the others undone. In other words, you apply the 80/20 principle to sorting out the small minority of tasks you should actually work on. For a business start-up, this is straightforward and means understanding the needs of the customers and acquiring more of them, as Adora Cheung's Y Combinator talk on managing time outlines.[5] In the case of a charity, it is slightly more complex, as the financial resources and the beneficiaries represent two distinct dimensions. In essence, four core task categories directly contribute to a charity start-up's success:

- Fundraising to obtain the financial resources to operate

- Applied research and direct feedback from beneficiaries to design a promising program

- Running a pilot program with solid monitoring and evaluation to understand your impact

- Operating a financially and legally compliant organization

Feel free to modify the list of core task categories to make them more applicable to your context, but resist the temptation to go above five categories or make them too broad.

Avoid any tasks that do not fall under these categories at all or do so only very indirectly. If you have a basic website, for example, updating or redesigning it is not a direct pathway to attracting more grants. Instead, the numbers of grant applications sent and warm introductions obtained are much more impactful. Similarly, at some point, desk research has marginal returns[6] and you would be better off talking to potential beneficiaries in the field and running a pilot with a strong monitoring and evaluation component. Finally, you might operate the

---

4 Lin Yutang, *The Importance of Living* (London: Duckworth, 2020).

5 Adora Cheung, "How to Prioritize Your Time," Jotengine, Sept. 2019, https://jotengine. com/transcriptions/ZaUOX0RT9hYxYLR0K3whsQ.

6 Karolina Sarek, "Are you working on a research agenda? A guide to increasing the impact of your research by involving decision-makers," Effective Altruism Forum, Sept. 24, 2019, https:// forum.effectivealtruism.org/posts/RZjGBHveK7rK8GLm3/are-you-working-on-a-research-agenda-a-guide-to-increasing.

most effective charity in the world, but if you get into trouble with tax or other government authorities, your future is uncertain.

The Eisenhower matrix[7] suggests prioritizing tasks according to importance and urgency. We extend this model by including the core task categories from above. This forces you to assign each task to a substantial success factor. This is a first filter against tasks not directly contributing to your charity's success. Moreover, we add effort, as this helps you identify low-hanging fruit.

Core task category	Importance	Urgency	Effort
• Fundraising • Research and feedback • Pilot with evaluation • Compliance	• High • Medium • Low	• High • Medium • Low	• High • Medium • Low

Follow these rules as you implement the grading framework:

- Avoid tasks that do not directly contribute to a core task defining the success of your organization.
- Prioritize tasks with high importance and high urgency.
- Do not neglect tasks with high importance but low urgency. Importance trumps urgency.
- Tasks with low importance and low urgency can often be postponed. Tasks with low importance but high urgency are suitable to be delegated.
- Effort is generally less important than importance and urgency. Yet among the important/urgent tasks, you want to prioritize those with the lowest effort first. Pick these low-hanging fruits.

See below an illustration of sample tasks assessed by importance, urgency, and effort. This assumes that you have already confirmed that each task aligns with at least one core task category. You first prioritize importance/urgency. In

---

7 James Clear, "How to be More Productive and Eliminate Time Wasting Activities by using the 'Eisenhower Box,'" *James Clear*, accessed Nov. 10, 2021, https://jamesclear.com/eisenhower-box.

each cluster, you then give priority to low-effort tasks.

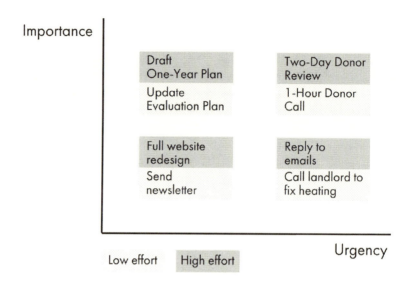

10.2. Don't reinvent the wheel

Are you really the best person to implement this task? Your co-founder might be better suited, and once you have employees you should try to delegate as much as possible anyhow (with clear task descriptions, responsibilities, and deadlines).

Outsourcing is another option that often gets forgotten. No need to spend the weekend reviewing hundreds of field expenses when you can delegate this to a contractor. You can easily find affordable remote freelancers on platforms such as Upwork.com. This works well for tasks such as simple review activities, basic bookkeeping, web research, or IT-related tasks (from developing Google Scripts to updating WordPress). In terms of more expensive contractors like lawyers, you might be able to find pro bono options (e.g., through TrustLaw[8]).

If you end up being the one implementing the task, make sure to check for existing advice and templates on the internet. For onboarding, you might consider looking at templates before drafting an Employee Handbook,[9] for

8 CAGI, "TrustLaw," International Geneva Welcome Centre, accessed Nov. 10, 2021, https:// www.cagi.ch/en/ngo/pro-bono-legal-assistance/trustlaw.php.

9 See Cinnamon Janzer, "7 Employee Handbook Examples You Should Steal From," Workest by Zenefits, Nov. 25, 2019, https://www.zenefits.com/workest/employee-handbook-examples/.

instance. Entrepreneurs love to set things up from scratch, but often, building on existing templates and guidelines can be more productive.

10.3. Use a task management tool

Don't be that person who jots down tasks on a random sheet of paper – or worse, tries to remember the task without documenting it anywhere. There are simply too many tasks in the life of an entrepreneur to remember them, and it is not the best use of your brainpower.

Using a shared Google Doc or Spreadsheet can be a decent way to track tasks and discuss them with your colleagues. However, this system faces severe limitations due to the lack of reminders and workflows.

It is best to use a proper task management tool and implement a simplified version of Getting Things Done[10] (GTD). In an unpublished talk for CE, Katriel Friedman of Charity Science Health notes that the key principle of GTD is to avoid "open loops." These are tasks that are uncategorized, not written down, or lacking a clear path to completion, and therefore may overwhelm and distract you. Create "buckets" that collect all your tasks in a few places (e.g., a notebook and the inbox of your task management app). Place new potential tasks in those buckets immediately, rather than trying to keep track of them using your memory. This way, rather than constantly carrying the mental load of many small tasks, you can review these buckets on a daily or weekly basis. Daniel Kestenholz and Peter Wildeford have written up great summaries of how they use a simplified GTD system in practice.[11]

Below we outline an even simpler form that works for those using a task management app.

---

10 Getting Things Done refers to capturing, clarifying, organizing, reflecting, and engaging the tasks at hand in order to effectively start and finish projects. Visit David Allen's website, https://gettingthingsdone.com/, for a more in-depth explanation. Accessed Nov. 10, 2021.

11 See Daniel Kestenholz, "Minimalist Productivity System," July 12, 2019, https://daniel-kestenholz.org/minimalist-productivity-system/, and Peter Wildeford, "How I Am Productive," Lesswrong, Aug. 27, 2013, https://www.lesswrong.com/posts/JTHe5oGvdj6T73o4o/how-i-am-productive, respectively.

How to deal with tasks

Type	Action
Meeting	Add to Google Calendar
Unimportant email	Archive in Gmail
Important email/article	Document it (e.g., assign to project folder/label in Gmail or save in related GDrive folder) before archiving
Two-Minute Task	Implement immediately
Task (no time to assign)	Keep the task in the inbox of your task management tool, i.e., write down the task without indicating an assignee or deadline
Task (time to assign)	Assign in task management tool to yourself or someone else and include a deadline. Provide additional context and links if necessary.

As you can see, this list already takes into consideration that many tasks will arrive in the form of emails. Instead of using your email inbox as your to-do list, you will be much more productive if you adopt Inbox Zero[12] and move any tasks immediately into your task management app. The Inbox Zero approach also rightly states that you only need to check your email client a few times per day to avoid distraction while implementing your tasks (see Deep Work below).

In terms of tools, you get a discount for Asana as an effective altruist organization through the EA Hub. Asana works great for large organizations. For personal usage or side projects, Todoist is a strong contender. If you would like to consider different apps, there is no shortage of options available to you.[13] In the end, it is less important which tool you pick than that you and your team stick to it.

---

12 Inbox Zero is an email management practice aimed at keeping the inbox empty, or nearly empty, at all times. See Ivy Wigmore, "Inbox Zero," TechTarget, June 2014, https://whatis.techtarget.com/definition/inbox-zero.

13 For a review, see Jill Duffy, "The Best To-Do List Apps for 2021," PC Mag, June 4, 2021, https://www.pcmag.com/picks/the-best-to-do-list-apps.

Box your time

Defining your high-value activities and turning them into tasks is important, but not sufficient. Let's say you have to finish a grant application in the next three days. You've got a critical task at hand with a clear deadline. The implementation, however, very much depends on the time needed to complete the task. In such cases, we can return to an old friend from Chapter 4.2. Time capping, or timeboxing, allows you to estimate the required time and book it in your calendar.[14] In this example, you might reserve a slot in Google Calendar one afternoon from 2 p.m. to 6 p.m. to finish the grant application.

Time capping works for any task, from research and decision-making to daily operations, and has a range of advantages. Time capping...

- Assigns a concrete time value to your task.
- Helps you avoid overspending time. You realize from the beginning that your time is limited, so you focus and stay within the timeframe. Hence, timeboxing is an excellent tool to force you to implement the 80/20 principle at the individual task level as well. Instead of going off on tangents, you remain focused on the core deliverable.
- Prevents paralysis and indecision. You have clearly defined how long you will spend on something. Sure, you might have to update your estimate, but this is very different from conducting tasks without any time estimates or deadlines.
- Gives you control. You are the one to define how much time to allocate. This enhances your feeling of autonomy, one of the key drivers of job happiness.[15]
- Enhances transparency in your team. Your co-founders see what you are working on and understand why you are busy.

Here are a few best practices in implementing timeboxing:

- Use one calendar for all your assignments and meetings and share the calendar with your team.

---

14 Joey Savoie, "The Importance of Time Capping," Charity Entrepreneurship, Dec. 16, 2018, https://www.charityentrepreneurship.com/blog/the-importance-of-time-capping.

15 Paul E. Spector, "Perceived Control by Employees: A Meta-Analysis of Studies Concerning Autonomy and Participation at Work," *Human Relations*, 1986;39(11):1005-1016. doi:10.1177/001872678603901104.

- Work at least two hours per day on your top goal, ideally more. Pick times when you are most productive, say, in the morning.

- If you use Calendly for scheduling meetings, restrict slots to times when you have less energy, for example, late afternoon.

- Combine similar shorter tasks into one block (e.g., review applications for an intern and a full-time position).

- Include breaks and logistical slots such as lunch and transit. You are not a robot, and your calendar should reflect that.

Review your progress

Each day – and more extensively, each week – check your progress on task management by going through this checklist.

☑ How much time did I spend on different tasks?

You should compare the time "boxed" with an estimate of the actual time spent based on your calendar. You planned, for example, to spend three hours on updating your monitoring and evaluation strategy, but exceeded that slot by two hours. Noting whether you systematically under- or overestimate time for certain tasks gives you helpful guidance going forward. For example, preparing a 1:1 meeting with an employee usually takes me around 30, not 15, minutes. Advanced users can use a time tracking app such as Clockify.me to get accurate numbers on time spent per task/category.

☑ Is the actual time spent in line with your focus on high-impact tasks? Check against importance, urgency, and effort again.

You might reassess a task after realizing how time-consuming it is (effort). Other developments at work might have corrected the task's importance upward or downward.

☑ Is there anybody that could help with or finish this task for me?

Based on your progress, you might reconsider delegating a task or getting help from a contractor/freelancer.

☑ Based on the answers to these questions, how do I need to change the deadlines and assignments in my task management app?

The progress made and your reevaluation of the task define whether updates regarding assignee and deadline are necessary.

☑ What are the implications for timeboxing for the next day/week?

Finally, the reevaluated task with an updated deadline gets more or less time allocated in your calendar. In the case of an important task for which you continue to be the lead, you might timebox larger slots to meet a deadline. In another case, you might delete a timebox, as you decided to delegate finishing a task.

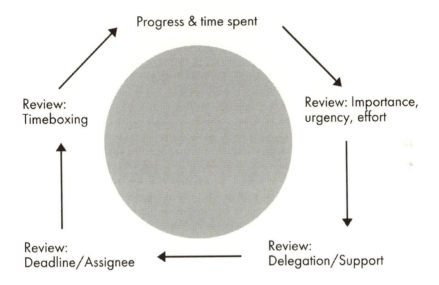

Progress & time spent

Review: Timeboxing

Review: Importance, urgency, effort

Review: Deadline/Assignee

Review: Delegation/Support

10.4. Work in deep mode

Working on your fundraising strategy and responding to emails while helping out your new colleague over instant messaging – does this sound like your typical workday? If so, you will want to consider Deep Work,[16] as presented in the classic by Cal Newport.[17] The basic message is one that intuitively resonates and has been proven in studies: multitasking and distraction undermine productivity (and flow experiences that contribute to a fulfilled work life).

16 Fadeke Adegbuyi, "The Complete Guide to Deep Work," *Doist*, accessed Nov. 10, 2021, https://blog.doist.com/deep-work/.

17 Cal Newport's book *Deep Work: Rules for Focused Success in a Distracted World* (New York City: Grand Central Publishing, 2016) coins the term Deep Work and explains the influential concepts discussed here.

Newport's *Deep Work* suggests building your whole day around carrying out important tasks without interruption: "Instead of scheduling the occasional break from distraction so you can focus, you should instead schedule the occasional break from focus to give in to distraction."[18]

Timeboxing, introduced above, is a key tool to arrive at deep work. You should also stop checking your email and turn off notifications from instant messaging like Slack as you focus on the activity at hand.

Another key concept is productive reflection, whereby you give yourself time to think about a certain problem. This is not your typical work task, as it is less linked to a specific outcome such as writing a report. Yet it is also not leisure, as you contemplate a work challenge from various angles. Productive reflection can take place in relaxed settings, say, on a walk or under the shower. For some, this comes naturally. If, however, you find yourself running from one task to the other and lack time for thinking through problems creatively, make sure to dedicate at least one to two hours per week to productive reflection. As an example, your outreach to fish farmers might not have been as successful as hoped for. In productive reflection, you approach the problem from a high level (Why do you need to talk to fish farmers? What are all the theoretical ways to reach them?) and consider different alternatives (What if we set up a hotline instead of sending email newsletters?). The goal is to consider many options in brainstorming mode and follow first principles.[19]

10.5. Reduce or structure meetings

Meetings are often not the setting to create the building blocks for your charity start-up. When was the last time you created an M&E[20] strategy or fundraising plan in a meeting? As Paul Graham points out, frequent meetings can interrupt quiet work on the outputs you need to deliver.[21] Nobody would dispute that meetings are essential for some coordination or even some crea-

---

18 Newport, *Deep Work*.

19 "First principles" refers to the idea of breaking down complicated problems into basic elements, and then reassembling your reasoning from the ground up. See Farnam Street, "First Principles: The Building Blocks of True Knowledge," Farnam Street Media Inc., accessed Nov. 10, 2021, https://fs.blog/first-principles/.

20 M&E refers to monitoring and evaluation.

21 Paul Graham, "Maker's Schedule, Manager's Schedule," July 2009, http://www.paulgraham.com/makersschedule.html.

tive problem-solving tasks. But in many work settings, they still take place too frequently and in an unstructured manner.

Here are some basic guidelines for getting the most out of your meetings:

- Apart from weekly team meetings and one-on-ones,[22] generally don't schedule regular meetings where there is no obvious need for in-person coordination. Team meetings as well as one-on-ones have an important social component, so it matters less if there are no important topics for discussion.

- At least, prepare an agenda before the meeting and document decision points after the meeting. These decision points can be turned into tasks in your task management app.

- At best, someone prepares options for decisions before the meeting and shares them with all participants. An extreme form of this is practiced at Amazon, where employees write multi-page memos[23] ahead of meetings.

- In terms of meeting scheduling, a best practice is to schedule for 25 and 50 minutes. This allows you to switch location and refresh after each meeting.

10.6. Don't forget the other (more) important stuff

This chapter covers task management and productivity in a relatively narrow sense. The focus is on the immediate work setting and delivering results. While the tools presented here are impactful, more holistic strategies might be even more important. The good news is, you are already fully aware of them. You might just need to commit to implementing them (see summary of James

---

22 To make the most out of your one on one meetings, see Lighthouse, "One on One Meeting Questions Great Managers Ask Their Teams," accessed Nov. 10, 2021, https://getlighthouse.com/blog/one-on-one-meeting-questions-great-managers-ask/.

23 Carmine Gallo, "How The First 15 Minutes of Amazon's Leadership Meetings Spark Great Ideas And Better Conversations," Forbes, June 18, 2019, https://www.forbes.com/sites/carminegallo/2019/06/18/how-the-first-15-minutes-of-amazons-leadership-meetings-sparks-great-ideas-and-better-conversations/?sh=238001e54ca9.

Clear's *Atomic Habits[24]*).

- Sleep well
- Eat well and plant-based
- Spend time with friends and family
- Exercise or at least move (as a workaholic, consider Steve Job's famous walking meetings[25])
- Outsource chores (e.g., see Joey Savoie's time saving assessment[26])
- Take weekends off and schedule vacations during which you completely disconnect
- Practice mindfulness/meditation (indeed, it would not be an article about productivity without at least one reference to meditation)

As you implement most or some of the practices introduced here, you have every right to add the title Pareto Productivity Pro to your business card and LinkedIn profile. You might not yet be an ordained monk in the order of productivity, but you are slowly getting there.

---

24 Notes on James Clear, *Atomic Habits: An Easy & Proven Way to Build Good Habits & Break Bad Ones* (New York City: Avery Publishing, 2018), available through Nathaniel Eliason, "Atomic Habits by James Clear," accessed Nov. 10, 2021, https://www.nateliason.com/notes/atomic-habits-james-clear.

25 Steve Jobs reportedly held meetings while strolling around the company's California neighborhood.

26 Available at https://bit.ly/CEtimesave.

Putting it all together in the charity world

My overarching approach to project management was to ask myself, "What do I need to know? When do I need to know it?" and then, make sure that I would know it at the right time.

My co-founder had a different approach. He would ask, "What is the one biggest opportunity right now?" and tackle it in an aggressive sprint. I like to think it was a complementary combination that let us move fast where needed while also steadily advancing longer-term goals in the background.

The key tools:

1. A running list of all our outstanding and active goals that I would read through once a week and ask what I could do to advance toward them. These varied in scope from "Understand barriers to vaccination demand" to "Get X employee off the company bank account." When I realized something was important, I'd put it on the list. Then I'd know it would stay on my radar even if I ignored it that moment.

2. A running list of my next actions, with 1-4 priority rankings that I added at the time of putting the task on my list – only things that I thought could be done in one sitting. That way, whenever I had unstructured time, I knew where to start.

3. A way to get reminded of specific tasks on specific dates. Reminder dates can be more important than due dates. If you have an application due in six months, you want to be reminded about it in four months, not in six months. We used Asana, but the specific software isn't important – you could do this reasonably well with a pair of Excel sheets and Google Calendar.

Although it might seem like setting up a complex system takes a lot of time, this approach paid off by ensuring we got done the things that just needed steady, periodic attention.

– Katriel Friedman, CEO of Charity Science Health

11. Problem-solving

Every great project and decision will require problem-solving skills. A large and consistent part of entrepreneurship is getting good at solving a wide range of problems as they come up. Like duct tape, your problem-solving skills will get you out of a jam and temporarily fix many issues as you create space for more thorough and long-lasting solutions. Aspects of problem-solving can be used for almost every decision or challenge encountered.

11.1. Six steps to problem-solving

Problems will inevitably arise as part of any complex project. In the context of founding a charity, it could be that a donor you were counting on does not fund the project, a key employee leaves the job, or a government agency requires a document you have never heard of. Underneath the shiny website and carefully branded social media pages, most organizations face a consistent stream of diverse and novel problems. A big part of being a well-rounded and talented charity founder is the ability to solve these novel problems effectively.

When you encounter a problem:

1. Determine how important it is
2. Define the problem
3. Generate solutions (divergent ideation)
4. Compare solutions (convergent ideation)

5. Implement your solution(s)

6. Upstream problem-solving

Determine how important the problem is

When you detect a new problem, first determine how important it is to solve. There will always be more problems than you have time to address, so it's necessary to prioritize. As a useful heuristic, ask yourself, "What is the cost of not dealing with this?" If your computer mic is broken so you have to find headphones every time you Skype, the cost might be mild irritation. But if you just learned that a key piece of program software is down across multiple states, not addressing the problem might mean losing the trust of your users and the impact of your program.

The more important the problem, the sooner you should get around to it and the more time you should dedicate to solving it. Often, it's worth putting more time into problem-solving than your intuition suggests, as problems tend to get bigger when ignored.

Define the problem

Once you've decided a problem is important, define what exactly you are trying to achieve. Do you need to answer a legal question, change a habit within your team, fix a malfunctioning piece of your program operations, or something else? What do you want to optimize for? Having a clear understanding of your goal will help you to be more creative in coming up with solutions, and more decisive when comparing those solutions in order to land on the best one. Consider the popular mythical race between the US and USSR to develop a tool for writing in space. Was the goal to build a gravity-resistant pen (requiring complex and expensive novel engineering) or to create something that would make a mark on paper? In the latter case, the solution already existed in the form of a pencil.

You may realize at this stage that you don't yet fully understand the problem. If so, gather any additional information you need. Let's say your employee is underperforming. Do you understand why that is? Are they lacking tools, support, confidence, skills, space, or something else? Can you speak to someone who has faced a similar problem in the past, or who has a different perspective on the same problem you are facing?

Generate solutions (divergent thinking)

Now that you've defined your problem, it's time to get creative. Often, some potential solutions will come to mind quickly, but finding the best one might take some out-of-the-box thinking. Imagine you're trying to figure out what to do with that underperforming employee. Maybe a couple of ideas come up right away: you could a) fire the employee, b) ignore the problem, or c) do a performance review with them and help them work through the issues. These might seem like decent solutions, but dig a little deeper and plenty more will arise.

At this stage, it's worth being creative about possible solutions. Adopt the mantra "no idea is a bad idea." The time for judging them comes later – now is the time for generating as many ideas as you can. There are a few things you can do to help boost creativity at this stage:

- Go for a walk. Research shows that the act of walking (indoors or outdoors) stimulates your ability to come up with creative uses for an object.[1] Maybe you can have a walking meeting, or take a quick walk right before you start.

- Frame the problem as a question constructed to find solutions, e.g., if too few strong candidates are applying for your job roles, ask, "How can we ensure that our job ad gets into the hands of as many people as possible who are a great fit?"

- Brainstorm as a team. Many of the best creative ideas arise when one person riffs off another – often at the intersection of their personal areas of expertise, or where their different thinking styles complement each other well. Get the (virtual) whiteboard out, appoint someone to plaster it with key words from the conversation, and encourage everyone to bounce off each other's ideas.

- Start with a creative primer. Come up with a fun exercise to get everyone's creative juices flowing, for example: "Imagine a monkey is stuck in a tree. How many different ways can we think of to get him down?"

- Keep it fun. It's worth making a special effort to ensure everyone in the room feels confident making creative suggestions. Challenge everyone

---

1 May Wong, "Stanford study finds walking improves creativity," Stanford News, April 24, 2014, https://news.stanford.edu/news/2014/april/walking-vs-sitting-042414.html.

to come up with at least one ridiculous idea, keep the session light-hearted (criticism of ideas should be forbidden at this stage), and lead by example in proposing ideas you know to be silly. You could also set a team challenge, e.g., "Can we come up with 30 ideas in five minutes?" Once again, the goal here is quantity, not quality.

- Bring in outside perspectives. While your team may have a deeper understanding of the context surrounding your problem, your advisory board, family, or housemates might bring a different perspective based on their own backgrounds or experiences. Talking to other people in your life can be a helpful way to add some diversity of thought.

Compare solutions (convergent thinking)

Now that you have a long list of possible solutions, it's time to get critical and break out your decision-making toolkit. You will likely want to make a comparison spreadsheet or a simple pros-and-cons list. This will be made easier by the work you did earlier to define the problem clearly and what you want to optimize for in your solution.

How much time to spend comparing solutions depends on the difference in expected value between your top option and the next-best one. But keep in mind that generating and comparing ideas are likely worth 10% of the time the solution will take to implement.

Remember that solutions are not exclusive – your plan might involve trying one low-cost solution first, then implementing another if that doesn't work. By the end of your comparison, you should feel comfortable talking to an advisor or trusted friend (and often this is a good thing to do) about the options you considered and why you came to the solution you chose.

Implement your solution(s)

The first step in implementing a solution is communicating the plan clearly to everyone it involves. In some cases, this might be no one, but usually, you will have to explain to your team why you have gone with this plan (good thing you have practice from when you explained it to your friend). The solution is best presented clearly, assertively, and confidently. You do not need always to be confident you have made the right call – everyone makes mistakes. But when you are confident in your process, you can confidently say, "I think this is the best call given the time I was able to put in."

Many solutions require habit forming. There are great resources on how to do this, including James Clear's previously mentioned book *Atomic Habits*. Many require changing your team's mind on key issues (our favorite book on this is Dan Heath's *Switch*). This can take time and patience. Most of the time a solution will not be universally liked by everyone, but over time and with encouragement, people will adapt.

For example, say you are getting your team to switch to a new task management system. You might plan to speak about it at a regular team meeting. Start with the "need," or why this is happening. "As you all know, our team has been struggling to stay on top of all the work we need to do. A few important things have fallen through the cracks."

Next, you briefly want to explain your process in coming to the solution, drawing the person along on the journey you went through. "I talked to a few other organizations and spent some time researching possible solutions. One thing that came up was our type of task manager and the way it's used. I compared about a dozen task management systems, and it seems as though quite a few of them would give our team big benefits."

Finally, explain the transition and implementation of the idea. Small steps are often good. "We are going to try this new system for a week with our communications team and reevaluate after that. If it seems to help with some of our problems, we will switch everyone over." To help ease the change, document the new processes by writing standard operating procedures. This way, everyone is on the same page about how things should be done.

Acknowledge possible flaws or complaints, but be reassuring and firm and remind them of the benefits (particularly the long-term benefits). "I know it will be a pain to move all our old tasks over, but once we transition, we will get more done every week. And the more we can do with our limited resources, the better we can achieve our goals as an organization and save lives."

At this point, you might think your problem is solved and you can move on. But you can't quite yet.

Upstream problem-solving

The last step is solving the problem upstream. Solving problems can be categorized in two ways: upstream problem-solving and firefighting. So far, the process we have talked about is mostly firefighting steps. Upstream problem-solving refers to actions that can be done to prevent problems from arising, like getting a flu vaccination to lower your chances of getting the flu. Firefighting, on the other hand, refers to reactive actions taken after the problem occurs, like going to a doctor after you feel ill. Most often, an ounce of prevention is worth a pound of cure, and the more problems you can solve upstream the easier it will be to fight the (still inevitable) others that come up downstream. Sometimes you have to experience the flu to realize the importance of preventing it the next time. For every problem you solve, you should think: "Does this have a chance of coming up again? How can I prevent this sort of problem from reoccurring?"

A lot of upstream problem-solving comes from realizing recurrent patterns and recognizing problems as "another one of those" instead of a unique situation. Of course, each situation is somewhat unique, but that does not mean the same underlying problem cannot be causing it.

Say you're looking at three problems on your desk. One is that your operations team is falling behind on their monthly bookkeeping. The second is a promising new idea that you would love to pursue, but you don't have any staff to spare for it. The third is that your communications team is not responding well to emails sent to your website; many of them seem to fall through the cracks.

These may seem like unrelated problems in unconnected departments, but they could also be a sign that you have not built in enough organizational slack to deal with a changing and dynamic workload. A firefighting solution might be to pull an all-nighter responding to the emails and doing the bookkeeping. An upstream solution might be to hire more staff or narrow the scope of your project, freeing up organizational time.

Upstream problem-solving does not come naturally. It's not trained in school or practiced in most workplaces. There are few resources aimed at teaching upstream problem-solving, but *Upstream* by Dan Heath is a deep guide both to the barriers – i.e., the mindset that a problem is unavoidable, "not my problem," or can't be dealt with right now – and to some solutions. Key questions to ask in upstream problem-solving are:

- How do we bring together the right people?
- How can we change flawed systems?
- What's the leverage point?

- How can we spot problems before they happen, steering clear of false positives?
- What does success look like and how do we avoid "ghost victories" (i.e., failures in the trappings of success)?
- How do we avoid causing harm in flow-through effects?
- If nothing happens, who foots the bill?

More materials, including a summary and the first chapter of the book, are available on the author's website.[2]

11.2. Steelman solitaire

To deal with the strongest version of a problem, you often have to steelman it.[3] Steelman solitaire consists of arguing with yourself, alternating between writing a steelman of an argument, a steelman of a counter-argument, a steelman of a counter-counter-argument, and so on and so forth.

Benefits

Structure forces you to do the thing you know you should do anyway. Most people reading this already know that it's important to consider the best arguments on all sides instead of just considering the weakest on the other. Many already know that you can't just consider a counter-argument, then consider yourself done. However, it's easy to forget to do so. The structure of this method makes you much more likely to follow through on your existing rational aspirations.

Clarifies thinking. I'm sure everybody has experienced a discussion that's gone all over the place, and by the end, you're more confused than when you started. Some points get lost and forgotten while others dominate. This approach helps to organize and clarify your thinking, revealing holes and strengths in different lines of thought.

More likely to change your mind. As much as we aspire not to, most people, even the most competent rationalists, will often become entrenched in a position

---

2 See heathbrothers.com for notes on Dan Heath, *Upstream: The Quest to Solve Problems Before They Happen* (New York: Avid Reader Press / Simon & Schuster, 2020), and other works.

3 As discussed in Chapter 6.2, Steelmanning views refers to constructing the strongest possible argument from a given viewpoint.

due to the nature of conversations. In steelman solitaire, there's no other person to lose face to or to hurt your feelings. This often makes it more likely to change your mind than a lot of other methods.

Makes you think much more deeply than usual. A common feature of people we would describe as "deep thinkers" is that they've often already thought of our counter-argument, and the counter-counter-counter-etc.-argument. This method will make you really dig deep into an issue.

Dealing with steelmen that are compelling to you. The problem with a lot of debates is that what is convincing to the other person isn't convincing to you, even though there are actually good arguments out there. This method allows you to think of those reasons instead of getting caught up in what another person thinks should convince you.

You can look back at why you came to the belief you have. Like most intellectually oriented people, we have a lot of opinions, sometimes so many that we forget why we came to hold them in the first place (but we vaguely remember that it was a good reason, we're sure). Writing things down can help you refer back to them later and reevaluate.

Better at coming to the truth than most methods. For the above reasons, we think that this method makes you more likely to arrive at accurate beliefs.

The broad idea

"Strawmanning" means presenting an opposing view in the least charitable light – often so uncharitable that it does not resemble the view that the other side actually holds. The term "steelmanning" is a counter to this. It means taking the opposing view and trying to present it in its strongest form. The alternative belief proposed by a steelman isn't necessarily what the opposing side actually believes. For example, there's a steelman argument stating that the reason organic food is good is because monopolies are generally bad, and Monsanto having a monopoly on food could lead to disaster. This might indeed be a belief held by some people who are pro-organic, but a huge percentage of people are just falling prey to the naturalistic fallacy.[4]

While steelmanning may not be perfect for understanding people's true reasons for believing propositions, it is very good for coming to more accurate

---

4 The naturalistic fallacy is the idea that things found in nature are basically good, and in fact better than their "non-natural" counterparts, with no real evidence to support it.

beliefs yourself. If the reason you believe you don't have to care about buying organic is that you think people only do so because of the naturalistic fallacy, you might be missing out on the argument about the dangers of monopolies that may convince you.

However – and this is where steelmanning back and forth comes in – what if buying organic doesn't necessarily lead to breaking the monopoly? Maybe upon further investigation, Monsanto doesn't have a monopoly. Or maybe multiple organizations have copyrighted different gene edits, so there's no true monopoly.

The idea behind steelman solitaire is not to stop at steelmanning the opposing view. It's to steelman the counter-counter-argument as well. As has been said by more eloquent people than myself, you can't just consider an argument and counter-argument. There are very long chains of counter^x arguments, and you want to consider the steelman of each of them. Don't pick any side in advance. Just commit to trying to find the true answer.

This is all well and good in principle but can be challenging to keep organized. This is where the tool Workflowy comes in.[5] Workflowy allows you to have counter-arguments nested under arguments, counter-counter-arguments nested under counter-arguments, and so forth. That way, you can zoom in and out and focus on one particular line of reasoning, realize you've gone so deep you've lost the forest for the trees, zoom out, and realize what triggered the consideration in the first place. It also allows you to look at the main arguments for and against quickly.

Tips and tricks

That's the broad-strokes explanation of the method. A few pointers:

- **Name your arguments**. Instead of just saying, "We should buy organic because Monsanto is forming a monopoly and monopolies can lead to abuses of power," call it "monopoly argument" in bold at the front of the bullet point, and then write the full argument in normal font. Naming arguments condenses them and gives you more cognitive workspace to play around with. It also allows you to see your arguments from a bird's eye view.

- **Insult yourself sometimes**. We usually (always) make fun of ourselves

---

5 See https://workflowy.com/s/DIeJ.FbSGQb5osE, accessed Nov. 10, 2021, for an example.

or our arguments while using this technique, just because it's funny. Making your deep thinking more enjoyable makes you more likely to do it instead of putting it off forever, much like including a jelly bean in your vitamin regimen to incentivize you to take that giant gross pill you know you should.

- **Mark arguments as resolved** as they become resolved. If you dive deep into an argument and come to the conclusion that it's not compelling, then mark it clearly as done. Our team writes "rsv" at the beginning of the entry to remind ourselves, but you can use anything that will let you know that you're no longer concerned with that argument. Follow up with a little note at the beginning of the thread, giving either a short explanation detailing why it's ruled out or, ideally, just the named argument that beat it.

- **Prioritize ruling out arguments**. This is a good general approach to life and one we use in our research at Charity Entrepreneurship. Try to find out as soon as possible whether something is going to work. Take a moment when you're thinking of arguments to come up with the angles that are most likely to destroy something quickly, then prioritize investigating those. That will allow you to get through more arguments faster, and thus, come to more correct conclusions over your lifetime.

- **Start with the trigger**. Start with a section where you describe what triggered the thought. This can often help you get to the true question you're trying to answer. A huge trick to coming to correct conclusions is asking the right questions in the first place.

- **Use spreadsheet decision-making.** If you're using the spreadsheet decision-making system (laid out in Chapter 5), steelman solitaire can help you fill in the cells comparing different options.

- **Use for decisions and problem-solving generally**. This method can be used for claims about anything, but it can also generally be applied to decision-making and problem-solving. Just start with a problem statement or decision you're contemplating, make a list of possible solutions, and then play steelman solitaire on those options.

Putting it all together in the charity world

Fall in love with problems and you will fall in love with entrepreneurship. It took me a while to embrace this lesson, but there is something to it. Naturally, solid problem-solving techniques go a long way in letting you deal with this reality.

Based on my own experience and those of the charities I've worked with, the following lessons on problem-solving have been particularly helpful:

- Be brutal in prioritizing the problems you deal with

Your team will confront you with many urgent problems throughout the workday. Don't fall for the trap of urgency and stick to the important problems instead. It took me a while to neglect my wish to be hyper-responsive and start delegating urgent non-important tasks or dealing with them at one set point during the day instead of as they came in.

- Give more time for creative solutions

Rapid implementation is a key trait of a successful charity. However, it is worth spending more time looking for creative solutions, as it saves time and energy. The book *A Whack on the Side of the Head* helped me practice out-of-the-box thinking.[6] Questioning the core assumptions is key: should we try to make a boring meeting more engaging or, rather, move this type of communication to Slack? Should we distribute deworming pills instead of textbooks to boost education?

- Solve problems upstream

Prevention is better than cure. This is what we define as upstream problem-solving. A risk register outlining the key threats to your organization can be an excellent starting point for this – otherwise, there are just too many problems to solve preventatively. Once you have your priorities set, solving problems preventatively often involves defining processes as Standard Operating Procedures (SOPs). How I've come to love these endless lists of instructions!

– Patrick Stadler (charity mentor & entrepreneur)

---

6 Here, Patrick is referring to Roger von Oech's 1973 creativity classic.

12. Creativity

Creativity is more of an art than a science. Using it is often a softer process of searching an area rather than the hard edge that most tools bring to the table. When you start a new project, you will face challenges neither you nor anyone else has faced before. A flashlight helps you see something that is not obvious at first glance.

As a charity entrepreneur, you will often have to think outside the box to accomplish something others believe is impossible. Acts of creativity can be as large as a huge organizational change or as small as a workaround to get a form more quickly through a snarled bureaucracy.

Creativity is often thought of as an innate quality, shrouded in mystery. But of course, like most other things, it's a trainable skill. We're going to go over five ways to think more creatively about running a charity (or anything else you do in life).

12.1. Creativity soup

To create a creativity soup, you need both the ingredients and the right mix. Every successful person stands on the shoulders of giants, and creativity doesn't magically emerge from the ether; it builds on what has come before. Even the most original artists, writers, and musicians take inspiration from other creatives, mixing and re-mixing ingredients to create something new.

The best way to gather ingredients is to hunt far and wide. The most common ideas (the salt and pepper of your field) will be regularly used and readily accessible. The special ingredients will be harder to find. Thankfully, there are a couple of reliable ways to be exposed to them.

Questions are a great source of creativity. Why does that work the way it does? How did someone else work around this challenge? Practice infinite curiosity to improve the number of great ideas you get.

Creativity often stems from connecting areas in new ways. Learning from others can give you access to ideas from far-reaching places. Many creatives get their best ideas from talking to someone in a completely different field, stumbling across a concept that might not be used in their own.

Having a lot of different ideas from wide-ranging disciplines kicking around in your brain means that a lot more mixing happens naturally. In addition to chatting to people in different fields, you can introduce new concepts to your mind by watching documentaries, reading non-fiction books, or mastering an area outside of your top focus. (The creative benefits of mixing can even be some justification for having a messy desk – "I am facilitating a randomized mixing of ideas!")

Over time, you will get the hang of which ingredients are key information that might come in handy later and which can be discarded. Remembering a celebrity's favorite color will rarely be a useful ingredient, but knowing that an electric bike does not require a driver's license just might be.

12.2. Generate lots of answers

Most creative gems come with huge numbers of solutions and ideas – in this case, quantity really does correlate with quality. It could be that generating ideas works your creative muscles, or that it's only after twenty solutions that you start hitting the really original ideas. Either way, this is an easy technique to apply. Is your charity struggling to choose its logo? Come up with a hundred ideas. Most of them will be horrible, but you only need one to be great. Writing a blog post? Come up with ten options for the title before settling. Wondering whom to ask for advice? Brainstorm five times as many people as you plan to talk to. Your best option can only be the best of the options you have considered.

Generating a lot of answers involves thinking outside of the box – way outside of the box. Most people will have been taught in school that doing this means looking at the same information slightly differently, like completing a puzzle by turning it upside down. Real-life creativity looks far more like leaving the classroom, going to the dollar store to find a beach ball, and attaching the pieces to that instead. Your teacher might not be happy, but that's the point. If it's inside the box enough that it's expected, it's not really that creative.

Don't fall in love with an idea too quickly. If you love your third idea, you're unlikely to put in the hard work to come up with a thirty-third. Hold off on judging your ideas till you have a large number in front of you.

12.3. Toy with ideas and be okay with failing

Creative people tend to be both curious about the world and playful in their approach to it. We have two friends, Fred and Ezekiel, who play board games completely differently. Fred is highly concentrated on winning the game in front of him. He uses proven tactics with small tweaks, slowly trying to master his strategy. Ezekiel is quickly bored by an established strategy and tries something radically different each game. He loses far more often than Fred, but comes up with completely new ways to play the game. This experimental mindset can cross apply to even the hardest problems.

Toying with an idea doesn't mean it's unimportant; it just means that looking at it from different angles will generate valuable concepts. Sometimes a charity can undergo a large-scale flip due to a change in perspective. One of our team members used to work with a charity that sent out vaccination reminders. They had to go door to door to sign people up to the program, which made up the bulk of the cost. One day the CEO of the charity realized, "We're spending all our money going door to door. Maybe we should think about the most impactful thing to provide given the network we have in place." This flipped the original question – "What is the best way to sign people up to a vaccination program?" – and they changed the nature of their intervention entirely.

Toying with ideas involves thinking about them more softly and fluidly. It also involves being okay coming up with bad ideas. At the start of a research year, we often compile hundreds of ideas for how to help. Some are good; some less so. If you give yourself permission to come up with wacky ideas, you can sometimes end up with gems. One idea we came up with to help animals was flyer dog, a cute dog who could be trained to hand out flyers on animal rights.

Flyer dog, although an entertaining idea, was not nearly cost-effective enough. But it did lead to a deeper conversation about different ways to hand out flyers, and some genuinely promising ideas.

12.4. Ride the wave

Some tasks take the same amount of time no matter when you do them. Vacuuming the house takes me just as long whether I'm excited or indifferent. However, this is not true of creativity. Sometimes you'll find yourself able to think more creatively. When these moments come, ride the wave. Many creative people always carry around a notebook, or jot down ideas on their phone. We have a Google document called "Idea bucket" that's our go-to for any ideas we have, no matter how ridiculous. We periodically come back to the document and discard some ideas, flesh some out, and share some with others. The idea of a charity entrepreneurship handbook was written down in that bucket before it appeared anywhere else.

It's one thing to ride the wave, but how about creating one? You might be able to notice certain trends in your creativity. Maybe you get your best ideas in the morning, when talking to someone, or when listening to music. Try to make note of when a creative wave hits and why that might be. Some individuals come up with the vast majority of their ideas while talking to others, particularly people they know well who have a different background from them. Others come up with their best ideas when they have some time and space to themselves – in the shower, for example. Sometimes, a creative activity in a different area can put you in the creative mode. Painting a picture or working on a fiction book can get the creative juices flowing, which can then help solve problems relating to your charity.

Putting it all together in the charity world

Creativity has been a constant theme in our organization. At Canopie, we're building an app-based digital mental health intervention that requires a lot of workarounds to make for a good user experience. This has exercised our creative muscle constantly. One thing we've noticed is how easy it is to lose creativity, or the ability to find creative workarounds, when you're stressed or have decision fatigue. Sometimes just talking to an outsider, hearing their left-field ideas - someone who can pull you out of your own thoughts - can be a way to get your creative juices unstuck. Basically, creativity works best when we're in the right frame of mind first.

More broadly, in our journey, it has paid off to break some of the rules that other organizations follow to chart our own path. Creativity has been the tool we have used to stay laser-focused on our mission and the impact we hope to have on the world, while other forces (status quo, for example) would have had us going another way.

For example, we realized very early on that even though behavioral health and physical health in the US are very siloed, the most cost-effective distribution channel for our maternal mental-health intervention would be through pediatric offices, as doctors screen for maternal mental-health challenges four times in the first year post-birth. Unfortunately, the referral process falls apart after that (due to lack of good maternal mental-health resources), which means 85% of new mothers who need support don't get it. We saw an opportunity to address this problem for doctors, while also ensuring that our program would get in front of mothers and be trusted, by using doctors as our distribution channel and the screening process as the point of referral.

Despite the apparent barrier, we were able to successfully engage reputable doctors' associations and established partnerships with dozens of pediatric clinics within several months.

– Anne Wanlund (co-founder of Canopie)

13. Long-term planning

Every great project needs to be sketched out before its creation. A pencil lets you draft, erase, and change as you learn. The same will be true of your long-term plan, which will update as you go. All great plans will go through numerous iterations throughout the year. However, having a sketch of your endline project is equally crucial for both decision-making and practical projects.

13.1. Theory of change

A "theory of change" explicitly articulates the assumptions that underlie your plan to achieve a specific goal, and lays out a method to test them. It is generally represented in the form of a cause-and-effect diagram. A well-designed theory of change allows you to communicate clearly what your activities are and why they lead to the outcomes that you and your supporters want.

Example 1: Research organizations

Imagine you want to start an organization that uses research to make a difference. Without an explicit theory of change, your implicit mental model of how you might make an impact may go something like this:

Do reviews of literature →Find insights that seem useful → Publish them

This is not a good theory of change. It doesn't properly outline your goal, it doesn't explain how your actions will lead to that goal, and it doesn't explain how you will measure what you are doing. Presumably, your final goal is to impact living beings positively, not just publish papers. Even if you work very hard and put out many widely cited papers, it's possible that you will not make any difference. If you want a more in-depth explanation of how this theory of change could be improved, head to the EA Forum to read about increasing the impact of your research from CE's research director, Karolina Sarek.[1]

A good theory of change draws the full causal chain from your actions to the final impact, which is your end goal.

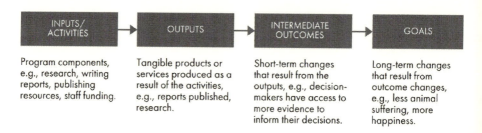

INPUTS/ ACTIVITIES	OUTPUTS	INTERMEDIATE OUTCOMES	GOALS
Program components, e.g., research, writing reports, publishing resources, staff funding.	Tangible products or services produced as a result of the activities, e.g., reports published, research.	Short-term changes that result from the outputs, e.g., decision-makers have access to more evidence to inform their decisions.	Long-term changes that result from outcome changes, e.g., less animal suffering, more happiness.

After going through Charity Entrepreneurship's curriculum, the Happier Lives Institute published a theory of change that follows the above principles.[2]

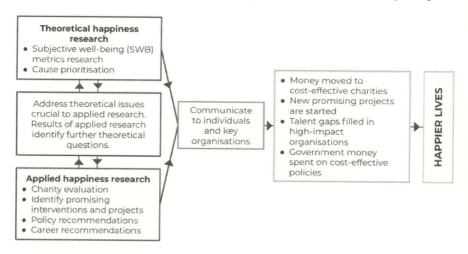

---

1 Sarek, "Are you working on a research agenda?"

2 Happier Lives Institute, "HLI Has Hatched: Strategy Update after the Charity Entrepreneurship Incubation Program," Oct. 29, 2019, https://www.happierlivesinstitute.org/blog/hli-has-hatched-strategy-update-after-the-charity-entrepreneurship-incubation-program.

On the left, you can see the core research agenda of the Happier Lives Institute at a glance (the inputs/activities). On the right, you can see some measurable metrics such as money moved, new projects, and hires made (intermediate outcomes) which lead to the final impact – happier lives.

It is clear from this diagram that "communicating to individuals and key organizations" is an important part of this process. Ultimately, the goal of doing research is that someone will read it and become able to allocate a grant in a better way, or start a new project in a more promising area.

Making this explicit is important because it allows the research agenda to proceed with clear goals and objectives in mind. If you are well aware from the start that one of the major goals of a specific research project is to improve grant allocation, you can contact those grantmakers before beginning the research and get a sense of what sort of information might help them make better decisions.

Formalizing your theory of change means that your research will be much more likely to have an impact.

Example 2: Cash transfer organizations

Below is a theory of change for an organization that uses cash transfers to increase immunizations.

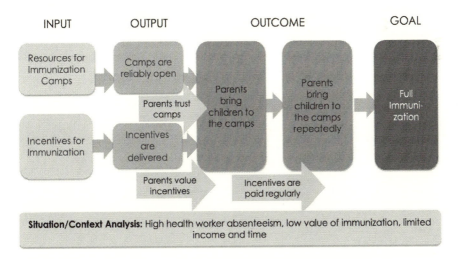

They have two "input" actions: providing resources to keep immunization camps reliably open, and providing cash incentives to people who get vaccinated.

There are also several measurable "outputs and outcomes."[3] You can send someone to check and see if a camp is reliably open. You can create a verification system to check if incentives are delivered. You can count how many children come to the camps, and how often they return for their booster shots. If something is going wrong, you can check your assumptions (e.g., surveying parents to see if they trust the camps).

When designing measurement systems, keep in mind how much they cost. If a measurement is expensive but isn't meaningfully informing your decision on whether it's worth investing more resources in this intervention, cut it. Do try to measure things in more than one way, however, especially if there's scope for a particular measurement to be misleading.

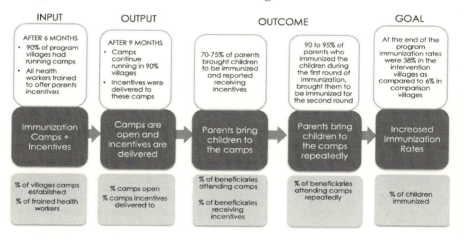

Common errors to watch out for

Don't forget the endline metric. The above example is a good theory of change, but can it be improved? Immunization isn't the end goal – saving lives and improving quality of life is. This may seem obvious, but it is very important to note it explicitly so that you remember to model how much disease is actually prevented and how many lives are actually saved by increasing immunization in a region.

---

3 ToC images on pages 151 and 152 sourced and unchanged from 2017 J-PAL/CLEAR South Asia Evaluating Social Programs, "Theory of Change," Course lecture, J-PAL/CLEAR South Asia at IFMR, Delhi, July 2017, https://www.povertyactionlab.org/sites/default/files/Lecture%202-THEORY%20OF%20CHANGE.pdf. The images here are licensed under the Creative Commons Attribution 4.0 International License. To view a copy of the license, visit https://creativecommons.org/licenses/by/4.0/.

If you skip this step, you might (for instance) end up choosing a location that maximizes the number of people you can immunize, rather than one that maximizes the number of lives you can save (e.g., by picking a location with a high child mortality rate).

Effective organizations are built by systematically examining many simple, perhaps obvious-seeming considerations, and the theory of change is an important step in that process.

Beware of mission creep: This theory of change actually has two interventions: opening camps and incentivizing people to attend them. Sometimes, this is appropriate. But suppose it turns out that building camps provides most of the benefit, even without the incentive? In that scenario, you might divert the money that goes into incentives and use it to build more camps, and vaccinate more people and save more lives. Or, suppose it turns out that incentivizing preexisting camps would provide most of the benefit of creating new camps at a fraction of the price? In that scenario, you could divert resources you might spend building camps toward just handing out conditional cash transfers, and therefore vaccinate a lot more people and save more lives.

Suppose as this hypothetical nonprofit grows larger, they begin to think: "If we have the camps, why not also provide vitamin supplements, or distribute essential medicines, or have the workers build latrines to prevent the spread of disease?"

Sometimes adding more programs is efficient, squeezes more impact out of fewer resources, and does make sense! It also often looks good on paper and impresses some donors to have a more comprehensive and holistic program. However, be sure to do an explicit cost-effectiveness analysis first. There are exceptions, but generally speaking, if you are considering multiple interventions, one of those interventions will be more efficient than all the others and you shouldn't divert any resources from it.

Stay specific and skeptical: Don't allow any hand-wavy[4] steps in your theory of change. Some examples of hand-wavy steps are:

Publishing research → lives are saved. As covered above, you need to add steps where you explicitly model who is going to use it and what actions they

---

4 Missing important details or logical steps, instead relying on lackluster evidence like intuition alone, examples, or the perception of common sense.

will take, and you need to actually talk to these decision-makers. And, you need to quantify the impact of these decisions on living beings.

Raising awareness → less suffering. You should explicitly model and measure, or at least estimate, the rate at which this translates to behavioral changes, voting changes, policy changes, etc. And, you need to quantify the impact of these changes on living beings.

Changing people's views → impact. You should outline the mechanism of how changing attitudes influences living beings, and estimate or measure the degree of this impact.

Don't just assume that one step will lead to another. Don't overestimate the probability that one step will lead to another. Find an objective way to verify it. Get feedback from someone you know to be skeptical.

13.2. Three levels of long-term planning

What changes do you want to bring to the world this year? What about in five years?

Your theory of change specifies steps along the path to accomplishing your organization's goals and achieving impact. Many of these actions may involve complex projects that require a sequence of smaller tasks over a long period of time. However, most people have a tendency to underestimate how long a task will take and the difficulties they will face. This phenomenon goes by many names ("planning fallacy," "Murphy's law") and it can lead you off track, failing to achieve your goals due to pursuing projects you don't have time for.

Making a plan will help keep you organized and focused on your highest-priority tasks. Even if you work a lot, it's easy to get sidetracked with stuff that is not important for your main goals. Keeping track of time will help you use it well. By estimating and then keeping track of how long you thought things would take vs. how long they actually took, you will improve your ability to strategize actions taken by your organization.

Plans can also encourage you to anticipate problems before they happen. We recommend doing "pre-mortems" as part of your planning: imagine that your charity failed, think of the most likely reasons why this might have happened, and come up with some ways to prevent this outcome.

We recommend three levels of planning: an aspirational five-year plan, a brief but precise one-year plan, and a more detailed month-to-month plan.

Five-year plan

CE's five-year plan establishes specific benchmarks for what we want to accomplish as well as how many staff it will require (and therefore the approximate cost).

Stating your long-term goals, and criteria for success and failure, beforehand will keep you honest about whether or not you are meeting them. In this way, you can avoid moving the goalposts – changing the criteria for "success" to fit whatever you did achieve. For instance, say you've completed a counterfactual impact evaluation, which specified that you had to achieve a certain goal in order to consider your activities sufficiently high impact to be worth doing given the alternatives. Five years later, you have not achieved it. Though tough, it will be easier for you to acknowledge this failure to yourself if you've set non-negotiable criteria beforehand.

Our five-year plan also incorporates testing and scalability. In addition to its direct importance in realizing long-term impact, having a clear vision for the longer-term future is essential when communicating with donors and grantmakers. Many will want to know whether the project will be **sustainable** (Will it eventually be able to continue without their support?) and **scalable** (Does it have the structure to grow cost-effectively?).

Circumstances are guaranteed to change over time, so there's no need to be too detailed and specific with a five-year plan. It should provide you with a solid strategic trajectory and guide your more immediate goals, including those in the one-year plan.

One-year plan

A one-year plan tends to include the following elements:

- A set of very specific, measurable goals and clear timelines for achieving them. It also includes a plan for how any progress on the goals will be measured.

- A budget. Funding is typically given out on a yearly basis, so one-year plans are often part of a fundraising ask. It may be wise to include a rough outline of who you are hoping will fund this budget.

- An explanation of how these goals tie into past activities and connect with longer-term future goals

You will often need to make a one-year plan as part of a grant application. Keep it concise (one to three pages) so that other people can read it easily. It helps to talk about how this year's activities tie into the bigger picture over the next five years.

Month-to-month timeline

You should roughly plan out what you will do for individual months. This becomes especially important as your organization gains more staff members. Each one has a limited number of hours, so it helps to make sure that this time is being allotted to tasks that will help them have the highest impact.

Below is an example of one of our month-to-month timeline templates. You should plan out start and end dates for each project. You might also specify who or how many full-time staff equivalents[5] will be working on the tasks.

Your timeline doesn't necessarily need to be very detailed in the early days, but it's good to have a sense of what everyone is working on during any given time period. You might also encourage individual staff to make weekly plans for themselves, and share them with close collaborators.

In addition to helping you plan, having a legible timeline can help your staff understand the internal parameters that they are working with. The more infor-

---

5 Capacity expressed in full-time staff: e.g., if two staff members work on a project at a 50% capacity, that is equivalent to one full-time staff member doing the same work.

mation your staff has about the big picture, the more connected they will be to the work, and the better they will be able to take initiative, manage themselves, and prioritize their time correctly.

Tracking progress and evaluating next steps

Every month, it's worth going through your monthly and one-year goals. Try highlighting things that are "on track," "not on track," and "seem unlikely to happen" in different colors. After seeing how the month went, you can refocus. You should also go through this process before adding any new goals that are likely to take a lot of time, so you can remind yourself how long tasks take.

You should also build longer, more in-depth reevaluation points where you deeply question all your core assumptions.

- Which goals did you meet this past year?
- Do you still think this is the most impactful project you can work on, and if not, how can you pivot or scale down?
- Which aspects of your process worked well, and which need improvement?
- Did you learn any new information, and how should you change what you are doing based on that info?

Reevaluations should also be done when a major organizational change occurs or a new key piece of information is discovered.

13.3. To scale, or not to scale: that is the question

As we look for ways to maximize our impact, the enormity of the problems we confront yawns before us. Animal advocates are faced with the cold reality that seventy billion animals are farmed each year – not to mention those we pull from the oceans, whom we measure in tons rather than in individual lives. One in four of us will suffer from mental illness in our lifetime, and stigma prevents many from seeking help. Today, health-care systems groan under the weight of a pandemic, as COVID-19 swallows up normal life.

Next to the statistics, our efforts can seem like a drop in the ocean. This is why scaling up is so urgent: the more we grow, the more we can help. But what if we're focusing on the wrong thing? In their article for the Stanford Social Innovation Review, Alice Gugelev and Andrew Stern shift the conversation away from scale-up and toward the concept of endgame. They observe that, while scaling up can certainly increase your organization's impact, scale and impact are imperfectly aligned. Essentially, through thinking consciously about our endgame, we can better map action onto impact and do good more effectively.[6]

Before exploring the concept of endgame, let's look at some of the challenges associated with scaling up. Stern and Gugelev point out that the barriers here are immense and structural in nature. For a nonprofit, the leap from early stages (where budget is capped at roughly $5 million) to breakout ($5-$10 million) or full scale (upward of $10 million) presents an enormous challenge. The authors describe this gap as the social capital chasm, and highlight four aspects of the nonprofit sector that create it:

- Incentive structures (e.g., lack of equity/stock options) make attracting managerial talent difficult.

- There is usually no overlap between the funders and direct beneficiaries, so charities must "win two games."[7]

- An emphasis on minimizing overhead can undermine operational capacities.

- Funding is erratic, since grants are normally allocated to specific programs rather than to broad missions.

As an EA organization, some of these challenges might affect you less, since staff are often motivated to accept lower salaries and overhead is less of an issue. But growth is often only possible outside the narrow world of EA donors. And even if an organization can overcome the social capital chasm, challenges remain. There's scaling and there's scaling well, for example. How do you ensure that you scale up sustainably, without watering down your impact?

At this point, with snares on all sides, nonprofit work is starting to look a bit disheartening. So let's turn to the endgame. First off, what does it mean to

---

6 All references to this concept within this chapter sourced from Alice Gugelev and Andrew Stern, "What's Your Endgame?" Stanford Social Innovation Review, 2015, https://www.philan-thropy.org.au/images/site/misc/Tools__Resources/Publications/2015/Winter_2015_Whats_Your_Endgame.pdf.

7 In a for-profit company, there's only one customer, who gets a benefit and pays for it. In nonprofits with beneficiaries and donors, you must please the donor and, in parallel, provide impact for the beneficiary – and the donor does not always have the same endline vision as your organization.

focus on the endgame? As Stern and Gugelev define it, the term endgame refers to a nonprofit organization's intended role in solving a problem. While scaling up traditionally looks more at your organization's direct impact, the endgame examines the part you play in shaping the broader sector.

To illustrate the concept, Gugelev and Stern sketch out six possible endgames.

- **Open source.** An organization cultivates new ideas and interventions through research. Knowledge and resources can then be shared with other organizations.

  - o For example, Charity Entrepreneurship extensively researches interventions and supports co-founders to start the most effective through our Incubation Program. CE's research and handbook for entrepreneurs are both publicly available to extend impact beyond program participants.

- **Replication.** An organization creates a model or product that can be easily reproduced. The original organization can offer certification and training, and act as a center of excellence.

  - o Charter school networks in the US use replication centers to teach their model to other educators, whose preexisting infrastructure and embeddedness within a community mean that they may be better positioned to implement the model.

- **Government adoption.** This endgame is appropriate for an intervention that can be delivered at scale and requires lobbying to influence policy and budget. After the intervention is adopted, the organization may continue in an advisory role or as a service provider. Yet the ultimate goal is for the government to be in charge of financing and decision-making.

  - o Suvita partners with state governments (as well as with other NGOs) to ensure the sustainability of their intervention, which involves sending SMS reminders for vaccinations. At some point, the government might be able to adopt the intervention itself, run it through the Ministry of Health, and fund it with tax income. While the Suvita model is very lightweight, government adoption is even more important for harder-to-scale programs involving the distribution of cash or in-kind aid.

- **Commercial adoption.** An organization explores a potentially profitable product or service, which commercial organizations can then adopt and expand.

  o   The Good Food Institute (GFI) works to expand the market for plant-based and clean meat, supporting companies and innovation by connecting experts to opportunities. A project supported by GFI, Counterfactual Ventures, aims at creating for-profit start-ups in the field of clean meat.

- **Mission achievement.** Once an organization has reached a clearly defined, achievable goal, it then winds down its activities. The organization may also pivot if there's another problem it can effectively tackle with its resources and knowledge.

  o   Recognizing that fundraising work was no longer neglected within the EA community, the team behind Charity Science Outreach wound down the project[8] and shifted their focus toward Charity Science Health and, ultimately, Charity Entrepreneurship.

- **Sustained service.** Although this tends to be the default, sustained service is only appropriate if the public or private sectors cannot meet a need. In this case, a nonprofit organization fills the gap, and must constantly build on the efficiency of its program.

  o   The Nigerian Government is currently not able to fund widespread cash transfers for vaccinations, and the private sector cannot operate a sustainable business model in this field. GiveWell top charity New Incentives will continue to serve as many beneficiaries as possible.

Now that we have a sense of what an endgame might look like, let's look at how we can incorporate the concept into our work. For nonprofits, Gugelev and Stern outline three basic imperatives:

- **Define your endgame early.** Having a clear path forward will keep

---

8 Charity Science Foundation, "Scaling Down Charity Science Outreach," Aug. 12, 2016, https://www.charityscience.com/operations-details.

your organization on track for impact. Working on your endgame will also help refine your theory of change.

- **Focus on your core goals.** Ensure that your organization's activities move you toward your endgame.

- **Prepare your team.** As a nonprofit, your responsibilities are first and foremost to your beneficiaries. But you're also responsible for your employees. Unless your organization's endgame is sustained service, its budget should level off or shrink – this has implications for your staff.

All too far off for you? Many funders will only support you if you have a clear path toward an endgame. "We'll just grow indefinitely as an NGO" is usually not an answer they like to hear. So, thinking about the endgame has a direct impact on your startgame.

Gugelev and Stern's exploration of the endgame provides a valuable lens through which to view our work. And as well as allowing us to clarify our impact, it acts as an important reminder. The ultimate goal of nonprofit work is our own obsolescence. We dream that the disease we're fighting will be eradicated; that no animals will be born into brief and pain-filled lives on factory farms. Such goals are our lodestar. Reflecting on our endgame brings them back in focus

So yes, the problems that we face are huge, but we can't lose hope because of them – and here, centering our endgame helps. In asking, "*How do we scale up?*" we spotlight the problem. "*What's our endgame?*" spotlights its solution.

Putting it all together in the charity world

Fortify Health aims to reduce anemia and neural tube defects in India by facilitating wheat flour fortification in the open market and in government safety net programs. At Fortify Health, we have engaged in different levels of planning, particularly in the lead up to evaluations for funding. We also regularly track and document progress against goals through spreadsheets and updates to GiveWell, which helps us evaluate our next steps.

In the lead up to our second GiveWell incubation grant evaluation, our team put a lot of time into our one-year plan for Fortify Health's open market strategy. To project our mill outreach for the following year, we put together a miller scale-up plan. Within this, we asked each member of our team to provide their own scale-up projections for the next year across differently sized mills. Each team member was given a total of twelve mills to distribute. With these twelve mills, we invited each team member to add their best assumption for: a) how many mills in each production band we could partner with, and b) what proportion of production we could extend fortification to within those mill bands. We then took the average of the team members' individual projections. This was the first step toward putting together Fortify Health's one-year plan.

Based on the miller scale-up plan, we projected the program costs, and the costs of the subsequent projected growth in our team. From these cost estimates, we developed a budget, which included a total for a modest (low-bound) and a more optimistic (high-bound) scale-up.

When we reached out to GiveWell for evaluation for an incubation grant in 2019, the miller scale-up plan and the budget made up the major aspects of our 1-year plan presented to GiveWell. Using our projections, GiveWell developed a value of incubation grants sheet, that analyzed the worth of an incubation grant to Fortify Health.

– Nikita Patel (co-founder of Fortify Health)

14. Cost-effectiveness analysis

Sometimes you need a closer look to understand the details. In the world of woodworking, you might use a magnifying glass to inspect more closely an aspect of the project. When it comes to entrepreneurship, a formal cost-effectiveness analysis (CEA) offers this closer look.

Cost-effectiveness analysis is commonly used in economics, health economics, and charity evaluation. It calculates a ratio of the cost of a given action or intervention relative to its impact. Cost is usually measured in dollars, with impact often measured in something like DALYs or lives saved. More cost-effective interventions generally have a lower ratio of costs to good done and are considered better than less cost-effective interventions (all else being equal).

CEAs are particularly useful because they allow us to quantitatively compare different interventions. However, they can be prone to errors and fail to adjust for prior views.

Imagine two charities. One can train one guide dog to assist one blind person for each additional \$1,000 donated. The other can perform one vision-restoring cataract surgery for each additional \$35 donated. While these are two very different interventions, once you recognize that they are both fundamentally aimed at alleviating blindness, you can confidently say that performing cataract surgeries is a more cost-effective way to achieve that goal.[1]

---

1 Boris Yakubchik, "It is Effectiveness, not Overhead that Matters." 80,000 Hours (blog), Nov. 4, 2011, https://80000hours.org/2011/11/it-is-effectiveness-not-overhead-that-matters/.

Example CEA, produced in Guesstimate.

Total WP affected per $
34
31 to 38

Total chickens helped per $
1.8
1.6 to 2

Probability of success
0.26
0.15 to 0.41

Total expected WP affected
72M
42M to 110M

Total expected chickens helped
3.7M
2.2M to 5.9M

Total expected costs
2.1M
1.2M to 3.3M

Salary founder
32K
25K to 40K

Salary other staff
18K
13K to 25K

Number of other staff
2

In-country travel costs
720
530 to 1000

Office space
2800
2300 to 3400

Subscription costs
2600
490 to 9100

Subsidization costs

Average subsidisation costs
0.34
0.33 to 0.39

Total cost of supplementation per farm
27K
23K to 32K

Optimistic

Cost of calcium per kg ($)
0.27

Required calcium (kg)
$7.4 \cdot 10^{-3}$

Required calcium per year (kg)
0.261814

Cost of calcium supplementation per year ($)
0.0706897

Pessimistic

Cost of calcium per kg ($)
0.27

Required calcium (kg)
0.04
0.03b to 0.04

Required calcium per year (kg)
1.4
1.3 to 1.5

Cost of calcium supplementation per year ($)
0.38
0.35 to 0.42

Data

Amount of chicken feed eaten per year per chicken (kg)
35.3802

Average flock size on Indian layer farm (2017)
25.5K

Average growth rate of Indian egg industry
0.07
0.02 to 0.08

Average flock size on Indian layer farm (2019)
58K
53K to 64K

14.1. Strengths & weaknesses

Modeled vs. true cost-effectiveness

It is important to distinguish between the true cost-effectiveness of an action and the modeled cost-effectiveness. The true cost-effectiveness of an action – if known – would be a highly relevant metric and could be weighted very heavily when making a decision. However, we often lack important data about the world, or a sufficient amount of it. The closest we can usually get to the true cost-effectiveness of an intervention is through constructing a model – an imperfect estimate.

Models can certainly be helpful and can be used as a type of evidence that an intervention should or shouldn't be considered. However, given the shortcomings of modeled cost-effectiveness, it's important to take into account other forms of data.

Why is cost-effectiveness analysis useful?

When you are considering investing a lot of resources into a course of action, it is worth approaching the issue with deeper rigor. Cost-effectiveness analysis lays the foundation for further quantified estimates of the best path forward.

When attempting to compare the effectiveness of different interventions, it can be useful to create a formal and detailed model with a single endline number output, i.e., one unique final result.

Benefits of CEAs (from strongest to weakest):

Clearly connect to endline goals: Ultimately, our goal is to do the most good per dollar spent. A CEA may be an imperfect model, but it speaks directly to our key question. Compared to other models such as consulting experts or a WFM (as explained in Chapter 5), it has the clearest theoretical correlation with good done, even if model errors weaken it in practice.

Can be used to compare difficult-to-compare interventions: Doing an analysis that results in a ratio is useful because it allows for a direct numerical comparison to be made. In other words, CEAs provide a way to quantitatively compare interventions that may seem qualitatively incomparable (e.g., from different cause areas).

Allow formal sensitivity analysis: A sensitivity analysis can locate the most important assumptions, variables, and considerations affecting the endline conclusion – the factors that could most radically change the amount of good achieved.[2] Formal sensitivity analysis can be done quickly and easily on a CEA, showing the key parameters that are the most important to get right.

Encourage quantitative analysis more broadly: By default, most people (including experts) do not think in quantitative terms. For example, when asked if an event will happen, most people think of this as a binary question (yes/no) rather than answering with the probability of the event happening. CEAs require quantitative inputs for each variable, which encourages quantitative thinking and calibration (e.g., an event being 20% vs. 80% likely).

Underused in many evaluations: Quantified consideration in general, and CEAs more specifically, takes considerable amounts of time and requires a decent mathematical understanding. Likely for this reason, CEAs are often unused in situations that could benefit from them, especially in charitable areas with less established research bases. This allows CEAs to add a useful and unconsidered or under-considered viewpoint.

Give a transparent picture of the evaluator's rationale: Cost-effectiveness models provide a high level of transparency. Since each input is identified and clearly quantified, an outsider can see where assumptions are being made and more easily assess the validity of the conclusions.

A respected tool in multiple fields: Experts in many fields are in strong agreement that CEAs are a useful tool. These include those in economics, medicine, and – most relevant for our purposes – charity evaluation.[3]

Consider scope: Humans are notoriously bad at properly understanding scope,[4] so it's a major concern that many non-CEA models don't take it into account. If one charity has the potential to grow one thousand times bigger than another, a different type of model may not successfully reflect that it could be one thousand times more important to start the former over the latter.

---

2 For further understanding, see Ozzie Gooen, "Visual Sensitivity Analysis in Guesstimate," The Guesstimate Blog, May 17, 2016, https://medium.com/guesstimate-blog/analysis-view-with-guesstimate-4afadd87f72c.

3 GiveWell, "Cost-Effectiveness," last modified Nov. 2017, https://www.givewell.org/how-we-work/our-criteria/cost-effectiveness.

4 Wikipedia, "Scope neglect," last modified July 28, 2021, https://en.wikipedia.org/wiki/Scope_neglect.

Reduce some biases: CEAs are less susceptible to certain human biases that affect other analyses. For example, a well-used CEA can reduce the base rate fallacy,[5] conjunction fallacy,[6] and hyperbolic discounting.[7]

Can lead to novel conclusions: CEAs can often lead to unintuitive conclusions and, thus, the consideration of new ideas or approaches that might have been quickly ruled out by other methodologies or "commonsense" approaches.

Why we shouldn't rely solely on cost-effectiveness analysis

Concerns with reliance on CEAs in charity evaluation have been discussed in depth in other posts. GiveWell offers the most comprehensive coverage of the theoretical concerns,[8] and Saulius Šimčikas, the practical concerns.[9] Below we have listed the flaws of CEAs (from most to least significant):

Subject to the "optimizer's curse": All estimates are prone to error, and these errors compound.[10] An intervention whose CEA yields a high cost-effectiveness is more likely to have had errors in its favor. This means that the most and least cost-effective interventions are likely to regress closer to the average upon further examination. Overweighting CEAs in your decision-making could lead you to neglect good opportunities that did not have as many favorable errors.

Necessarily involve value judgments: It is surprising how much value judgments can differ. For example, GiveWell assumes that the "value of averting the death of an individual under 5 [years of age]" is 50 times larger than the value of "doubling consumption for one person for one year."[11] Reasonable estimates

---

5   When given general "base rate" information on prevalence and specific information, people may ignore the base rate and focus on the individuating info alone.

6   A situation in which people will point to a more mathematically unlikely scenario as being more likely to be true when it contains an easily recognizable heuristic.

7   A time-inconsistent model of delay discounting where people weight the "nearness" of receiving some reward against its actual worth.

8   Holden Karnofsky, "Why we can't take expected value estimates literally (even when they're unbiased)," The GiveWell Blog, July 25, 2016, https://blog.givewell.org/2011/08/18/why-we-cant-take-expected-value-estimates-literally-even-when-theyre-unbiased/.

9   Saulius Šimčikas, "List of ways in which cost-effectiveness estimates can be misleading," Effective Altruism Forum, Aug. 20, 2019, https://forum.effectivealtruism.org/posts/zdAst6e-zi45cChRi6/list-of-ways-in-which-cost-effectiveness-estimates-can-be.

10   J.E. Smith and R.L. Winkler. "The optimizer's curse: skepticism and postdecision surprise in decision analysis." *Management Science* 52, no. 3 (2006): 311-22.

11   GiveWell, "Research on Moral Weights - 2019," 2019, https://www.givewell.org/how-we-work/our-criteria/cost-effectiveness/2019-moral-weights-research.

could be as large as six times this amount, using life-satisfaction years. If all value judgments are subjective preferences that vary among individuals, then CEAs are only generalizable insofar as the researcher's values align with the reader's.

Model uncertainty: Cost-effectiveness models are necessarily simplifications of reality. This is both a strength and a weakness. Although it allows us to get a clearer understanding faster, it also means that they do not accurately capture reality. Adjustments in the variables used will change the final value of the CEA. One way to combat this is to create several models and see if they converge.

Prone to mistakes: Mistakes are inevitable, due to human error and/or poor information quality. Although small mistakes usually only translate to small problems on their own, these mistakes compound in a multivariate model, thus exaggerating the consequences. For example, GiveWell once found five separate errors in a DCP2 DALY figure for deworming that contributed to an overestimation of the intervention's cost-effectiveness by one hundred times.[12]

May not be generalizable to other contexts: Some CEAs rely heavily on randomized controlled trials (RCTs) for their data, and in some cases, this can be problematic. If an RCT was conducted in one particular region or with one particular method, the effect size may change dramatically in different regions or with other methods.

Make it hard to model flow-through effects: It is difficult to model flow-through effects in CEAs properly. Indeed, a common tactic is to ignore them entirely. The currently proposed ways to incorporate flow-through effects take vast amounts of time or are prone to error.

Can be misleading in many ways: If researchers fail to consider important factors or are not transparent in their reasoning, CEAs can yield misleading results. For example, a CEA looking at expected value needs to incorporate the probability of success. A CEA that only reports expected value makes no distinction between a 50% chance of saving ten children and a 100% chance of saving five children. This fails to account for any level of risk aversion.

Subject to researcher bias: CEAs are resistant to certain biases but susceptible to others. The researcher conducting a particular CEA may (consciously or unconsciously) bias the results toward their own views of its strengths. A

---

12 Alexander Berger, "Errors in DCP2 cost-effectiveness estimate for deworming," The GiveWell Blog, Feb. 3, 2014, https://blog.givewell.org/2011/09/29/errors-in-dcp2-cost-effectiveness-estimate-for-deworming/.

researcher's desire to find novel, cost-effective interventions may also have this result.

May bias you toward interventions with more measurable results: Effects that are difficult to measure may increase the error rate or be neglected. This can lead us to underestimate the effectiveness of interventions with hard-to-measure outcomes.

Ninety-percent confidence intervals can be misleading: Depending on how well calibrated researchers are, the worst-case scenario, the best case, and the 90% confidence interval (CI) may be incorrect. CIs are particularly susceptible, as we are likely to underestimate the range of uncertainty. Worst case and best case are no better, as these may rely on many unlikely events happening, meaning the probability of either occurring is minimal.

How often is cost-effectiveness analysis the right tool?

Given that CEAs have many benefits and flaws, it is important to use them only in conjunction with other methodologies. CEAs are great as one of three or four components used. It's worth considering the convergence of these components, i.e., in which direction the different models point overall. We expect CEAs to be more useful in areas where quantitative differences can be very large and where analysis based on our other evaluative criteria is less reliable.

14.2. How to create a cost-effectiveness analysis

There are few great resources on how to become good at creating cost-effectiveness analyses. Most experts we have seen have built their skills by playing with and making many, many models. We will go over some of the basic steps, but your first CEA will, in all likelihood, be terrible. Don't let that discourage you – it takes time, but you'll improve.

Software

We considered several software programs and combinations for our cost-effectiveness modeling. The two easiest to rule out were Google Documents for back-of-the-envelope calculation, and STATA, a complex modeling software. These had either too little or too much complexity for most charities' purposes.

Some tools can be great for certain more specific use cases (e.g., we love Causal[13] for time series models). For general CEAs, Google Sheets and Guesstimate seem to be the best tools.

Google Sheets is fast and simple to work with, and easy to get the hang of without much prior knowledge. While spreadsheets are a common way to generate number-based models, they lack a few of the key features we need for our more in-depth CEAs. **Guesstimate** is a less commonly used system but offers advanced Monte Carlo and sensitivity analysis features. It is too slow to use for very quick CEAs, but can be handy for models with high levels of uncertainty.

For important models, we recommend using Google Sheets and Guesstimate in combination. Create an initial CEA in a GSheets spreadsheet, and then remodel the data using Guesstimate for sensitivity analysis and simulated endline point estimates. Using two models decreases the odds that an error in one model will have a very significant effect on the overall outcome, particularly since the software packages require somewhat different formatting.

Formatting

It's good practice to use consistent formatting across all of your CEAs, even keeping it consistent with other models your CEAs might be compared to (e.g., GiveWell's or CE's).[14] This way, anyone familiar with GiveWell's CEAs will have an easier time understanding yours (and vice versa).

Color coding

Certain cells are color-coded to reflect the sources of those numbers.

Yellow: Value and ethical judgments

These numbers could change if the reader has different values from the researcher. For example, reasonable people could disagree about the answer to the question, "How many years of happiness is losing the life of one child under five worth?" When making these judgments, we generally consult the available literature, but there is often no clear answer.

Green: Citation-based numbers

---

13 See casual.app. Time series models, as the name suggests, study changes over time.

14 GiveWell, "GiveWell's Cost-Effectiveness Analyses," last updated Sept. 2021, https://www.givewell.org/how-we-work/our-criteria/cost-effectiveness/cost-effectiveness-models.

These numbers are based on a specific citation. If we found and considered multiple citations, the best will be hyperlinked to the number, and the others will be included in the reference section. If a number is an average of two other numbers, both numbers will be entered into the sheet, and the average will become a calculated number with a different color format.

Blue: Calculated number

These numbers are calculations generated from others within the sheet. Calculated numbers involve no more than five variables, both for readability and to allow for sanity checking. Generally, it is harder to err when making a higher number of subtotals rather than a single very large, multi-variable calculation.

Orange: Estimated numbers

Sometimes, no specific numbers can be found for a parameter. In this case, the number is estimated by one or more staff members. These estimates will often be the numbers within a CEA that we have the lowest confidence in.

Discounting

On paper, two interventions might show a similar number of QALYs,[15] welfare points, lives saved, etc. In practice, they might be supported by different levels of evidence, occur over different time frames, or have other extenuating factors that change your view of their true cost-effectiveness.

Applying discounting factors is one way to address these issues. We try to keep our discounting clear and separate from the original number in the CEA, as these discounts are generally subjective. Discounting is common and can be seen in many other detailed CEAs (again, see GiveWell's). The items listed below are not the only types of discounting used in our models, but they are some of the most common.

Certainty discounting: If a source of evidence suggests one number but the source is extremely weak, we might apply a certainty discount to it. This is based on the assumption that, in general, numbers regress as they get more certain. Thus, using a very weakly evidenced number in one estimate and a strongly evidenced number in another will systematically favor the areas with weaker evidence, as these numbers will be more positive.

Generalizability discounting: Often, sources will be based on a situation

---

15 Quality-adjusted life-years.

that is not identical or even similar to the situation we are considering when using a source. For example, if a study was run in one country, the results will not be identical if it were run in another, even if all other factors are held constant. Thus, when generalizing evidence more than is common in our other comparable CEAs, we apply a generalizability discount.

Bias discounting: If a citation comes from a source that we suspect has some sort of bias, we might discount this number. For example, every charity has a strong incentive to make their program and progress look better. Thus, charity-reported numbers tend to be far more optimistic than the same activity analyzed by a study or outside actor.[16]

Time discounting: Time discounting is the practice of discounting future benefits compared to immediate effects. Even with zero time preference, in terms of utility, it can still make sense to discount based on time. For example, income in the near term can be invested and used for increased consumption in the future. Additionally, there is always some probability that an accidental death will occur before the future utility is realized, and therefore, it is worth less than in the present.

Organization

Each broad idea will have its own CEA tab being evaluated within the sheet. The most important numbers of each tab will be pulled into a summary tab.

Summary tab: The first tab will be a summary that allows quick comparison between the charities and describes the three factors that could most change the CEA, as determined by a sensitivity analysis, and the factors considered the least certain by the CEA's creator. The summary tab will include two endlines. One is a metric that is easily understandable and directly connected to the intervention – for example, "number of chickens' life-years lost from being in a caged vs. a cage-free system." The other endline will be a cross-comparable metric, such as welfare points, that can be used across the entire cause area. This metric can be used to determine which interventions look most cost-effective in a given area. There is also a column to describe the overall uncertainty level, which is the CEA creator's estimate of how confident they are in this CEA

---

16 Robert Wiblin, "Most people report believing it's incredibly cheap to save lives in the developing world," 80,000 Hours (blog), May 9, 2017, https://80000hours.org/2017/05/most-people-report-believing-its-incredibly-cheap-to-save-lives-in-the-developing-world/.

COST-EFFECTIVENESS ANALYSIS

relative to others within the cause area.

Row, columns, and sections: The spreadsheet will generally be read across a given row with the first non-empty column containing a title or description. The column will generally be consistent across multiple rows. Specific sections will be put into boxes to increase readability. Generally, the last column and row of a given section will be used for notes or descriptions. Every CEA will generally have a benefits, costs, and counterfactuals section.

Optimistic, pessimistic, and best guess: Throughout the spreadsheet, an optimistic, pessimistic, and best-guess estimate will be identified. The most time will be put into the best-guess numbers. The endline summary will be generated using a Monte Carlo simulation. The optimistic and pessimistic estimates will be used for the range of the 90% confidence interval. The relative position of the best-guess within this range will be used to determine the probability curve.[17]

Sensitivity analysis: A sensitivity analysis will be conducted on each CEA to determine which factors most affect the estimate. The CEA creator then pulls out the factors that have a large effect and seem more likely to change based on new information or research. These factors will be listed on the summary sheet.

Referencing: The most important or relevant reference will be linked to the cell. All references will be stored in a section of the reference sheet. Each cause-level CEA spreadsheet will have a consistent reference page as its last sheet. Our tracking of references will be consistent with our system that is used across other methodologies.

Using external CEAs

There's a lot of diversity among CEAs, in both quality and formatting. This diversity means that CEAs are basically never directly comparable, although this doesn't mean they aren't useful. We see CEAs at roughly three different levels: informative, suggestive, and predictive.

Informative CEAs: Many CEAs, even those of low quality, can be informative to generate ideas or find citations for key numbers. For this level of CEA, the endline itself isn't informative or even suggestive of the intervention's impact. However, if we are investigating an area, it's worth considering the variables and

---

17 See Charley Kyd, "How to Create Monte Carlo Models and Forecasts Using Excel Data Tables," ExcelUser, Inc., accessed Nov. 10, 2021, https://exceluser.com/1157/how-to-create-monte-carlo-models-and-forecasts-using-excel-data-tables/, for an in-depth explanation.

citations used in informative CEAs. Quick or back-of-the-envelope calculations will often fall into this category.

Suggestive CEAs: Many CEAs are of decent quality, but assess different metrics or look at a different situation than what we're interested in. These CEAs might suggest the promise of an idea. Often we can update our views based on a suggestive CEA. We view the DCP3 CEAs[18] as suggestive, so if their models indicate that an intervention is cost-effective, that makes us think that related charities and intervention areas could be promising. Even so, we do not take the endline numbers literally or even as comparable. If DCP3 says intervention A is better than B but that both are cost-effective, we would do our own comparative research.

Predictive CEAs: Some CEAs are of high enough quality or sufficiently close to our own methodology and endline measurements that we take them as predictive. A predictive CEA might hold considerable weight in our research process, and we might use many of the same numbers and inputs when creating our own. If an organization has created multiple high-quality CEAs, we would view their CEAs as useful in predicting which areas are more promising. CEAs in this category include those done by GiveWell.[19]

CEAs and endline values

Straddling the border between a question about ethics and a question about tools is what metric you build your CEA around. Many CEAs use QALYs (quality-adjusted life-years) and DALYs (disability-adjusted life-years), which composite multiple measures of health and well-being to arrive at a single number. Others use income or subjective well-being. Different fields and cause areas tend to use different metrics. When CE started working on animal advocacy, we had to build our own DALY equivalent ("welfare points") to compare many interventions.[20]

The different metrics bring their own unique strengths and weaknesses. More specific metrics are generally more reliable, but less generalizable; more common metrics are more readily understood, but less likely to include the most recent data. Picking your endline value is sometimes clear for a charity (e.g., number

---

18 See DCP3, "Economic Evaluation Methods," accessed Nov. 10, 2021, dcp-3.org/economic-evaluations, for an overview.

19 GiveWell, "GiveWell's Cost-Effectiveness Analyses."

20 See previously mentioned blog post by Charity Entrepreneurship, "Is it better to be a wild rat or a factory farmed cow? A systematic method for comparing animal welfare."

of preventable deaths stopped), but other times might be a long conversation with your co-founder and many trusted advisors.

14.3. Common CEA mistakes

Cost-effectiveness analyses are not necessarily intuitive. Over time, we've noticed some mistakes that tend to be made repeatedly. We've tried to list some of the most common ones here.

Taking cost-effectiveness estimates literally

You might have noticed that cost-effectiveness analyses involve many judgment calls – not only in philosophical matters regarding morality and epistemology but also in much more arbitrary decisions about how to count things and which particular equation to use in a given scenario. In reading about this, we hope you've developed a bit more of an intuition for why you can't take expected value estimates literally (even when they're unbiased).

Comparing dissimilar CEAs

Because of all the aforementioned semi-arbitrary decisions involved in creating a CEA, the precise numbers you get are often an artifact of the methods you used to get them. However, if two interventions were evaluated using the same CEA methodology, using similar models that operate under comparable assumptions and judgment calls, they can be directly compared in a productive manner.

If one were to compare two completely different CEAs that were constructed under completely different methodologies, it's quite likely that the differences in the final numbers are mostly a result of methodological artifacts, not real differences in the impact that the interventions have on the real world.

If you want to compare your CEA with a CEA created by GiveWell or another organization, you ought to model your own CEA to be sufficiently similar. Equal application of rigor is essential when comparing two interventions.

Committing the 1% fallacy

The 1% fallacy is a phenomenon in which entrepreneurs pitch investors on a big, speculative idea, and then claim that even if they could only capture 1% of the market share or have a 1% probability of success, it would still be a good investment. Investors know not to fall for this pitch, because "to capture 1% of the market share" is actually an ambitiously large claim. "1%" is often a lot bolder and less reasonable than it seems.

Cost-effectiveness analyses for interventions that are difficult to measure and aim to have a massive effect (for example, policy change or corporate campaigns) can be vulnerable to this issue. The problem with the "even if we discount this by 99%" defense is that in real life, realistic probabilities can be and often are much lower than 1%.

Simplistic discounting/probabilities

Proposing to accomplish something that has enormous benefits and then simply adding, "I conservatively assume a 1% chance of success in this endeavor," will lead to incredibly optimistic estimates.

Discounting and incorporating probabilities must be done separately for every assumption in your process, not just tacked on to the end of your analysis. If your intervention relies on ten separate assumptions to be true, and each of those assumptions comes with a 50% discount, the cumulative discount is actually 0.098% – an order of magnitude less than 1%.

Simplistic worst-case scenarios

Your analysis rests on knowing the values of several difficult-to-estimate quantities (e.g., the efficacy of an untested antidepressant, the number of crustaceans that exist, or the externalities of an unprecedented policy change). Suppose you tried doing your cost-effectiveness analysis under worst-case assumptions for these unknown values, where for each assumption you are 95% certain that reality is more favorable than your inputs.

What's wrong with this? The more assumptions you add, the more hopelessly optimistic your so-called worst-case analysis becomes. If you have five worst-case assumptions where you are 95% certain that reality is more favorable, there's actually only a $95\%^5 = 77\%$ chance that one of the factors isn't catastrophically worse than you thought it was – that's hardly a worst case. Any average-case or best-case analysis using these methods runs into similar issues.

When dealing with a probabilistic range of values, put them into Guesstimate. Guesstimate is a tool that allows you to describe the probability distribution of possible values and then run a Monte Carlo simulation to find the range of likely outcomes.

Double counting impact

When multiple people and organizations are working in a similar space, they can all end up taking credit for something that any one of them might have accomplished alone. This results in every organization having inflated cost-effectiveness analyses because the endline impact is subject to double/triple counting. Any CEA attempting to model the value of meta-activities needs to take into account the direct impact and counterfactual replaceability of those actions to determine whether they are really tackling the limiting factors to direct work. Without accounting for these considerations, you can get strange outcomes like more lives saved in a location than the total population.

Assuming your impact lasts forever

Generally, anything you build will eventually fall apart — either due to failure, or the world changing and moving on. Just because you got a farm to pledge to fortify their chicken feed now, doesn't mean they will keep fortifying it for decades. Just because you passed a government policy change, doesn't mean that the policy won't be reversed in the future.

On a similar note, it is often the case that someone else might have eventually implemented your intervention had you not done so. So it's often best to model your impact as speeding up the arrival of an intervention. Few models do this, but without it, you might estimate a much higher impact than is reasonable.

Incorrect assumptions about trends and distributions

Not every distribution is a normal distribution.[21] Many statistical techniques will go wrong if you assume something has a normal distribution when it doesn't. Trends that seem linear will often hit diminishing returns eventually. Trends

---

21 A normal distribution assumes the highest concentration of values around one average, with tails leading off either end.

that seem exponential will often turn out to be sigmoid (S-shaped) curves.

Forgetting time, management, and operation costs

Staff time is expensive, not only in money but in opportunity costs.[22] It's common for people to think that if something does not come with a large bill, it's free, but spending a lot of staff time on something is actually very expensive. It's also easy to focus on the costs of the intervention itself and forget that things like managing staff or registering a charity or processing donations and payments also cost money, in the form of occupying the time of paid staff members.

Overgeneralizing evidence across contexts

Findings from one country, or even one village, often don't generalize to other settings. On the other hand, a single focused study in a highly applicable and adjacent context is also shaky ground on which to establish an intervention. Unfortunately, evaluating evidence correctly is difficult, and experts won't necessarily agree on the right way to do it. The best way to avoid mistakes is to learn a lot about your intervention and the particular mechanism by which it operates so that you can make these judgments on a case-by-case basis at least as well as any other expert in the field. In the ideal scenario, you would be able to combine your own RCT with prior evidence from studies on similar interventions around the globe, but this evidence will not be available for all interventions.

Creating overcomplicated or illegible CEAs

The more moving parts your CEA has, the more likely there is an error. It is extremely common for simple accounting and copyediting errors to throw off the final estimate by an order of magnitude. It is always possible to add more modifying factors to a CEA – and you shouldn't shy away from accounting for complexity! But in most CEAs, generally a small number of important figures and key assumptions can mostly explain the final number.

You should be able to identify these major factors, and when explaining your CEA to other people, you should be able to describe them in a few sentences and a simple equation. Unless you're dealing with something that genuinely can't

---

22 The cost of not doing an activity that you would have otherwise done.

be reduced to a simple explanation, don't let your stakeholders wade through a complicated spreadsheet or Guesstimate model to understand what's really going on, only to find that the important bits could have been explained in a few lines.

Putting it all together in the charity world

Family Empowerment Media (FEM) develops radio-based health messaging to increase the uptake of modern contraceptives in Nigeria. At FEM, we have used CEAs to support all our big decisions.

We have found CEAs particularly helpful when evaluating the relative importance of hard-to-compare considerations. Let's say that the cost of radio airtime is 50% cheaper in state A than in state B, but experts tell us that it is harder to work in state A, and the maternal mortality rates are 20% lower. How should you weigh these factors against each other? In a CEA, the difference in airtime costs affects the total cost of your intervention, expert opinion impacts your execution difficulty discount, and the maternal mortality estimates show up on the impact side. In the end, you end up with a single number that takes all the relevant considerations into account.

We have more than one CEA because different types of CEAs have different weaknesses and strengths. When starting, we developed a very complex model where we tried to capture all the benefits of our intervention. This model helped us understand the total impact of our intervention and, equally significantly, the most critical variables that affect our impact. However, it has many assumptions, and it is so complicated that only the co-founder team has a good understanding of it.

Later we developed a simple CEA, which is 26 lines long. This model only considers the effects of our intervention on maternal mortality, and only captures between 20 and 50 percent of our impact. However, we have shared it with donors and other supporters interested in understanding our effectiveness, and we know it doesn't have any mistakes.

For us, CEAs have been a very helpful tool to evaluate hard-to-compare considerations. Being aware of the limitations and strengths of the tool has allowed us to produce the type of model needed for each decision, and also understand how to weigh its findings up against other tools.

– Anna Christina Thorsheim and Kenneth Scheffler (co-founders of Family Empowerment Media)

15. Measurement & evaluation

"Measure twice and cut once" is a phrase commonly used when working on carpentry projects. It is equally applicable to running a charity. Without careful measurement and thoughtful evaluation, a charitable project can be off by more than a few inches. It can fail to have an impact altogether.

Measuring your impact and progress before and during your project is crucial to success, yet the average decision-maker often skips this step. Good measurement and evaluation, also referred to as monitoring and evaluation, is one of the hallmarks of a great charity. We are going to talk about some of the dos and don'ts of monitoring and evaluation.

15.1. Metrics

So you want to create an effective charity. How do you know if it is effective?

A common answer is, "By detailed monitoring and evaluation." But this is harder than it sounds. While research is hard to get right in general, the difficulty starts just in the measurement alone. Which metric should you use?

The case of immigration reform

Imagine that we think improving immigration in the US is important for economic growth and the welfare of immigrants. So we set up an advocacy website that encourages people to write to their congressperson and urge immigration reform. How do we know if this website is effective?

One way is to measure web traffic. More traffic should be good, right? But what if we get a lot of visitors, but no one follows through and writes to their congressperson?

Okay, that's bad. So maybe we measure the number of letters delivered to congresspeople. That does measure our influence over the public process, but what if the petitions get ignored? How do we know our petitions lead to legislation change? What if the legislation would have changed anyway?

What we really want to measure is counterfactual legislation change. To do this, we construct an RCT where we randomly select some legislators to be targeted and some not to be. Then we see whether the targeted legislators are more likely to sponsor immigration reform than the non-targeted legislators.

Web traffic and the number of letters sent might contribute to immigration reform, but they could easily be unconnected. Only measuring the right thing helps us check.

Why might charities focus on incomplete metrics?

In the example of web traffic or letters sent, the metrics measured are incomplete – we can't clearly connect them with positive impact. A focus on incomplete metrics is the default in the charity world. Why would charities focus on these incomplete metrics? If we aren't careful, we too can fall back on metrics that are easier to measure, readily come to mind, and look more impressive for funders.

It's far easier to measure the web traffic to your advocacy website than to do an RCT on your legislative impact. It's easier to measure web traffic than even the number of petitions sent. Thus, an increase in web traffic is often cited as a criterion for success, even when it may not be connected to the charity's real goals.

Identifying the most important metrics can be hard, particularly when a charity's goals are a bit vague. This is true particularly with younger charities, as well as charities with less of a clear focus. When a charity is unsure what the most important metrics are, they might instead report on several less helpful metrics.

Reporting on several metrics looks more impressive because you are showing more data – even if the data is not reflective of the good your charity is doing. Additionally, the more metrics you have, the easier it is to cherry-pick the ones that are going well and downplay the ones that are not going as well. This kind of practice makes your organization more appealing to donors and members, even if it is ultimately an illusion.

Ways to avoid this mistake

The first step is to clarify your goals and identify the number one most important metric. This is hugely important as it makes clear what your organization is really aiming to do, and how you will measure it. Letting the public know your most important metric also allows them to focus on what really matters.

- **Be sure of the connection between your metric and real good happening in the world**

Even with a straightforward metric, you have to make sure that it really translates into good getting done. If your organization moves money, what charities does it move money to, and how much good do they accomplish with this extra donation? If you're using website traffic as a metric, how does it translate to the actions you want to achieve, and how do those actions correlate with impact?

- **Think about if it would be possible to cheat this metric**

How might someone game your metric, making it less valuable? For example, if we wanted to gain a bunch of website traffic, it would be quite easy for us to invest in non-targeted online ads or just directly buy views. Although this would boost our traffic, it's very unlikely to cause any real good on the metric we actually care about.

- **Watch out for counterfactuals**

An easy mistake to make is to measure metrics that have many possible causes. Given that many organizations are working toward the same goals, it is necessary to be able to isolate the impact of your organization when compared to the wider movement.

- **Be cautious of longer causality chains**

Consider an unconditional cash transfer charity. Their "chain to impact" looks like this:

We give grants of unconditional cash transfers to the global poor → The global poor spend the money on what they desperately need → They are happier because they could afford a basic necessity or invest in their future → Good is achieved.

Furthermore, we're pretty confident about each link on this causal chain because there are multiple studies supporting each link.

Now consider an organization that fundraises for the unconditional cash transfer charity and cites web traffic as their metric of success:

Website traffic → People are then more interested in donating → More people go to the cash transfer charity website to learn more → More money is donated → The transferred cash is spent on basic necessities or investments → People are happier → Good is achieved.

Not only is this chain longer, but there is also a huge problem in the assumption that website traffic results in more donations. While we can easily track website visits, it's very difficult to track how many of these visits translate into more donations, and it's easy for the metric to get cheated by getting large amounts of "lower quality" traffic. Generally, the more steps you have, the more confidence you need to have in each of the steps working.

Focusing on the right metrics in charity entrepreneurship

For folks like us interested in creating the most effective charities, we need to be careful about metrics. We care most about having the largest counterfactually positive impact on global well-being (for both human and nonhuman animals). We don't want to look at any incomplete metrics, like the number of people we help, the size of our budget, or how many people read our blog posts. But well-being isn't a very precisely defined metric. Instead, we can use proxy metrics like the impact of our charity on increasing longevity, reducing the burden of disease and disability, improving income, improving subjective well-being, etc.

Each of these metrics is a lot more nuanced than our earlier examples of web traffic and letters sent. Although none is an obviously incomplete metric, we do think that some are better than others at capturing the ultimate goal of global well-being.

The best metric for your new charity to use will depend on your cause area and intervention. We recommend researching a few different metrics, and if none seem adequate for your purposes, you might need to create your own.[1]

---

1 Again, see Charity Entrepreneurship, "Is it Better to be a Wild Rat or a Factory Farmed Cow? A Systematic Method for Comparing Animal Welfare."

15.2. Building an M&E process

Monitoring and evaluation, or M&E, shows you whether you are having an impact and how large that impact is. Sometimes it can also be used to clarify the mechanism behind your impact.

Some donors will require a detailed monitoring and evaluation system. However, few will have standards high enough that you will not want to go deeper to be sure your work is having the impact you intend.

The best M&E systems take measurements that will inform you about how to make progress on concrete decisions and reveal how you could improve your organization's structure. Remembering back, your theory of change describes various inputs and steps. Some of these are conducive to monitoring and evaluation.

For each point in your theory of change, try to introduce measurements to get feedback on whether your changes in theory are happening in practice. Typically, the further along in your theory of change (i.e., the closer you are to your endline goal), the harder but more important measurement becomes. A logframe template[2] will help you link your theory of change to M&E. (Don't worry – the template comes with detailed instructions.)

Find creative ways to incorporate measurement into your charity

You might imagine that M&E mostly consists of rigorous randomized controlled trials. But what if you don't have the time or money for a big experiment? If you randomly select five data points from a population, there is a 93% chance that the population median lies in between the lowest and the highest value. Measurement does not always have to be expensive or time-consuming, and even a small amount of data can be extremely informative. Generally, the less information you have in an area, the easier it is to get a somewhat informed view rapidly. And an imperfect sense of things is good enough, particularly at the start of your charity. You can find these and other tips in *How to Measure Anything*,[3] a book about finding creative ways to get figures without spending a ton of money or effort.

Remember that for many purposes, you don't necessarily need highly precise data. A focus group will give you qualitative anecdotal reports from beneficiaries

---

2 Available at https://bit.ly/CElogtemplate.

3 Douglas W. Hubbard, *How to Measure Anything* (Hoboken, New Jersey: John Wiley & Sons, Inc., 2010).

or workers who are in touch with facts on the ground. You can run surveys that solicit opinions from stakeholders. By choosing your measuring tools carefully, you can get very useful data without spending much time or money.

Keep data collection decision-relevant

It's often tempting to measure everything you can, or to collect data because it seems interesting. However, there's no need to take a measurement if it's not going to help you increase impact. Unnecessary measurements cost you in terms of design and administration. If you are collecting data from human beings, it also causes fatigue in respondents, making it more difficult to get the data you actually need. For each measurement, make explicit which decision it is helping you with.

Example: Suvita runs a vaccination reminder program. Their surveys don't need to include a question about the age of the child's parent, because knowing that number will not change any of their decisions. They do want to collect data about how many people a surveyor signs up for the program per day, because that number can influence decisions regarding how many surveyors to hire, show which to fire or talk to about underperformance, and help spot scams (for instance, some surveyors may fill in fake data or report an unrealistically high number).

Automation is good, but don't overdo it

Automation is an amazing tool, but be aware that it doesn't always mean less work. Automated processes can sometimes involve a time-consuming setup, extended maintenance, and software bugs that will require the attention of skilled and tech-savvy employees. When using automation, try to work with preexisting solutions built for exactly the purpose that you are using them and shown to work without maintenance, rather than trying to design automated systems from scratch. If you're conducting a survey, use tools like SurveyCTO (built on Open Data Kit). For a cheaper alternative, consider apps such as doForms[4] or even Google Forms, Skype, and a Skype Recorder[5] – but be careful of lock-in and issues down the road as you scale.

---

4 See surveyCTO.com, opendatakit.org, and doforms.com/mobile-forms/, respectively.
5 For example, voipcallrecording.com.

Social desirability bias

Any measurement tool that relies on human reporting is subject to social desirability bias. People will generally follow their own incentives, tend toward answers that show them in a positive light, and lean toward responses that put you and your organization in a positive light as well in order to avoid insulting you or hurting your feelings. Try to avoid social desirability bias by framing the question so that none of the responses are obviously a "bad" answer. Take answers to questions that are prone to this bias with a grain of salt.

Another way to get more accurate answers is to ensure privacy. Inform people in plain language that no identifying data will be shared with third parties. If you are working in an environment where a door-to-door survey would tend to draw a crowd of onlookers (common in the developing world), give the surveyor explicit instructions to ask the crowd to give some space and ensure the participant can answer sensitive questions anonymously.

Sometimes, you can sidestep this issue by using an objective metric as a proxy for a subjective one. For example, GiveDirectly has no easy way to figure out people's income without asking them. So instead, they use an objective metric (one of many): whether the person's house has a dirt floor.[6] In general, surveying housing characteristics is a common method of estimating poverty in developing-world contexts. This includes the materials of the roof, walls, and floor, the cooking method, the availability of electricity, and plumbing, amongst other criteria.

Assumptions and cultural differences

When interacting with different cultures and people who live very different lives from you, you might find that you hold many assumptions about how things work that turn out not to be true.

For example, at Charity Science Health, we implicitly assumed that people would know their date of birth. When we saw discrepancies in our data, we thought our surveyors were making mistakes. It turned out that people were giving rough estimates regarding dates of birth because they did not know when they were born, and perhaps didn't necessarily think of it as an important thing to keep track of or be precise about.

---

6 Michael Faye, "Metal Roofs - A Lesson from the True Poverty Experts," GiveDirectly (blog), Aug. 6, 2013, https://www.givedirectly.org/metal-roofs-a-lesson-from-the-true-poverty-experts/.

Another issue we encountered was working with different gender norms. The cultural norms of your respondents and surveyors will often influence who feels comfortable speaking to whom, and who feels comfortable going to which locations. Female respondents were not always comfortable speaking to an unknown male surveyor, while female surveyors did not always feel safe being sent into unfamiliar locations alone. These types of considerations are highly local, even varying from neighborhood to neighborhood. Talk to your staff and spend some time on site to get a sense of these issues.

15.3. Data collection methods

Focus groups

A focus group is a discussion among a small group of typically six to eight participants. Talking things over with a focus group is a great way to get key qualitative background information about how they experience the intervention. It's often helpful to get this sort of data before investing resources in more rigid and quantitative metrics, as it gives you a basic sense of the relevant and applicable considerations. For instance, without checking first in a focus group, the metric or question types used in a randomized controlled trial might be biased in ways you would not know about. The general rule here is: talk to many beneficiaries before you run sophisticated studies. To get started, see the Citizens Advice guide "How to run focus groups."[7]

Survey data

Once you get a sense of the relevant questions, quantitative surveys are a great tool to check various parts of your M&E process. Running surveys in contexts where resources are low comes with a few challenges.

Some common methods of survey data collection include:

- **Phone surveys:** Phone surveys are cheaper and less geographically constrained. It's also easier to monitor surveyors and prevent scams. However, it can be harder to get ahold of people, because cell phones

---

7 Citizens Advice, "How to run focus groups," Dec. 18, 2015, https://www.citizensadvice.org.uk/Global/CitizensAdvice/Equalities/How%20to%20run%20focus%20groups%20guide.pdf.

are often switched off in settings where people can't count on electricity or data is expensive. Additionally, phones may be shared among many people, so the wrong person often picks up. Some objective metrics (e.g., does the person live on a dirt floor) are harder to get over the phone.

- **In-person surveys:** In-person surveys are more expensive. It's hard to locate people – many regions do not have signs or street addresses, so you have to ask around to find a specific person. It's also harder to monitor surveyors and prevent scams. However, you can often give longer surveys in person, and get objective metrics.

- **Paper surveys:** Paper surveys typically have low response rates, and require participants to have high literacy. However, on paper, you have the advantage that questions are always asked in the same way, whereas in person or on the phone, surveyors often paraphrase questions in a way that might change the responses.

- **Online surveys:** Online surveys are much like paper surveys, but with the added advantage that you can randomize question order, which removes some sources of bias. They're also quicker to pull data out of. Of course, they are limited by respondents having internet access.

Miscellaneous tips for surveys in the developing world:

- Be mindful of scams. Build accountability into your system (e.g., if you have surveyors, deploy them in teams and give each team a trusted supervisor). You can also use tablets to record conversations and see how long was spent on each question. Err on the paranoid side here, and implement back checks for as many submissions as possible (e.g., 10%). Frauds you would never expect, such as surveyors filling out fake forms in their hotel rooms instead of in the field, are common.

- Factor into your budget that tablets often break, run out of charge, and get stolen.

- Respondents may not be accustomed to taking surveys and may feel nervous. Place easier and more impersonal questions near the beginning to make respondents more comfortable before delving into potentially more sensitive content.

- Aim for your surveys to take between five and 10 minutes. Following this rule will limit the questions you ask to what really matters and avoid combining too many topics in one survey.

General tips for all surveys

- Role-playing the questions with surveyors beforehand and directly observing the first few responses can help you work out kinks in your process.
- Some people don't take surveys seriously, don't pay attention, respond randomly, or make jokes. To prevent this, include some questions that are designed to weed out unreliable respondents.
- Don't fiddle with analysis methods to make your data look good. Pre-commit to your analysis methods beforehand (sometimes called "preregistration" of your study).

Running large-scale studies

Many global health, family planning, and mental health interventions will eventually need to run a randomized controlled trial (RCT) in order to establish evidence that they are working. This is usually the most complex and expensive part of any M&E project, and typically requires partnering with a university or an organization that focuses exclusively on evaluation. Although co-founders will benefit from a basic understanding of the process, don't expect to be the expert. If appropriate, you should run a large-scale study once your intervention is running as intended to find out whether it is worth scaling up the project.

Experimental and quasi-experimental design

Experimental designs aim to address the many sources of noise when determining the impact of your intervention. These experiments are expensive and time-consuming, so you should generally begin considering these methods when you are ready to decide whether to scale up. Below are just a few examples of experimental designs to give you a rough sense of what's out there.

Randomized controlled trials are generally the gold standard for evaluating impact. The design is straightforward: you randomly[8] assign one portion of the

---

8 "Randomly" here means, specifically, through random sampling; it's important to eliminate all sources of possible non-random grouping.

population to receive the intervention, and another portion not to. If performed correctly, confounding differences between the two groups disappear, and any observed differences might now be attributable to your intervention.

RCTs usually generate the highest-quality data, because they allow you to understand the counterfactual impacts clearly. If there's an economic downturn and your beneficiaries were worse off after your intervention, but people who didn't get the intervention were even more worse off, an RCT would still capture your positive impact. If your beneficiaries were better off after your intervention, but people who didn't get it were also better off and you had nothing to do with it, an RCT will capture that, too. Without a randomized controlled trial, it can be quite a bit more complex to figure out the true effect of your actions.

Discontinuity regressions take an intervention applied at some arbitrary cutoff and compare data points on either side of the threshold to determine the effect. For example, if you were to tutor every student who scored less than 70% on a given exam, you could look at the differences in outcomes for those who scored 69% vs. those who scored 71% to get a sense of the effect of the tutoring. This method is a type of "natural experiment" – a situation where two similar groups experience different things, and you quantify the effects of those differences. This method circumvents some of the expenses and ethical dilemmas surrounding random assignment but is vulnerable to confounding factors.

Difference-in-differences is a statistical technique that can be used to compare two groups that differ slightly from each other but are generally going through the same changes over time.

Suppose you have child mortality data from two villages but are running your intervention in just one of them. The two villages may not be the same – for instance, one may have a higher child mortality rate than the other. However, they may both undergo similar changes over time. They're likely to be similarly affected by variations in the national economy, changes in the weather, and natural disasters. If the two groups change over time but in similar ways, the method returns a null result, meaning that your intervention was ineffective.

The weakness of this method is that the groups you are comparing may change at different rates for reasons unrelated to the intervention. Remember that a positive result isn't necessarily attributable to the intervention or event that you're interested in, it only means that something changed.

Interrupted time series analyses compare the same population for a long period of time before and after an intervention. For example, because global

GDP generally rises at a somewhat predictable rate, you might try using an interrupted time series to check whether a global pandemic had a lasting effect on it a decade later. This is often a good method to use when there is no possibility of controlled randomization and no reasonable group that might serve as a natural control. However, there is a risk of unrelated events occurring at the cutoff point and contaminating the data.

Remember, science is messy. It's very easy for factors you did not predict to change everything in your results. It's also very easy to make mistakes with statistics.

Terms to know that might influence or confound your results include:

- **"Significance" vs. "effect size":** If a result is statistically significant, it means that what you're seeing might not be due to random coincidence. "Effect size" reports how big the effect actually is, and for your purposes, this will generally be what actually matters. Two programs that increase vaccination rates by 1% and 10% might both be statistically significant, but have very different effect sizes.

- **Correct for multiple comparisons:** If you run 100 statistical tests with a 5% chance of a false positive, you'll get, on average, five false positives. Sadly, running into a false positive in the scientific literature is common, because positive results are often more exciting than negative. You can combat this by preregistering your study before seeing the results, or by statistically correcting for multiple comparisons.

- **Generalizability:** Sometimes, results taken in one context will generalize to another. Other times, they won't. While a randomized controlled trial can demonstrate that an intervention works within a specific context (internal validity), you can't be confident that the results will apply in a different region (external validity).

More general tips are available via GiveWell's "How we evaluate a study."[9]

Organizations to know

If you are implementing a human-focused intervention, you don't have to

9 Holden Karnofsky, "How we evaluate a study," The GiveWell Blog, last modified Sept. 2, 2016, https://blog.givewell.org/2012/08/23/how-we-evaluate-a-study/.

carry out M&E on your own. In the effective altruism community, GiveWell often partners with IDinsight. In the broader development community, J-PAL, IPA, and CEGA have a network of academics who conduct high-quality impact evaluations. Having your work evaluated by a third-party organization well respected in the field can provide useful data for you and your organization and demonstrate your impact to donors.

What if a well-designed study says our intervention is low-impact?

Don't be afraid of shutting down the project if it isn't working. Your time, your staff's time, and your funding are valuable forces for good. When you have clear evidence that a different use of resources would improve the world more effectively, stop what you are doing and pursue that instead. Starting an organization is a high-risk, high-reward activity, so plan for both success and failure.

Putting it all together in the charity world

Animal Advocacy Careers (AAC) seeks to address the career and talent bottlenecks in the animal advocacy movement, especially the farmed animal movement. As a meta organization working to help other nonprofits, a lot of our work is quite indirect, with a long "chain of impact" from our actions to positive outcomes for animals. This makes M&E tough.

One of the services AAC offers is career advising calls. Although it's difficult to assess the cost-effectiveness of such a service, we are running a mini randomized controlled trial[10] and are optimistic about getting some good insights into several important steps in its hypothesized "chain of impact." We think we need to carry out this sort of evaluation to understand the counterfactuals. For example, someone might report that our advice changed their whole career plan. But if they're highly engaged with effective altruism and animal advocacy, they might have discovered similar information regardless of our support.

Another program we have measured is offering recruiting support to effective animal advocacy nonprofits. Here, we are much less worried about counterfactuals – most of the candidates we identify are not familiar with the organizations we are recruiting for, and not engaged with effective altruism or animal advocacy.

As well as attempting to retrospectively evaluate the impact of our interventions, we use surveys and interviews to determine the community's greatest needs, and therefore where we expect we can add the most value. The various forms of M&E all have their own strengths and weaknesses. Internally we find it helpful to use a variety of different forms of information gathering (e.g., surveys, RCTs, expert opinions) and decision-making tools (e.g., spreadsheets, cost-effectiveness estimates, Bayesian thinking) to prioritize.

M&E can be complicated, especially if your path to impact is pretty indirect. But with some creativity and a variety of methodologies, you can generate lots of useful information and feedback to help you to make your interventions as cost-effective as possible.

– Jamie Harris and Lauren Mee (co-founders of Animal Advocacy Careers)

---

10 Jamie Harris, "Pre-registration: The Effects of Career Advising Calls on Expected Impact for Animals," OSF Registries, June 29, 2020, https://osf.io/pwufc.

16. Summary: Making good decisions

You now have a set of tools to help you make better decisions, but the journey is far from over. The best decision-makers sharpen their tools, practice with them often, and replace the ones that don't work well anymore.

Our knowledge is always changing, and we should always strive to be better. Over time, we'll identify new tools and heuristics. For now, what does making consistently good decisions look like? How can we even know what "better" is?

16.1. What does good decision-making look like?

People are bad at judging how good they are at decision-making. Making a bad decision feels the same as making a good decision. But there are ways to tell the difference.

Making predictions

Making predictions is one of the fastest ways to judge decision-making. Think you've found a way to beat the stock market? Try investing a small amount of money in that system and review the outcome of your prediction. You can also predict simple things, such as the odds of something happening discussed informally with friends. Try putting real estimated numbers on these guesses and see how often you are right. If you win so often your friends stop wanting to play, that's a good sign.

You can also make predictions without any other actors. If you think there are two possible outcomes to a given event, try writing down an explicit probability. You'll likely find patterns that differ between reality and your predictions. Most people tend to be consistently optimistic or pessimistic in their predictions. Making predictions gives you a constant source of real-world data; just make sure to track them consistently so you notice both the hits and misses.

External review

You might not feel any different when making a good call vs. a bad one, but external actors sure will. Ask people you trust as good thinkers and decision-makers to review your process and conclusions. Many careful thinkers will recognize a solid reasoning process, even if they disagree with the conclusion.

Having a trusted external group of decision-makers also provides opportunities for feedback and growth. Keep in mind that your external reviewers won't always agree with all of your processes and conclusions, even the ones that are right. Even the best decision-makers can be biased, wrong, or underinformed. But on average, they'll be a better judge of where you have gone astray. And strongly heeding their advice for issues you cannot rapidly test is a wise idea.

Reviewing other people's work and getting a sense of their processes will also be well worth the time spent for the benefit it provides to your own.

Results

Ultimately, good decision-makers will recognize this fact in their results: they won't win every decision. Luck, both good and bad, will affect them. However, like a good poker player, they will do better with the cards they are given than others.

After many, many decisions, good decision-makers will often be more successful at accomplishing their goals (whatever those might be). This is a longer feedback loop, as it often takes considerable time to progress on the most important goals. Yet, ultimately, this is the key metric for good decision-making. Can you make decisions that maximize the outcomes you want? Such an individual will have more stable relationships and better habits, and found a more successful charity.

Weakness in one of these areas does not necessarily turn someone into a bad decision-maker. Yet, one of the easiest ways to judge someone's decision-making abilities is by looking at their luck-controlled results. A lottery ticket winner is no better a decision-maker than the average person (in fact, they are likely worse than non lottery ticket buyers), but the person who wisely picks a career that consistently maximizes their goals of impact and happiness very well would be.

16.2. Key principles

We only recall and use a fraction of the content we encounter. So what are the key principles to remember? This cheat sheet will help you recall the most important lessons of decision-making applied to charity entrepreneurship.

Frame your decision well before working on it, and sharpen your tools:

- Determine upfront how much time to put into activities and time cap based on importance.
- Set up reevaluation points at specific dates to reconsider your activities.
- If you are narrowing down from many options, set up rounds of iterative depth, time capping each one.
- Spend the most time on the key choices: co-founder, country, and intervention selection.
- Be ready for many of your decisions to be made with far less than 100% confidence.

Understand and utilize many different tools:

- Multi-factor decision-making – The Swiss Army knife
  - Create spreadsheets with different weighted factors to compare complex options.
- Rationality – The hammer
  - Think skeptically, and narrow down to the crucial considerations of the decision.
- Science – The screwdriver
  - Use evidence from as high up on the pyramid as possible, and set up falsifiability in your decisions.
- Effective altruism – The wrench
  - Consider the counterfactuals and limiting factors that could affect your impact.
- Independent experts – The cellphone
  - Be careful whose advice you believe, but seek it out from many.
- Task planning – The clamps
  - Have a task management system, and focus on the highest-impact tasks.
- Cost-effectiveness analysis – The magnifying glass

- - Create detailed CEAs populated with strong sources of data.
- Problem-solving – The duct tape
  - Create multiple solutions, compare them evaluatively, and try to solve problems upstream.
- Creativity – The flashlight
  - Play with pieces of the puzzle to generate many possible ideas.
- Long-term planning – The pencil
  - Create a focused theory of change and have a possible endgame.
- Monitoring and evaluation – The tape measure
  - Pick your metrics carefully, and set up systems to measure them often.

16.3. Twelve months in: Are you on the right track?

1. Are you focusing on a single very impactful thing? Or have you spread out between many areas, some of which are less effective?

2. Have you progressed fast enough to have started taking action in your implementation country? Have you spent at least a few months there?

3. Have you established a group of trusted advisors, so that you're getting good feedback at least once a month?

4. Have you progressed on your one-year plan, and completed at least half of it?

5. Have you spent less than 30% of your time on things that are not your primary objective?

6. Do you have an established system to track an important endline metric?

7. Are the co-founders of the project and the leadership team stable?

8. Are you making better decisions for your project than you were a year ago?

9. Do you have a long document of lessons learned?

10. Are you fast and effective at using three or more tools during decision-making?

Part III. Key decisions

The payload system carries what you want to bring to your destination. Our payload when founding a charity depends on the macro (our ethical views) and the micro (four key decisions). Or, put simply, what counts as "good" and "impact"? And more concretely, how do we then choose our Career path, Charity idea, Co-founder, and Country?

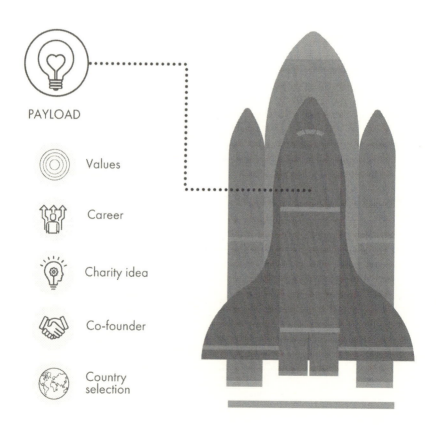

PAYLOAD

Values

Career

Charity idea

Co-founder

Country
selection

17. Knowing your values

Knowing your goal is key to accomplishing it efficiently. So what is the goal of founding a charity? It might seem simple: to help others and do the most good. But what is good, and who counts as others? How you answer such questions will impact key choices you make as you launch your organization.

One assumption held throughout this book is that the consequences of an action are highly important. This means charities need more than good intentions. They need to show that their results are helping people. This brings us to our first dilemma: how to measure our impact. Some suggest that asking about people's subjective well-being is the best way to measure, while others favor more objective health metrics such as DALYs (disability-adjusted life-years). But how important might it be to cure a disease versus to increase someone's income? What if someone has a preference for an activity that will harm them in the long term? Is it ethical to help them, or even permit them, to do it?

Although there are many open questions, some areas have consensus. Helping beings experience more positive emotions such as joy, happiness, and contentment is good, as is reducing negative emotions such as sadness, depression, fear. For many of the areas that charities work in, you don't need a deep moral understanding or specific moral view to see they are striving to do good. Curing diseases and reducing child mortality are fairly morally safe. There is a case to be made that charities that do well across a wide range of views might be the best ones to start with and the easiest to scale.

Whose lives matter?

A famous thought experiment by Peter Singer puts into perspective the choices before us. He asks us to imagine walking past a shallow pond, only to see a child drowning. The child would be easy to save, but at the cost of your clothing, your watch, and your phone in your pocket all being destroyed.

Almost everyone agrees that this tradeoff is not simply the right thing to do – it's the only ethical choice. It doesn't matter if someone else could have saved the child, or even if there are five children drowning. You would do everything in your power to save as many children as you could.

Although coming across drowning children might be rare, a slight shift in the question makes it relevant to our everyday lives. What if you could donate the cost of your clothing and gadgets, and be certain that the money would save someone on the other side of the world? GiveWell currently suggests that a life can be saved for around $3,000-5,000.[1] They use a highly rigorous process to ensure that each dollar donated does, in fact, make that difference. The power to save lives for such a small trade-off gives us both an opportunity and an obligation to help others.

Singer connects this point to W.E.H. Lecky's concept of the expanding moral circle – the idea that the number of individuals we consider it reasonable to help is growing over time.[2]

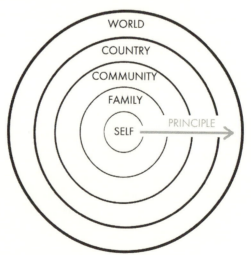

---

1 GiveWell, "Our Top Charities."

2 Peter Singer, *The Life You Can Save: Acting Now to End World Poverty* (New York: Random House, 2009). Available for download at thelifeyoucansave.org/the-book/.

Long ago, the expectation was that you would support yourself and your family. Animals, neighbors, and faraway humans would be considered a tool at best, or a threat to be eliminated at worst. But as time goes on, we recognize more and more beings as deserving of our help. The importance of caring about our community grew into caring about our nation, and over time, caring about humans all around the globe.

It's tempting to think that we're at the end of history and our circle now includes everyone we should care about. But there are many who, for all intents and purposes, remain outside most people's ethical circles.

Perhaps there are evolutionary reasons why we care about those closest to us, but does that make them right ethically? After all, there are evolutionary reasons for violence, and yet this is something we try actively to reduce in society. Imagine you are behind a veil, from which vantage point you know nothing about yourself, your natural abilities, or the position you hold in society. You might be a human from any country, or even an animal. What system would you want to design? How would you want others to act? If we knew nothing of our position in the world, we would probably not want to roll the dice and end up on the edge of the moral circles of those with power and resources.[3]

For the average person in the Western world, people living in the most extreme poverty fall at the outer limits of our moral circle – out of sight and out of mind. More and more actors are realizing the unacceptability of this fact. The Gates Foundation believes "all lives have equal value," and the organization's resulting actions focus on locations and people with the highest need, often far from its Seattle base.[4] This is quite different from the adage "charity begins at home" and closer to a policy of "charity begins with those in the most need."

Nonhuman animals fall into an even more distant ring in the moral circle, despite compelling evidence that many if not all animals suffer in very similar ways to humans. We treat the animals closest to us, such as dogs and cats, with an extremely high level of concern, often seeing them as beloved members of the family. But we give other animals far less ethical consideration. A person may own a pet mouse and yet still put out highly painful rodenticides around their house for mice who are not pets. One of the most abused populations in the

---

3 See Ethics Unwrapped, "Veil of Ignorance," Ethics Unwrapped Glossary, McCombs School of Business, accessed Nov. 10, 2021, https://ethicsunwrapped.utexas.edu/glossary/veil-of-ignorance.

4 Bill & Melinda Gates Foundation, "Our story," accessed Nov. 10, 2021, https://www.gatesfoundation.org/about/our-story.

world right now is the billions of animals in factory farms, who suffer intensely for much of their lives. Future generations will likely look back on our cruelty to farmed animals with shame.

When deciding where to focus, charity founders can encounter difficulties that donors do not have. The people who most need help may be on the opposite side of the world, in an unfamiliar culture and context. Perhaps it's easier to work at home, where you understand the government or policies better. But the fact remains that the most good can normally be done in countries with the most need. Does this mean you will need to learn about the country you work in and hire specialists on the ground? Of course – in fact, this would be necessary even if you grew up in the country you end up working in.

In the animal space, charity entrepreneurs encounter a different set of dilemmas. For one, the animal movement is both smaller and newer than the global health and development space. Large strides have been made for animal welfare, with many governments banning the most egregiously inhumane conditions. However, the best ways to help animals remain unclear – we simply don't have enough evidence. An issue as morally important as animal welfare must be approached with the same rigorous analysis that has led to huge health improvements over the last 50 years.

At the fringes of the moral circle, humans in far-flung countries and nonhuman animals need our help most. For a charity entrepreneur, personal passion or interest in a project may be important as motivation, but how important is it really, relative to a project that could help others more? Can you inspire yourself to pursue a more impactful idea?

In addition to such broad considerations, the moral circle will factor into many of the day-to-day decisions you'll make as a charity entrepreneur. Charity entrepreneurs have no boss and thus have considerable flexibility about choices like how much they pay themselves and how hard they work. What is the best way to think through these choices where your personal well-being might not always line up with the path to making the greatest difference? We know founders who are the lowest-paid staff member in their organization and work the longest hours. There is of course a limit to how hard we can push ourselves, but not all entrepreneurs find that limit – and it's worth exploring, for the sake of those many individuals who need our help.

At the end of the day, liking or agreeing with a group doesn't affect how much moral concern we should give to it. Someone who thinks differently from us in all ways still feels the same pain from injury. If it's in our power to prevent suffering and make the world a better place, we ought to do so. It does not matter how different they are or who caused the injury. Our circle should include all those who feel.

17.1. Trade-offs in doing good

Tricky questions arise when considering trade-offs. Every charity has limited resources and cannot work in every area. Some charities differ greatly in effectiveness depending on how you count their impact. For example, family planning is often seen as a good thing for its direct benefits, such as women's empowerment and reducing maternal deaths. However, on these metrics alone, other interventions can be even more effective. But, of course, there are many more flow-through effects of increasing family planning. How does one fewer child being born affect a low-income family who may already be struggling even without another mouth to feed? Would that child's life have been happy, so that it's bad they did not come into existence? Or would their life have been filled with pain, so that it's perhaps a good thing they were not born?

Taking a step even further out, how would that child affect their country and the broader world? Would they help or hurt the economy of the country? What would their environmental impact be? What about their effect on animals? The ripple effects from such an intervention can be highly complex. With some sane assumptions, family planning looks like the most impactful way to help the world; with other assumptions, it's not nearly as cost-effective as other global health-focused interventions.

One way to think through these tricky questions is by imagining a busy parliament house filled with 100 ministers. But instead of political parties, these ministers represent moral theories. Some theories you might put quite a bit of weight in, and thus many ministers are in that party. For example, our own largest parties would be utilitarianism[5] and prioritarianism, however, there are still seats for many other members of different ethical theories. When they come together, just like politicians, they make trades and alliances.

Our major parties might care less about some issues that more minor parties find very important. For example, typically we do not eat animal products, and

_____
5 See Utilitarianism, "What Is Utilitarianism?" Accessed Nov. 10, 2021, https://www.utilitarianism.net/.

many of our moral parties think this is the right thing to do. However, say an animal was raised in good conditions and treated well. For some of our parties (including the largest ones), this makes eating meat no longer a significant ethical issue – it might even be slightly net positive if it brings a happy life into existence. But smaller parties in the moral parliament, such as deontological parties, may have a rule that brooks no exceptions: "Don't kill others." They would thus still strongly maintain that we should not eat meat. Still other parties might be indifferent. The parliamentarians from virtue ethics parties might know that we have good intentions in both cases, and thus abstain from any votes.

Having a sense of your fundamental ethics in this way is a helpful exercise. And reading up on ethics can be a way to understand how you want to do good in the world – particularly because decisions can come up that pose a conflict in values, not in understanding.

A fortification charity we spoke to once faced a tough choice. Should they work in an area that they knew they would make progress in but would help fewer people, or an area that was more risky but would help far more people if successful? Comparing the expected value of these two options, the charity chose the riskier strategy with the potential to help many more people. From the perspective of co-founder happiness, it's better to have a successful charity that is less impactful than to be confronted with a significant chance of failure, but for the sake of helping as many people as possible, they made a different choice.

The right choice for the world and for all those on the edge of the circle is not the one that makes you look the best or that makes your family and friends the happiest. As a charity entrepreneur, sometimes you will need to make hard calls. Firing an underperforming employee whom you really like nonetheless is the right thing to do for the world, but on a personal level, it's far less pleasant than keeping them around. Your co-founder team will have to do unpleasant tasks that are important for your charity's progress.

Sometimes it's the hard choice that helps others, even at a cost to yourself or those closest to you. These can be the choices that separate good from great charities.

17.2. Doing good vs. doing the most good

Almost everyone wants to do good, and almost every charity does some good. However, many readers of this book are aiming higher. We want charities that do the most good – charities that are not just decent, but rather are leaders in their field.

If saving one life is good, saving two lives is better. Most people will agree with this simple statement, but our emotions often don't line up with this sentiment. A well-known quote remarks that "a single death is a tragedy; a million deaths is a statistic."[6] Our brains have trouble comprehending large numbers of suffering, and we certainly do not feel a million times sadder hearing about a million deaths than when hearing about one. Humans evolved in small groups, caring deeply about those closest to us. We did not evolve to handle large numbers or to emotionally understand the global community we are now a part of.

Let's go back to Singer's thought experiment of the drowning child. What if there were two children drowning? Does that change your actions? Even if there were so many children drowning that you could not possibly hope to save them all, you would swim until your arms gave out.

This is the moral imperative to do the most good. There is so much pain and suffering in the world that a fantastic charity can work as hard as it is able and there will still be problems. But that hundredth child saved, the last one you manage to rescue before your strength gives out, matters just as much as the first.

Doing the most good you can versus doing some good makes all the difference when we look at individual lives. The charity world may be more abstract than the drowning child, but the stakes are no less high.

17.3. Supporting your values

Bill is in his first year of college when he first thinks about founding a nonprofit. He gets excited about the idea through a local effective altruism chapter and ends up becoming a member. He takes a pledge to donate some of his income and accepts an internship at a young, but promising, charity over winter break to improve his skills. So far, Bill is on a great track to found a charity, and he holds it as one of his major life goals.

When Bill gets back from break, he hits a particularly rough year of school and really focuses on maintaining his GPA. His involvement with the EA

---

6 Attributed to a French diplomat in the essay "Französischer Witz [French Wit]" in Vossische Zeitung 23 Aug. 1925, according to Susan Ratcliffe, *Oxford Essential Quotations*, 4 ed. (Oxford University Press, 2016), eISBN: 9780191826719.

chapter drops off – he's too busy. The silver lining at the end of this rough year is that he starts a relationship. The person is smart and well suited to him, but does not share his charitable interest. Over time, Bill stops reading the NGO content he used to, and he never gets back into attending chapter meetings. After he gets his degree, he takes a job in consulting to build up some skills and found a charity later in his career, but he has a sense in his heart that it's unlikely to happen.

Bill's story is not uncommon. Knowing your values is only half the battle. The other half is supporting them.

We tend to think that the person we are today is who we will be in the long term. However, if you look back to how you were five years ago, you'll probably realize that your lifestyle and views have changed significantly. This applies to your values, too.

Sometimes change is neutral or positive, as you may deepen and confirm your understanding of your values. Other times, you might drift in your views or behavior away from your values, much like a healthy eater might drift toward junk food.

Value drift may be a problem that concerns the future you, but just as you want your future self to be healthy, you want your future self to be ethical. Thankfully, there are many ways to support your values and make it easier to remain the person you wish to be ethically.

Often, bad habits sneak up on us one inch at a time. Drawing a clear line in the sand such as "I will always donate XX% of income" might seem overly restrictive, but there is lots of evidence that setting specific lines or goals greatly increases the chances of sticking to positive habits.[7] Many of the most successful charity founders set specific goals for themselves for hours worked or other aspects that are easy to let slide when founding a new project.

Studies show that you can change your environment to support the actions you wish to do. Something as simple as putting healthy foods in a glass bowl or putting cookies on a hard-to-reach shelf can significantly improve your odds of choosing healthier foods. (A great book on this is Sunstein & Thaler's *Nudge*.[8]) Systems can make doing good the easy default action, such as setting

---

7 We again refer back to James Clear's *Atomic Habits*.

8 C.R. Sunstein and R.H. Thaler, *Nudge: Improving Decisions About Health, Wealth, and Happiness* (London: Penguin Books, Feb. 24, 2009).

up automatic donations instead of having to remember each month.

When it comes to founding charities, put yourself in an environment that will make it easy to keep doing the actions you wish to do; for instance, working at a coworking office or in a city with a strong drive toward charity and doing good, or building skills that are more useful in altruistic careers than others. Self-identifying as an effective altruist or charity entrepreneur and publicly committing to your plans can help you achieve your ethical goals.

There's a saying that you become the average of the five people closest to you. Lots of people vastly underestimate the impact of the social connections around them, but your relationships can shape huge aspects of your personality. Surrounding yourself with people who motivate and inspire you in your altruistic pursuits can be one of the best ways to have an impact long term.

Make an effort to have regular social interactions with value-aligned people (e.g., meet for lunch/dinner/coffee); engage with or start an altruism meetup or volunteering activity; attend conferences or social events; or get in touch with value-aligned people and communities online.

For the more adventurous, even something as radical as moving cities can be a fair idea to increase the community connection that you want to build. The current hub for charity entrepreneurship is London, UK, but there are altruistic and charity hubs all over the world.

18. Career area

Your journey as a charity entrepreneur starts with the four Cs:

- Career area - found a charity, or pursue another career path?
- Charity idea - what intervention should you implement?
- Co-founder - whom do you want to launch this charity with?
- Country selection - which geographical area will you work in?

More than half of your total impact will come from your answers to these questions.

The first and biggest choice of all the four Cs is career area. At Charity Entrepreneurship, we consider starting a high-impact NGO to be one of the most impactful ways to make a change in the world. But we don't consider changing plans along the way to be a sign of failure. If, for example, an RCT shows that your program is not making an impact, it could be rational to change gears. Even during and after the Incubation Program, there are many good reasons to reconsider one's future as a charity founder. So it's smart to constantly reevaluate the entrepreneurship path and have a plan B, and maybe even a plan C and D, ready.

Here are some of the reasons you might not become a charity entrepreneur:

1. There are drawbacks to entrepreneurship, ranging from uncertainty and poor work-life balance to high risk of failure. It is fair to recognize that you don't want to accept these downsides or that your personality might be too far away from the typical traits of an entrepreneur. Recognizing

this early on can spare you a lot of hardship later.[1]

2. You might not have found your ideal match in terms of a co-founder or charity idea, so may decide to hold off on starting an NGO.

3. Funding is a key bottleneck for charities. Some teams might not secure a grant after the program, or struggle to get additional funds from third parties. Such funding constraints can be overcome in the short term by working without pay or getting a paid job on the side. In the long term, however, this might not be sustainable.

4. As you work toward implementing a high-impact program in a particular country, you may notice that another organization is already implementing something very similar. Often, that charity would not meet EA standards and may not focus on cost-effectiveness or monitoring and evaluation. Yet in some cases, you will come across a strong NGO that is already implementing your desired program or could easily implement it based on its expertise. (For example, it might already have the infrastructure such as radio programming for health, so could easily add messaging for cause X.) In such instances, you could first explore a collaboration with this organization or join their team rather than launching your own venture.

There are legitimate reasons not to pursue the path of entrepreneurship or to stop along the way. Thankfully, there are fulfilling alternatives with a high-impact profile.

As you explore your career options, use the tools of decision-making to evaluate the most promising options. In Chapter 1, we looked at charity entrepreneurship from a range of perspectives, including cost-effectiveness analysis, expert views, track record, and neglectedness. We can use these and other heuristics to build a weighted factor model comparing different career paths as in our Career Decision Tool below:

	Total score	Short term impact (0.5)				Long term impact (0.4)			Happiness factor (0.1)
		CEA converted	Outside view	Competitive ad	Flexible skill building	Value drift	Building a team	Strength of feedback loops	Personal happiness
Factor importance		0.2	0.1	0.1	0.2	0.1	0.1	0.1	0.1
Option A	8.8	9	10	10	8	9	10	7	8
Option B	7.8	5.6	8	9	10	8	10	5	7
Option C	6.4	2.7	8	8	7	7	7	9	6
Option D	6.2	2.5	9	7	9	5	6	5	7
Option E	5.7	3.0	7	5	8	6	5	6	6
Option F	5.7	3.3	8	9	6	3	7	7	4
Option G	4.8	2.1	6	6	7	5	3	5	5
Option H	4.1	1	1	10	2	1	5	8	10

---

1 Flip back to Part I for a refresher on the disadvantages and typical traits of entrepreneurship.

In this example, options A and B are pretty close. Both are worth exploring more deeply and maybe even testing on a small scale. Other options can be considered only if there are major updates to the top two or a new important factor comes to light.

So what other career paths might you consider? In this chapter, we'll talk through some of the top options for people interested in charity entrepreneurship. We will start with the closest options, such as social entrepreneurship and for-profit entrepreneurship, and then open out to the broader nonprofit space and other impactful options.

18.1. Nonprofit, for-profit, and social entrepreneurship

There are countless ways to use entrepreneurship to make the world a better place. Our organization, Charity Entrepreneurship, launches new charities. But why charities and not social or for-profit ventures? In this section, we explain some of the differences between these areas, and what to consider when assessing your personal fit for each option.

Reading through the following tables, you might notice that, while there are differences between the various types of entrepreneurship, the boundaries aren't always perfectly clear cut. Some larger charities might raise money through running a charity shop (although this type of fundraising isn't suitable for a small start-up). Some for-profit organizations might become certified B Corps[2] (e.g., Ben & Jerry's), committing themselves to a triple bottom line of profit and a positive impact on society and the environment.

---

2 Certified B Corporations meet specific social, environmental, and transparency standards established by the nonprofit B Lab.

Fact files

Charity entrepreneurship

Definition	Founding charitable organizations.
Bottom line	Impact
Revenue structure	Donations
Examples	Against Malaria Foundation, The Humane League
Strengths	- Can help beneficiaries with low or no income - Can partner with governments - More neglected - Can focus model solely on impact - Historically has created huge amounts of impact
Weaknesses	- Has to fundraise to create impact - More limited scale - Disconnect between funders and beneficiaries - More challenging monitoring and evaluation
Personal fit	- Have to think about measuring impact far more - Have to be strongly motivated by helping others

Social entrepreneurship

Definition	Founding projects that cause good in the world and can financially sustain themselves.
Bottom line	Double bottom line of profit and impact
Revenue structure	Sales or a mix of sales and donations
Examples	Wave, Living Goods
Strengths	- Can offset the costs of soliciting donations, allowing a donation to go further - Some opportunities can be run much like a for-profit, with impact achieved through long-term indirect effects (i.e., flow-through benefits) - Gives a lot of flexibility in revenue structures - Often easier to gain traction compared to nonprofits
Weaknesses	- Can have a divided focus, making it hard to compete on impact or profit metrics - More limited pool of investors - Mixed track record (e.g., microloans) - Complex tax structures, depending on the country
Personal fit	- Ideally have a broader understanding of both nonprofit and for-profit norms - Need to have a strong ability to make trade-offs

For-profit entrepreneurship

Definition	Founding projects geared toward profit.
Bottom line	Profit
Revenue structure	Sales and income
Examples	Google, 23andMe
Strengths	- Can grow to truly extreme sizes - Can cause massively increased spending and focus on key areas - Does not take money from the charity sector - Success is easier to measure - Profits can be donated to make a direct impact
Weaknesses	- Can typically only focus on creating products that individuals with income want to buy - Highly competitive space compared to others - Higher risk of value drift
Personal fit	- Requires strong communication skills - Have to be comfortable moving fast and lean

Our overall views on impact

Our goal (and likely one of yours if you're reading this book!) is to have the greatest possible impact with our time. So, the most important difference across these areas is the possible and average impact.

Charity entrepreneurship

Example: Against Malaria Foundation

Confidence: Our confidence in this area is much higher than in the others. We have made explicit and detailed models and spoken to many experts about how to execute impactful projects.

Average: The impact of the average charity could be very low or even net negative. Unfortunately, money fundraised for one charity typically means funds are redirected away from another charitable organization. This means that if a new project is less impactful than those its donors would have given to otherwise, it could easily be a net negative.

Top founders: We have modeled the impact of charities founded via the CE program, which is highly competitive and aims to only launch highly impactful charities. Our best estimate suggests that our average founder creates as much value for the world as about ~$200k of donations to the most impactful charities in their space. However, this number has considerable range, with our top founders creating 5x that value in impact.[3]

Overall: The bar for impact set by projects going through the CE program is very high relative to most other career paths, including other types of entrepreneurship. However, we do think there are a few other careers both within and outside of the entrepreneurship space that can equal it in impact and, thus, could be a better choice, depending on personal fit.

For-profit entrepreneurship + donating

Example: 23andMe

Confidence: Our team has far less experience in this area. However, the estimates for impact are comparatively easier to calculate, as it is primarily

---

3 Here we again refer to the CE Team's internal "Early 2021 CEA."

achieved through donations. This can be broken down as earnings and donation percentages. 80,000 Hours and Founders Pledge have both considered this impact and created some relevant resources. Overall, this is the area we are second most confident in speaking about.

Average: Earnings in this career are extremely power-lawed.[4] The average US entrepreneur earns about 18% more than similar people who remain in salaried jobs.[5] With this estimate in mind, going down this path while maintaining a donation pledge (such as 10%) can be a solid way to have an impact. Our best guess is that starting an average for-profit and donating is more impactful than starting an average nonprofit.

Top founders: 80,000 Hours found that people who have received venture capital funding[6] or entered Y Combinator,[7] on average, earn millions of dollars per year. One complexity is that these earnings typically derive from increases in the value of the stake in the company. There are often restrictions on how such earnings can be used as opposed to donatable cash in hand. Depending on donation percentage, this could compete with being a top charity entrepreneur (e.g., if percentage is 50%).

Overall: We think this is a strong career path for those who are interested in entrepreneurship but do not attend the CE Incubation Program, or those who get into a program like Y Combinator and plan to donate a large percentage of their income. We do have concerns about value drift in this career path, so think it is vital to be an active member in communities focused on doing good.

Social entrepreneurship

Social entrepreneurship has likely the messiest definition, sometimes including many charitable projects. Depending on the type of social entrepreneurship, our current sense of its impact varies greatly. To talk about its impact, we are going to break social entrepreneurship into two types: flow-through effect social

---

4 Meaning that a small number of entrepreneurs will make a huge profit, while the majority will make substantially less.

5 Benjamin Todd, "Career reviews: Tech startup founder," 80,000 hours, Aug. 2014, https://80000hours.org/career-reviews/tech-entrepreneurship/.

6 Ryan Carey, "The payoff and probability of obtaining venture capital," 80,000 Hours (blog), June 25, 2014, https://80000hours.org/2014/06/the-payoff-and-probability-of-obtaining-venture-capital/.

7 Ryan Carey, "How much do Y Combinator founders earn?" 80,000 Hours (blog), May 27, 2014, https://80000hours.org/2014/05/how-much-do-y-combinator-founders-earn/.

entrepreneurship and double bottom line social entrepreneurship.

Confidence: Our confidence in impact for both of these areas is lower, as we have seen fewer successful examples of social entrepreneurship. Additionally, Charity Entrepreneurship, and the EA movement as a whole, has done less research on the topic.

Flow-through effects of social entrepreneurship

Example: Beyond Meat, a for-profit company, creates flow-through benefits by reducing the number of animals farmed for human consumption. Other organizations in this category include Wave, which facilitates access to financial services in emerging markets. Projects in this group can compete from a for-profit perspective and, if they succeed, will create significant benefits outside of their revenue generated.

Average: We expect that on average, successfully launching such a project would be more challenging than for-profit entrepreneurship, as the flow-through effect consideration adds another factor to reflect on when founding. The impact of projects like these also occurs more at scale. This means that unsuccessful projects would likely only generate impact via the donations made by founders and employees in the meantime.

Top founders: For top founders, we feel pretty optimistic, but with low confidence about this type of social entrepreneurship. Our best estimate is that this option could be on par with other top entrepreneurship paths if (i) the project has significant positive flow-through effects, (ii) it gets into incubation programs like Y Combinator, and (iii) its founders donate ~25% of their earnings.

Overall: We are cautiously optimistic about this type of entrepreneurship, although we think the band of people[8] who would be a good personal fit for it is likely more narrow than for nonprofit or for-profit entrepreneurship.

Double bottom line social entrepreneurship

Example: Living Goods, a nonprofit that supports community health workers by using mobile technology and financial incentives to ensure quality care. This type of social entrepreneurship generally cannot succeed without donations and

---

8 Ben Kuhn, "Why and how to start a for-profit company serving emerging markets," Effective Altruism Forum, Nov. 5, 2019, https://forum.effectivealtruism.org/posts/M44rw22o5dbrRaA8F/why-and-how-to-start-a-for-profit-company-serving-emerging.

profits. Thus, it has to maximize a double bottom line made up of profits and impact. Often, these bottom lines will pull in different directions and require hard trade-offs.

Average impact: We expect the average impact of projects like these to be quite limited. We've seen many projects in this space struggle to gain traction and achieve impact.

Top founders: Some impact can be had from founding projects in this space. However, we generally do not see it as competitive with the other entrepreneurship options, and would generally encourage people toward those paths instead.

Overall: We are fairly pessimistic about this type of entrepreneurship.

Each of these options is worth considering, and has many of the same benefits and drawbacks as charity entrepreneurship.

18.2. Impactful alternatives to entrepreneurship

Entrepreneurship is far from the only option for people pursuing high-impact careers. Depending on personal fit, you might opt to seek employment in another organization in the nonprofit sector (an effective charity or foundation), work on policy in the public sector, or earn to give. Some of these options might also be a good way to build skills to move into charity entrepreneurship at a later point in your career.

Working at CE

Our organization, Charity Entrepreneurship, operates at a meta level, so staff members support not one but various charities. If you are a research-oriented person, you would likely be happy at CE, because we offer full-time researcher positions. Jobs at the average incubated charity lean more toward operations. Furthermore, at CE, you are close to the incubated organizations and might be able to jump back into entrepreneurship at some point.

These roles are quite competitive. However, in the past, we have offered jobs to candidates who have gone through our program but determined that entrepreneurship is not or is not yet a good fit for them. We also offer remote internships that can help test out an aspect of founding a charity in a lower-commitment way.

- Check out Ishaan Guptasarma's 2020 post "What is it like to work at Charity Entrepreneurship" on our blog to learn more.

Working at a CE-incubated or otherwise impactful new org

Why found your own charity when you can join an existing impactful NGO? Talent with an entrepreneurial mindset is in high demand at young organizations. You might be able to join a fast-growing organization as one of their first staff members, which gives you considerable influence.

Joining an existing charity means the probability of success is likely higher, as the initial battles are already behind it. You're still part of a highly dynamic organization, but with more structure as some systems are already set up and co-founders will provide guidance. It is also one of the best ways to build up future skills for running your own project.

Working at another effectiveness-focused or EA charity

The advantages of working at an EA charity outside the CE network are very similar to those of working at one within it. The main difference might be that the charity is less influenced by the "CE spirit" and more influenced by other streams within the EA movement. Look into:

- Animal charities such as The Humane League, in roles recommended by Animal Advocacy Careers (AAC). Fundraising and operations roles are in high demand.[9] Additional details can be found in AAC's 2019 talent bottleneck survey.
- Mental health charities, based on career tips from the Happier Lives Institute[10]
- GiveWell top charities (or GiveWell itself)
- Research roles at impact-focused poverty research organizations, e.g., IDinsight, J-PAL, or 3ie

The importance of fundraising highlighted in animal advocacy applies to other areas, too. In fundraising roles, we believe you can have particularly high leverage.

---

9 Animal Advocacy Careers, "Effective animal advocacy nonprofit roles spot-check," Oct. 19, 2020, https://www.animaladvocacycareers.org/post/effective-animal-advocacy-nonprofit-roles-spot-check.

10 Happier Lives Institute, "Career Advice," accessed Nov. 10, 2021, https://www.happierlivesinstitute.org/career-advice.html.

Working at another charity or foundation

Another option is to work for a charity in CE's recommended cause areas. To have the maximum impact working for these charities outside the EA movement, look for two factors: First, that this organization is very well established and moves funding in the millions or tens of millions per year; second, that your role is sufficiently influential so as to shape the organization's trajectory. These boxes are hard to check. Most NGOs are small, and at a large organization, your impact potential is often negligible. However, this can be an attractive option if you are able to steer a large organization in a positive direction.

Picking an NGO that already has some history of evidence-based programming might be a safer choice than battling windmills starting from zero. You could, for example, advocate for cash programming at an established development organization. Often these NGOs have some cash programs already, but they make up only a small portion of overall programming. It's often easier to add a new program than to take one away. With many opportunities, it will be best to add effective programs to the list of projects or supported organizations.

The same approach applies to foundations. In the best case, you could direct millions of dollars to evidence-based recipients. Foundations also have the hidden benefit of being able to donate a decent amount of money, and thus doubling as earning to give options.

How working at a foundation can top earning to give

- You make $90,000 as a Program Manager at a foundation. You live off $20,000 per year and turn your $70,000 donation into $100,000 through an employer donation matching program up to $30,000.

- You direct a budget of $1,000,000 that is, on average, 10% as effective as GiveWell top charities. With your inputs, the cost-effectiveness doubles (2x). You end up redirecting $200,000 in terms of GiveWell-equivalent funds. ($1,000,000 * 0.1 * 2)

- Add the $100,000 to the $200,000 and you end up moving $300,000 to GiveWell-like opportunities.

- This calculation improves further if you manage more than $1 million, which is realistic at many foundations.

Working in policy

Several CE charities work on policy. If this interests you, working in government could be a good fit. You can pursue the role of a civil servant or politician/activist. This career generally provides more stability, but requires persistence. One's impact should be calculated on the basis of decades rather than years. As national regulations impact millions and governments spend billions each year, your impact can nevertheless be considerable.

If you're interested in learning more about this option, head to 80,000 Hours for their review of policy careers.[11]

Earning to give

While fundraising might be less of an issue in some areas (e.g., existential risk or animal welfare), there is still a demand for funding in general, particularly in areas such as global health. An earning to give (E2G) career can provide funding to jump-start many CE charities, e.g., through contributions to the Charity Entrepreneurship Fund or to Charity Entrepreneurship itself. While it's most effective if you focus on a particularly lucrative career (e.g., medicine or law[12]) you can still pick an area where you can maximize your strengths and job satisfaction.

An extremely quantitative person might enjoy working with complex models at a hedge fund more than getting into the weeds of start-up operations. So E2G might increase your job satisfaction compared to charity entrepreneurship.

Moreover, the period between the first funding and major follow-up funding is a difficult one for commercial and nonprofit start-ups alike. As an E2G donor, you can help charities move through this phase, commonly known as death valley.

E2G is generally a better option the more you can donate. If you can give upward of $100,000 per year, it becomes a very strong option. This is possible with a salary of $135,000 or $150,000, which applies to some jobs. Of course, the sweet spot would be a job where you make upward of $200,000 and could

---

11 See the drop-down option "Government and policy in an area relevant to a top problem" in 80,000 Hours, "Our list of high-impact careers," accessed Nov. 10, 2021, https://80000hours.org/career-reviews/#government-and-policy.

12 Benjamin Todd, "Which industry has the highest paying jobs?" 80,000 Hours (blog), May 2017, https://80000hours.org/articles/highest-paying-jobs/.

donate even more. This more limited set of jobs can be a good fit for some in the finance community, for example.

While replaceability is a concern for most EA careers, it is less so for E2G. There is no limit to positions that allow motivated individuals to donate large amounts of their salaries to EA causes (although there is a possible limit to the number of underfunded and cost-effective interventions).

Career capital

Some people are positive that charity entrepreneurship is not a fit for them now, but think it might be in the future. **We generally advise against putting off your charity founding plans**. Some exceptions would be if you have previously tried to found a charity and run into a block based specifically on lack of experience, or if trusted advisors recommend building up certain skills. In this case, getting a **short-term job or internship** can help you build skills and good habits quickly.

We recommend working at a small, well-run, impact-focused nonprofit, ideally in the approximate cause area you're interested in. Small nonprofits will give you a better feel for working as a charity entrepreneur, both work-wise and culturally. You'll build a wide range of experiences, as you will often wear a lot of different hats (a key skill for charity entrepreneurship). Many small charities will end up giving you more responsibility within a shorter time frame. They also tend not to use the more established seniority-based systems that larger nonprofits often do, so individuals can grow more freely. Culturally, they tend to be less rigid and have less established systems. Overall, working in smaller nonprofits will stand much closer to simulating the first few years of founding a charity than working in the larger ones.

What about advanced education? Although we think most education programs are not well built for teaching charity entrepreneurship, there is one exception. The MIT MicroMasters in Data, Economics, and Development Policy[13] is unusually focused on practicalities, has a sliding-scale cost based on income, and can be done even without a BA if you have nonprofit experience. Going through this program can be a good, small-scale way to test your fit for charity entrepreneurship. Other options like studying economics, medicine, or

---

13 MITx MicroMasters Programs, "About the Program," accessed Nov. 10, 2021, https://micromasters.mit.edu/dedp/.

statistics can also be good choices but are typically a very slow way to learn the skills you need.

Facing a question as big as career area, many worry that their choices today will determine the rest of their working career. This makes a hard question (What career should I follow for the next few years?) a much harder question (What do I want to do for the rest of my life?). Although thinking long term can be valuable, mapping out one's whole career in advance is impossible without a crystal ball. Instead, experiment with different avenues and steadily spend more time in the most promising ones.

Try to view charity entrepreneurship like any other job offer at a normal company. Like many jobs, you might start with a trial period – attending an incubation program, for example, or working on a project over the summer. After the trial period, you might escalate to a longer-term commitment, spending a year testing out the project, and so on.

Even if you're confident that you want to move forward with charity entrepreneurship as a career path, knowing about adjacent options (and having a fleshed out plan B) will give you greater confidence in taking risks and going for big wins.

19. Charity idea

Landmines and typhoid and bridges, oh my!

Many people start charities based on something that has personally affected them. But given the size of the world and its range of problems, it's highly un-likely that the best way to save lives will be something that affects you personally. Most of the strongest charities were founded using a very different process. We can use the tools of good decision-making to make an informed determination of which charity the world needs most.

19.1. Cause area profiles

Cause area is the umbrella term for a broad problem. To clarify, mental health would be a cause area, depression reduction would be an intervention, and a cognitive behavioral therapy app to reduce postpartum depression would be a charity idea. Each cause area has its strengths and weaknesses, and it's hard to compare them reliably due to the many assumptions (both ethical and epistemic) that must be made. This chapter offers a starting point for such comparisons. We focus on five cause areas that our research has identified as particularly promising: mental health, family planning, animal welfare, health policy, and meta-charities.

Mental health

Mental health directly influences happiness and can fill large happiness gaps in both high- and low-income countries. Despite limited historical work on determining the most cost-effective interventions, the evidence base looks promising. Interventions within this cause area could include delivering guided self-help for mental illnesses, distributing antidepressants such as SSRIs, or training stakeholders to help prevent suicide.

Animal welfare

Farmed and wild animals are victims of huge suffering and extreme neglect. There appear to be many promising ways to improve farmed animal lives massively. Now seems like a uniquely good time to found new animal organizations. Example interventions include addressing footpad burn and feather pecking among factory-farmed birds, improving water quality for farmed crustaceans, and campaigning for more humane rodent control.

Family planning

Family planning has a range of positive effects on health, wealth, empowerment, and more. The area looks highly promising and is growing dramatically, but has not yet received as much attention as other areas of global health. Ideas could include offering family planning services to women postpartum and postabortion, providing vouchers for contraceptives to increase access, and implementing a social and behavior change media campaign.

Health and development policy

Leveraging government resources can make a significant, large-scale impact. Health policies can be evidence-based and extremely cost-effective. This could include ideas like campaigning for lead paint regulation, lobbying to lower alcohol or tobacco consumption, and advocating for better foreign aid.

Meta-charities

Meta-charities are one step removed from doing direct good. For example, Charity Entrepreneurship's training program does not cause impact directly; instead, it supports charities that then go on to cause impact. Meta ideas include charity evaluation, conducting research on key areas, and grantmaking.

Weighted factor model – comparing cause areas

So let's start to compare these very different areas. The table below shows our weighted factor model framing for each of these cause areas. Each area is color-coded from strongest to weakest.

Area	Direct cost-effective-ness	Relevant evidence	Limiting factor*	Execution difficulty	Non-captured externalities**
Mental health	Moderate	Some	Funding (1)	Easier	EA movement (3)
Family planning	Low	Moderate	Logistical (4)	Complex	Child, animals (4)
Animal welfare	High	Low	Talent (2)	Easier	Bar setting (2)
Health policy	High	High	Funding (3)	Complex	Precedent (1)
Meta charities	Moderate	Low	Logistical (4)	Easier	Moderate (3)

* If the number accompanying the limiting factor[1] cell is low, this means that the limiting factor will be met very quickly. Higher numbers mean that the factor will not soon become relevant.

** If the number accompanying the non-captured externality cell is high, this means that the externalities are large and positive. If the number is low, this means that the externality is small.

---

1 For an explanation of limiting factors, see Charity Entrepreneurship, "Why We Look at the Limiting Factor Instead of the Problem Scale," Jan. 28, 2019, https://www.charityentrepreneurship. com/blog/why-we-look-at-the-limiting-factor-instead-of-the-problem-scale.

We can also frame comparisons in terms of more specific key strengths and weaknesses.

Mental health

Strengths	Weaknesses
Directness of the subjective well-being metric and possible underrating of the area by other metrics	Uncertain cost-effectiveness compared to top global health interventions
Possible promising cost-effectiveness for both low- and high-income countries	More theoretical and philosophical work is required for assessment
Strong to moderate evidence base and background research, but limited prioritization work	More limited funding base, particularly in the EA movement
Could encourage EA movement to consider more cause areas long term	Evidence base has a wider range of metrics used, making it more difficult to compare

Family planning

Strengths	Weaknesses
Strong funding outside of EA Moderate evidence base Diverse range of positive effects (e.g., women's empowerment, un-born child benefits, family benefits, income benefits, etc.)	Maximizing multiple positive effects makes the charity harder to run Can be controversial Size of impact depends in part on unsolved population ethics questions
Under certain ethical views could be extremely impactful Area has more limited use of CEAs than others in global health, leaving promising subareas neglected	Evidence is spread out between a wide range of metrics, thus speculative conversions and comparisons need to be used

Animal welfare

Strengths	Weaknesses
Naive cost-effectiveness estimates generally show extremely high cost-effectiveness High levels of historical neglect mean many promising charity ideas are not yet founded Strong support both within and outside of the EA community Very strong case that animals should be given moral weight	Very low evidence base compared to other areas Some talent shortages in the movement that impair key charities More limited externalities and flow-through effects than other cause areas High rate of non-effectiveness minded activists in the area

Health & development policy

Strengths	Weaknesses
Naive cost-effectiveness estimates show higher cost-effectiveness than standard global health interventions and maybe all other human-focused areas	Extremely complex space resulting in a much higher than average chance of a charity having limited or no impact
Evidence base fairly strong if confidence is established in causal relationship of lobbying	More limited externalities and flow-through effects compared to other cause areas

Very high bar of charities already working in the space |

Meta-charities

Strengths	Weaknesses
Can allow a larger impact than direct interventions

Can create impact across a number of different cause areas, allowing hedged bets | Have a low evidence base

Often require a higher level of M&E ability to determine their impact

Can have more political elements than direct delivery charities |

Another way to compare these cause areas is to consider key ethical and epistemic assumptions. Three controversial ethical dilemmas might rule out or strengthen certain areas: animal lives, the lives of unborn people, and happiness vs. health vs. income.

Animal lives

Some people think that certain nonhuman animals do not feel pain or suffering, although this is becoming an increasingly rare view for larger animals (such as dogs and cats). The view gets more common when considering animals further from humans in the evolutionary tree. Should shrimp and bugs be given moral consideration? Often the same sum of money can save either many smaller animals or just one larger animal – but how can we weigh this trade-off ethically?

Another difficult question: could you motivate yourself every day to put energy into saving nonhuman animals when humans are still suffering? If not, this could rule out animal welfare as an area. However, if you're keen to help neglected beings who would otherwise receive little attention, animal advocacy could be a good fit. And if you morally value animals such as fish, shrimp, or bugs, you can help truly staggering numbers of beings by working in the animal space.

Lives of unborn people

Some interventions save lives, but others affect unborn people. Family planning has measurable benefits for the mother, but how does the unborn child factor into the equation? Is it a good thing that they did not come into a life where their parents would have preferred not to have them, or is this bad? In the longer term, do we want more humans on earth (maybe good for human welfare and economic progress) or fewer (maybe good for animals and the environment)? Intuitions on these sorts of questions can make family planning look either extremely promising or not very promising at all.

Happiness vs. health vs. income

There are lots of ways to measure impact, and not a lot of cross comparison between them. The DALY is used across many health interventions, but it's hard to compare it to income or subjective well-being (self-reported happiness). Certain cause areas do much better on one metric than others. Mental health looks extremely important from a subjective well-being perspective, but less so from a DALY perspective.

Picking a cause area is a complex choice that merits deep research and conversations with people who have worked in the space or faced similar choices. Some cause areas you might be personally excited about just might not look as effective once you review the evidence. Always try to keep in mind the endline goal: saving or improving as many lives as possible.

19.2. Comparing interventions

Let's narrow down a step and start to consider interventions within the same cause area. In many ways, this is a similar process but with more narrowly defined options. This tends to result in fewer ethical considerations and more evidence-based considerations.

We will look at two different causes in this section: global health and animal welfare. As in the previous section, the tables for each cause area show the weighted factor model and then intervention-specific strengths and weaknesses. These tables are from 2019, so some of these ideas have now been launched as new nonprofits.

Global health interventions

Area	Direct cost-effective-ness	Relevant evidence	Limiting factor	Execution difficulty	Non-captured externalities
Immu-nization reminders	Low	Moderate	Funding (3)	Easy	Limited (1)
Tobacco taxation	High	Mixed	Policy windows (1)	Complex	Precedent (4)
Iron and folic acid fortifica-tion	Moderate	Moderate	Logistical (4)	Moderate	Moderate (3)

Immunization reminders

Strengths	Weaknesses
Highly flexible and has great feed-back loops. For example, can move from SMS reminders to SMS + gossip (community) reminders	High cost-effectiveness can be hard to achieve (e.g., higher than Give-Directly but not as high as other GiveWell top charities)
Has a spectrum of success (unlike lobbying-based organizations) Many impactful opportunities are still on the table due to the newness of the intervention Easier to get government buy-in on large-scale projects	Behavior change makes concerns about external validity stronger Almost all benefits are in saving lives of children under five, so limited externalities

Tobacco taxation

Strengths	Weaknesses
Possibility of being extremely cost-effective	High-risk opportunity with a high chance of failure
Provides learning opportunities as well as the ability to set a precedent if success is achieved	Agents (i.e., tobacco companies) actively push against interventions in this space
Often regarded as one of the most effective global health policy interventions that is not consistently applied in all countries	The evidence base for the best strategies for getting tobacco taxes raised is unclear
The evidence base that tobacco cessation prevents a massive DALY burden and tobacco taxes reduce tobacco use is very strong	There are major difficulties in assessing the impact of a single organization in the space when multiple organizations are working in the same location

Iron & folic acid fortification

Strengths	Weaknesses
Nutrition as a broad area is seen as highly promising by a wide range of external experts, including GiveWell and the Copenhagen Consensus	Certain locations are highly effective to run this intervention in (e.g., northern Indian states), but fewer gaps than other interventions
Iron affects a wide range of health outcomes, often leaving it undervalued in standard calculations. One example of this would be iron's effects on depression rates.	Medium-risk opportunity with a medium chance of failure
	Sub-standard fortification may lead to a limited or non-impactful effect
There are large gaps in fortification in lower-income countries	There are many other nutrition-focused organizations, although none focusing on iron & folic acid in India

Animal welfare interventions

Area	Direct cost-effec-tiveness	Relevant evidence	Limiting factor	Execution difficulty
Dissolved oxygen for fish	Moderate	High	Logistical (4)	Moderate
Feed for-tification for laying hens	Low	High	Logistical (3)	Low
Ask re-search	High	Moderate	Talent (1)	Moderate
Animal careers	Moderate	Low	Replicability (3)	Low

Dissolved oxygen (DO) for fish

Strengths	Weaknesses
Has a precedent in recent similar cage-free and broiler asks	Upfront research required to determine key variables (e.g., optimal range of DO)
Extremely cost-effective when compared to other animal-focused interventions. The most cost-effective direct intervention we measured.	Heterogeneity between species of fish makes it harder to generalize DO or other interventions
Strong evidence base	Finding talent on the research side will be challenging in the animal space
Has strong pathways to funding, as many donors consider fish a promising focus area	Fish-focused charities would likely eventually get started, so the counterfactual impact comes from the sub-focus areas
Has the possibility of shifting the animal movement's fish focus in a much more effective direction	

Feed fortification for laying hens

Strengths	Weaknesses
Strong evidence base relative to other interventions in the space	The timing might not be optimal due to recent cage-free campaigns
Less initial research needed before this organization could be founded	Lower cost-effectiveness than other animal charities
Feed cost is the largest single-item cost in poultry production	Some concerns regarding counterfactual replaceability of the industry improving feed
Room for scaling to other food-related interventions	

Nutrition is a well understood and cost-effective intervention	There is a wide range of possible nutritional improvements, with exact effects on pain of birds being less clear

Ask research

Strengths	Weaknesses
There's limited research in the animal movement as a whole, and even less directly focused on asks that can be made of govts or corps	The impact depends strongly on the effectiveness of corporate and governmental campaigns
This type of research seems tractable and, compared to other research, has quick feedback loops	Impact relies on NGOs and organizations updating based on research
Given the low cost of a research organization focused on this and the possibility of affecting large corporate campaigns, it could be highly cost-effective	Founders will have to be very strong in both research and communication skills
Effective altruists have a strong competitive advantage for this idea	Relatively few asks are chosen annually, so the feedback loops are slow compared to direct intervention charities, and there is downtime between key choices

Animal advocacy careers

Strengths	Weaknesses
Meta-charity that could lead to other charities being founded	Relies on other charities in the animal movement being net positive and effective
Has models that can be replicated as a starting point (CSO in testing ideas, 80,000 hours in organizational scope)	Requires a high level of communication skills
Has a low floor for failure (even if done moderately well, could have major benefits)	Co-founders will have to be comfortable with interorganizational interaction
Likely the charity idea the largest number of funders and activists will be excited about	Requires a broad understanding of a diverse movement
Could be very cost-effective if you take surveys of employee demand at face value	Many will not understand the charity idea or how it helps the movement
Can be done in a wide range of locations effectively	Impact is indirect and hard to measure
	Very limited historical research in the area, so starting from scratch in many cases

19.3. What if I have a charity idea already?

We often get asked for advice about charity ideas. Every charity and entrepreneur will need different guidance, but the most cross-applicable advice that virtually everybody could benefit from is:

- Compare at least ten different options.
- Really research your ideas – and try to destroy them.

Compare at least ten options

There are untold numbers of ideas out there; the odds are vanishingly low that any one idea is the optimal one. Furthermore, your choice can only be as good as the best option you have on the table. If there are only two, that puts hard limits on your potential upside.

To come up with a truly good idea, think of at least ten different options. The "at least" is important. Ideally, you should try to think of dozens, then whittle them down. The more ideas you generate, the more likely it is you'll come across something truly outstanding.

Starting a charity is a really big commitment, and the idea is the largest driver of impact. You could execute flawlessly, but if you're running a charity distributing homeopathic medicine, you won't be helping anybody. You want to make sure you're committing to something worth the effort. Changing your direction later on is difficult, both logistically and psychologically.

When you brainstorm options, **don't limit yourself to charity ideas**. You should also **include alternatives** such as working for a direct charity, earning to give, starting a for-profit, and any other pursuit you think might plausibly have an impact.

One more tip: Test out multiple ideas.

People tend to settle on an idea and get married to it. If at all possible, try working on an idea for a bit before settling on your choice. This can even be worthwhile for cause areas. Many founders come into our program with one idea in mind and come out being more excited about a different one. Sometimes, finding a co-founder or working on a project for a bit can make a big difference in which idea you end up working on long term.

Really research your idea – then try to destroy it

This may seem obvious, but most people we have spoken to have not really done this. They stumble into an idea, then ask a few people what they think. Those people don't want to be critical and "crush your dreams," so the hopeful entrepreneur dives straight in.

If you really want to know if it's a good idea, research it. This is what EAs specialize in; play to your strengths! You can learn a lot about your idea before proceeding.

In fact, you can learn enough beforehand to know that you shouldn't actually do it in the first place. You should approach this with the attitude of trying to destroy your idea before you end up investing in and wasting time on something that you could have ruled out far faster.

Even more importantly, you want to rule it out before you become emotionally invested, or it will be far less likely that you'll ever be able to see that it's not a good idea. This is one of the greatest dangers lurking in the waters of charity entrepreneurship. If you are running a for-profit and it isn't making money, you'll eventually find out, no matter how much it hurts to admit. With a charity, the results are very rarely obvious. You could run something that has no impact, indefinitely, and fool both yourself and your donors.

While you can set up systems to check and make sure you are indeed helping,[2] it's easy to ignore them, move the goalposts, rationalize the results away, or use systems that don't actually falsify your program's impact, all in subtle ways that are hard for you to notice.

Of course, don't just try to destroy your program idea. Try to rebuild or strengthen the weaknesses you uncover. Returning to Chapter 11, play steelman solitaire: steelman counterarguments, then steelman counter-counterarguments, and so forth. Maybe your idea won't work because you don't have experience in the area. How could you get around that? Maybe you could find a co-founder who does? Maybe you could do a few months of intensive study in a very small area? That there is a problem with an idea does not necessarily mean that the problem is unsolvable.

For any idea, odds are somebody else has already tried it. See if you can find them. Google it, and ask people in the area. If it's been done, learn as much as you can about what happened. If it didn't work, why not? Is it something you could plausibly solve, or should you abandon the idea? Is it already being run well, such that it might be better simply to support the existing program with money or time? Alternatively, if it's being run well but only in a small section of its potential scope, you could use its success as a reason to scale it up, or run a similar program in a different location.

Another alternative is to start a charity based on research recommendations.

CE has put in thousands of expert hours into identifying top interventions.[3] Choosing one of them will give you a huge head start, alleviate analysis paralysis, and greatly increase the odds that your charity will succeed in making the world a better place.

---

2 For further reading, see Mary Kay Gugerty and Dean Karlan, *The Goldilocks Challenge: Right-Fit Evidence for the Social Sector* (California: OUP USA, 2018).

3 Check out Charity Entrepreneurship, "Charity Ideas," accessed Dec. 10, 2021, https://www.charityentrepreneurship.com/charity-ideas.html to see our up-to-date recommendations.

20. Co-founder

Each organization is, in essence, the people behind it. In the case of a start-up, those are the co-founders. Whom you pick as your partner will greatly affect decision-making and culture at your charity. Does your partner care about evidence? Are they energetic? These characteristics will reverberate across the organization as you recruit and manage staff, and interact with stakeholders.

There are many advantages to having a co-founder. Your partner will broaden your skill set, make your daily work fun, and increase the likelihood that you will stick through rough parts of the journey, as you can mutually support each other. Some start-up accelerators even have rules that recognize the comparative advantages of a partner: for instance, it is hard to get accepted at Y Combinator as a solo founder.

While you can reverse many decisions you make, the one about your co-founder is hard to turn around. A co-founder embodies part of the organization, so a departure can result in a loss of vision, implementing power, and atmosphere. It is no surprise that co-founder issues and split-ups are a common failure point for start-ups in the for-profit world.[1] In our experience, this finding translates to nonprofit start-ups as well.

---

1 Bretton Putter, "Startup due diligence begins with your cofounder(s)," Forbes, Feb. 25, 2019, https://www.forbes.com/sites/brettonputter/2019/02/25/cofoundd-startup-due-diligence-begins-with-your-cofounder/.

20.1. The ideal number of co-founders

Two is the sweet spot, according to many start-up connoisseurs. You get the benefits of a team with less of the friction of larger groups. However, this is no scientific rule: the evidence in the literature is mixed and depends on the context. A 2018 study, for example, concludes that solo founders outperform others in business settings.[2] So, these reflections should be taken with a grain of salt.

The friction of larger teams occurs in terms of both decision-making and burn rate. The more people there are, the harder it becomes to make decisions, as there are more opinions and points of view. There is also the danger of coalitions forming within the founding team; for instance, two co-founders could habitually vote against the third. Rapid decision-making is a key success factor for a start-up,[3] so anything that slows this down is a threat.

Besides decision-making, another factor that usually constrains charity start-ups is funding. Paying three instead of two salaries can be difficult at an early stage. The team might need to dedicate more resources to fundraising, rather than testing in the field. The pressure to scale an unproven concept will also be higher, as you might need to justify the bigger overhead to donors and to yourselves. With resources divided among more people, the salary of each founding team member may also be lower than in the two-person scenario. This, in turn, could affect motivation or cause financial difficulties.

In sum, you likely don't want to be a solo founder, and you need some additional justification for having three or more co-founders. Such larger teams might be more common in the world of tech or pharma start-ups, where very specific, hard-won expertise is required, and a team of three might combine business, tech, and science backgrounds. In the world of nonprofits or common businesses, two members should be able to cover the basic skill sets required. Perhaps most relevantly, in our experience running the CE program, two-person founding teams have worked better than solo or three-person teams.

---

2 Jason Greenberg and Ethan R. Mollick, "Sole Survivors: Solo Ventures Versus Founding Teams," Jan. 23, 2018, http://dx.doi.org/10.2139/ssrn.3107898.

3 Sam Altman, *Startup Playbook*, accessed Nov. 10, 2021, https://playbook.samaltman.com/#execution.

20.2. Aligned goals and values

The brightest and most successful co-founder candidate cannot be a match if they do not align with your values and goals.

You both need to be fully convinced about the cause area and intervention that your charity pursues. Consider both the rational and emotional levels: An EA co-founder might be sympathetic to the idea of switching from a poverty to an animal charity from a rational perspective, but if they are not fully bought-in emotionally, it could get tricky in trying times. Similarly, you set yourself up for many arguments if your co-founder has never been fully convinced of the specific intervention area, such as animal food fortification. Of course, the debate about the most effective intervention is vital at the beginning of a venture. But it should be settled within an agreed-upon timeframe, and not constantly pop up during daily operations. You will hit many roadblocks with any intervention, and this should not be an excuse to switch back and forth.

You need to share the same personal goals and timeframes. It will be a recipe for conflict if you see yourself leading a charity for five to 10 years, but your co-founder is interested in "trying out" charity entrepreneurship for only two. Watch out for co-founders who don't understand that setting up a new organization takes years, or who are already planning their next big thing.

You should share the key values of evidence-based charity entrepreneurship and effective altruism. Cost-effectiveness, solid impact measurement, tractability, and transparency all fall under this category. Don't trade these values for expert status or experience. Such compromises can be made at the level of your field staff, but at the co-founder level, ignoring these values will lead to poor decisions or value drift.

Grit: a short word with profound implications.[4] Pick a co-founder who has shown grit and tenacity in their professional and private life. Start-ups are often uncomfortable and hard, and you don't want your co-founder to jump ship when the first clouds appear.

There are many intelligent people out there, but your co-founder needs to combine intelligence with a proactive attitude. Pick someone who can get sh… done over the smartest person in the room. The journey of a start-up involves a lot of trial and error, and only moving forward will help you get the necessary

---

4 See Angela Duckworth's TED talk "Grit: The power of passion and perseverance."

feedback on your journey to success.

As in relationships, financial preferences are a common cause of conflict between co-founders. Ensure that yours has similar ideas on expenses. Lean toward frugality, as a high burn rate limits your time to test your program, while a modest budget attracts donors.

Pick someone who shares a similar perspective on work-life balance. There does not need to be perfect overlap here, but avoid going for someone who prefers to work much more or less than you, as this will lead to frustration or burnout. Of course, you can adapt your idea of work-life balance as your organization matures, but it helps to have a shared general understanding at the beginning.

20.3. Complementary skills

You both graduated from an Ivy League school in business administration, both like to work on headquarters-level tasks, and neither of you has ever worked in a developing country. This might not be the best setup in terms of complementary skills and interests. Ideally, in the case of a poverty charity, for instance, one co-founder brings experience and interest in working in the field. It is also helpful to have previous involvement in the area you are working on. For example, it is beneficial if at least one co-founder at an animal charity has been engaged in the space before. It is common in for-profits to have a technical founder who is responsible for software and product, and a non-technical founder responsible for the business side. At nonprofits, a well-balanced team can often consist of a founder with a background in research/programming and another with a background in business/communications.

It's unlikely that you'll achieve perfect overlap in terms of complementary skills. But strive to build a team where you have unique strengths and weaknesses. In the best case, you understand who is going to lead which domain from the beginning. One might be uniquely qualified for fundraising and other HQ-level tasks, while the other excels at program implementation in the field.

Consider the following skills and interests as you look for a co-founder fit:

- Cause-area experience
- Cost-effectiveness analysis
- Budgeting and financial planning
- Operations

- Fundraising
- Stakeholder relations
- Communications
- Human resources (incl. recruitment)
- Managing people
- Planning and task management
- Monitoring and evaluation
- Research
- Negotiations
- Customer focus and user experience

Complementary psychology

Potentially even more important than complementary skills are psychological traits that align within the co-founding team. This does not mean that you should be twins – it might well mean that you have opposite psychological traits. Someone might be more easy-going, while the other always has strong opinions. Someone might be more enthusiastic about new ideas, the other more skeptical and suited for reality checks. Someone might have many ups and downs, while the other is more steady. The team goes beyond its members.

On the other hand, differences in psychology can cause conflict. If one partner gains energy from heated disputes while the other would prefer to discuss disagreements more calmly, you will need to find a way of dealing with these differences.

All sounds a bit complex and fuzzy? Just consider whether you enjoy spending time with, and tackling challenges with, the person in front of you. If so, you might have found a good match from a personality perspective. As a step further, imagine that your charity has failed after many years of hard work. Would you still have enjoyed the journey together as co-founders? There is no need to be best friends, but don't go into this if you need to justify the decision to yourself ("We might not click, but the opportunity is too big to pass up…"). That's a bad start, as in the end, a venture is all about people.

Logistical factors

So, you've found your perfect match, but he or she lives on a different continent. Is this a dealbreaker? Start-up wisdom holds that you should be based in the same location. In-person communication often allows you to move faster and build stronger personal ties. Yet, there are examples of business (e.g., Zapier) and nonprofit (e.g., New Incentives) start-ups that had a remote setup from the beginning without experiencing substantial disadvantages.

If you are looking for a co-founder, you still want to prioritize someone with whom you can work in person. This includes candidates who may not already live in your location, but are willing to relocate – and, importantly, who have the necessary citizenship to get a visa. Unfortunately, this last factor restricts your choice and is unfair to potential founders from certain countries. Yet, experience shows that visa status should be considered. Several previous CE Incubation Program graduates struggled with this issue.

Real work

As with recruiting staff, your impression of a candidate from their CV and conversations might be misleading. The real test comes only with real work. As a result, you will want to test your co-founder working relationship with minor common assignments before you jump right in. You could, for instance, work on a short research summary or an overview of the planned intervention. It's a great sign if such a test collaboration is inspiring to both sides and results in a strong outcome that goes beyond what you each would have achieved as individuals.

The longer you have known a person, the more certainty you have about their suitability. However, if you're considering starting your charity with a good friend, consider the following questions:

- Has your relationship included common work assignments, or was it limited to fun leisure activities? Of course, you would want to consider how the other person performs in a work situation.
- Are you fine with your start-up impacting your friendship? If you launch a venture with a good friend, both of you should acknowledge that this could go incredibly well, as you know and respect each other, but it could also mean the end of a dear friendship. Be sure you both understand that in case of conflict, the charity's future, not your friendship's trajectory, will likely be the deciding factor.

20.4. How to find your co-founder

Charity Entrepreneurship's Incubation Program prioritizes various activities aimed at successful co-founder selection. Team-building exercises and projects are crucial to help you get a strong understanding of your co-founder before you make the decision that defines your charity and, potentially, your professional life.

If you plan to start your charity outside the Charity Entrepreneurship program, we recommend modeling your process similarly.

- Make meeting potential co-founders a priority, and go about it systematically. Don't expect the first person you meet at a random event to be your match made in heaven.
- Go through the list of characteristics above together.
- Make use of questionnaires aimed at picking a co-founder. FirstRound's "50 Questions to Explore with a Potential Co-Founder" is a good option. It is geared toward for-profits and includes some questions that don't apply to a charity, but it is still a helpful resource.
- Respond to more general questionnaires. Even those that originate in the field of dating, like *The New York Times'* "The 36 Questions That Lead to Love," add value when picking a co-founder.
- Take personality tests to identify potential areas of overlap, complementarity, or friction. OpenPsychometrics is a great resource.
- If you are confident that you have found a match, start discussing a Founders' Agreement (outlined in Chapter 32).

Having a clear process and defining what you are looking for is a solid starting point. At the same time, be realistic. You are not looking for a superwoman or superman, but a human being who has flaws like you. Ask about whether you complement each other well, and whether both or all potential co-founders are a good fit for (charity) entrepreneurship. So instead of trying to find someone who stands out in all areas, define your own set of co-founder must-haves and nice-to-haves as you go about your search.

If you don't immediately find a co-founder you are looking forward to working with, give it some time. You can always start working as a solo founder and bring someone on board later. This still trumps settling for a poor choice. Eventually, you will find your perfect match.

Happy searching!

21. Country

Your choice of location can make a big difference to your chances of successfully overcoming initial logistical hurdles, as well as to your estimated cost-effectiveness in later stages. Once you pick a location, it can be difficult to change it. Aside from general expenses, many location-specific networks and skills may not transfer from place to place.

21.1. The greatest addressable need

How many potential beneficiaries stand to benefit from your intervention? When working on global health interventions focused on humans, you can usually help the most people if you work in an area with a large population that suffers from severe poverty, and especially where people suffer from easily preventable health issues. A proportionately smaller number of people who are in need live in more affluent locations such as New York, London, or Tokyo, and it is generally more difficult to alleviate those types of suffering using a very small amount of money.

It's often also helpful to work in locations that present fewer logistical challenges. Locations such as Syria, South Sudan, Afghanistan, or the D.R.C. have many people who are suffering from issues such as malnutrition and disease, which may at face value seem easily preventable. However, it is often difficult to alleviate this suffering cost-effectively, because violence, political instability, and lack of infrastructure make it difficult to operate in these countries (though certainly possible – for instance, Against Malaria Foundation distributes nets in both Sudan and the D.R.C.[1]).

Finally, it's important to work in a population where there's a large number of potential beneficiaries for your intervention. Before pivoting to using conditional cash transfers for vaccinations, New Incentives used cash transfers to incentivize HIV-positive pregnant women to give birth in a clinic, where appropriate procedures can minimize the risk of disease transmission to the infant. While the intervention was cost-effective, the organization was unable to scale because there wasn't a large enough population of potential beneficiaries – and they were spread out across hundreds of clinics.[2]

Organizations working in areas with a high burden of very harmful but easily preventable issues are able to use money to do good more cost-effectively.[3] Working in locations such as New Delhi has the advantage of juxtaposing the infrastructure of a city (for instance, medical supplies, helpful government agencies, qualified staff) and close access to extreme poverty. These are also locations with large populations and high population densities, ensuring a large pool of potential beneficiaries. In these regions, you will often find situations where you can accomplish a great deal of good for many people at low cost. Populations in such locations will often be served by other organizations, and it's worth keeping track of who else is working in the space.

Remote regions are often poorer than large cities. Even these areas are usually relatively easily accessible from nearby towns (within a few hours' drive). Northwest Nigeria, where New Incentives operates, has several larger towns that function well as operational hubs, and Kano is a megacity with access to international flights.

This advice can change quite a bit depending on the particulars of what one is working on. When working on policy interventions, population size and disease burden often still matter, but the degree of affluence might be less important. It might be cost-effective to work in middle- or even high-income countries. When working with animals, it's still worth thinking about the total number of animals

1 Against Malaria Foundation, "Net Distributions," accessed Nov. 10, 2021, https://www.againstmalaria.com/Nets.aspx.

2 Elie Hassenfeld, "New Incentives update," The GiveWell Blog, Feb. 12, 2021, https://blog.givewell.org/2016/10/06/new-incentives-update/.

3 GiveWell, "Your Dollar Goes Further Overseas," accessed Nov. 10, 2021, https://www.givewell.org/giving101/Your-dollar-goes-further-overseas.

involved and the severity of the welfare issues in various locations, but there are new logistical considerations. Many logistic issues overlap (e.g., safety issues), but some are distinct. Two locations may have a similar number of animals, but convincing a single corporation to implement a change in practice across their production facilities is different from convincing many unregulated small-scale farmers to do the same. It's good to make a list of which considerations are most likely to apply to your intervention.

21.2. How location influences logistical hurdles

Running a highly cost-effective intervention generally means you must make use of local resources rather than build everything from scratch. If you want to distribute vaccines, you don't open an entire hospital – you work with an existing one to subsidize or incentivize treatment. If you want to fortify food, you don't open a mill – you work with existing mills and enable them to fortify. When it comes to infrastructure, common factors that might make a difference include:

- General infrastructure: This depends on the intervention you are working on, but it's tough to work with hospitals, schools, and other institutions that are chronically understaffed. This problem can be fairly severe in some cases – for example, some cash transfer programs pay health workers more to incentivize them to show up to work.[4]

- The "informal sector": In low-income countries, it's common for the majority of the population to work in the "informal sector." That means that they start businesses or are employed without any formal contracts with or recognition from any government. Informal supply chains have many implications for interventions based on lobbying and corporate campaigns.

- Access to financial services: Any intervention that requires exchanging money with beneficiaries becomes easier if they have access to some form of financial service.

- Phone access: Many interventions require you to be in contact with

---

4 For an overview, see The Cash Learning Partnership, "The State of the World's Cash 2020," accessed Nov. 10, 2021, https://www.calpnetwork.org/resources/collections/state-of-the-worlds-cash-2020/.

your beneficiaries. Also note that having a phone means that beneficiaries may have access to mobile financial instruments (for example,
M-Pesa, a branchless banking service).

- Access to electricity: Low or inconsistent access to electricity spells
  trouble for many interventions. It might be difficult to keep medicine
  refrigerated or aerators for fish running (many fish farms are just holes
  dug into the ground, nowhere near electricity). This also means that
  beneficiaries will often have dead phone batteries, and so are uncontactable.

- Proximity to talent: If you want to hire skilled people who live near
  your intervention site and share a language in common with you, it's
  often easier if the intervention site is near a large city where a lot of
  qualified people might live.

In addition to those relating specifically to interacting with your beneficiaries,
there are also logistical hurdles to consider regarding the day-to-day realities of
running an organization.

- General lack of standardization: Some locations may use multiple
  languages, with dialects changing sharply from place to place. You
  often can't rely on buses and trains being consistent or predictable.
  In some places, you can't take for granted the idea of "addresses,"
  which can make finding beneficiaries tough. People might not use
  the same calendar as you – or any calendar. Legal standards are often
  inconsistently applied as well.

- Corruption: In some places, it is difficult to do anything without being
  asked to pay bribes. This can happen even when dealing with law en-
  forcement, government officials, and other authorities one might seek
  out for recourse. (It goes without saying that bribery is not acceptable
  for a charity entrepreneur!)

- Bureaucracy: Some places have bureaucratic systems that are difficult
  to navigate. You may find yourself struggling to do things such as open
  a bank account or phone line.

- Health and safety: You and your staff may hesitate to work near certain places due to health and safety concerns. Some factors that may be detrimental to health and safety might include low availability of medical care, local diseases, food safety, availability of drinking water, high traffic conditions, air pollution, targeted harassment due to race, gender, or sexual orientation, military conflicts, and crime.

Not all of these factors will matter to you, and there will likely be additional factors not listed here that will. When choosing a location, do some thinking about the logistics of your intervention[5] and try to get data on the factors likely to be most relevant to you.

If you are able to overcome the initial logistical hurdles and set up your charity, the next challenge is to achieve a level of cost-effectiveness sufficient to justify scaling. Location makes a big difference when it comes to these factors.

The yearly chance of being infected with pertussis in Northwestern Nigeria is 30%. In India, it is only 10%. This is obviously an important consideration when thinking about the relative importance of providing vaccinations for this disease to those in Northwestern Nigeria vs. India. (However, bear in mind that this reflects the choice to use statistics for "India" as a whole – a more localized analysis would reveal that different Indian states have wildly different health outcomes.)[6]

This can lead to the cost-effectiveness between locations being orders of magnitude different from each other, even with the exact same intervention. If we enter data from India into an otherwise unchanged cost-effectiveness estimate of New Incentives in Northwestern Nigeria, it will change quite a bit. The benefits would reduce, because the former as a whole has a better baseline vaccination rate than the latter. The costs would reduce as well, because Delhi is more affordable than Lagos. Our new hypothetical charity would end up being about 25% less cost-effective.

5 For further reading, see Charity Entrepreneurship, "How Logistics Will Influence Which Intervention You Pick," April 17, 2017, https://www.charityentrepreneurship.com/blog/how-logistics-will-influence-which-intervention-you-pick.

6 See GiveWell, "Charity Science Health - Exit Grant," Dec. 2019, https://www.givewell.org/research/incubation-grants/charity-science-exit-grant-july-2019, for CSH's CEA.

21.3. Geographic selection templates

Studying examples can be the best way to create your own process for choosing a location. Your crucial considerations will be specific to you, but we've compiled some helpful examples from our previously incubated charities for you to get an idea of how they came to a decision.

Fortify Health's Country/location selection decision spreadsheet, pictured below, includes the DALY burden of anemia (remedied by iron), neural tube defects (remedied by folic acid), and malaria risk (because iron supplementation may increase this risk) in each potential location. It also estimates important logistical factors, such as centralization of wheat supply chains, cooperativeness and effectiveness of the government, and safety, as well as personal factors particular to the founders, such as language barriers and preexisting networks of helpful contacts. Finally, there are estimates regarding crowdedness in the field with regard to supplementation programs that already exist.

metric	DALYs Rate (/100,000 population)	DALYs	DALYs	Prevalence Percent	Deaths Rate	Deaths Rate	Deaths Rate	Population (millions) Number	DALYs Rate	Greatest untapped potential of centralized fortification (g/person/day produced in industrial mills not currently fortified)	Political barriers and conflict (these were rapid subjective ratings initially used for country selection - see adjacent columns with worldbank data for improved objectivity)	Government Effectiveness	These data (presented as z-scores) corroborate subjective scoring used in initial selection, but were added to this sheet post hoc for comparison — Political Stability and Absence of Violence/Terrorism	population (log scaled)
view as		Rate	Rate		Rate	Rate	Rate		Rate					
condition	Iron-deficiency anemia	Neural tube defects	Malaria	Iron-deficiency anemia	Iron-deficiency anemia	Neural tube defects	Malaria	People	IDA + NTDs					
Average of top 20 after first											1.06	-0.67	-0.48	0.39
Average of top 5 after first											1.20	-0.51	-0.22	0.31
Filter/sort in this row -->								Y						
India	1235	26	248	33%	0.03	0.06	3.65	1324.2	1261	94.8	0	0.1	-0.955	0.99
Tanzania	697	125	2279	24%	0.06	1.07	29.42	55.6	822	19.8	0	-0.55	-0.408	0.56
Mauritius	655	25	0	27%	0.01	0.08	0.01	1.3	680	296.4	0	0.958	1.048	0.04
Chad	1336	671	3574	37%	0.04	7.31	44.32	14.5	2207	0.0	2	-1.494	-1.206	0.37
Mauritania	918	354	509	30%	0.03	3.61	6.44	4.3	1272	118.0	2	-0.787	-0.736	0.20
Zambia	561	88	2440	18%	0.07	0.65	31.28	16.6	649	113.8	2	-0.658	0.183	0.39
Ghana	922	237	5133	28%	0.70	2.27	69.67	28.2	1159	4.0	2	-0.202	-0.162	0.46
Ethiopia	472	85	118	17%	0.07	0.55	1.31	102.4	557	47.3	2	-0.639	-1.569	0.64

Fortify Health's State selection decision spreadsheet[7] goes into greater detail regarding the consumption and supply chains of atta (wheat flour). It narrows down which states have a confluence of anemia and high consumption of atta from centralized supply chains (such that it would be easy to introduce and monitor fortification in just a few mills and have a large impact).

Charity Entrepreneurship's preliminary country research[8] will be generally helpful for animal-focused organizations. This includes data on farmed meat production by species in number of individuals, consumption by species in weight, legal protections for animals, trade agreements, public attitudes, English

---

7 Available at https://bit.ly/FHstatetool.
8 Available at https://bit.ly/CEcountrytool.

proficiency, and other useful metrics.

Fish Welfare Initiative used a five-step process based on CE's country research:

- Generate a longlist of promising countries
    - Pick countries that do well on the spreadsheet, as well as countries that experts or respected sources recommended.
    - Enter in some other countries, especially those that are unusual in some way, to test the validity of internal metrics.
- Create a middle-list
    - Spend 30 minutes reading each CE report (found in the Country Rating subspreadsheet) and 15 minutes writing up pros and cons for each item on the longlist.
    - Eliminate half of the least promising options.
- Create a shortlist
    - Spend two hours identifying crucial considerations and researching them or asking experts. (Crucial considerations[9] can radically shift your estimates about how likely something is to work. In this case, some crucial considerations included "Do interventions involving oxygenators work on a farm with inconsistent electricity?" or "How centralized is the production of fish in each region?")
    - Eliminate the least promising option.
- Create a top five
    - For each remaining item, spend two hours reading and talking to experts until you can identify the top five.
- Rank the top five. Visit the top five countries if it helps narrow them down. Spend 12 hours writing up reports based on the findings.

---

9 Check out Pablo Stafforini, "'Crucial Considerations and Wise Philanthropy,' by Nick Bostrom." *Pablo's Miscellany*, last updated Feb. 2, 2020, http://www.stafforini.com/blog/bostrom/.

22.   Summary: Key decisions

We have now put our tools into action, applying them to some of the hardest questions an aspiring charity entrepreneur will need to consider: career, charity idea, co-founder, and country.

Underpinning the choices you make are your values. Ethical concern is likely one of the reasons you picked up this book. But ethics can be complex, and your views can significantly affect your charity's payload.

22.1. Values

The expanding moral circle illustrates the gradual increase in the number of beings we hold morally relevant. For many of you reading this book, moral concern reaches beyond our family and communities, covering continents and even crossing the boundary of species.

Often our actions impact multiple groups, and we need to make trade-offs in doing good. In such cases, a moral parliament, i.e., imagining a parliament house filled with 100 ministers representing ethical perspectives rather than political parties, can help you figure out the best path forward.

One death is a tragedy, and a million deaths, a statistic. We're bad at comprehending suffering at scale, but we can't let this hold us back. It's not enough to do good; we must try to do the *most* good.

How can we maintain our ethical principles and avoid value drift?

- Draw a line in the sand (e.g., commit to always pledge X% of your income)
- Surround yourself with people who share your values and drive for impact

22.2. Career area

For career area, it is important to map out the impact of your options in a quantified way, such as using a CEA or WFM, but also to take into account softer factors like personal fit, expert views, and feedback loops while following your chosen path. Having a sense of your best options and how they compare will allow you to see if charity entrepreneurship is at the top, or even a good fit overall. Considering at least a dozen careers on at least five tools is a good baseline for such an important call.

There are several alternatives to charity entrepreneurship. Some might suit you better; others might be a good interim solution until you jump back into your next co-founding adventure. The key point is that entrepreneurship is not necessarily "now or never." You should not only consider the next few months but also your longer-term career trajectory.

Some key advantages of several careers:

Career	Advantages
Founding a charity	· Extremely high impact · Builds a lot of skills in many different areas · Personally rewarding for people who are a good personality fit
Work at CE	· Support various future charities · Research-only positions available · Option to jump back into a charity at some point
Work at a CE-incubated charity	· Higher likelihood of success · Dynamic, but slightly more structured · CE spirit
Work at another EA organization	· Higher likelihood of success · Dynamic, but slightly more structured

Work at other NGO or foundation in a chosen field	· Potentially much more established and high funding volume · Ability to shape non-EA org
Work in policy	· More stable environment (e.g., public servant) · High amounts of leverage · Higher standard of living
Earning to give	· Focus on your key strengths and factors for job motivation · Funding gaps are prevalent in certain areas · Low risk of replaceability · Higher standard of living
Career capital	· Get ready for future leadership role at an evidence-based charity · Some earning to give potential · Higher standard of living

Questions to ask yourself:

1. Have I deeply considered multiple paths?
2. Have I tried out a couple of paths to test for fit?
3. Do I have a specific idea of what job a given path would lead to?

22.3. Charity idea

There are countless charity ideas out there, and using research to narrow them down will give you the best shot at starting a high-impact one. Some of the factors relevant to choosing an area are ethical, particularly at a higher level like cause selection, but as you gather more options, narrow evidence and cost-effectiveness become bigger factors. Although it's hard to know exactly which charities or cause areas are the most impactful, we can take a good guess at areas and ideas that are in the top tier of effectiveness. Researching a charity idea takes major time, and it's often worth largely deferring to research that has already been done in the space when it comes to specific implementation.

If you're considering starting a charity, begin with the fundamentals before thinking about how to fundraise and register as a not-for-profit. Figure out if your idea is a good one in the first place. Make sure to consider at least ten options and then research them, looking for disconfirming evidence before making the leap.

Questions to ask yourself:

1. How much research has been done in this area?

2. Is this an area I would be highly motivated to work on?

3. Do I know why one charity idea is more impactful than another, or what factors would push a person one way or the other?

Area	Direct cost-effective-ness	Relevant evidence	Limiting factor	Execution difficulty	Non-captured externalities
Mental health	Moderate	Some	Funding (1)	Easier	EA movement (3)
Family planning	Low	Moderate	Logistical (4)	Complex	Child, animals (4)
Animal welfare	High	Low	Talent (2)	Easier	Bar setting (2)
Health policy	High	High	Funding (3)	Complex	Precedent (1)
Meta charities	Moderate	Low	Logistical (4)	Easier	Moderate (3)

22.4. Co-founder

A co-founder will be your first team member and your co-captain, driving your charity forward. You both need to enjoy spending time and working with each other, as well as bring useful tools to the table.

Why is it important? Your choice of co-founder isn't easily undone, and co-founder friction is a common cause of start-up failure. A good co-founder complements your skills, makes your work more fun, and helps you stick through hard times.

What do you look for? In most cases, aim for a team of two co-founders total. You should have aligned goals and values (e.g., cost-effectiveness, proactive attitude), complementary skills (e.g., the field experience you lack), complementary psychology (e.g., enthusiastic if you are skeptical; similar conflict resolution behaviors), and a visa to work in person as a co-founder team. Experience working together is a helpful tool as it gives you a real-life sense of how well you jive, so start with some trial tasks if you have never collaborated prior to your start-up.

How do you look for them? CE's Incubation Program is an ideal setting, involving team-building exercises and work projects to test out your fit. If you plan to start your charity outside the program, design a similarly systematic co-founder search process.

Questions to ask yourself:

1. Do we have complementary skills and psychology, but shared values?

2. When we collaborate, do we produce great work?

22.5. Country selection

Selecting a location is one of the most important decisions you will make about your intervention. Logistical hurdles differ from place to place, and choosing a location with many hurdles can make the initial setup and scaling of your charity challenging. Location considerations can also dramatically alter the ultimate cost-effectiveness of your charity when the time comes to scale. Choosing correctly can make the difference between success and failure.

Once you have identified the location-driven factors that are most important for your success, both in terms of logistics and cost-effectiveness, you are ready to begin researching which location is best suited for you to operate in.

Studying the examples of how some of our other incubatees have chosen their locations will likely be the most helpful starting point for creating a research process of your own.

Questions to ask yourself:

1. Is the location I am considering a good fit for the problem? This usually means low baseline rates of, e.g., vaccinations, and high poverty, which results in higher mortality.

2. Is it easy to scale work out of this location? This usually means, first, high population numbers of affected individuals, and second, ease of scalability (e.g., high mobile phone penetration rates for a vaccination reminder charity, government openness to your program, safety, etc.).

3. Do I have any networks that will make it logistically easier to operate out of a given location?

Part IV. Gathering support

The propulsion system is the fuel that gives your rocket speed. This corresponds to your ability to gather support and communicate. Without fuel, it will be hard to gain funding or staff, and your accomplishments will slow. Even if you're heading in the right direction, you won't get there fast.

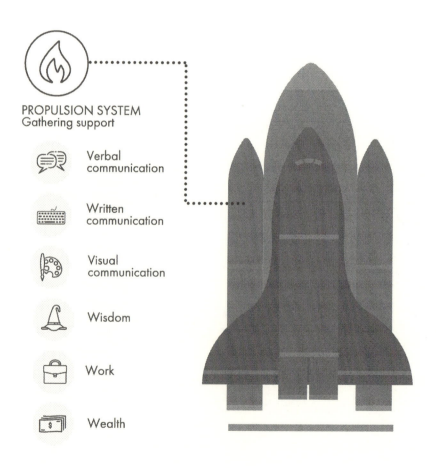

PROPULSION SYSTEM
Gathering support

Verbal communication

Written communication

Visual communication

Wisdom

Work

Wealth

23. How to be a people person

The most common form of communication is verbal. It's also the one that most people find intimidating – public speaking is often ranked as a top fear.

We tend to think of verbal skills as an innate talent. But, although some people are more naturally charismatic, good communication – like anything else – can be learned. A big part of this is practice and thinking consciously about presentation. Of course, there's no magic formula; it's crucial to think critically about each unique situation. But some general principles are worth keeping in mind.

In this section, we go through some actionable tips about active communication. Fundamentally, communication is what we're doing all the time – swapping information, ideas, stories. Active communication means being thoughtful and deliberate. This can help you relay your ideas and listen more effectively, which in turn can help you strengthen your relationships and better achieve your goals.

23.1. Getting your point across

The six Ws are what, who, when, where, why, and (an honorary W) how (and in Chapters 26 and 28, we introduce wealth and wisdom as well). In the context of communications, it means asking the following questions:

- What message am I trying to convey?
- Whom am I trying to reach?

- When is the best time and where is the best place to have this conversation?

- Why do I want to communicate this point, and why to this person?

- And bringing all these together: How am I going to adapt my communication strategy to get my point across most effectively?

You don't want to walk into an important conversation without thinking about what message you want to convey.

What: It seems like a no-brainer, but you want to be really clear on this. Write it out in a sentence for yourself so as to help you not lose sight of your point in the midst of its packaging. Before talking to an important mentor, you might formalize your thinking: "I want to convey that my organization is young but promising, and could use their help."

Who: An effective altruist is more likely to be interested in the data and evidence. So think about adopting a highly rational style, and emphasize the numbers. Someone else might be more interested in stories than in numbers: to better reach them, you might anchor your data in concrete details of individual lives. The more familiar you are with your audience, as a group or as an individual, the more you can fine-tune your message. "Normally I talk to academics and am careful to hedge my statements. But for this group of Silicon Valley for-profit entrepreneurs, I should try to be more bold and decisive in my claims."

When & where: 4:50 p.m. on a Friday might not be the best time to raise a delicate issue, but could be good for a quick end-of-the-week check-in. Sometimes a general announcement will get your point across without singling anyone out; other times a private meeting is more appropriate. Use your judgment and try to be understanding – there might be something else going on (e.g., a recently underperforming employee might be feeling under the weather). "What time zone is this person in? Maybe I don't want to book the earliest or latest slot open on their calendar."

Why: It's worth thinking about your motives to make sure that you're approaching this conversation for the right reasons, and that it is indeed important. You should consider why they would care about what you have to say. "When talking to a new possible hire, I should let them know how their job would contribute to the impact of the organization as a whole."

How: It's vital to tailor your strategy to the situation and the individual(s) involved. Is this a quick and simple message that you can send via Slack? Or is it more complex, worth discussing face to face to minimize misunderstandings? Another thing to think about here is whether to opt for a direct or indirect communication style. In the interest of tact, it's probably better to start out indirectly, by dropping hints. Generally, people are more likely to change their behavior if it's their own idea rather than one imposed on them. Bring out the sledgehammer as a last resort: if you focus on communicating positively and constructively, you'll often find that problems resolve themselves without confrontation. "I need to have a difficult talk with employee B about their slow work. I should probably bring this up in a one-on-one meeting so I can be sure to use a friendly tone."

23.2. Strong relationships

To build solid working relationships, you'll sometimes need to give others feedback (and be ready to accept feedback on your own performance).

Providing positive feedback can guide others and amplify their strengths. So when someone does well, highlight what they did that was good, and note why you liked it. Often, they will then build on that strength in other areas of their work, preempting your input. Feel free to give positive feedback publicly or in front of the team. During our weekly meetings at Charity Entrepreneurship, each member of our team talks about what they worked on, but also what they are grateful for. Often this is work done by someone else on the team, making this practice a simple way to build lots of positive feelings in a team.

As you integrate positivity into your relationships, the piggy bank model can be a useful framework. Imagine that each positive experience with someone puts, say, $1 in a piggy bank. But each negative experience takes, say, $5 out.[1] (You don't need to keep score religiously here – the piggy bank is just a helpful mental image to get a sense of scale.)

To stay in the black, you want to be proactive about sharing positive experiences. This might mean recognizing someone's hard work and thanking them for it. It might mean organizing team lunches or social events, like drinks or board game nights. Essentially, the goal is to cultivate a positive atmosphere, rather than letting negativity take root. You also need to build up some currency before

---

1 Bridget de Maine, "How Many Good Experiences Finally Outweigh a Bad One?" Collective Hub (blog), May 15, 2017, https://collectivehub.com/2017/05/how-many-good-experiences-finally-outweigh-a-bad-one/.

having harder conversations. The piggy bank starts at zero, but if you build up some strong savings you will be able to have the more difficult conversations and still remain in the black.

Extend this positivity as broadly as possible – try to maintain it when problems inevitably arise. If someone has done something to irritate you, ask yourself: could this be a simple miscommunication? Should I just let it go, or should we talk about it? Open communication channels will help here.

To make sure you're addressing any issues constructively, it's best not to let things simmer. This will help you avoid starting a discussion when you're angry (always a bad idea!). Try to check in with people once a week, both to see how things are going and to give yourselves an opportunity to discuss anything that might come up. If you feel heated and need to talk about something important, try to sleep on it. You'd never make an important decision without thinking about it for 24 hours. The same should be true for important conversations.

Sometimes conflict is inevitable, but it doesn't have to be aggressive. Think about Marshall Rosenberg's theory of nonviolent communication. In brief, frame issues in terms of how you feel, rather than rushing to criticize the other person.[2] For example, instead of saying, "By being late, you're being inconsiderate and not valuing my time," you might say, "When you're late, I feel neglected because I want to use my time productively."

If possible, try to address conflict in person (or, if working remotely, via video). Communicating tone is difficult via text, and you want to make sure that neither of you misinterprets the other.

23.3. General principles

Many great writers speak about the value of getting to practice their work in person with a live audience. This allows them to cut elements that are weak or boring and pick out the gems to focus on. The same technique can be used in any verbal conversation. Did that joke you just tell fall flat? Maybe you don't tell it again, or try a different crowd. Does someone seem hurt by what you just said? Now might be a good time to soften the claim and reassure them.

Tuning in to how other people respond to you allows you to get feedback on

---

2 Marshall Rosenberg, *Nonviolent Communication* (California: Puddledancer Press, 2015). You can view a summary and analysis on Shortform.com.

your communication skills. So practice! Have you explained your charity idea to your friends, your parents, the people you meet at conferences? Practicing with a wide range of groups and audiences will give you the skills you need to explain your idea to anyone, and the more you practice, the better you'll get. A strong communicator can adapt their style on the fly to the type of person they are talking to.

Getting feedback can also help you become more self-aware – an important quality for a charity entrepreneur. It can help your work: if you know that you're a procrastinator, you can set up workarounds. And it can help your relationships: taking in an outside perspective on yourself can help you understand where the other person is coming from.

Part of self-awareness is thinking about how you present yourself. On the most basic level, make sure you're clean (e.g., aim to shower a few hours before an important in-person conversation and get some xylitol mints) and dressed appropriately for the situation (err on the side of formal if you are unsure). Beyond these basics, consider the more complex questions about your identity and how it may be read. For example, trying to do the right thing can be perceived as holier-than-thou – think about the negative connotations of the word "do-gooder," or "vegan." Knowing that this might be a risk, you can navigate accordingly in your self-presentation – be humble, perhaps, and recognize that moral perfection is unattainable. Hopefully, you can then avoid making others feel defensive and thereby alienating them.

So how do you become more self-aware?

- Make sure that you're open to feedback. You can do this simply by listening, but you can also actively seek it out. However, asking for feedback can make even close friends and family feel awkward. If you do want to ask someone, make sure they know that you respond well to criticism by being appreciative of feedback in other contexts.

- Be conscious of your thoughts and feelings. Practicing mindfulness or meditation can help with this, as can journaling. (As a bonus, building these habits can help your mood and happiness more broadly.)

- Consider taking a personality test. The point is not to take the outcome as gospel truth – there are tons of doubts about how accurate such tests are. It's more to get you reflecting on who you are as you answer the questions.

24. Writing to be read

Trillions of words float around the internet. And in all this flood, your words need to stand out. How do you get people to read what you've written?

The best way to improve your writing is to practice. Beyond that simple rule, this chapter offers you some more specific guidelines on how to write well. The overarching takeaways are that you should think about your priorities, audience, word choice, and presentation. And throughout, aim to write in plain English.

Let's go into these points in a bit more detail. (Embracing the irony that our book does not consistently follow all these principles!)

24.1. Prioritize

Ideally, every word and sentence you write is painstakingly crafted. But deadlines exist. If you're under time pressure, get the most important bits perfect, and the rest right.

Far and above the most important sections of any article are the title, the lede (journalist's lingo for the opening line, also written as lead), and the final sentence(s). Crafting them should take a while and multiple attempts. Shoot for ten if possible, and get feedback on which is best.

Frontload key takeaways. Sometimes when we're reading, life gets in the way. Make sure your readers get the most important information ASAP – we're all busy.

24.2. Think about your audience

Always. When you're communicating with a specific person or group, you can tailor your communication style to each individual. But if you're publishing an article online, for example, you don't know who exactly will stumble across it, and **what's intended is less important than what's understood**. In this case, writing for your audience means appealing to a broad swathe of people, probably skewing toward an analytical bent.

The first question to ask yourself is: what does your audience want? Write about how you can meet these wants, rather than focusing on what your organization needs. For example, instead of "it would be great to get some funding for X," write that "we can help you implement X." Simple reframings highlight for your audience the value of your organization, plus allow you time to reflect on your impact and goals.

As well as taking the specific point of view of your audience, it's worth being more generally aware of how people think. Necessarily, your audience is human – and that means that cognitive biases creep in. For example, compassion fade can mean that as the numbers increase, a tragedy becomes a statistic. That we humans are bad at comprehending suffering at scale doesn't mean you shouldn't talk about it, but it does mean that you'll want to think carefully about how to convey your message without losing its power to inevitable human biases.

No matter how beautifully you tailor your message, you won't get your point across if by contortuplicated syntax and needlessly eruditical language it is obscured. (Wasn't that painful to read?) Writing for a broad audience means writing in plain English. This does not mean dumbing it down, but rather keeping it clear. In some ways, writing in plain English is harder than hiding behind a more complicated writing style. But it's the best way to get your point across.

- One plain English tip is to keep your sentences short. Generally, cap them at 20 words or so.

24.3. Choose your words carefully

Plain English is also something to be aware of as you choose your words. Bear in mind:

- Connotations make or break – think of the difference between a terrorist and a freedom fighter.

- For animal advocacy in particular, compare "marketing" and "outreach"; "vegan" and "plant-based"; "diet" and "lifestyle."

- Strong verbs reinforce your meaning; don't over-rely on adverbs. The same goes for nouns and adjectives.

- Instead of "negatively affect," what about "damage" or "harm"?

- Try to avoid long words or phrases when a shorter one does the trick – e.g., "use" vs. "utilize," "after" vs. "subsequent to."

- Watch out for nominalizations: instead of "give consideration to," "consider"; instead of "have a discussion," "discuss."

Decide which point of view to use. For example, you might want to opt for "we" rather than "you," which can come across as accusatory. Using "we" also has the benefit of creating a connection between you and the reader: it implies you're in this together. On the other hand, you might choose "you" to try and galvanize your audience into action by highlighting their role in a situation (e.g., your donation helps xyz). This is a perfectly legitimate choice, but you might then phrase things more cautiously to avoid alienating your reader.

24.4. Presentation

No matter how perfectly you've chosen your words, readers will balk at un-friendly formatting or huge blocks of text. The format you opt for depends on the information you're trying to convey. Would this topic be better addressed as a listicle, or a formal report? Once you've chosen your format, make sure to match your tone. A more conversational style might be appropriate for a blog, but not for an official report. Feel free to use contractions in the former, but not the latter.

A shorter article is more friendly to someone scrolling the web at the end of a long day. But you don't want it to seem like you're trivializing a complex problem. Usually, a good option might be to strike a middle ground. Section headings, bullet points, and shorter paragraphs can help you keep things accessible with-out oversimplifying, allowing readers to navigate to topics that interest them.

It goes without saying, but always triple check grammar and spelling. Think too about nuts and bolts like consistency – do you use American or British English, for example? What's your policy on hyphenation? Put such things in a house style guide so that your charity's voice doesn't fluctuate wildly. You can also use your style guide to set out formatting preferences: little details like which font you use, and what point; when to bold or italicize. These details might seem tiny, but they're worth getting right.

- Tip: to set up your default styles in Google Docs, go to Format -> Paragraph styles -> Options -> Save as my default styles. To align a document (new or preexisting) to these defaults, navigate again to Options -> Use my default styles.

Final points

Putting it all together, your writing should aim to be:

- Concise
- Clear
- Compelling
- Consistent
- Error-free

Thinking about priorities, audience, word choice, and presentation will help you with this. But beyond these starting points, good writing is good editing. This means both editing your own work and getting outside input. If possible, do this at several stages of the process – as you're writing, and after you've produced the first version.

- Draft aloud. Reread aloud. Does it sound natural? Can you cut or rephrase?
- Make it strange. Write it out and leave it for a few days (deadlines permitting). When you come back to your writing, a different headspace makes it easier to see which parts might be unclear.
- Circulate documents throughout your team. Use as many pairs of eyes as possible to catch those slippery mistakes, as well as to ensure your charity's voice is consistent.

25. The 90/10 of looking good online

One of the most common start-up mistakes is **focusing on building the perfect product** (i.e., website, branding, blog) before **putting effort into** outreach or **community building**. We are constantly surrounded by millions of dollars worth of advertising, and it can seem like without the help of a graphic designer, developer, and a large budget, we will not look professional as an NGO. Nothing could be further from the truth.

This chapter will show you where to start when creating your charity's brand online. It will prove that at the beginning of your charity's journey, you don't need professionals or big budgets to reach people successfully. Things like building a website, creating a logo, picking color schemes and fonts, and producing leaflets, posters, reports, and presentations, you can all do yourself or with the help of an intern.

In time, you might need some help building graphic projects for bigger campaigns and website pages with a more complex user experience, but even then, getting outside help doesn't need to be costly. Services like Fiverr and Upwork can help you find the right person for a very reasonable price.

Your online presence is a journey. **The most important thing is reaching your target audience as fast as possible, because building a community and support network takes time and trust.** So drop the perfectionist's approach and get things done. You can and will improve everything as time passes.

25.1. First steps: Designing your website

There are several services that you can use to create your website without the help of a developer. After reading multiple comparisons and testing a few of the main providers, we recommend starting with Wix. It will allow you to build a simple website, which you'll need as soon as you found your charity. Just make sure to limit your time spent on designing, especially if you have very few visitors. Focus on your main tasks, as you can always revisit when you get more traffic.

Prepare the content

Before you start designing, prepare some basic content for the website. You should at least have:

1) Your charity's name.

Online articles offer tips on how to go about creating a business name, including using acronyms, word mash-ups, telling a story, or even using Latin.[1] You can also use a name generator that creates names based on keywords and brand type preference. **Pro tip:** Before establishing your organization's name:

a) Google it. Check if any other charities or brands are already using it (it might be trademarked, so you could be penalized if you use the same one) and how popular it is (if it's a very common word, there is a chance your charity will be very far down in the Google search results).

b) Check if the **.com** domain for the name is available. We recommend buying both the .com domain name and the .org, keeping your website as a **.com** and redirecting anyone that might accidentally use **.org** to the main website.

c) Ask ten people about it and see if they raise any issues. We don't recommend doing a large public survey, as people will adapt to a name much more quickly if they don't see the other options considered.

2) A logo (we'll explain how to design a simple logo below).

3) A tagline.

For a great tagline, follow this simple rule: [Who]…[what we do]…[for whom]…[how we do it].

---

1 Vistaprint, "How to come up with a business name," accessed Nov. 10, 2021, https://www.vistaprint.com/hub/business-name-ideas.

Let's look at the tagline of our incubated charity, Fish Welfare Initiative:

Fish Welfare Initiative aims to improve the welfare outcomes of billions of fish through **researching and executing targeted, highly-scalable welfare interventions**.

4) A short description of your goals and what you work on.

5) Short team bios (yours and your co-founder's) + photos.

6) Contact details.

Make sure your email looks professional. Use your website domain so it looks like this:

yourname@yourorganizationname.com

And not like this:

john87@gmail.com

7) Newsletter sign-up.

This is all the content you need to start your own website. With time, you'll be able to add sections like a Blog, Donate page, and Reports page, but remember this is a process – start with the basics. **A simple website is more professional than no website!** And it's better to create a small website well than a big one poorly.

Pro tip: Your content needs to be near perfect when it comes to spelling and grammar. Visitors are quite forgiving when it comes to design, but highly averse to linguistic errors. Everyone makes them, so run your content through applications like Grammarly or Hemingway Editor before publishing, and get another pair of eyes to look it over. For reports, try to find a volunteer editor to check them before they're available online.

Website body

The fastest way to design your website is by picking a ready-made template[2] where you can focus on minor changes like text, header image, and photos. Wix already has some dedicated to nonprofits, but you can also use Wix ADI, an automatic website creator that helps you design a template based on your aesthetic preferences and logo colors.

---

2 See examples at https://www.wix.com/website/templates, accessed Nov. 10, 2021.

Before starting, look for inspiration. Check well-designed charity websites like GiveWell, The Humane League, The Life You Can Save, and Anima International, or follow one of the many examples collected and curated at Dribbble, Behance, Pages, or Lapa. Since Wix has a lot of customizable pieces, you can try to recreate parts of your favorite designs. (For the sake of time, we recommend adjusting available templates or, again, using Wix ADI.)

Pro tip: If you're using any photos on the website, remember to optimize their size. The website needs to weigh as little as possible so it runs smoothly on multiple devices. You can download an application for optimizing pictures in bulk like ImageOptim. To test your website weight and speed, use services like PageSpeed Insights.

Logo

One of the key elements of your website is the logo. A logo is a graphic description of your charity; something that identifies it and can be immediately recognized. It represents what you do, but it's not as important as your message, which is why it can be abstract and almost anything.

For the nonprofit sector, your logo should be:

- simple
- distinctive (it should not remind people of other charities)
- practical (you want it to work on Facebook, your website, and paper)
- appropriate

At this point in your charity, designing a logo should not take you more than two to four hours. Your logo is not a lifetime commitment, and many organizations change theirs as they grow.

1) Start with brainstorming.

2) Do your research: Google ideas, i.e., if you want to design a logo for an animal charity that will focus on chicken welfare, search "chicken logo," "chicken logo abstract," etc.

3) Sketch an idea that you have in your head.

4) Design a few versions using free tools like Canva (an application for graphic design with several free logo templates that you can modify).

5) Poll your target audience (potential supporters or donors).

You can also use other free services like Logo Garden, Logomaker, and FreeLogoServices, or paid ones like DesignEvo and Wix Logo Maker. They are cheaper than hiring a professional, and decent is enough for your first few years.

See below a few examples quickly generated in Canva.

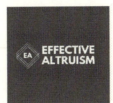

Website colors

If your logo is ready, you can use its color scheme as a starting point for picking your website colors. Colormind will help you generate a color palette based on your primary or accent color and allows you to preview how it will look on a sample design. (Wix ADI can also help with matching website colors to the logo.)

For the logo and website colors, you can draw inspiration from the most iconic brands through BrandColors or by searching color palettes on Dribbble.[3]

Typography

There is a whole philosophy behind picking the right fonts for your online projects, but you can stick to a few simple rules.

1) Decide if you want to use serif or sans serif fonts on your website.

This is a serif font (e.g., Merriweather, Times New Roman), and

---

3 Start at https://dribbble.com/, accessed Nov. 10, 2021.

this is a sans serif font (e.g., Arial, Raleway, Proxima Nova).

Sans serif fonts do not have the small projecting features that you can see while reading this book (written in a serif font). They tend to be perceived as more simple or modern. There are different schools of thought on choosing **serif vs. sans serif** fonts, but we would recommend:

a) Using sans serif fonts for your website since they are clean, simple, and reader-friendly.

b) Using serif fonts for larger bodies of texts like reports. Serif fonts guide the eye better through lines of text. They're also popular in the scientific literature and effective altruism publications.

2) Use at least 16 to 20px font size for your website's body copy. Font size matters, and it's common for inexperienced designers to use fonts that are too small.

3) Put 50 to 70 characters maximum in one visible line. More words means that the text will be harder to read, and may lead to people abandoning your website quite quickly.

4) Use a maximum of three fonts on your website (and two in your other designs). Be very consistent with using them in everything you publish.

5) The font pairing should not be random. Check out a few articles[4] for the most common and user-friendly examples. We also encourage you to test some pairings using tools that automatically generate complementary combinations.[5]

25.2. Graphic materials

Choosing a handy application

Whether it's a presentation for an important conference or a leaflet for an outreach event, you can design it yourself with free, intuitive applications like Canva, or paid ones like Visme, Crello, or Piktochart. We've opted for Canva because it is versatile and registered charities can get the pro version for free.

We use Canva for almost everything. It's intuitive, has ready-made tem-

---

4 See Canva, "Canva's ultimate guide to font pairing," accessed Nov. 10, 2021, https://www.canva.com/learn/the-ultimate-guide-to-font-pairing/, for a great example.

5 https://fontjoy.com/ is a great place to start. Accessed Nov. 10, 2021.

plates, a huge library of royalty-free photos, videos, and music, and allows you to prepare everything down to the final step: exporting your designs as graphics and print PDFs. However, if you need to put together an extensive report with a lot of references, you might want to stick with Google Docs or paid programs like Visme or Adobe InDesign (since Canva can't generate a clickable table of contents, which is important for long publications). If you need advanced data visualization, we recommend two apps: Tableau and Power BI. Tableau seems more intuitive and flexible; however, it's on the pricier side. But again, in both cases, you can apply for nonprofit discounts.

Here are a few tips that we find useful while working in Canva:

a) Remember the ready-made templates. To stay consistent, try to always use the same fonts and colors within any template you choose. We crafted a quick example below:

b) When you want to print your design, e.g., a leaflet, download a PDF Print version of the file and check "Crop marks and bleed" (see picture below). This means the design will have a few millimeters of margin on all edges for the printer cut. Nowadays many services (like Helloprint, which we use for our leaflets) offer a very useful preview so you can check your design before printing.

c) If you need a photo in your design, you can use Canva's repository. It has a huge selection of royalty-free resources (especially the pro version for nonprofits).

Pro tip: Remember always to use **royalty-free** photos in your designs. These photos are not copyrighted, so you can modify and use them without gaining permission or attributing them to a source. If you want to use photos you took yourself, you'll need to check which laws apply to using them for commercial purposes. For example, you usually need permission to use any portrait photography or close-ups. You can publish photos taken in public spaces, like parks, without permission if it's hard to recognize particular people. However, we still recommend getting permission from photographed people and precisely listing where you'll use the photos in the agreement[6] you ask them to sign.

You can also check other services that provide royalty-free photos like Unsplash, Pexels, Pixabay, and unDraw (which collects SVG illustrations – great to use on your website, as they adjust to the size of your page). We also recommend repositories of free resources like Design notes, UI Goodies, and Caio Calderari's Medium blog.[7]

---

6 See TemplateLAB, "50 Best Model Release Forms (Free Templates)," accessed Nov. 10, 2021, https://templatelab.com/model-release-forms/.

7 Caio Calderari, "Design Resources - Growing List," *Caio Calderari Medium*, Aug. 3, 2018, https://calderaricaio.medium.com/growing-list-of-design-resources-67c72a5d4f56.

25.3. Visual design

If you're not a graphic designer, it's best to stick to the ready-made templates offered by your program of choice. However, we've noticed that this can still lead to poor-quality designs if you don't follow some simple principles.[8] With a few tips from the experts and a good online application, though, you should be able to produce professional designs without any help and look good enough online.

a) Visual hierarchy

Your design should guide the eye from the most to least important elements. Visual hierarchy can be implemented through, for example, size, colors, or spacing.

Let's look at two examples of the first page of a three-fold leaflet. They both have the same content, but different visual hierarchies. You can clearly see that one is more successful in guiding your eye from the most to least important information:

b) Balance

This one is more tricky and a bit harder to learn, but again, platforms like Canva come in handy here. Balance in visual design is about the proportion of

---

8 Check out Kelley Gordon, "5 Principles of Visual Design in UX," Nielsen Norman Group, March 1, 2020, https://www.nngroup.com/articles/principles-visual-design/ for a more detailed starting point on these concepts.

the elements on the canvas, i.e., making sure that there are not too many "heavy" elements in the top or left side of the design.

In the example below, you can see a Facebook post with unbalanced (left) and balanced (right) proportions.

c) Contrast

This one is fairly simple. You use a contrasting element, e.g., a bright color on your "donate" button, to grab viewer attention.

Contrast also can involve font colors (for instance, you should use dark grey for your font colors instead of pastel green and yellow). Interestingly, experts recommend using an almost black color (i.e., #333333) for body text and not pure black, which apparently is harder to focus on.[9]

d) Coherence

As already mentioned, to create great visuals for your charity, you need to be coherent in your designs. Use the same type of fonts, colors, logo, and style in most designs.

9 Read about these and more tips from Marc Hemeon, "How to not suck at design, a 5 minute guide for the non-designer," Startupgrind, April 30, 2017, https://medium.com/startup-grind/how-to-not-suck-at-design-a-5-minute-guide-for-the-non-designer-291efac43037.

25.4. Social media

In our experience, **Facebook** is the most popular social media platform for the effective altruism community, mostly because of the numerous themed groups created over the years (the EA Hub has a working list of popular EA groups[10]). Therefore, it's a great place to start your community building. The most relevant platform for outreach and networking is now **LinkedIn**. You can get visibility faster than with Facebook, which prioritizes paid content. Although Twitter is not that popular in the EA community, it can be useful in reaching out to politicians, influencers, and potential donors. You can manage it with Buffer or Hootsuite. We don't recommend it as a starting point, because it's a time-consuming medium that requires a lot of engagement in ongoing debates.

When your charity is much bigger and wants to reach out to different demographics for donations, you can think about using Instagram or TikTok. But when you're just starting your journey as an entrepreneur, they're not worth your time. For now, LinkedIn and Facebook groups are the way to go.

Social media goals

Your social media presence will often be a significant part of your outreach efforts. In Charity Entrepreneurship's experience, posting on social media is actually the second-best outreach method. The first is direct and online meetings, either as scheduled one-on-ones or organized and facilitated during conferences.

The main goals of your social media presence are:

- increasing awareness of your organization
- generating and increasing leads (e.g., newsletter sign-ups)
- generating or increasing donations
- building an engaged community

Social media content – what works

At the beginning of your journey, we recommend focusing on LinkedIn. It works similarly to Facebook, but with more benefits like showcasing value to

---

10 EA Hub, "Connect and Keep Up to Date," last updated June 8, 2021, https://resources. eahub.org/learn/connect/.

potential donors, connecting with future co-workers, and gaining trust as an expert in your field. Facebook is still helpful for creating groups and staying engaged within the established community, but it becomes harder to work with every year.

a) Organic reach on Facebook is low.

Some sources say that organic reach (the number of people that will see your posts without you paying for advertising) can be as low as 6.4%, and it may have decreased even more in the last year (to as little as < 2%).[11] A recent Socialinsider study also observed that the bigger the profile, the less engagement it will have.[12]

b) Preferred activity on Facebook is defined as "meaningful interactions," which implies that the reach of your posts will be bigger if people comment and share them with friends.

Pro tip: Don't use content that produces false engagement. Examples of this include trying to "game the system" by asking people to vote with a reaction or share your post. You can be punished by the algorithm for doing so, and may even get shadowbanned (which means your posts will be visible to almost no one).

c) What content does work on Facebook?

It's always best to google the latest trends, but you should probably focus on:

- Posting in relevant Facebook groups.

- Videos that are longer than 1 minute (**Pro tip:** Don't repost videos from YouTube or other platforms. It will make your reach even lower than usual. Always upload videos directly to Facebook.)

- If you can, try to avoid outbound links in your posts. In general, Facebook wants people to stay on Facebook, so in-website content will do better.

- Live videos. For example, organize a webinar and stream it from Zoom directly on Facebook and YouTube (a tool like StreamYard can help).

---

11 Maxwell Gollin, "How the Latest Facebook Algorithm Changes Affect Marketers," Falcon.io, May 7, 2021, https://www.falcon.io/insights-hub/industry-updates/social-media-updates/facebook-algorithm-change/.

12 Teodora Lozan, "[Study]: 101,421,493 Posts Show How To Write The Best Content On Facebook vs. Instagram vs. Twitter In 2020," Socialinsider, Nov. 14, 2019, https://www.socialinsider.io/blog/social-media-content-research/.

- Don't forget about stories. Vertical videos are still on the rise.
- Use image carousels, emojis (if appropriate), and concise writing.

Remember that organic Facebook reach allows you to engage with only 5-6% of your existing community, and paying for ads is now a standard practice. That's why we recommend moving more of your attention to LinkedIn (which has fewer advertisements and guarantees a more engaged audience) while using paid Facebook ads for bigger campaigns.

25.5. Newsletter

Your newsletter is the number one online marketing tool for your charity, so you should start using it as soon as you can. It's also a very popular source of information in the EA community (if you're not yet subscribed to the famous EA newsletter, you should do so right now). You can even start using your newsletter before your website is officially ready. Just add it to your landing page and note that the website is in development, but people can subscribe for updates on your progress.

Why is your newsletter so important? It has the best conversion rates, meaning that people subscribed to it are kind of your biggest fans. You can count on at least some of them for support (whether it be responding to your job ad or call for donations, or just reading your latest research and giving some useful feedback). In general, these people are interested in what your charity is doing and cheering for your success. That's why staying in touch with them is so important.

How to set up a newsletter

The platforms you'll use for building your website usually have their own templates for newsletter sign-up. In Wix, just click the "+" sign in the left-hand side menu and choose -> **Contact Forms** -> **Subscribe** to add a section with a newsletter.

Very important: your newsletter must be GDPR (General Data Protection Regulation) compliant. GDPR protects the personal data of European citizens and residents. If your website is viewed by anyone with a European IP address (which almost all websites are), it will have to be compliant. You can read more about this via TermsFeed.[13]

Before you start sending out your newsletter, we recommend that you integrate it with Mailchimp, which you can later use to email your subscribers. Again, Wix has this option already built in.

How to send a newsletter

Initially, you will probably only send out a newsletter when you have something important to announce (e.g., launching your website, introductory blog posts about your organization). With time, you will probably want to update your subscribers on a more regular basis. We recommend a frequency of no more than once a month. There are multiple services that you can use for collecting emails and sending out your newsletter, like GetResponse, Sendinblue, and Mailchimp. At CE, we use Mailchimp. It's a great program to start with, allowing up to 2,000 subscribers for free.

Newsletter content

You've probably received hundreds of newsletters in your life. Some were spammy, so you unsubscribed; some you continue to follow for the latest updates. With your charity start-up, the goal of the newsletter is to build an audience of supporters. This audience will include donors, friends, hopeful effective altruists, and random people who just liked the idea of your charity. In time, you'll probably divide your audience into segments and send out dedicated newsletters for each group.

When designing your newsletter, follow the example of those that the community already likes, like the EA newsletter's archives[14] or Lewis Bollard's farm animal welfare research newsletter.[15] Notice that their designs are very simple, and the content is focused on important information and announcements. Standard charity newsletters will look more like that of The Life You Can Save

---

13 TermsFeed, "Setting Up Newsletters for GDPR Compliance," Dec. 23, 2020, https://www.termsfeed.com/blog/gdpr-email-newsletters/.

14 These can be found at Effective Altruism, "The EA Newsletter," accessed Nov. 10, 2021, https://www.effectivealtruism.org/ea-newsletter-archives/.

15 Open Philanthropy, "Open Philanthropy farm animal welfare research newsletter," accessed Nov. 10, 2021, https://us14.campaign-archive.com/home/?u=66df320da8400b581cb-c1b539&id=de632a3c62.

(see their Newsletter Archive).[16]

In general, your newsletter should have:

- a catchy title and subject line (a great way to arrive at something click-worthy is to come up with 10 options and test the top two to three on a friend)

- a colorful, well-designed banner (recommended dimensions: 600x400px)

- the most important message at the top, usually with a big button to click on (e.g., "Donate to Support Here")

- clear sections (use a divider)

- a color scheme that matches your logo/website

- announcements (starting a new project, fundraising), latest articles, new job opportunities, successes, or learnings

- it's common practice and a nice personal touch to place a photo of the author at the bottom of the newsletter

- links to your social media channels at the very bottom

- an encouragement to sign up for people who have been forwarded the newsletter

25.6. Summary

Use ready-made solutions: take advantage of graphic and website design programs that you can learn quickly, ready-made templates, and royalty-free photo repositories.

Keep your design clean: use simple rules of visual hierarchy and contrast to make small changes in the templates, remembering that less is more.

Be consistent: to look professional, use the same logo, font styles, and color palette in your designs. Create templates for any content that you'll be repeating.

Be present on LinkedIn and Facebook groups: for bigger campaigns, pay

---

16 The Life You Can Save, "Newsletter Archive," accessed Nov. 10, 2021, https://us3.campaign-archive.com/home/?u=30da440b4264260fc5f00ebc3&id=d8f0721547.

for Facebook advertising; organic reach is now very limited. However, keep in mind that this can be tricky, and often requires testing with larger budgets.

Send out a newsletter: always keep in touch with your most engaged supporters, but make sure to stay GDPR compliant.

Look good enough online: focus on the bare minimum that will allow you to look professional (simple one-page website, no spelling mistakes, neat reports for potential donors, two to three blog posts). There will be time to improve everything, but in the beginning, "good enough" is actually perfect.

Useful resources: Social Media Examiner, Social Media Today, Content Marketing Institute, and Snov.io's list of social media experts to follow.[17]

---

17 Paul Shuteyev, "Top 15 Digital Marketing Experts To Follow In 2021," Snov.io Labs (blog), last updated Aug. 18, 2021, https://snov.io/blog/digital-marketing-gurus/.

26. Wisdom

The wizard brought to the group neither strength nor speed. What he did bring was years of experience and a thoughtful disposition, enabling the team to go down the right path.

As a founder, you will have to make countless decisions. Although this book has armed you with some tools to make better ones, your most important choices will greatly benefit from good thinking from outside the co-founder team.

Wisdom is the least fungible of the Ws. A dollar from one donor is much the same as a dollar from another, and there's a near endless pool of people interested in working for a charity. Wisdom depends much more on the source; advice can save you significant time and trouble, but it can also be counterproductive.

At the highest level, we distinguish between two structures: an advisory board and a legal board. Your advisory board includes a broad range of mentors and advisors without any legal decision-making power. Your legal board, on the other hand, fulfills the lawmakers' requirements in terms of overseeing a charity.

The most formalized way to obtain wisdom is through your legal or advisory board, both of which shape the ongoing direction of your charity. However, you can also do so in a myriad of less formal ways. Mentors and advisors with specialized expertise in a key area can benefit an organization even in one short annual advice session.

How do you make sure your advisors are leading you in the right direction?

- Look at their own accomplishments. For instance, have they grown large charities with limited impact? They'll likely give good advice for scaling, but less so when it comes to impact.

- Consider why your advisor is giving you advice. Do they care about you personally? Their advice might value your interests more highly than other co-founders. Are they being paid to? They might lean toward things that take more of their hours.

- "Be careful whose advice you pay for, but be open to those who give it for free." Your best advisors will typically not be paid consultants, but rather passionate and impact-driven contributors to your project.

26.1. Advisory Board

This sounds more formal than it actually is. Despite its official term "Board," your advisory board simply incorporates your mentors and advisors. In a broad sense, it includes all the advisors that you rely on. This might be a list of 10 to 20 people. In a narrow sense, it captures only your five to 10 most valuable or high-profile advisors. The result of the latter is a list of distinguished individuals that you would, for instance, publish on your website under the title Advisory Board.

Members of this public Advisory Board have no legal authority. They cannot vote you out of your CEO post, and you are free to disregard any advice they give. Yet they are instrumental in providing insights and recommendations, especially as you start out on your journey as a charity entrepreneur.

Advantages/roles

An Advisory Board has several advantages. You can think of each advantage as a role that you want to fill with a suitable candidate.

- **Signaling:** As a start-up, you are a small, unknown organization. Showing that you are acquainted with and taking the advice of well-known individuals helps you increase the perceived legitimacy and importance of your organization. This can include individuals known to the broader public, for example, a famous philosopher, or those well-respected in a particular subfield such as animal welfare or development economics. Such positive signaling increases your success in attracting funds, negotiating agreements with governments, and finding talented staff.

- **Fundraising:** Fundraising provides the lifeblood of every charity. An advisor can add value in this arena in three ways: first, as a wealthy individual contributing directly; second, as someone well-connected who makes introductions to foundations and private donors; third, as an expert in fundraising tactics. These three characteristics can be spread out over multiple advisors, or combined in one. Regarding the first category, wealthy individuals, it often helps to approach them for advice before asking for financial contributions. By building a relationship, they will get to know you and your project better, which facilitates future fundraising requests.

- **Domain expertise (research):** As an evidence-based charity, you build on the available research, conduct your own impact evaluations, and incorporate new findings from third-party studies. Researchers in your area of interest can help you with all of this. In addition to their domain expertise, some of them will also be able to guide you on your monitoring and evaluation plans, including how to run solid impact studies.

- **Domain expertise (operations):** Most charity start-ups are not research but implementation focused. It is therefore critical to have operators in your field as advisors. This could include a senior executive of a nonprofit organization who will be able to shed light on solving operational puzzles in your domain.

- **Start-up experience:** Advisors can also include successful start-up operators from the for-profit or nonprofit world. You might consult them about successful decision-making under high uncertainty, managing your time as a leader, or scaling up an organization from scratch.

While not necessarily a public role, make sure that you also add an advisor who can give you tips on your emotional well-being and resilience. This might be a separate person, or one of the advisors listed above with a particular talent for psychological support.

In terms of prioritizing the various roles, a public advisory board should put particular emphasis on signaling and fundraising value. Less-known advisors can provide input in the background as well, but once you include an official Advisory Board on your website, make sure you have some heavyweights in there. In terms of fundraising, having this official board raises the likelihood that members feel committed to helping out. The advisory position becomes part of their identity, and they start to have skin in the game.

The advantages of advisors are wide-ranging, but what about the **disadvantages**? The main pitfall is that you link your organization's name with those of your advisors. If one of them is suddenly implicated in a controversy, that could then also affect your brand. In the best-case scenario, you can carry out reference-checking within your community regarding mentor candidates. You should also set clear expectations with your advisors. They should not perceive themselves as running the organization, as they are not in the decision-maker's seat. Similarly, advisors should be transparent about their affiliation with your organization. They do not speak on behalf of the organization, so, for example, they should consult you if they are asked to provide a quote to the media or represent you at a conference.

A suitable strategy to avoid these pitfalls is to **test advisors** before you add them to your formal board. This also aligns well with the natural progression of your start-up. In the beginning, you will scramble to recruit advisors. Eventually, you will end up with a diverse group that matches the roles listed above. You can then pick the best candidate for each role and make your Advisory Board public.

Finding advisors

CE's Incubation Program connects you to established mentors with expertise in all recommended cause areas and the key functions of a charity. The program ensures that you have a skillful, motivated mentor with time reserved to advise you.

Below we list some additional guidelines in picking mentors, including those for founders not participating in the program.

First, distinguish between **general and specific mentors**. The latter is an expert in a particular domain; for example, fish farming, or a certain country. Such a person might be able to provide excellent guidance in their area of expertise; for example, how to engage with fish farmers in India. They might not, however, be the right person to elaborate on the strategic outlook of your charity. For that, you will want to have a small set (usually only 1-3) of general advisors, while you can have a greater number of specific advisors. General advisors excel at tackling cross-cutting issues, such as the implications of your impact evaluation on your fundraising strategy. These individuals often have a background in entrepreneurship and can share firsthand lessons learned in operational and strategic challenges, based on their own journey. Given their broadly applicable skill set, they often make good members of legal boards (see below).

In terms of the **traits** you are looking for, the person's reputation or availability is usually secondary. Some of the best advisors might be very busy or not have fancy titles. Instead, optimize for the following: concern for your mission, tendency to listen effectively to and understand your challenges, ability to provide informed advice and connections, and understanding that their own experience might not apply in a particular situation (self-reflectiveness).

Make sure to get a good mix of mentors in terms of **style**. You need some harsher or more skeptical mentors to help you identify blind spots, but encouragement and motivation are also important aspects of a mentoring relationship. The entrepreneur's journey is sufficiently challenging. For this reason, have both harsher and less harsh mentors.

Don't forget to consider advisors from your country of operations. **Local advisors** help you understand the preferences of your beneficiaries and navigate stakeholders. This can increase your program's effectiveness and strengthen government buy-in. Examples include the CEO of a national NGO, a government official, or a professor of an in-country university with good connections to the government.

Managing advisors

Once you have identified a potential mentor, reach out with a specific question and a suggestion for a brief conversation (e.g., 15-20 min). Mentors are usually very busy and don't have time for broad and time-consuming requests (i.e., don't go for "let's have coffee and chat about malaria bed nets"). Once you have established a personal connection through shorter interactions, longer conversations might become a possibility if you hit it off. As you approach new mentors, think back to the piggybank analogy. Don't just subtract, in the sense of constantly making requests. Try to be helpful by, for instance, sharing relevant articles, offering introductions to valuable members of your network, and reaching out with simple messages of appreciation (without an embedded request).

If you would like to add someone to your formal Advisory Board, make sure to get permission to use their details and photo on your website. Ask via email to create a written record. Even better, create a Terms of Reference template that each advisor signs. This clarifies expectations regarding duties, time commitment, and usage of their names for public communications and fundraising. You can reference a template from CE-incubated Charity Science Health.[1]

In your regular interactions with advisors, it's helpful to consider the following:

- Prepare an agenda for calls with your mentor. This helps you focus on key topics and not waste valuable advisor time.

- Don't use your 30 minutes with an advisor for issues that are only pertinent between co-founders.

- Share data ahead of or during the call to help your advisor understand the facts. This also improves the quality of their advice.

- Understand the limits of advisors. Don't use specific mentors as general mentors (see above). Acknowledge that every mentor will typically be less familiar with your particular context.

- Don't outsource decision-making. You are in charge, and you have the best understanding of your situation. Combine different viewpoints from different advisors with your own, and then opt for the most promising approach.

- Capture the advice provided in a Google Doc and structure it by date or topic. For your closest general advisors, you can also use a stricter template such as the CE Mentor Canvas.[2] This keeps you accountable to yourself and your mentor on key performance metrics.

26.2. Legal Board

While an advisory board has no formal authority, the legal board is responsible for the oversight and legal governance of your charity.

If you work in two countries (e.g., HQ and field operations), you will likely

---

1 Available at https://bit.ly/CSHterms.
2 Available at https://bit.ly/CEmentorcanvas.

have to set up two different legal boards. Both bodies are responsible for ensuring that the organization adheres to its mission and to the respective country's laws. In the case of any violations, board members (also known as directors) can be held legally accountable.

Key responsibilities of a legal board include:

- Reviewing finances on annual returns and submissions to national tax authorities (e.g., IRS 990 in the US)
- Hiring the executive team (in particular, the NGO's CEO), evaluating their performance, and determining their compensation[3]
- Providing advice and/or strategic decisions brought up by the CEO and discussing mitigation measures for the organization's major risks, ranging from financial, legal, and operational, to security

Board 1.0

As you start out with your charity, it is best to keep your investment into the legal board version 1.0 light, and focus on the fundamentals. First, make sure the board remains small and has members you fully trust, including yourself. Remember, the board can dismiss you or negatively affect your strategy. It could, for example, force you to move away from an evidence-based intervention toward an unproven one. Second, ensure through the board that your organization is fully legally compliant. Just cover the essentials here, and avoid getting into trouble with an influential government agency such as, for instance, the tax authorities by submitting your annual returns late.

In terms of legal minimum requirements, most countries require at least one board meeting per year, written meeting notes (minutes), and at least three members (sometimes they must be citizens of the country). You should also strongly consider general liability insurance, as board members are liable for legal issues. While the threat of successful legal action against individuals is low, it cannot be excluded. Having a Conflict of Interest policy from the beginning is helpful, too.[4] Additional policies such as Whistleblower Protection and Docu-

---

3   For specifics, see BoardSource, "Executive Evaluation and Compensation," accessed Nov. 10, 2021, https://boardsource.org/fundamental-topics-of-nonprofit-board-service/executive-evaluation-compensation/.

4   See National Council of Nonprofits, "Conflicts of Interest," accessed Nov. 10, 2021, https://www.councilofnonprofits.org/tools-resources/conflicts-of-interest.

ment Retention can be added later if you are time-constrained.

Board 2.0

As you grow, you have more resources to professionalize and expand your legal board. Approach proven members of your advisory board and ask them if they would like to join the legal board. In addition to expert knowledge, they will also need a certain willingness to take on legal responsibility and deal with formal issues. Importantly, you still want them to be on your side and share the values of evidence-based charity entrepreneurship. In this respect, be careful with having too much intellectual diversity in the legal board. Rather, implement it in the advisory board, which does not steer your organization.

Lawyers and finance executives can add a lot of value in managing your organization's legal compliance. Ideally, they bring specific domain expertise in the field of nonprofit accounting/law to the table. An executive experienced in nonprofit accounting might, for example, take on the role of treasurer. Treasurers oversee all matters related to finance, accounting, and auditing in the board and work closely with the CEO/CFO.

As you professionalize your board and bring in increasingly seasoned executives, you will likely still keep positions pro bono. The time commitment is reasonable, especially for members without special functions. You may want to consider a board member contract to outline roles and responsibilities clearly.[5]

In terms of finding talented candidates, you can use your community's network (e.g., the 80,000 Hours Job Board[6]), traditional employment channels (e.g., Idealist), and platforms tailored to finding Board members.

Here is a list of recommended Board member recruitment platforms tailored to US charities:[7]

- Impact Opportunity (free)
- BoardNet (free)
- AdvisoryCloud (free search, paid referral of $2500)

5 See Jan Masaoka, "A Board Member 'Contract,'" Blue Avocado, Oct. 9, 2009, https://blueavocado.org/board-of-directors/a-board-member-contract/.

6 80,000 Hours, "Board Posting & Matching Programs by Region," accessed Nov. 10, 2021, https://80000hours.org/job-board/.

7 See https://impactopportunity.org/jobs/, http://www.boardnetusa.org/public/home.asp, and https://www.advisorycloud.com/, respectively. Accessed Nov. 10, 2021.

Platforms outside the US can be found through BoardSource.[8]

Finally, LinkedIn Recruiter Lite is an excellent service to headhunt for specific board member profiles like, for instance, treasurer candidates with experience in nonprofit accounting. The subscription is expensive at around $100 per month, but a free one-month trial is available.

---

8 BoardSource, "Board Posting & Matching Programs by Region," accessed Nov. 10, 2021, https://boardsource.org/fundamental-topics-of-nonprofit-board-service/composition-recruitment/board-recruitment/board-posting-matching/.

27. Work

Your nonprofit's biggest driver will be the hours put into it. Some of them are put in by a board or volunteered by close contacts, but the majority of hours will come from paid staff.

A good staff member can speed up your organization in countless ways. A bad one can be an anchor, dragging you down. (Or, to keep with our metaphor of the rocket, a reverse thruster rather than an anchor – but this just doesn't have the same ring to it.) Staff affect the long-term speed and culture of your organization – this is particularly true of your earliest hires. Your staff will also often start as your biggest cost.

Why should I work for you?

Even someone new to fundraising knows that you need to make a good case for your charity when speaking to a possible donor. But many forget that you need to do the same when speaking to a potential hire. The nonprofit sector is full of people looking for work, but the best hires often have many options to choose from. Just like when fundraising, you'll need to know your competitive advantage – why they should choose you.

Is your mission inspiring? Can you make a case that it's higher impact than other options? Do you offer something that other jobs do not? As a new nonprofit, you will often not be able to compete with market rates for salary (even NGO market rates!), but the flip side is that there are other benefits you can bring to the table that some jobseekers might weigh more heavily. Small NGOs tend to be more flexible, less bureaucratic, and able to give more freedom to their employees. What you want to offer, and your answer to the question of "Why should I work for you?" should be tied to traits that will also help you identify the right person for the job. Don't imply the role is stable if it is not. Instead, highlight its flexibility and ever-changing nature; you'll find a better fit.

Promises are cheap. Anyone can put "a great place to work" on a job ad, so get specific. Do your employees have a shared pancake breakfast on Mondays, or a training program for how to break down problems? That's something to highlight. Are you more like a Silicon Valley start-up, or an academic think tank? Different organizations have different cultures, and you want to attract the right person for the job.

Whom should you hire?

Just as you should try to calculate the costs and expected value of your organization as a whole, consider explicitly calculating the costs and expected value of an additional employee. Hiring employees is generally the most expensive thing you will do as an organization, so it's definitely worth putting some time into calculating what you expect to get out of it.

What type of person do you want to hire? What do they value? What tasks are they focusing on? What specialized skills do they have (if any)? What salary are they going to expect? Think through this carefully. Especially in the early stages, you will work very closely with this person, so it's a lot like choosing a co-founder. It helps to pick someone with aligned values and complementary skills.

Think about how each person's strengths, weaknesses, and personal quirks might interact with your team. If you and all your current staff struggle to give speeches or come across well in meetings, hiring someone charismatic could provide a huge advantage in representing your organization. If you and your current staff tend to be too blunt and direct, hiring someone who struggles to accept criticism might exacerbate the problem.

As a general rule, the more positive qualities you ask for, the fewer options you will have, so it helps to think about which traits and skills are most important to you. As always, we recommend making a spreadsheet to help yourself reason through which criteria are important to you (like in our example below), since assigning values to qualitative judgments can help you clarify your thinking.

Role	Skill (fill in your own)	Value alignment	EA knowledge	Verbal ability	English skills	Organized	Research skill	Charisma	Self-starter	Intervention/country-specific knowledge
Co-founder		10	10	8	4	5	8	7	10	4
Operations		7	6	5	6	8	7	3	4	3
Research		8	7	9	4	3	10	4	6	7
Program manager		6	5	6	4	7	5	6	3	9
Copy editor		4	6	9	10	5	4	2	2	1

The purpose of this spreadsheet is primarily to help you reason through all possible criteria and their relative weight, so it's important that you come up with the criteria yourself. While you probably won't use this spreadsheet directly, it might help inform your thinking about what sorts of metrics you can use to evaluate candidates. It's also good practice for getting in the habit of using spreadsheets to systematize your thinking.

Generalists first, specialists later

If you are a new and inexperienced founder, you may feel overwhelmed by the fact that you lack the expertise necessary for the goals you wish to accomplish. Your first instinct might be to hire a specialist with a résumé filled with years of experience and a technical background that applies to the exact thing that you are working on, one who has the connections and intuition you lack. However, bear in mind that if you are a small organization of only one to three people and lots of diverse tasks, it may be more important to hire generalists who are pretty good at everything rather than specialists who are really good at one specific thing. (Instead, get that specialist on your advisory board.) This allows you to remain flexible and avoid finding yourself shorthanded when it comes to tasks outside of your employees' specialization. The ideal, of course, is a specialist who is also generally good at everything else, but it's rare to find someone who meets all criteria.

If you over-value specialization and experience, you will have a smaller set of candidates to choose from. That means you won't be able to be as selective regarding other qualities. Someone looking for a "charismatic effective altruist writer who is a specialist in the field" will have far fewer options, if any at all, compared to someone who is looking for just a charismatic effective altruist writer. Because the first person added the "specialist in the field" requirement, they may need to compromise on the charisma, writing skills, or alignment with effective altruism.

If you do decide that it is important to hire a specialist, keep in mind that it can be tough to evaluate skill in an area you yourself may not be competent in. You may need to consult someone you trust who is more skilled than you in that particular area. A member of your advisory board might be able to help.

It's important to be aware that specialists are often more comfortable working in larger organizations able to spread out tasks among a large group of people. Be sure to test any specialist hire for start-up compatibility. If a candidate asks you many questions about benefits and established processes/protocols, it could be a sign that they are more accustomed to working at larger organizations.

Hire people who will make aligned decisions

In an early hire, we recommend prioritizing not only for competence but also for mission alignment. Remember that employees don't simply do tasks – they autonomously make important decisions for the entire organization, often without very much input or oversight from you. If your hire doesn't particularly buy into the notion of measuring impact and ranking interventions according to cost-effectiveness, the organization as a whole will shift in that direction. Whatever you envision the core mission of your organization to be, there are certain roles where you want to preferentially hire people who "get it" and don't need to be convinced to buy in.

It's common for people to prioritize things other than maximizing impact, such as "growing bigger" (commanding a bigger budget or hiring more people), because they are accustomed to the prestige signals and incentive structures of the corporate world or even many parts of the nonprofit sector. Well-intentioned people who are not accustomed to thinking about what it means to "maximize" impact will often want instead to maximize intermediate metrics that aren't directly tied to impact, or expand the program to cover multiple interventions rather than focus on the most cost-effective one. Sometimes a quick explanation will be enough to change a person's mind, but other times these disagreements are deeper and more ingrained.

You don't necessarily need only to hire self-proclaimed "effective altruists." However, do consider the value of having some people on your team who speak the language of effective altruism well enough to communicate with large EA funders, or who understand why you might do something like turning down counterfactually heavy funding. Fields such as economic studies, medicine, and public health also ascribe to values like impact and prioritization, and might be good pools to hire from.

If a trait isn't important for the job, don't consider it

If you are influenced by traits that don't really matter,[1] you will further cut down your options and may miss out on the best person for the job. For example, attractiveness and English skills (assuming a role that doesn't directly involve those things) are examples of traits that are not relevant to every job and can easily bias an interview process.

Here are some traits we look for when interviewing for the Charity Entrepreneurship Incubation Program:

- Alignment with effective altruism
  - History of involvement with the EA community. Big points for volunteering, hosting a meetup group, going to conferences, writing forum posts, or donating a large portion of your income.
  - History of involvement with altruistic causes in general. Any form of volunteering would be taken as a positive, even if it was unrelated to EA.
- Self-starter, takes initiative, builds own structures in addition to following other structures
  - A major project of any form outside of traditional school or employment.
  - Online courses, blogs, organizing groups of any sort.
- Prioritization and systemization skills
  - Tries to identify the crucial considerations that matter in a task (as opposed to spending too much time getting lost in one or two details that will not influence the overall impact).
  - Demonstrates or describes using systematic processes during interviews or test tasks.

These are not necessarily the same traits we look for when hiring staff for

---

1 Charity Entrepreneurship, "What People Overvalue When Hiring," Sept. 25, 2014, https://www.charityentrepreneurship.com/blog/what-people-over-value-when-hiring.

Charity Entrepreneurship as an organization. For junior operations roles, we might still emphasize alignment with effective altruism and prioritization skills, but we may not care about self-starting and instead be more enthused by a history of successfully managing logistically complex things.

Think about the unique needs of your organization, not just what you might stereotypically associate with a role. You might ordinarily consider a "researcher" to be someone with a PhD, for example. But when hiring researchers, in some cases it's worth putting more weight on performance in a five-hour "shallow review" test task than on successfully publishing several highly cited studies in prestigious journals. It all depends on whether or not you are aiming to produce papers for academia, as the skill sets involved can be quite different.

When not to hire

While hiring employees is an important part of building an organization, don't rush into it. Employees are expensive, and hiring too quickly can undermine your org's financial stability. It might make sense to hold off if:

- Your strategy and intervention are still very much up in the air. The co-founders first need to get more clarity on where the organization is headed. Y Combinator, for example, discourages hiring during the three-month accelerator program, as any activity other than finding product-market fit would be a distraction.

- An additional hire would undermine the financial stability of the organization.

- You are not really looking to recruit an employee but outsource a specific task to a contractor/freelancer. E.g., for reviewing expenses and adding them to a bookkeeping software, it might make more sense to hire a part-time contractor or freelancer on a platform such as Upwork.

- You have not been able to define a clear job profile for your first hire. Without a clear role, it will be difficult to identify the best candidate. Don't expect someone to be a superb researcher for three months and then switch to a completely different profile of a highly flexible operations generalist. You are setting yourself and your employee up for failure if you want a superman or woman that ticks all the boxes.

Force yourself to think clearly about your key pain points as an organization and what hire could best address them.

How to hire the talent you need

When you're a small team of one to three co-founders, you'll be taking on all the tasks necessary to achieve the organization's goals on your own. Eventually, you may discover that the main bottleneck on your progress is the speed at which you can work and the amount of time and energy that you are able to devote to the job. When that time comes, consider making your first hire.

Hiring well is no mean feat. Finding key staff who want to work for your organization can be difficult even at the best of times. But, virtually every successful founder says it's worth taking large amounts of upfront time to get the right employees. The next few pages walk you through a process that will get you hiring better than most other new organizations. Naturally, your process will grow and change as you get larger (e.g., having dedicated staff for hiring); however, this will give you strong bones for when one of the co-founders is doing the bulk of the hiring – which will likely be the case for the first few years.

For every role, design and execute the following six steps:

1. Build hiring metrics
2. Create a job ad
3. Design an application form
4. Conduct interviews
5. Set test tasks
6. Make the final call

27.1. Building your hiring metrics

A meta-analysis on individual differences in work performance estimates that "in low-complexity jobs, the top 1% averages 52% more [productivity] than the average employee. For medium-complexity jobs this figure is 85%, and for high-complexity jobs it is 127%," with some jobs such as sales having ratios that are even more skewed and not normally distributed.[2] This variation

---

2 J.E. Hunter, F.L. Schmidt, & M.K. Judiesch, "Individual differences in output variability as a function of job complexity," *Journal of Applied Psychology*, 75(1), (1990): 28-42.

suggests that you can be quite a bit more productive if you hire the right people, yet most interview processes are conducted with essentially random metrics. In the 1980s, it was common practice for firms to hire on the basis of "graphology," which purported to derive a person's traits from their handwriting.[3] We are not immune to making similar mistakes today, as it is now common to use various unscientific personality tests and compatibility metrics. Top-performing companies like Google once used quirky "brain teasers" as interview questions, only to find that they didn't end up predicting anything – although many hiring managers still use them.

Given the fact that so many organizations conduct essentially useless candidate processing, use caution when designing an application process. One that is badly designed will trick you into thinking you are selecting the best candidates when in reality you are wasting their time and yours.

Pick metrics that are supported by both common sense and research

The most highly cited meta-analysis regarding what works is the work of F. Schmidt & J. Hunter (1998).[4] Schmidt also recently published an updated meta-analysis (less frequently cited).[5]

The research is constantly changing. For example, while the 1998 data favor more structured interviews, the 2016 update claims that structured and unstructured interviews are of similar usefulness. The 1998 data claims that combining work tasks with general cognitive ability tests gives the greatest combined validity, while the 2016 update claims that once you add a cognitive ability test, work tasks become redundant and give no additional information. Where the research is not consistent, you will have to use common sense as your guide.

These authors conclude that the best interview processes combine general mental ability tests with either "integrity tests" (which purport to measure ethical behavior) or structured interviews. They also found that education and

---

3 Aaron, "Graphology as a Personnel Selection Method," EffortlessHR, May 5, 2017, https://www.effortlesshr.com/blog/graphology-as-a-personnel-selection-method/.

4 F. Schmidt and J. Hunter, "The validity and utility of selection methods in personnel psychology: Practical and theoretical implications of 85 years of research findings," *Psychological Bulletin* 124 (1998): 262-274. https://doi.org/10.1037/0033-2909.124.2.262.

5 Frank Schmidt, "The Validity and Utility of Selection Methods in Personnel Psychology: Practical and Theoretical Implications of 100 Years of Research Findings," (2016), https://www.researchgate.net/publication/309203898_The_Validity_and_Utility_of_Selection_Methods_in_Personnel_Psychology_Practical_and_Theoretical_Implications_of_100_Years_of_Research_Findings.

experience matter less than you might think, and job experience hits sharply diminishing returns after five years. Meanwhile, they found that reference letters and education tend not to matter much.

However, you shouldn't blindly trust research to tell you what works. This data generalizes performance from tasks that differ dramatically from the ones you are hiring for, such as carpentry, waiting tables, or sales. It measures "productivity" in ways that may not make sense for the context in which you want to apply it. Consult your intuition – studies suggest[6] that common sense is a useful guide as to which research will replicate.[7] Consider scientific research as a check on your intuition, a way to prevent yourself from picking useless metrics or trying something completely untested. Choose methods that are both backed by research and intuitively appealing.

We tend to rely on structured interviews and work test tasks to carry the bulk of the application weight, with some ability questions mixed into the first round form.

27.2. The perfect job ad

What makes the perfect job ad? Most people think it's the one that attracts the most candidates. And although attracting candidates is indeed important, a job ad is also the first filtering opportunity. You want it to attract people who would be a good fit and discourage those who would not be, saving both you and them time. When designing a job ad, you really want to accurately reflect what your workplace looks and feels like.

The first step of creating your ad should be looking at templates and other job ads. We've created a generic template for a job advertisement.[8] It was originally for a copyeditor, but all the organization- and job-specific aspects have been highlighted with instructions to help you rewrite them for your needs. It can be a good use of time to look at job ads hiring from similar organizations and for similar roles. It will give you a sense of the market, what to include, and

---

6 Ed Yong, "Online Bettors Can Sniff Out Weak Psychology Studies," The Atlantic, Aug. 27, 2018, https://www.theatlantic.com/science/archive/2018/08/scientists-can-collective-ly-sense-which-psychology-studies-are-weak/568630/.

7 Jesse Singal, "Want To Know Whether A Psychology Study Will Replicate? Just Ask A Bunch Of People," Research Digest, Oct. 16, 2019, https://digest.bps.org.uk/2019/10/16/want-to-know-whether-a-psychology-study-will-replicate-just-ask-a-bunch-of-people/.

8 Available at https://bit.ly/CEjobad.

how your position might differ from others offered.

Every job ad should include the following details:

Job title: A job title should succinctly communicate the role that the person is going to play in the organization. Spend some time researching common titles to ensure that you are using terms that others will understand – it should reflect the type of work and the level of responsibility implied.

Your organization: Help potential candidates understand the basics of what you are trying to accomplish. This is also a good opportunity to impress them with some of your past accomplishments. Keep it brief – they can always read more on your website.

Role responsibilities: Outline the core responsibilities of the position. You've hopefully spent some time thinking about this before putting up an ad. In addition to being informative, this section should be interesting. Picture your ideal candidate and try to figure out what their dream job would be.

Impact of the role: Effective altruists and others in the nonprofit sector generally care first and foremost about making a positive difference to the world. This is the most important section, and the main draw that motivates qualified candidates to apply. Think of it like applying for a grant or a donation, but for human resources (time) instead of money. You should have already spent some time explicitly modeling the impact of making a new hire – this is a chance to present your work.

Qualifications: Do you need them to already know about effective altruism? Do they need to live in a specific city? Do they need a specific language? Give your applicants some cues as to whether they are a good fit. Distinguish between requirements and nice-to-haves.

Benefits: Individual applicants prioritize things like skill building, intellectual challenge, autonomy, and work-life balance differently. Give them a sense of the perks of this position. Think about whether you want to list a salary or leave it as negotiable – there are pros and cons to both.

Application process: Give them a link that they can use to apply, and mention any deadlines. (Setting a deadline is better, even if it's rolling – far fewer people apply if there's no deadline.)

27.3. Designing an application form

After you create a great job ad that would get someone excited to apply, you need an application form. Asking for a résumé is standard practice for almost every job application. We have found cover letters far less useful than targeted application forms for getting at the important key questions. And if you expect a large number of applications, a form can offer the benefit of scoring candidates automatically.

Typically, you link your application form at the bottom of your job ad. There are plenty of templates within Google Forms (a good program to use for this sort of thing) and across the internet. To get you up and running, we've made a template for an application form in Google Forms, available at https://bit.ly/ CEapptemplate. To start, navigate to the menu (the three dots in the top right corner) and click "make a copy." You now have your very own application form that you can edit!

You will need to customize it with some top (quick answer) questions to narrow down the pool. You don't want your application form to take more than 2-15 minutes, depending on how many applications you expect to get. For a more clearly desirable position, you can get away with a long initial application. But when you're just starting out, it's better to make it as easy to fill out as possible.

Do for every application

- Collect both a name and email: Make sure this is a required question.

- Have them upload a CV or link a LinkedIn profile into the form: This allows you to have all the application information in a single spreadsheet later.

- Check for basic understanding: You can use a basic understanding check to filter out the large number of people who are simply sending résumés to every application they can find. A good question might be, "Please describe in one sentence a previous role you have held that is most similar to this one."

Do for most applications

- Logistics questions: Can the candidate work in a specific location? Will they relocate? What visas do they have? When can they start? If they plan to work part time, how many hours per week do they have in mind?

- Knowledge questions: If there's anything that the candidate should already know coming in, you can include it here as a basic filter for applicants who won't work. For example, you probably shouldn't hire a copyeditor who doesn't know the difference between "their" and "there," or an animal welfare specialist who doesn't know what cortisol is. You can use multiple such questions to get an overall quiz score.

- Problem-solving questions: You can use problem-solving questions as a filter for general ability. These could be multiple choice with a single correct answer, or a long answer allowing a candidate to showcase their creativity or methods. These are especially helpful if you want a candidate who can demonstrate understanding of a specific complex topic (e.g., counterfactual impact, cost-effectiveness analyses, monitoring and evaluation, etc.). Just make sure you can grade them quickly.

- Connect your results to a spreadsheet: Connecting a spreadsheet to the form will help you systematically rate applicants to keep things consistent. Google Forms can do this automatically, making it easy.

Don't do for any application

- Ask for information you are not legally allowed to ask for: This includes things like race, sexual orientation, and marital status. Make sure to check for topics you are not allowed to ask about.

- Ask for information that is easy to find on a résumé: Wasting a candidate's time is no fun. If you are going to look at their resume, don't ask them to write out parts of it again into a form. It just creates frustration.

- Have hard cutoffs: Very few factors will rule out a job applicant 100% of the time. When auto scoring, make sure no one factor can rule an applicant out. Generally, a strong candidate is near the top in most categories, but that doesn't mean they have no areas of weakness.

How much to weight it

The application form will be your first impression. Hopefully, between the form and the résumé you'll be able to rule out at least 50% of applications.

However, as you get more data points, its weighting in your endline call will move closer to 10%.

27.4. Structured interviews

An interview can provide valuable information about a candidate's social skills, their ability to think on their feet, and their first-impulse responses. It also offers the opportunity to test the candidate under conditions where you can clearly observe them. Unfortunately, interviews are also where factors that do not necessarily matter to every job (e.g., charisma, assertiveness) can bias a decision.

The goal of a structured interview is to minimize the biases caused by first impressions and random factors, generating responses that can be systematically compared between multiple types of interviews. You'll interview all candidates who make it past your form. We typically recommended having one short interview (15 minutes) and another, longer one (60 minutes) later in the process. Both should be structured.

Designing the interview

Plan to record the interview: Ask the candidate if it's okay for them to be recorded. This is a legal requirement in many countries. Recording interviews can be very helpful later on when you want to compare between two neck-and-neck candidates and need a refresher on what happened during the interview. If you want multiple people to grade an interview, or want to forward an interview from lower-level to higher-level staff during a multistage hiring process, having a recording allows you to do so. It can also help you write down information that you missed while it was live.

Design the questions: Laszlo Bock of Google has conducted internal studies regarding what works in hiring and written guides on structured interviewing,[9] as well as some sample questions.[10] Read through them for ideas.

---

9 Laszlo Bock, "Here's Google's Secret to Hiring the Best People," Wired, April 7, 2015, https://www.wired.com/2015/04/hire-like-google/.

10 Richard Feloni, "Google HR boss says asking these questions will instantly improve your job interviews," Business Insider, April 15, 2015, https://www.businessinsider.com/google-laszlo-bock-interview-questions-2015-4.

- **Softball questions**: Keep it easy and generic for the first few questions. This helps put the interviewee at ease. For example, you might ask, "How did you hear about us?" or "What made you interested in working here?"

- **Skill-focused questions**: Include some semi-focused questions that give the applicant the opportunity to tell anecdotes about the skills you are hiring them for. For example, when hiring someone who will need to manage, you might ask: "Tell me about a time when you effectively managed your team to achieve a goal. What did your approach look like?" (Follow-ups: What were your targets, and how did you meet them as an individual and as a team? How did you adapt your leadership approach to different individuals? What was the key takeaway from this specific situation?)

- **Negative questions**: You can also try questions that explore more negative emotions, such as, "When was the last time you got into a conflict with a coworker, and how did you handle it?" Some candidates will not be able to answer these questions gracefully and may tell an anecdote that focuses on putting down others, which is useful to know.

- **Knowledge questions**: How much do they know about you as an organization? How much do they know about effective altruism in general? How much do they know about the intervention you're doing? Design some questions that allow them to demonstrate this knowledge.

- **Find out their values**: Having shared values is important in an impact-focused organization. You'll want to know not only what they value morally in a philosophical sense, but also how they will practically make decisions. Examples: "If you could change one thing about the effective altruism movement, what would it be?" "How should employee salaries be decided?" "Do you think it is important to have diversity within an organization, and why?"

- **Miniature test tasks**: If you're recruiting a copyeditor, for instance, you could ask them to edit a short document during the interview. You might also ask them questions that test their intelligence or creativity. Be careful, as it's really easy to get carried away and ask questions that don't predict anything.[11] If your organization is facing a real problem, this might be a good time to ask them for advice on how they would solve it so you can get a sense of their problem-solving methods. In general, the closer the test task is to the real tasks, the better.

Create rubrics and scores for each question: Oftentimes, people's responses to questions are predictable and similar to each other. In these cases, you can create a rough map of expected answers and grade them accordingly. This will also help you take fewer notes during the interview. Most importantly, a structured scoring table allows you to be more neutral and unbiased. Of course, some candidates will surprise you with unusual answers, which you can write down and grade later. We created an interview rubric template to get you started, available at https://bit.ly/CEinterviewscore.

What resources on effective altruism have you read or are you reading?	Hasn't read anything about it	Has read an article or two	Familiar with concepts, has read a book or many articles	Read extensively, can name favorites
	0 points	1 point	2 points	3 points

Scheduling an interview

We recommend using Calendly or an equivalent software to allow multiple applicants to book you during preset time slots. It lets you display the times you are available to be booked and condenses the "when are you free" back and forth down into a single step.

Always be mindful of time zones when booking a long-distance meeting. Googling "London 2 p.m. to Chicago" will tell you what time it is in Chicago at 2 p.m. in London, or use Every Time Zone to make doubly sure everyone is on the same page about when you're meeting. To avoid confusion, write dates in

11 Jena McGregor, "Companies turn to quirky interview questions - even after Google says they don't work." The Washington Post, March 29, 2016, https://www.washingtonpost.com/news/on-leadership/wp/2016/03/29/companies-turn-to-quirky-interview-questions-even-after-google-says-they-dont-work/.

long-form (e.g., "January 2nd, 2020"), because different countries use different abbreviation systems (e.g., Christmas is written 12/25 in the USA, but 25/12 in the UK).

If you're conducting interviews in a country where people don't really use video chat software, you have the option of getting a phone number through Skype or Google Voice to connect to people's phones via the internet.

Tips for conducting an interview

Make sure you practice everything with friends a couple of times before conducting your first interview.

Before you begin, make small talk to put the interviewee at ease. Don't forget to ask them if it's okay to record. Rewatching interviews can be incredibly time-consuming, so you will save a lot of time if you can conduct the interview in a structured manner:

1. Integrate your scoring guide into a Google Sheet that for every question leaves a) one cell for the answer and b) one cell for the grade (with preset scores through the data validation function in Google Sheets).

2. Ask each question and enter the key points of the answer in the answer cell.

3. Grade the responses immediately after the call. During the call, you will likely not have sufficient time as you'll be busy writing notes and managing the conversation.

Access the "interview" tab of our scoring template at https://bit.ly/CEhiringtemplate to get started. Ask questions that rule out many people in the first interview (e.g., the most important or easiest to judge). You can keep the others for the second interview.

By the end of your hiring process, the first short interview will likely account for around 10% of the total score. The longer interview will remain important; you might weight it as much as ~20% in the final call.

27.5. Test task

A test task, also known as a "work task" or "task-based interview," is a small project to ascertain how suited a candidate is for a job. Performance on a test task is typically the most revealing piece of information that you will get during the application process. Another benefit is that setting a test task forces you to identify the most important responsibilities of your future hire. Hiring managers often have too broad or insufficiently clear expectations. A test task brings the discussion down from high-level areas of responsibility to the day-to-day work.

The main drawback of test tasks is that they often take a long time to complete, and also a long time to evaluate. If the candidate plans on working with you locally but is doing the test task from a remote location, it's also difficult to perform the test task in a controlled environment that mimics work. This is part of why test tasks tend to be done with fewer candidates later in the process.

Creating a test task

When sending out a test task, remember to give 1) a deadline for submission and 2) a sense of how long the applicant should spend on the task. It's best to keep it short. In most cases, a test task of one to two hours will give you a solid understanding of the candidate's ability. Even a shorter task of 15-30 minutes can be helpful. For crucial positions with various responsibilities, you can also consider one or multiple test tasks of five to 10 hours in total.

Here are some example test tasks, which should take no more than three to five hours each:

- **Research role:** Evaluate the expected counterfactual impact of starting an organization that lobbies for raising taxes on tobacco.
- **Communications director role:** Part 1: Contact one chicken farm and find out the following 10 pieces of information, plus any other info you think might be relevant. Part 2: Which farm do you think would be a good target for launching an intervention: the one you called, or the one described in the report below? Why?
- **Operations role:** Our lease is expiring, and we have to change offices in December. We have 15 staff, all of whom are able to relocate within the city come December. We will want to stay in the new office for one year. Using real listings that are currently available in this city, decide which office we should rent.

The ideal test task closely resembles the type of work that the candidate will be doing in practice, or otherwise draws upon a similar set of skills. You might even think of the first couple of tasks you would give them and see if any of them can be made into a test task.

Evaluating a test task

Because each test task is different, there's not necessarily a single way to evaluate them all. Come up with a set of criteria that makes sense for your task, and rate the responses via those criteria. You can access the "test task" tab of our hiring template to get started,[12] which consists of three scoring components that feed into an overall score for each candidate.

Name	Notes	Score	Accept?	Part 1 spreadsheet (link)	Write-up (link)	Score component 1	Score component 2	Score component 3
Applicant 1	Notes for task	13	A	LINK	LINK	4	5	4
Applicant 2	Notes	10	A	LINK	LINK	3	2	5
Applicant 3	Rejected for task	7	R	LINK	LINK	3	3	1
Applicant 5	Notes for task	14	A	LINK	LINK	5	5	4

Because test tasks are important and tricky to evaluate, it helps to have more than one person rate them.[13]

27.6. Making the final call

Each step of your candidate's application process will give you a piece of data. If you follow our process, that would mean one application form, a CV, a short and a long interview, and one or two test tasks. You can store the scores for each of these in the same spreadsheet and see which areas a given candidate does well on.

For the final three top candidates, you will want to call references and add that data in as well. We tend to weight each piece of data as follows:

- CV - 10%
- Application form - 5%
- 15-minute interview - 10%
- Two-hour test task - 25%
- 60-minute interview - 20%

---

12 Available at https://bit.ly/CEtasktemplate.

13 You can learn how to integrate multiple ratings and other tips in Assessments Made Easy With Google Spreadsheets, available at https://bit.ly/CEassessments.

- Five-hour test task - 25%

- References - 5%

These weights are not binding. If someone does well but comes back with really worrying references, we might still rule them out.

Even for a great candidate, it's a good idea to start with a trial hire or probationary period, particularly if you haven't done much hiring in the past. A good hire can make your charity and a bad one can break it, so the upfront time investment really pays off.

28. Wealth

Acquiring the funds to support a project is easily the fuel that most scares nonprofit leaders. As a co-founder, it will be your job to raise the bulk of funding for your project for the first couple of years. How hard this is depends greatly on the cause area, but across all cause areas you need strong communication skills to fundraise effectively.

An important and often forgotten factor is that a dollar saved is a dollar earned. In nonprofit terms, this means the fatter your budget, the better you need to be at fundraising. Start small, and fundraising will be a lot easier than if you start with scaling to the moon. The first funding Charity Science ever got was a $12k donation from a high-net-worth donor. Although this doesn't seem like much, it meant everything for the project. If we had asked for $50k, it might never have gotten started.

Starting lean and scrappy will lower the expectations funders set for you and the amount of time you need to spend fundraising. A good budget can be one of the best ways to improve your ability to fundraise.

28.1. Layers of fundraising and alignment

Some funders are large, others are small; some are quick to fund, while with others it's always a long process. Every organization's fundraising path is different, and different cause areas have different fundraising prospects. In this section, we will go over five different funding sources and some of their unique characteristics:

- Small funders
- High-net-worth funders
- Corporate giving
- Foundation funding
- Government funding

We will not talk about earned money (e.g., through running a charity shop) as it is a less common funding stream for early-stage organizations going through our Incubation Program. You can find a more thorough breakdown of nonprofit revenue sources in an infographic via the National Council of Nonprofits.[1]

Small funders

Who they are

Small funders are often the first donors that come to mind. Most of us have been small donors for an organization at one point or another. Your first offered donations will likely come from small donors, ranging from friends and family to people who find out about your charity online.

Exactly what counts as a small donor often depends on the size of the charity and the funding gap. To a multimillion-dollar charity, someone giving $10,000 might still be considered a small donor. For a small charity, it would be a very large one. We'll use $10,000 as the cutoff between small and large donors.

How organizations generally get their support

Small donors tend to build up like a snowball. You can actively recruit them using methods like door-to-door or mail campaigns, but often they come even without active outreach as your organization becomes more established and better known. Small donors will often be built up through your mailing list or

---

1 National Council of Nonprofits, "Nonprofit Impact Matters: How America's Charitable Nonprofits Strengthen Communities and Improve Lives," accessed Dec. 9, 2021, https://www.nonprofitimpactmatters.org/site/assets/files/1015/nonprofit-impact-matters-infographic-sept-2019.pdf.

converted from website traffic, and may also be volunteers. In some cases, later large donors will start off as small donors.

Characteristics

- Small donors are diverse. Funding from small donors encompasses a much wider spread of reasons for donating compared to large donors and is affected in different and smaller ways by organizational changes. Although small donors will be affected by things that affect large numbers of people (e.g., an organizational scandal or economic depression), this source of funding is generally more stable than other more unified ones.

- Small donors will often have less time to invest in considering charitable choices, so they will fund an organization based on its core mission as opposed to the details of its execution.

- Within the EA movement, small donors will be effectiveness-oriented. Outside EA, however, most donors will not be as focused on this aspect of the organization.

- Most small donors will give with no specific earmarking or restrictions. Frequently, this means that their funding is uniquely helpful, as it can be used to fill less glamorous funding gaps.

How best to leverage them as a new organization

There are lots of ways to acquire small donors actively, but they are often time and resource intensive. It's likely not worth the time to run active campaigns to recruit them unless you have a very specific project that's a great fit (e.g., one that strongly appeals to a certain demographic that follows your charity). However, it is worth creating a pathway for these donors to support your organization. For example, having a donate page on your website and a donate button on your social media channels is a good, low-cost way to start building up support. This can not only start the snowball of small funders, but also build up goodwill among a larger audience of potential employees, larger funders, mentors, and volunteers.

High-net-worth funders

Who they are

High-net-worth (HNW) funders are people who generally earn a lot and give large donations. They might have a private foundation or a donor-advised fund, but usually will not have full-time staff working with them to distribute funding.

High-net-worth funders are a very common source of funding for new organizations. Charity Science's first donation was from a high-net-worth individual (HNWI) who had a pretty strong understanding of our team and organizational goals. HNW funders often place a premium on knowing the team and co-founders. In most cases, they will personally know one or both of the co-founders, and will often talk to them about issues outside of the direct charity they are all passionate about. Some of the more successful fundraisers connect with HNWIs through hobbies, like tennis or golf; activities, like meeting at parties or events; or certain topics, like talking about a certain country or mutual interest area.

Many people are afraid that interacting with HNW funders just gives them more chances to mess up the relationship. The truth is often the opposite. The longer and better any donor knows you and your team, the more enthusiastic they will be to support it. This does not mean you should pressure HNWIs to spend time with you – often they are busy folks. But it does mean that you should not shy away from connecting on more social issues as well as the ones directly connected to your charity.

How organizations generally get their support

High-net-worth donors most often come from mutual connections, but may also grow out of mailing lists and groups of small donors. You can also meet them at conferences or events.

It's worth keeping in mind that it is not clear from the outside who is an HNW donor and who is an interested small donor or someone interested in volunteering. The best system is just to treat as many people as you can with respect and thoughtfulness, answering their questions intelligently and leaving them impressed with you and your project.

In addition to specifically targeting certain individuals at events, you can make use of your network. If someone is keen on your project (whether they are an HNWI or not), you can mention to them that you are seeking funding and would appreciate being introduced to anyone they think might be interested in financially supporting a project like yours. More often than you would expect, that person will offer some funding right there, and if impressed with both you and your project, they will very often introduce you to someone who could be a larger funder.

Characteristics

- HNW donors tend to be comfortable with risk, keen on a personal connection, and enjoy an understanding of the project.

- They often have groups of other HNWIs and people they respect whom they talk to about funding options. Being well regarded by one HNWI can therefore help others learn about and become interested in your project.

- Usually, they don't have a formal process and thus can be fairly quick donors.

- They tend to attach fewer restrictions to funding than governments or foundations, but more than small funders.

- Often, they support a number of charities. Many HNWIs start with smaller donations to a new group and donate more over time. This is a common trend across all larger funders.

- Some HNW donors will ask for highly detailed information, tailored to what they are most interested in. In some cases, this is worth creating. In other cases, it can be a larger time investment than it's worth. With HNW donors, it's important to respect their time, but it's fair to ask the same of them.

- Make sure your personal habits are on point when talking to an HNWI – particularly one you do not know well. Dress smartly, be on time, and share the conversation.

- A good conversation with an HNWI might have a similar atmosphere to talking to your favorite teacher or a friend you don't see as much as you would like. It should not feel like a dragon's den or timeshare pitch.

How best to leverage them as a new organization

HNW donors are generally a good fit for new organizations as they can donate quickly and involve fewer legal constraints – something that can be challenging early on. You should try not to rely on a single HNW donor, since one person's feelings or financial situation can change dramatically year to year. However, there's a good chance that they will make up the first couple of large sums of money you get. HNWIs tend to give in yearly cycles and like to reevaluate projects frequently.

HNWIs can also be great mentors and additions to your advisory board if they have knowledge relevant to your area or generally give solid advice. You do not want to add an HNWI to your board if all they bring to the table is money, but if they are a supporter and also someone you trust to give good advice, they can be a perfect fit.

Keep in mind that HNW funders are just like every other person, they just happen to have more money.

Corporate funding

Who they are

Corporate donors are, generally, sections of companies looking to do some charitable giving. Very large companies will set up independent foundations that look more like foundation funding than anything else. However, small companies will just have some staff within their for-profit entity in charge of distributing funds. In some countries (such as in India), social responsibility is a mandatory requirement, which means that a large number of companies have corporate funding programs.

How organizations generally get their support

Corporations are often more keen to give pro bono services than cash. They may donate to organizations that they feel will give them good press or connect them with more customers.

Compared to other sources of funding, corporate is often the most focused on "what's in it for me." Corporate donors will generally be quite risk-averse and unlikely to give to controversial causes. Most will be linked to you through a relationship you have or make with an employee in the company from a non-fundraising-focused connection.

Characteristics

- Risk-averse and reputationally careful.
- Want to fund things local to them or connected directly to what they work on. For example, a phone company might fund text message health reminders.
- Often concerned with how many people will see their brand or how much recognition they will get.

How best to leverage them as a new organization

It's hard to get corporations on board with many of the most effective ideas. However, small organizations can have success with pro bono services or corporate funding of events (often with the trade-off of advertising). Corporations that have a personal connection to someone on your team and do for-profit work in a nearby area will be your best bet.

Foundation funding

Who they are

Foundation donors are organizations whose purpose is to give away funding. They typically range in size from having a couple of full-time staff to hundreds of staff and dozens of different teams. Large corporations (such as Coca-Cola) and extremely wealthy individuals (such as Bill and Melinda Gates) have set up full-time foundations to distribute and monitor large amounts of funds. Foundations typically give out money in grants with a high number of restrictions and legal requirements relative to other sources of funding.

How organizations generally get their support

There is some debate in the fundraising community as to whether funding can be acquired from cold applying for a foundation funding round or whether they are more often determined informally, with the grant application completed afterward as a formality.

Foundations often have open granting rounds, to which organizations that are a good fit are encouraged to apply. These can often read somewhat like job ads. Some organizations send out a large number of fairly uncustomized applications (similar to how many people apply for a large number of jobs using the same cover letter). However, these sorts of applications generally have very low success rates.

Normally, a handful of foundations will operate in and fund the space you are working in. It's best to spend the vast majority of your grant application time on the top five.

Characteristics

- Many foundations are run by people successful in the for-profit world. They like novel projects that do things a bit differently. This novelty drive can sometimes lead to nonprofits trading foundations, moving from one to another with each foundation only funding it for a couple of years. This way, each foundation can claim credit and feels as though they were the catalytic funding for the organization.

- Foundations commonly state they want a project to be sustainable, often meaning that they do not want to fund it long term. They would rather fund it for a bit before moving the burden of funding to another.

- Foundations tend to give grants for a small number of years (e.g., 1-3). Legal paperwork and granting forms need to be filled out annually, showing how funding has been spent.

- Foundations are characterized by their staff. Even fairly long and formal funding processes very often come down to what the staff or founders think of the idea.

How best to leverage them as a new organization

Foundations are a pretty good second step after a couple of donations from HNWIs. The application process for foundations is generally longer (3-12 months), so organizations will often need some funding before applying. The lengthy process can be hard for organizations that are continually changing.

Sometimes, the need for funding will be different by the time the foundation is able to process the grant.

We generally recommend getting to know the major foundations in your space (e.g., donors in global health and the broad EA community)[2] and speaking to them about what ideas they are most keen on. If there is a connection between those ideas and the projects that are highest impact for your organization to work on, speaking more to them and, eventually, formally applying is a good way of scaling up.

Government funding

What it is

Government funding is money given by a government, typically a department focused on charitable giving. It is almost always given as a grant contract with a very high level of detail and restrictions. Applications can often take a year or longer to finalize.

How organizations generally get it

Multiple websites post government grant opportunities. The biggest key here is just to keep an eye on them and look for alignment with the work that you are hoping to do. USAID and DFID are the top two to watch out for, although other countries will often have specific interest areas. For example, Canada is unusually interested in micronutrient fortification (perhaps because it fits our fairly helpful but boring mannerisms).

Characteristics

- Government funding tends to be extremely risk-averse and prefers organizations working on the same program for a long time in a fairly consistent way.
- Unlike foundations, they often do not like new projects or innovative ideas and are known to be more conservative funders.
- Governments will often have contracts with such a high level of speci-

---

2 Available at https://bit.ly/CEkeydonorsgh and https://bit.ly/CEkeydonorsea.

ficity that applying is more like applying to be the executor of an idea, rather than convincing them of a specific idea or approach.

- Many will call you an implementing partner. Some of their grant processes specifically look for contractors that carry out particular programs, e.g., in the field of HIV prevention and treatment.
- Governments often have unusually specific geographical constraints on funding.
- They often give very large grants over long periods of time (3-10 years).

How best to leverage it as a new organization

It will typically be hard for new organizations to acquire government funding. Many of the skills learned from getting foundation funding will apply to government funding, but at an even higher level.

Transitions over time

Every organization will have a different path, and cause area greatly impacts your exact way forward. But a common trajectory in terms of how to use these funders over time might be:

- Starting with HNW donors for the first year or two while slowly building up a small-funder network.
- Getting your first corporate grant or two a few years into your organization's life cycle, replacing some of the HNW donors who have now moved on and allowing your organization to grow larger. A next step could be focusing on foundations.
- After running for 3+ years, your organization might start to apply for government opportunities while also maintaining a donor base split between small, large, and foundation donors.

As mentioned above, it is usually not a good idea to set up a fundraising machine that tailors to small donors, as it requires substantial investment to generate returns. For example, two high-net-worth donors might give you $50,000, but to get the same amount from small donors you might have to convince 150 individual people. Corporate donors fit better than individual donors but are generally less promising than, e.g., foundations, as the funding tickets are usually lower and the application procedures drawn out.

28.2. Preparing to fundraise

Whether you like it or not, a significant share of your time as a co-founder will be spent on fundraising. It can be scary, but making sure you have a plan and knowing where you're going can help you reduce the uncertainties.

This section outlines how to prepare yourself to fundraise effectively. It includes tips for defining your fundraising strategy, tools to make sure you are ready when opportunities come up, and advice on how to learn to do better.

Prioritize

As a co-founder, it will be hard to delegate fundraising to somebody else, and you will have many other responsibilities to manage. There are multiple different sources to fundraise from, and because they each require efforts on different fronts, you will not have time to explore them all. For example, you may be attracted to the corporate social responsibility (CSR) sector in the country that you operate in as a source of funding, which will require a lot of meeting and pitching on your idea in person. Or you may want to reach out to private international foundations, who will want to see a written summary and an annual report before they agree to have a call with you. These options require putting your time into very different activities. That's why it is important, as a team, to decide which sources of funding you will pursue, limiting these to two; and the strategies you will adopt to approach these funders, limiting these to three or four. You can focus 100% of your efforts on these chosen sources and strategies for a limited period of time, after which you may reevaluate and adapt based on what you have learned (more on this below).

Find what might work best for you

There are no universal rules on which source of funding is most promising for nonprofits. However, it is common among successful charities to see specialization. This means that a nonprofit finds a type of fundraising that works for them, develops expertise in it, and draws a large part of their funding from it.

You need to assess your options based on what could work best for you. This will depend on:

- **The type of organization you are**: As an EA charity aiming to maximize impact, you may not be willing to compromise on your program to get funding. So, you may want to seek more flexible and unrestricted donations.

- **The sector, geography, and intervention you focus on**: You might need to identify which type of funders tend to prioritize the work that you are doing (e.g., if your country is neglected by international donors, you may want to explore CSR within the country), and if your intervention overlaps with certain types of businesses, you may want to explore networking among these (e.g., if your program relies on a new technology, reach out to the largest ICT businesses for advice).

- **The stage of your project**: At an early stage, your likelihood of getting support from large bilateral donors (e.g., DFID or USAID) is low, and you may want to seek support from private foundations and HNWIs until you are more established.

- **The qualities of your team members**: Think about what the people on your team bring to the table. For example, someone might have a large network within the business or NGO sector; they might have excellent written communication skills; etc.

Taking all this into consideration, you will end up with different strategies, even across EA entrepreneurs. For example, Charity Science Health adopted a strategy focused on connecting with wide-ranging impact- and evidence-oriented foundations, through going to conferences, their direct network, and cold contacting online. On the other end, Fish Welfare Initiative put most of their effort into private donors, through giving talks at events, communicating during Giving Tuesday, and setting up calls with EA-aligned people who were excited to support a novel idea. As they progress, they will start to explore larger funding bodies such as Open Philanthropy.

Work allocation

Fundraising is hard to delegate to other members of your team. Funders often prefer to talk to organization founders or directors, partly because they care about the quality of the leadership and conversations are a way to assess that. Once you have determined which strategy/source of funding to focus on, you'll need to identify the few tasks that can be delegated and allocate work between you and your co-founder. This might be based on what you are good at (e.g., in-person vs. written communication), but there might be things that you will both have to work on at the same time, such as activating your network through your direct connections.

Strategies for early-stage EA entrepreneurs

Some strategies may be promising for early-stage EA entrepreneurs to prioritize:

- Activate your network: Reaching out to people in your primary network is one of the best ways to connect with funders because they are people you know well, making the introduction more natural. You can also try people you know from someone else, or with whom you have something in common (university alumni, previous company/org's alumni, EAs, etc.).

- Conferences: Going to conferences is also an effective strategy, as it allows you to make in-person contact. This is always better than emails or phone conversations, and provides an environment where you share common interests. Reach out to attendees beforehand to plan meetings, and don't be afraid to target the most important people there. Scheduling meetings in advance is key to ensure you have a quality interaction with them, making the exchange more natural and private (meeting in a quiet room vs. trying to engage in conversation spontaneously in the crowd). It also increases your chances of being able to talk to them, since they might not have time if asked on the spot.

- Cold contacting a large number of aligned funders: This is an interesting strategy. It is low effort and can, surprisingly, result in promising leads. Once you have identified funders with whom you think your charity is well aligned, you can message people working there, asking to learn more about their work, either on LinkedIn (using the pro plan, you can send messages to anyone on LinkedIn who is not in your network; without pro, you can directly ask to connect and send a short note), email if you can find them, or even the contact form on their website. This has the advantage of being easy to time cap – you can set yourself a goal of two hours a week. Since funders usually get thousands of NGO requests, if they reply it is a good signal that they could indeed be interested. In such cases, you should put a lot of effort into creating a connection with them.

- Maintain relationships: This is not a strategy to decide on, but something you should always do regardless. It's important to keep this in mind, because it's easy to get excited about promising new leads and forget about those you already have. Although it might make sense to prioritize additional funding leads in the present, maintaining relationships with existing funders is important to sustaining funding in the long term. You can do this by sharing updates on the organization via email (e.g., setting up a newsletter with Mailchimp or personalized updates with MailMerge, which allows mass mailing out of Gmail) and scheduling meetings to make sure you stay in touch. December and the New Year are good opportunities to follow up, as you can share your wishes and it's the giving season. You can also use their own work and project timelines to follow up (e.g., "How is your work on the social project mapping going? I would love to hear your findings if you have some time in the next few weeks.").

Some strategies are less promising as a start-up organization:

- Written grant applications are rarely worth your time. Thousands of NGOs will apply to the same request for proposals, and application forms are usually very time-consuming. Most NGOs have entire teams working on polishing these applications. You should identify a few grant applications a year that you think are highly promising, and only apply to those. And if you do decide to apply, always try to get in touch with someone there for additional information on the review process. People are usually happy to share information as they care about transparency, and some donors (e.g., Global Innovation Fund) even have an option for internal review if you know someone at the organization.

- Fundraising campaigns among the general public might also be difficult as a start-up. You do not have the strongest communications/ outreach team at this point, and you do not yet have the credentials that will help the general public trust your project. It is also harder to track the counterfactual impact of donor funding with a large number of small donations.

Keep track of leads and stay organized

It's important to be organized early on to make sure you don't lose track of promising leads that you need to follow up with or miss out on well-aligned funding opportunities. Even when you have set your priorities and defined your strategy, it is easy to get lost and not know what to focus on day to day. Putting a system in place that allows you to prioritize which opportunities to pursue based on deadlines, your funding needs, and likelihood of success will come in handy.

Keep track of funding opportunities

Your system here can take the form of a spreadsheet tracking all opportunities and include a function to rank them in order of priority. You can refer to a template used by Charity Science Health at https://bit.ly/CSHtrackgrants for guidance. You can add anything funding related: funding organizations, people you are connected with who might be able to donate or connect you to funders, and one-time grant opportunities. When it comes to creating a priority order ranking, you may want to take into account the following factors:

- The amount of funding available;

- how aligned the mission of the funder and grant is with your own;

- your likelihood of getting the funding (based on the points above, but should also include considerations related to competition and concentration: see the number of applicants in the past application round or check how spread out vs. concentrated their portfolio is in terms of grantees);

- the deadline for applications;

- and what part of your program you will be able to fund through this, and how important it is compared to everything else you could be doing.

Aside from these factors, make sure the sheet allows you to add in any opportunities you hear about such that it contains those you have identified as promising, those you think should NOT be pursued (for reference in the future, since you will not remember names of all funders), and those you have not had time to assess fully yet. Ideally, you should also use this tracker as a way to document the status of the relationship: when you last spoke to them, who in the charity is responsible for the relationship, whether you have submitted a concept note to them already, etc.

As much as possible, this should be a tool you can consult at any time to know something about a funder in relation to your charity, which means it should be updated regularly.

Make sure to get in the habit of documenting what happened after each meeting with a potential donor. You will also need to have a system in place to ensure that you don't miss out on new requests for proposals, or just regularly research funders you may not know about yet. Assigning someone in your team, an intern for example, to spend a few hours each week to look for more opportunities could be useful. Consider subscribing to the newsletters of your top 10 funders and aggregators (e.g., Global Innovation Exchange) to stay up-to-date with the latest opportunities.

Create and maintain fundraising material

Each donor is different and will want different material. Ideally, you should adapt your material to each based on their preferences and expectations. That being said, it will be hard to do this every time. When it comes to moderately aligned funders, you may prefer to send something that is not really tailored as opposed to nothing at all. For this reason, creating template reports accompanied by pictures, a summary pitch of what your organization does, and two to four pages of concept notes can be very useful. Annual or biannual reports and a summary pitch come in handy to facilitate an introduction if, for example, a connection offers to put you in touch with a funder. A concept note might be the next step in terms of what funders ask for, and because it's short can easily be changed to meet different funders' needs.

When it comes to full proposals, it makes more sense for you to wait until a funder actually asks you for one, since they will have very specific requirements and details are harder to adapt.

Manage tasks within your team

Staying organized as a team is particularly important for fundraising as it's one of the aspects of your work for which the timeline is not under your control. You might get unexpected requests from funders, or unexpected opportunities you won't want to miss out on. Here are some things you can do to be better prepared:

- Set fundraising goals on a weekly and monthly basis and share them with the rest of your team. Make sure that beyond the unexpected, you will contact X number of people in your network and cold message at least X funders. These tasks are difficult and often lead to procrastination because they can be socially awkward (nobody likes to ask for favors). Setting goals and sharing them with your team can help you overcome this difficulty.

- Assign responsibilities within the team when it comes to meetings and reviewing proposals. Between you and your co-founder, this might be more about who is responsible for which funders. But between you and your employees, it might be deciding who writes the first draft of a concept note or email, who reviews it, and who needs to approve the final version.

Learn to do better

Although it might be true that fundraising is one of the skills you gain on the job/with experience, it may be inefficient just to go with your intuition and see how it turns out. From the very start, think of your fundraising as a topic of research – something you should ask experts their opinion about and conduct your own M&E on.

Ask advice from professional fundraisers

When joining the world of entrepreneurship, you may come in with a variety of skills, but it is unlikely that fundraising is your area of expertise. There are people whose job has been fundraising full time for the past ten years, so they may have a lot of advice to share. It might be especially useful to contact people who do this for successful/fast-growing organizations implementing similar programs, have a similar mission (EA focused), or work in a similar country.

Test it yourself

Acknowledging that you are new to this is great, but every organization is different, and relying only on external advice will leave you with incomplete information. You need to test what works for you and adapt your strategy based on your successes and failures. This can be done by tracking the time and money invested in each strategy and biannually evaluating the results yielded from each. In terms of metrics, you may not be able to measure your success in terms of the amount raised, especially in the first year since you might've created useful relationships that will yield results in the longer term. So, you may want to look at the number of strong connections you have made through each strategy. Based on these two pieces of information, decide which strategy looks the most cost-effective.

Having this framework in place to make sure you learn from your experience relieves the burden of having to decide once and for all which fundraising strategy to go for, and can remove some stress. If you are particularly worried about your ability to fundraise enough to meet your organization's needs, you can adjust your plan based on results (e.g., if I do not manage to create X promising connections by this month, I will reevaluate or try a different strategy). An evaluative framework also leaves more flexibility for you to try out less common strategies alongside your main methods:

- Reach out to the business world directly: Instead of targeting CSR, find the right people within companies whose work has some overlap with yours and reach out to them for advice. They might be better connected than you to the CSR branch of their company, or even just funders in this sector in general.

- Reach out to high-net-worth individuals.

- Ask your partners to connect you: If you are implementing your program in partnership with a government or other NGOs, you can ask them to refer you to one of their donors for an introduction. This is something they might be willing to do because if you are partners in implementation, more funding for you benefits them, too.

- Create online profiles: There are a lot of evaluators, aggregators, and networks of NGOs out there. Many funders do not accept unsolicited proposals and just do their own research to find NGOs instead, and having an online profile increases the chance that they see you. Submitting a profile and joining these networks can be a good way not only to increase your visibility but also improve your credentials (e.g., Innovations in Healthcare). When a funder hears about you for the first time, they will look for signs that you are credible and trustworthy. Having some external mention can help with that. Reviews from charity evaluators like GiveWell would be ideal, but might be hard to get at first.

Summary

Fundraising can be stressful. There are three ways to make sure you are prepared for it:

- **Prioritize**: You may be excited to try everything, but you're better off focusing on exploring a maximum of two sources of funding and three/four strategies to approach them. Find the sources that make the most sense for your organization. Activating your network, going to conferences, and cold contacting well-aligned foundations are promising strategies you may want to prioritize.

- **Keep track and organize**: Have a system in place to track funding leads, create general material that you can share with all potential donors, assign responsibilities within your team, and share individual fundraising goals with everyone.

- **Learn to do better**: Fundraise more effectively by learning from professionals and testing what works for you with quality M&E on your efforts and results.

29. Summary: Gathering support

You now have the basic information on gathering support for your organization. Every organization wants to gather more support, so it is a competitive space. Nonetheless, it's possible to beat the market by hiring thoughtfully, acquiring wise advisors, and fundraising from effectiveness-minded donors. Going through the CE Incubation Program also gives you a head start on connections and funding, plus an ongoing selection of possible hires.

29.1. The journey toward scale

The journey toward scale is long. Different factors will limit your growth at different times. Some years it will be funding, others talent; sometimes, it'll be management ability or bandwidth. Growing large is an aspirational goal, and there are many paths to impact. You will face an ever-changing landscape and have to move resources around to gather more support in the areas you are most lacking.

Do not neglect trusted advice ("wisdom"): it will not stop your charity as quickly as running out of funding, but weak advisors will lead you down paths that result in the same ends.

Keep in mind that a good employee can be worth triple their weight in funding, and a bad one painfully toxic to your organization.

29.2. Key principles

Wealth

- You can never be too good at communication.
- Start small and grow bigger both in team/program size and in funds.
- Spend every dollar intelligently and fundraising will always be easier.

- Put yourself on the same side as your funder and work together to solve the problem.

Wisdom

- Acquire expert advisors and generalized advisors, and stay in contact with them often.
- Learn from your mistakes, and share them so the community can learn from them as well.
- Listen to a lot of advice, but be careful about whom you trust.
- Set up both an advisory board and a legal board – they will likely consist of different people.

Work

- Manage expectations and motivations, not just people.
- Hire slowly, fire fast. Having the wrong employees has a huge cost.
- Take care of your employees and yourself, but don't put them ahead of impact.
- 90/10 your online presence and your outreach efforts.

29.3. Twelve months in: Are you on the right track?

- Do you have at least three trusted advisors you can ask for help on a range of topics?
- Do you have at least two sources of significant funding, with ideas on how to diversity funding such that no one source supplies over 50% of your budget?
- Have you made your first organizational hire?
- Have you set up a less formal form of engagement with the help of interns, volunteers, or a mailing list?
- Have you connected with other key organizations in the space?
- Do you have a polished fundraising proposal, a one-year plan, and a

five-year plan?

- Have you received a piece of feedback significant enough to change your direction?

- Have you registered as a charitable organization in the country you expect to receive funding from?

- Has one of the founders become a strong communicator you would be happy to send to any conference?

- Is your budget impressive in both its organization and the amount it gets accomplished for its size?

Part V. Operations

The structural system is the metal skeleton that holds everything together. Without a strong, well-planned structure, your rocket will fall apart when it experiences tough shocks. This section on operations covers everything from budgeting to day-to-day project management.

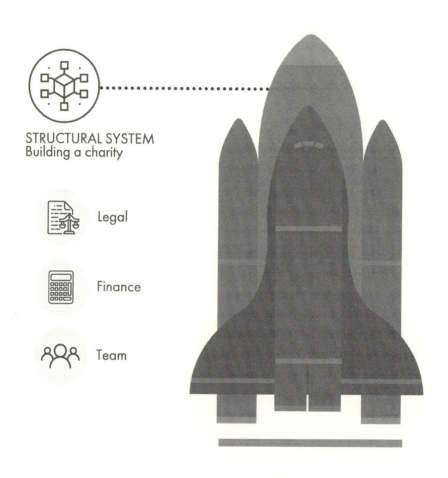

STRUCTURAL SYSTEM
Building a charity

Legal

Finance

Team

30. Running a legally compliant charity

Starting up a new organization involves bringing a legal entity into existence. Doing so, and then ensuring that that entity remains compliant with relevant laws, involves navigating the world of compliance. Understanding the applicable rules is key to creating the right type of organization, keeping that organization on the right side of the law, and performing the organization's essential functions.

While compliance rarely elicits great excitement, and reading up on charity law might not be quite the glamorous kind of activity you looked forward to when starting off, it's important. At worst, compliance work can just look like a series of bureaucratic obstacles that distract from your mission and should be gotten through as efficiently as possible. However, there is some sense and logic behind most regulations, and staying on top of compliance work can result in an organization that is well-governed, financially sound, and that manages risk well. Regardless of how you come to see compliance, falling afoul of relevant regulations can present substantial, even existential, risks to your organization, and to all the good you want to do in the world. Taking some time to learn the relevant rules and build compliance into your organization from the start can help make this work relatively frictionless.

In this section, we will cover the essentials of:

- Choosing a legal structure, including differences between nonprofits and charities, and the fiscal sponsorship option
- Registering as a charity, including whether it's even a good idea

- Reporting requirements to regulators
- Organizational policies, including staff policies and data protection
- Receiving grants and donations
- Giving out grants and moving money, including cross-border flows
- When and how to seek professional help and advice, including for free

First, a couple of disclaimers:

None of this should be interpreted as legal or tax advice, and we encourage you to seek counsel from qualified professionals in the relevant domains.

The specifics of compliance work vary from jurisdiction to jurisdiction. Every country regulates nonprofits and charities slightly differently. What is presented here are the broad strokes and commonalities, and introductions to general concepts. Make sure you understand the specific rules in the jurisdiction relevant to your organization and the work it is doing, as well as your organization's own governing documents.

30.1. Choosing a legal structure

If you're going to found an organization, what exactly is it that you will be founding? In a legal sense, you'll be bringing into existence some kind of entity that will be registered in a certain jurisdiction and have specifically defined capabilities and responsibilities. It is this entity and – insofar as you will be working for the entity – not you who undertakes the activities, and that receives and spends money. It is worth considering what kind of entity you want to found as part of your business plan, as this will impact how your organization operates and what it can and cannot do.

Incorporation: Incorporation is simply the act of creating a corporation. A corporation can be for-profit or a nonprofit. Why might you want to incorporate? The main reason is to limit personal liability. There are variations on the concept, including forms like limited companies and limited liability companies. In essence, though, a corporation protects its owners (or, in the case of a nonprofit corporation, its governing board of directors or trustees) from personal liability. The corporation has legal standing independent from that of its owners/directors. Any agreements into which it enters – with employees, with a supplier, with a lender, with a partner organization – is on its own behalf.

Therefore, if it gets into trouble and, say, gets into debt that it's unable to pay back, it is the corporation and not the owners/directors that is liable for those debts. (It is important to note that this does not absolve owners/directors of their responsibilities. They can be held liable if they fail to uphold their duties in those roles, like if they are negligent in their governance, or if they direct the corporation to do something illegal.)

Nonprofit vs. charity: These terms are easily confused, and colloquially are often used interchangeably. In fact, however, there are important differences. Generally speaking (allowing for slight differences in definition in different jurisdictions), a nonprofit is an organization whose profits, whether from donations or business activities, cannot be used for the personal benefit or interest of any individual. Nonprofit earnings are spent on some common purposes, reinvested into the nonprofit itself, or spent on some general or public benefit. Nonprofit earnings cannot be distributed as dividends or otherwise used to reward shareholders. A charity is a specific type of nonprofit that has tax-exempt status. All charities are nonprofits, but not all nonprofits are charities.

Nonprofits can usually be incorporated and registered relatively easily, typically involving a small fee and online registration. Registration happens through a jurisdiction's corporate registry, which might be at national or sub-national levels (for example, in the US this typically happens at the state level, while in Canada an entity can elect to incorporate with either federal or provincial corporate registries). The process can often be completed in a day or two.

Registering as a charity, on the other hand, is a long and complex process, described in the next section in further detail. The key is that a charity must expend its resources only on activities that are considered "charitable" according to that country's laws, which typically means they must pursue activities only in a number of predefined charitable categories for broad and public benefit. A nonprofit, on the other hand, is allowed to expend its resources on a broader range of activities. For example, organizations like labor unions, homeowner's associations, and private clubs, all of which serve the collective interests of a group but not the public at large, are usually nonprofits that would not qualify as charities.

Fiscal sponsorship: An alternative to setting up a brand-new organization from scratch is to enter into a fiscal sponsorship relationship with an existing one. These types of arrangements are not common in every jurisdiction. They seem to be fairly popular in the United States, and also exist in India, while they seem to be uncommon in the UK and Canada. The idea is for an existing charity that has already gone through the onerous registration process to lend the benefits of its charity status to a new entity.

As the founder of a new venture, you could quickly create a nonprofit corporation, which could then enter into a fiscal sponsorship agreement with a fiscal sponsor (alternatively, you could, as an individual, enter into a fiscal sponsorship agreement, but know that this would expose you to personal liability). This would create a "fictitious entity" that would exist under the aegis of the fiscal sponsor and benefit from their tax-exempt status, without having to go through its own charity registration process. It would be able to operate tax-free and offer its donors the tax incentives on donations to charities.

What's the catch? Fiscal sponsors charge fees, ranging anywhere from 2-15% either of expenditures or revenues. These are sometimes charged on a sliding scale, so a fiscal sponsor might charge 12% on the first $30,000 but only 5% on any amounts above that. There may also be minimum annual fees, or other service and setup fees. There is a whole spectrum of fiscal sponsorship options available, from the more involved, in which fiscal sponsors take care of all accounting and compliance, to the relatively removed. These options are priced accordingly.

Is this worthwhile? It might be, especially while your organization is small and just getting started. In your first year or two, you may want to focus on your core programming and interventions, and build off of the existing systems fiscal sponsors offer. Charity registration can take many months, and you might want to take advantage of a fiscal sponsor's tax-exempt status while waiting for your own registration to be completed. When you get big enough, though, you may have developed the capacity to perform the services a fiscal sponsor provides for less than they charge, at which point it may make sense to break away and become fully independent. Therefore, before entering a fiscal sponsorship relationship, make sure you have an exit strategy, like making sure all the assets held by the fiscally sponsored entity are spent or having the ability to transfer the assets out to your new, independent entity.

Where to set up your organization: For some types of organizations, this can be a difficult choice. If your founders are, for example, based in a high-income country but wish to operate in a low-income country, how do they decide where to create their organization? You'll need to consider (a) where and how you will be fundraising, and (b) where you will be operating.

If you are going to register as a charity, the tax incentives available to your donors will typically only be available to those from that same country. So, if you are a registered charity in the United States, you can offer donation receipts to US-based donors but not donors from other countries. Likewise, it may be easier to receive grant funding from foundations in the same jurisdiction in which you are registered. They may have rules requiring that they only grant to charities registered in the same jurisdiction, or that additional due diligence be carried out on charities registered in other jurisdictions. If you are only setting up a nonprofit and not a charity, this is a less important consideration.

If you want to operate in a different country than where you are doing most of your fundraising, and especially if you want to employ people, you may need to set up an additional entity in the country of operation. Some countries may allow you to set up an entity as a subsidiary or joint venture of the "parent" organization. Some lower-income countries have systems whereby foreign entities can register to operate in their country. Often, there may be requirements to have a certain number of local citizens or residents on the organization's board. There may also be restrictions on moving money across borders from both the giving and receiving countries (more on this below in Chapter 30.6). Hiring staff in a different location can be tricky, given each country's unique labor laws and requirements for employers to remit taxes and contribute to social security schemes. It is difficult to generalize too much here, and there is no real substitute for familiarizing oneself with the relevant rules in each jurisdiction.

30.2. Registering as a charity

While specific definitions may vary by jurisdiction, generally speaking, a charity is a nonprofit organization that has tax-exempt status. This means that it generally doesn't need to pay taxes, and can also offer some kind of tax incentive to its donors. How does an organization become a charity? It will need to undergo an application process to the official regulator of charities in the relevant jurisdiction.

Should you do it? Registering as a charity can be a lengthy process. Once registered, your organization will have additional reporting requirements to the charities regulator. You'll have to show how its resources are being expended and how its activities continue to meet the jurisdiction's legal definition of "charitable." However, becoming a charity does afford the organization substantial financial and reputational benefits such that, in the long run, it is probably worthwhile for most organizations that pursue activities that do meet the definition of "charitable." A good approach is to get started right away, either through a quick nonprofit incorporation and/or use of a fiscal sponsor, and focus on core activities and programming. Once underway, you'll have a better sense of if and when registering is worthwhile. Then, you can get your charity registration process going in the meantime while still pursuing your core activities.

Benefits of being a charity: The immediate tangible benefit is that the organization becomes tax-exempt, leaving it with more resources to fulfill its mission. It can also offer its donors tax incentives. Additionally, becoming a charity can make it easier to receive grant funding. Many foundations are bound by their own rules only to give grants to organizations that are registered charities, or they may require additional due diligence on grantees that are not. In general, having charity status confers reputational benefits. This can signal to donors and potential partners that the organization is credible, in that it has been recognized and continues to be regulated by authorities as an organization pursuing charitable activities.

Charities can often also access other benefits. For example, in the UK, they can qualify for substantial reductions in their "business rates" (a type of tax). Charities are often eligible for discounts on services, fee-free bank accounts, and free advice from professional associations (see below for more on getting free advice). Once you have registered as a charity, always be sure to ask if there is a discount for charities whenever you're buying anything.

Responsibilities of being a charity: Besides the fairly onerous process of registering as a charity, once your organization is registered, it will continue to be overseen by whichever agency regulates charities in that jurisdiction (this is expanded on below). The regulator will be concerned with ensuring that your activities fall into the purposes or objects that were specified in your governing document when you registered as a charity.

Charitable purposes, or objects: A charity's purposes, sometimes called objects, set out the limits of the activities to which it can devote its resources. The purposes are written in the charity's governing document. As part of the registration process, the organization will need to draft its purposes such that they (a) encompass all the activities the charity wants to undertake, and (b) meet the legal definition of what is "charitable" in that jurisdiction.

Charities regulators often set out a number of sample descriptions of purposes that charities can use as their own. For example, the Charity Commission for

England and Wales provides 13 sample descriptions of purposes (along with a 14th general description for "any other charitable purpose"). A charity can borrow the language found in these descriptions to use for its own charitable purposes.

When you apply to register as a charity, the charities regulator will closely scrutinize the charitable purposes you've selected. If you are doing activities that fit straightforwardly into one of the stock categories or descriptions, it's best just to use similar language to signal that your purposes fall neatly into its established categories. For example, if your organization works in global public health, its purpose could fit well into the Charity Commission's purpose #6, "The advancement of health or the saving of lives."

If your organization's activities are a little more complicated, they may not fit so neatly into any one category. Charity Entrepreneurship, for example, does research, provides training, and gives out grants. In these kinds of cases, you can choose purposes from several pre-established categories and/or use the catch-all category (though this will invite added scrutiny and questioning during the registration process).

It's a good idea to browse the registry of existing charities (usually freely accessible online), find charities with similar types of activities, and see how they have worded their purposes. It is perfectly acceptable to copy their wording, and doing so will signal to the charities regulator that your purposes are the same as those of an organization they have already approved for charity status.

If, further down the road, you decide you want to change your charity's activities such that they no longer fit within the original purposes, you will need to apply to the regulator to have the purposes updated. This can also be a long, drawn-out process. Therefore, it is advisable when first registering to try to think ahead about whether your activities might change, and if it might be better to register under purposes that allow some leeway for such future changes.

How to register as a charity: To become a charity, an organization will have to go through an application process. Application forms require a lot of detail on your proposed activities, governance, finances, and how these all meet the standards required of a charity. In many jurisdictions, getting a response to an application can take months, and usually the response is to provide further information and detail. A long process of back-and-forth can ensue. We are aware of organizations that have taken more than a year to become registered charities.

In preparation to register, the organization will need to have selected board directors or trustees, about whom the application may require further information. It can also be useful to have crafted certain policies. These may include a conflict of interest policy and policies that pertain to the organization's activities, like a research policy or process document for a research organization, or a grantmaking policy for a grantmaking organization (see Chapter 30.4), etc.

It can be useful, though not strictly necessary, to seek professional advice during the registration process. This is especially helpful if your organization's activities are a bit complicated and its purposes do not fit straightforwardly into a predefined category of charitable activities (see 30.7 below for more on getting professional advice).

30.3. Reporting to the charities regulator

In most jurisdictions, charities are required to do some kind of reporting to the charities regulator and maintain their financial records to a certain standard. Failure to do so can result in penalties and/or the revocation of charity status. Regulators will want to be assured that the organization is being well-governed, that it is maintaining adequate books and records, and that its resources are being devoted only to its charitable purposes.

Typically, this will come in the form of an annual report or return. In jurisdictions where the charities regulator is the same agency as the tax authority (as in the United States with the IRS, or in Canada with the CRA), you may hear these reports sometimes referred to as tax returns, though this is a misnomer as charities are tax-exempt; the charity report for the Canada Revenue Agency, for example, is properly called an Annual Information Return.

Reports will generally cover the organization's annual finances, some details on programs and activities, information about board directors/trustees and top executives, and affirmations of compliance with regulations. The level of detail required on the charity's finances may depend on the size of the charity. For example, US charities under $50,000 in annual revenue can file an "e-Postcard," those between $50,000 and $200,000 can file a simplified report, and over $200,000, a full report. Financial statements may be required, and might, depending on the size of the organization, need to be examined or audited by a professional accountant.

It's always helpful to keep in mind why charities regulators need to oversee charities. You might have the best intentions in the world, but they are on the lookout for bad and incompetent actors. Charity status confers considerable advantages, and regulators want to make sure that charities are not just businesses in disguise or funding nefarious activities. Insofar as charity status signals a measure of public trust, they also want to be sure that funds donated in good faith by members of the public are being spent competently and responsibly on things that are actually charitable.

30.4. Required and recommended policies

Your organization may be required to have certain policies, depending on where it is registered, what kind of organization it is, and what it does. Some policies may be legal requirements, others may be helpful for setting organizational culture and expectations, and still others may simply be so commonplace that it can look bad to donors, regulators, prospective employees, beneficiaries, and the general public if an organization doesn't have them in place.

If your organization has employees, it will likely need to offer them the minimum legal required amounts of leave in various categories. These can include vacation days, sick leave, parental leave (maternity and paternity), dependents leave (to care for dependents), compassionate leave (to attend a funeral or care for a relative), and civil engagement leave (for jury duty). It is a good idea to have and use a disciplinary procedure and a grievance procedure, based on legal requirements, so that when incidents come up you have a legally compliant set of processes already in place to follow. Policies on equal opportunities or equity diversity and inclusion, anti-harassment and bullying, anti-corruption and bribery, and whistleblowing are all fairly standard and expected to be in place.

If you have staff and a physical location, you may be required to meet minimum requirements and/or have a policy on health and safety in the workplace. If you keep employee, donor, or beneficiary data, or even simply have a website, you'll need to follow rules on data protection and should have privacy policies in place to cover all these groups. Policies on conflict of interest, financial controls, and expenses are useful for making sure your finances are managed with accountability.

How should you draft policies? Free templates of many types are available online. You may also be able to get policies from other friendly organizations just by asking. However, be sure that any you're copying are just a starting point for drafting. You need to ensure that the policy is relevant to the rules in your organization's jurisdiction and your type of organization.

Generally, compliance actually depends on an organization's actions and not just on whether it has written a policy and put it in place. Having written policies is a good signal to internal and external parties that the organization is serious and professional. But be sure to actually follow and enforce them, especially where doing so is a legal requirement.

30.5. Receiving grants and donations

Receiving large grants and donations: Depending on the jurisdiction, an organization may be required to conduct a certain minimum due diligence on its donors, especially from large funders or grantors. This may be a legal requirement, but it also may help mitigate reputational risk. Likewise, a grantmaking foundation may want to conduct due diligence on your organization before granting it funding. It may request much of the same information that a charities regulator would. Having charity status in the same country as the grantmaking foundation may sometimes allow you to bypass these types of checks.

Tax incentives for donors: Donors to registered charities are often eligible for some type of tax incentive. This is usually either a tax deduction or a tax credit for the amount (or some percentage of) the donation. The charity sends the donor a donation receipt, which the donor can use as proof to claim a deduction or credit on their taxes. In the UK, there is also the Gift Aid system, whereby UK taxpayers donating to UK-registered charities can claim "Gift Aid," effectively giving the charity an extra 25% of the value of the donation (there are additional details, so if you're a UK charity, familiarize yourself with these rules). These tax incentives are usually reserved for donors from the same country as the charity. So, if you're a US charity, only funders from the US are eligible for these incentives.

Donation receipts: A registered charity is responsible for issuing donation receipts (often called tax receipts) to eligible donors (typically, those from the same country). These should be issued soon after the donation is made, though for recurring donors it may be permitted to issue a cumulative receipt at the end of the year. Each country will have rules on when receipts must be issued, as well as what information needs to be included on them. Templates are freely available online, and receipts can usually be issued by email.

30.6. Giving out grants and moving money

Money leaving a charity can be a sensitive issue for charities regulators. Generally, they want to see that the charity's resources are expended only on charitable activities, and only on those within the ambit of the charity's registered purposes. Giving money to other charities, and to nonprofits engaged in charitable activities, can also fall under those definitions (especially if the charity is set up as a foundation whose purpose is, say, to make grants to organizations that themselves promote a specified charitable purpose). However, there are often specific rules to follow, which, as always, may vary by jurisdiction.

Giving grants to other charities: When charities regulators refer to "charities," they usually mean only the charities that are registered in their same jurisdiction. To the Canada Revenue Agency, a "charity" means a Canadian charity, and any other entity, including a German, Swiss, or British charity, is considered a "non-charity." Charities regulators like to keep charitable money within the charitable sector. For that reason, it's relatively straightforward for one charity to give to another within the same country. In some jurisdictions, there may not be any specific steps to follow besides ordinary financial recordkeeping. In some cases, a charity's grants may only be granted to another charity that advances the same purpose, so a charity whose purpose is to advance animal welfare wouldn't be able to grant to a charity that works on caring for the elderly. The best practice is to create a grant agreement that sets out explicitly what the grant funds will be used for.

Giving grants to non-charities: Giving grants to a non-charity, which could include a charity that's registered in a different country, a nonprofit that is not a registered charity, or an individual undertaking some personal charitable activity, is a bit more complicated. Regulators may require the granting entity to put in place more thorough measures to ensure the funds are spent only on the granting charity's purposes, including detailed grant agreements and regular reporting requirements.

Moving money across borders: There may be further additional requirements if the grant recipient is located in a different country. For example, Canadian charities regulators require that funds given to a foreign entity be spent only on the granting charity's own activities, and for the recipient entity to act as an intermediary or agent on the instructions of the grantor. For charities with entities in multiple countries, it is important to recognize that the charities regulators may not necessarily recognize your affiliation unless you have made some specific provision, as per their rules. If you have a charity in the UK and a charity in South Africa that, to you, are operationally acting in concert, the UK charities regulator may still simply see a charity and a non-charity. So, if you are moving money between the two, they may require you to treat your affiliate as any other foreign non-charity.

30.7. Getting help and advice

Fortunately, charities and even nonprofits can often benefit from help and advice from professional associations and firms – sometimes even for free!

Pro bono legal help: Most big law firms have pro bono programs that can be surprisingly easy to access through services available online, like TrustLaw and Advocates 4 International Development (A4ID). Personal contacts can be another good way to get access to a firm's pro bono program. You might also check professional associations like the Law Society in the UK and the American Bar Association for advice on how to get pro bono help.

Some big firms have expertise in many areas of the law. So, if you're able to engage them to, say, help you register as a charity, they may also be able to refer you internally to, for instance, their employment team to help you draft staff policies. They can also likely refer you to other law firms that have expertise in other areas. Some may offer a "legal health check" service (this is available on TrustLaw) where they check your organization on various elements of the law to see how compliant you are with all areas, some of which you might not be aware.

Charities networks and professional associations: Big networks or associations for charities and nonprofits can be a wealth of resources. Organizations like the National Council of Nonprofits (US) and the Small Charities Coalition (UK) have free information on their websites like how to register as a charity, how to choose the right legal structure, and guides on how to stay compliant with charities regulators' rules. They often run seminars and workshops educating nonprofit staff on these issues. Professional organizations like TrustLaw (for legal) and Charity Finance Group (for finance) connect nonprofits with professionals looking to volunteer. In the UK, there is an organization called Ethical Property just to help nonprofits with property-related issues. The Effective Altruism community also has a vibrant wealth of operations practitioners sharing helpful advice, how-tos on various areas of compliance, and reviews of professional service providers like insurers and accountants.

31. Running a financially sound charity

Financial management is a big topic. If you're starting an organization and only have one or two staff members, you'll probably need to wear several hats and perform a lot of different functions that in a bigger organization would be split among various types of financial professionals.

Even when you grow and are able to delegate some of these tasks to other people, you'll still need to have a good understanding of financial management in order to provide proper oversight and assess the financial health of your organization. This chapter offers a shallow look at budgeting, banking, bookkeeping and accounting, expenses management, financial controls, and some considerations about receiving money as a nonprofit. It also offers tips on efficient financial management for a small organization, easy ways to cut costs, how to set starting salaries, and thoughts on financial safety nets for founders.

This information should be understood in complement with the previous chapter on compliance, especially with respect to accounting and reporting. It can and should be supplemented with more in-depth courses and readings on these topics, many of which are freely available online.

31.1. Budgeting

General approach to budgeting

The budget is the core element of the financial planning process. Without it, any higher-level financial planning, including annual reports, is impossible.

Your budget defines what you expect to spend to carry out your charity's activities. Your **context** heavily influences your budget and its scope.

- Is your organization in a pilot, growth, or expansion phase?
- What is your current fundraising trajectory and the fundraising potential of your cause area?
- What are your annual goals and how many staff members will you need to implement them?

Answering these questions will help you start budgeting at the right level. You don't want to under-budget, as you might run out of funds to continue operations and pay salaries. You don't want to drastically over-budget either, as you might turn off potential donors or end up with a substantial amount of unused funds – a sign of operational failure in traditional donor circles. If you have to err on one side, be a bit too conservative, as running out of funds is obviously worse than ending up with unused funds. Another reason to be conservative is that you will likely not account for every cost that will come up as you implement your program. For example, imagine you're operating in a country where you need to start contributing to a pension scheme above five staff members. Initially, your operations might have been fine with four staff, but suddenly you realize that you need six. This unexpectedly turns you into a pension contributor for all six staff members. Proper budget planning and a conservative general approach will help you deal with such situations.

Focus on one overall budget that includes program and administrative costs. In terms of defining your detailed program costs that feed into the overall budget, it might help to list these in an activity budget. If you run different programs or conduct an impact evaluation, you might eventually need separate budgets, but hopefully, you can reduce complexity in the beginning by working with just one overall.

Use the most **realistic scenario** in your budget. This scenario includes your current funding and a reasonable fundraising trajectory (depending on previous fundraising success, your fundraising network, and the general ease of fundraising in your area). It should further account for program costs that allow you to carry out an effective pilot of your program. Once you have this realistic scenario outlined, you can add a maximum and minimum scenario. The **minimum scenario** cuts wherever possible but still allows you to test your intervention. Cutting all field staff, for example, would not count, as you could no longer meet your goals. The **maximum scenario** envisages an upper limit of funds you could reasonably spend to test your intervention. The maximum scenario could, for instance, include more beneficiaries to enhance the statistical significance of your pilot. It would, however, still respect your limits in terms of managerial and staff capacity. Don't turn this into the "let me spend $1 million in my first year" scenario.

Don't go into fundraising without a basic budget in hand. As you prepare your budget, also consider your **fundraising sources**. In general, be more hesitant to ask for substantial funds from evidence-based donors than traditional donors. Evidence-based donors have many other proven high-impact options, e.g., GiveWell's top charities, so they should primarily be tapped for initial testing of impact at a young charity. Once an intervention has been proven to be cost-effective, but less so than the current top charities, more traditional donors make more sense. In this case, you will not crowd out the most effective programs and will still stand out in terms of cost-effectiveness.

The overall budget captures a **horizon** of one to two years and therefore allows for monthly planning. If you need a five-year budget, work with annual instead of monthly numbers. In general, a five-year budget can give you some indication of how expensive your program is at scale and whether you should consider cheaper implementation methods given future fundraising needs. From a practical planning and fundraising perspective, the five-year projections will, however, be of limited value. You should be fine with a one- to two-year plan initially.

There is a trade-off between **detail and overview**. Ideally, you capture up to 10 header categories in your budget (e.g., Office) and between 25 and 100 positions, called **item categories** here (e.g., Office HQ). This also heavily depends on the program you implement. If your intervention consists of giving advice, the budget will be easier to draft (mainly personnel cost). The opposite is true for complex programs in the field, say, distribution of drugs or cash transfers. Remember that you have the activity budget so don't need to list, for instance, ten categories for different IT supplies in the overall budget. The **item categories** that you define here will show up in your expense management app, i.e., when a staff member tracks an expense she will be able to describe the purchase (e.g., printer paper) in a free text field and then select the corresponding item category from a drop-down list (e.g., Office HQ). The item category will also be used to compare your budget vs. actual expenses. Hence, make sure that you define the item categories at the right level (not too detailed, as you will end up with too many item categories, but not too high-level, as you will not be able to identify where your program costs more/less than expected). Your staff members should also be able to understand and use the item categories when tracking expenses.

A solid overall budget already links to the **Chart of Accounts** from your accounting system (e.g., QuickBooks). This facilitates your planning, reporting, and auditing processes considerably. More on that further down.

Include a category for **Contingency**, which comes in two forms and can be a lifesaver. It could consist of, for instance, 10% added to your overall budget. This is recommended for all charities. For important budget categories, you might also include a category-specific contingency (e.g., 10% on staff salary). Alternatively, you may choose to opt for an overall contingency and increase it (e.g., to 15%).

Also include a **buffer,** another safety net, which should not be confused with the contingency. While the contingency accounts for unexpected or higher costs, a buffer gives you extra runway for your charity of, say, six months. This comes in handy if your fundraising does not go as planned.

Your budget will change over time as you get more information on accurate costs and adapt your programming. In these instances, make sure not to delete or make previous versions unfindable. Use **versioning** in Google Sheets under File/Version history for smaller updates. Create a different tab in Google Sheets or a new spreadsheet for larger updates such as a new budget cycle.

Calculate with **full costs**. Don't forget taxes and social security contributions. Common costs include social security, pensions, and health insurance. Each country has different standards; in some, there might also be contributions to a national housing or training fund. The fact sheets for employers by international auditing firms such as PwC, KPMG, and Ernst & Young are a good guide for an initial, quick overview. PwC, for instance, publishes Tax Data Cards. Many countries including the UK, US, or former colonies know the PAYE (Pay As You Earn) tax, where deductions for income tax are made directly from the salary by the employer. This means that you are responsible as an NGO for deducting and forwarding tax payments for your staff directly to the tax authorities.

Banking, moving money, and investing

Choosing a bank account: Choose a bank account that meets your organization's present and future needs. Keep in mind that, in some countries, opening an account with a traditional bank can take some time. Consider, does your organization expect to make a lot of transactions? In cash, or electronically? International payments? Accounts in multiple currencies? A bank with brick-and-mortar branches, or one that's used to operating online? A bank with branches or connections in different countries? A bank that offers investment accounts? Different banks will have different offerings and fees associated with these services. As a charity, always ask if there's a fee-free option or special charity account that will better meet your needs.

Moving money: If you have several accounts for different functions, for example, in different currencies, make sure you're keeping enough in each to cover any automatic or upcoming expenses. This might seem obvious, but it's easy to lose sight of if not checked regularly. Got a big office rent payment coming up? Make sure to move enough money into the right account.

In terms of moving money internationally, try services like Wise or Monzo, which offer better rates than traditional banks. Always try to avoid exchange between currencies through traditional banks. For example, if your bank account is in GBP and you're receiving a big grant from an American foundation in USD, receive the money first in a USD balance with Wise or Monzo, convert it to GBP within the service, then transfer it to your main GBP account.

Note that there may be capital controls and restrictions on charity-related cross-border transfers. You can return to Chapter 30.5 for a refresher on this. As a general point, remember that charities regulators like to keep money within a country's charitable sector, and extra procedures may be necessary before moving it to a foreign entity.

Investing: This should not be interpreted as investing advice. We are not investment professionals. We just want to offer a few basic thoughts about investing assets as a nonprofit. When your money is sitting in a checking account (or a Wise or Monzo balance) earning little-to-no interest, it's effectively losing value every day due to inflation. At the very least, you can move your money to a savings account that earns a little more interest, and just keep what you need in the short-term in your checking account.

Interest rates as a whole are very low these days, and so even savings account rates earn barely anything. You can explore specialized, usually online-only banks with higher savings account interest rates. You can also consider investing to get higher returns. Of course, higher returns come with higher risks. At the lower-risk, lower-return end of the spectrum are instruments like term deposits, guaranteed income certificates, and money market funds. At the higher risk, higher return (or loss!) end of the spectrum, you can pick individual stocks, or even borrow money to do so. There are lots of different types of instruments in the middle of the spectrum that might be right for your organization.

How much could you invest, and for how long? If you always maintain a six-month runway of reserve funding, you could invest that more or less indefinitely, but only if you are reasonably certain you'll never need to withdraw before those six months. The longer you are able to invest your money without needing to sell, the higher-risk investment you can expose your organization to.

A few things to keep in mind before investing your organization's money:

- Are your donors okay with this? Check your grant agreements.
- Is your board okay with this? Ask them. Check your constitution and bylaws.
- Is your charities regulator okay with this? Check the rules. There are often regulations about how much charities can save/invest vs. how much they must spend on charitable activities within a year.
- Do your research first and/or consult a professional. There are investment funds available specifically for charities that you could look into, like the Charities Aid Foundation in the UK for example (this is not an endorsement).

Banking, accounting, and expenses management

Bookkeeping and accounting: Bookkeeping refers to the recording of the entirety of the organization's financial transactions – all its income and expenditures. Accounting refers to summarizing, analyzing, and reporting on all those transaction records. It's a good idea to use accounting software like QuickBooks or Xero, which allows you to record all of your transactions (bookkeeping), and facilitates some aspects of accounting as well.

You'll need a way to track all your expenses and revenues (more on expenses management below). But, basically, you should have records of most, if not all, of your transactions from your bank records. All money going in and out should be in your bank statements. Many banks can be linked with accounting software like QuickBooks such that transactions are automatically imported. This simplifies your monthly bookkeeping task so that each month you need merely to go down the list of imported transactions, make sure they seem right, and categorize them properly. For bank accounts that cannot be automatically imported into accounting software, you can manually enter transactions from your bank statements. Alternatively, if you are tracking transactions in a spreadsheet, you could format it to be importable into your accounting software.

Reconciliations: Once all your transactions are recorded, you should do monthly bank reconciliations. This is a standard method of verifying that the amounts recorded in your accounting software match the amounts in your bank accounts. After recording the transactions in your software, you check the closing balance for that month's bank statement. The closing balance in the accounting software should be the same as on the bank statement. Accounting software has features to facilitate bank reconciliations.

Chart of Accounts: The chart of accounts is a list of all the different "accounts" that your organization has identified as useful to classify its finances. These include "Balance Sheet" accounts for Assets (like cash held in bank accounts) and Liabilities (like debt), as well as "Income Statement" accounts for Revenues (like donations) and Expenses (like salaries, rent, bank fees, etc.). These are usually expressed as a number followed by a description, like "59100 Payroll salaries."

There are some existing conventions in the numbering and naming of accounts, but you can also come up with your own. You can make your financial management a lot simpler by standardizing financial categories across your budget, your accounting, and even your annual reports to charities regulators. This makes it easy to compare your budget with actual spending and fill out fields on your reports. For example, if you have an account in your Chart of Accounts called "30100 Rent," it can be matched with the budget category for Rent so you can compare budgeted and actual spending. When it's time to fill out your annual report to the charities regulator, if their form has a line to show all expenditures on Rent, you can easily find it under the "30100 Rent" account. This is also convenient with revenues; if you set up your Chart of Accounts to match required fields on your annual report to the charities regulator like, say, donations from domestic entities and donations from foreign entities, when the time comes to fill out your report you won't need to go back and figure out which donations were from individuals, foundations, or foreign entities because you were tracking these categories all along.

Expenses management: If you have a lot of staff members making expenditures, and especially if they are doing so in person and with cash, you may need to implement more advanced expense management systems. There are apps available for tracking expenses at greater levels of detail, some of which are quite user-friendly, for example, allowing any user on their phone to add an expenditure and upload a picture of the receipt quickly. This allows you to facilitate a large number of staff members making expenditures without having to give them access to (or train them on) the accounting software. Records taken through an app can feed directly into a spreadsheet, which can be imported into the software.

However, if you have a small number of expenses, or if most of them are made by the same person or electronically, your expenses management can be relatively simple. Expenses will show up in the statements of your bank accounts and credit cards. Using an expense management system outside your accounting software does add a level of complexity, creating the possibility that information might be lost if procedures are not followed properly. So, if it's not strictly needed, you may be better off simply working directly through accounting software.

If you are operating in a context in which it is not possible to make electronic payments either online or in-person using the organization's bank or credit cards, you may need to work through cash advances. Sometimes, staff members may also pay for organization expenses themselves and be reimbursed. Ideally, you want to minimize cash advances and reimbursements as much as possible and instead set up your systems so that expenses can mostly be paid directly from the organization's accounts. This reduces administrative burden as well as risk for the organization and employees. If you do need to use reimbursements and cash advances, be sure to have clear policies on who can approve expenses, what can be reimbursed, how long cash advances can stay open, and procedures for opening and closing them.

For every type of transaction, always keep your receipts, invoices, and other transaction records somewhere safe. For hard copies, take a picture and save it to that safe place. When you do your monthly bookkeeping, you can attach the transaction record to the transaction in the accounting software. Transaction records are proof that the money was spent or received in the way you claimed, which is helpful if you ever get audited and also good for your own internal accountability.

Financial statements: Financial statements are written records that summarize the financial activities and position of an organization in different formats. Understanding how to read financial statements is a good way for a manager to understand the financial position and health of an organization. You can search online for quick tips on how to read and understand financial statements in more detail. In brief, financial statements typically include three reports:

- **Balance Sheet** (also called the Statement of Financial Position): This provides a snapshot of the organization's assets and liabilities at any given point in time

- **Income Statement** (sometimes called Profit and Loss Statement, or Statement of Operations): This covers a range of time (so for annual financial statements, one year) and summarizes revenues, expenses, and net income

- **Cash Flow Statement**: This shows the flow of money through the organization and how much cash is available for expenses each month

If your bookkeeping and bank reconciliations are up to date, your accounting software should be able to generate these reports automatically. Financial statements may be requested by the organization's board, its donors, and/or the government charities regulator in order to understand the organization's financial health and position. They may even ask for independently audited financial statements, in which case the organization would need to hire an auditor to thoroughly review the organization's finances.

Receiving money as a nonprofit

Recordkeeping: In your accounting software, it's a good idea to set up accounts for different types of revenues. These can include separate categories: for example, for donations from donors (directly), donors (through a third party platform), and large institutional donors providing grants. You can also set up different Classes or Tags in your accounting software in case some funds are earmarked for specific sub-projects.

Receiving donations from the public: Lots of payment processing platforms are available to facilitate the receipt of donations from the public to nonprofits, including services like iATS, PayPal, Charity Engine, and Stripe. Generally, they charge small fees on transactions. You can also use charitable donation platforms like GiveIndia, CanadaHelps, CharityChoice, or Findly. For these, donors can find and donate to your charity through their website, or you may be able to put a donation button on your site for donations processed through them. Some such services take care of issuing donor receipts on your behalf, meaning that the actual donation is made from the donor to the donation platform, which then makes a gift to your organization.

For bigger donations, it may be worthwhile to direct donors to get in touch with you so you can provide them instructions to make a direct bank/wire transfer, which might save on fees from donation/payment platforms. Consider asking your donors if they want to set up monthly donations, which can be automated through donation/payment platforms, or their bank if doing a bank transfer.

Receiving big grants from foundations and institutions: These could include grants from philanthropic foundations, government agencies, and companies. Such grants tend to come with reporting requirements attached. These can include financial reports, narrative reports, and regular progress on key metrics on a quarterly, semi-annual, or annual basis. These reporting requirements can be fairly onerous, especially if the guarantor is a government agency. Large international development NGOs that receive a lot of their funding from governments and multilateral organizations employ whole departments of people to apply for grants and fulfill reporting requirements.

It is important to understand reporting requirements from the moment the grant is first received, as your organization may be required to track expenses in certain ways or categories from the beginning. Likewise, there may be restrictions you'll need to know about from the start. For example, it is common for expenditures on overhead costs to be required not to exceed a certain proportion of the total grant.

Efficient financial management processes

You'll want to regularize and automate your financial management processes as much as possible. This may not seem necessary when you're just starting out and the number of transactions and quantities you're dealing with are small. But when you begin to grow, you'll be thankful that you automated the processes you needed to earlier on. Getting things regularized from the start will help keep administration simple and prevent your administrative costs and hiring needs from growing more than necessary.

Here are just a few simple tips you can implement from the start:

- Get all your bills on direct debit payments that automatically withdraw from your bank account, or have them automatically charged to a credit card

- Get your payroll on the same schedule and pay everyone monthly or biweekly on the same dates, regardless of when their contract started. Use a payroll service (check for charities discounts or free versions!) to manage tax remittances and social security contributions for you.

- Use forms like Google Forms or JotForm to cut down on dozens of disorganized requests coming into your financial manager via email, Slack, text message, etc. Use forms for:

  ○ Recording employee contact details

  ○ Recording employee bank details

  ○ Recording expenses

  ○ Employee reimbursement expense claims

  ○ Records of cash advances

  ○ ... anything else you can think of!

- Outsource complicated and time-consuming tasks using platforms like Upwork

  ○ For example, maybe you don't know how to do bookkeeping, or you're just learning and it takes you a long time. A professional bookkeeper might be more cost-efficient, freeing up your time or saving you from making a deeper commitment by hiring another staff member.

31.2. Five ways to cut costs

The fundraising pitch went well, and thirty days later, you shout in excitement as a six-figure number pops up on your e-banking app. But don't get too pumped. Now begins the quest of spending your resources diligently.

Spend only on one to two high-impact projects

As a curious founder, you see so many opportunities for your charity. It is tempting to pursue many of them at the same time. Yet that would be a mistake. By spending on various projects, you allocate funding to opportunities below the top choice in terms of impact. Why spend on the second, third, and fourth most cost-effective project if you can instead pool resources to the best choice?

As you spend on more than one project, you are not only reducing your monetary power but also your managerial focus. You already have limited bandwidth with one project as a charity founder. Don't stretch it further. So as a general rule, focus on one project at a time – or, in exceptional circumstances, on two.

Cut fixed costs

A trendy office in the heart of London: doesn't this qualify as an investment in your staff and your organization's long-term success? But watch out before you sign that two-year lease in the glass skyscraper. While possibly obvious in this example, the decision on which fixed costs make sense is not always easy to spot. The problem with such costs is that they increase your overhead without having a direct relationship with the number of beneficiaries you serve. The size and interior of your office do not influence your potential to fulfill your charity's mission. Many organizations, including charities such as New Incentives, operate completely remotely. Others, like Charity Entrepreneurship, have successfully found affordable offices even in global cities such as London.

Reducing fixed costs applies to staff as well, most likely your number one expense item. Here, it is less straightforward, as you need skilled staff members to serve your beneficiaries. You also don't want to burn out or stretch your managerial capacity too much by not recruiting. Yet as an early organization, stick to the co-founding team for as long as possible. Your program might still iterate quite a bit, and new hires may not fit into an organization that has undergone a pivot. While staff increases capacity, it also requires more oversight on your end. Additionally, being a smaller team forces you to focus on your strategic decisions. And of course, fewer staff equal lower cost.

Use an activity budget

Your overall budget includes all expenses from program to overhead. Your activity budget, on the other hand, tracks all costs going into serving one beneficiary. As such, it allows you to track your unit costs. Working with unit costs helps you design a cost-effective and scalable program. If your beneficiaries are spread out over hundreds of villages or clinics, for example, you will have high transport costs. Noticing this in an activity budget will start the brainstorming process on how to serve beneficiaries in a more sustainable way (e.g., by organizing camps that bring beneficiaries together in fewer locations).

Start with a low salary

We sometimes get questions from applicants about whether they could assign themselves an annual salary of, say, $75,000. Technically, they can. After all, you call the shots as founder. Yet, this might not be the best idea. A relatively high salary at a start-up has several downsides:

- It limits your ability to pivot as your runway is shorter (all other things being equal).

- It makes fundraising harder by requiring you to raise potentially double or triple of what you would have asked for otherwise.

- Depending on your donor, it can be seen as too high for an organization with an unproven track record.

Therefore, we encourage our incubatees to start out with relatively low salaries. As an organization, we also believe in a culture that does not align seniority with a higher salary. Our co-founders, for example, are among the lowest-paid staff members. We encourage our charities to follow suit and actively decouple personal worth as an employee from the monthly paycheck.

Watch out for common cost drivers

Aside from salary and office, there are several other common cost drivers at charities.

- Field transport can be a crucial one. A developing-country context does not mean that transport will be particularly cheap, especially if you have many staff members who need to travel on a frequent basis.

- Electricity is another, as the grid can be unreliable in many countries and running a generator is expensive. As a modern organization, you likely run your program digitally, so you need to factor in the costs for getting each staff member at least a mobile phone and accessories like power banks.

- Finally, training costs can be higher than expected – you usually underestimate the duration needed to onboard new field staff, and facilities such as training halls are costly.

In sum, there are many ways to make the best of your charity's finances as a founder – so make sure to protect this six-figure number on your start-up's bank account for as long as possible.

31.3. More safety nets than you think?

Charity entrepreneurship is in many ways a less stable career than a traditional job. Charities in their early days will have limited runway (often under six months). At any point, results could come in showing that an intervention is not worth continuing. On the other hand, value drift is an important consideration. Losing motivation to achieve altruistic impact happens more quickly than one would expect. Hence, it is better to donate more to effective causes now than to accumulate a large safety buffer that you might later spend ineffectively in the case of value drift. So a question arises: how much personal runway or savings should someone have when becoming a charity entrepreneur?

In the case of any job, people will want enough safety nets to be able to transition securely from one position to another. The first fact to consider is the average length of time between jobs. It's worth looking at your past history and the history of similar peers. The second thing to consider is cash-based savings, but there are also many other, often forgotten safety nets. Monetary savings are only one of them – frequently representing a fairly small percentage of a person's overall safety net.

Often, when non-financial safety nets are taken into account, everyone's position looks substantially more secure, and thus more confident. Non-financial safety nets are things that exist in a peer group or world outside of a personal bank account that extend the effective time a person could be unemployed without considerable negative ramifications. Living on a friend's couch for months wouldn't be that thrilling, but it would be far from homelessness. Some factors to consider when estimating your current personal runway include:

Partner

For those who have a partner, this will commonly be the first level of safety net. Even if a major event throws your earning ability out the window, often a single earner (particularly in high-earning demographics) can cover the difference.

Cost-cutting

This is a strategy that likely would work in combination with any others. Few people are cutting expenses as much as they could if the need arose. Certain factors like rent might be hard to change quickly, but food and entertainment budgets are generally a lot more flexible.

Family

Not all families are able or willing to provide long-term support, but many are. Some people, due to having a partner or divorced parents, have multiple plausible families who could help out with things like free rent. And in many crisis situations, most would be more than happy to help for fairly long periods of time.

Friends

Not everyone has a group of friends that would be able to give a temporary place to live, or friends wealthy enough to offer a loan, but many people do. Those in the charity sector, in particular, tend to have more altruistic and high-talent peer groups. In many cases of serious distress, friends can pull a lot of weight.

Internal capacity

Some events requiring safety nets might completely destroy one's effective capacity to work. However, many would just lower the value of the job they would get if they had to find work in a rush due to financial pressure. For example, many people skilled enough to be charity entrepreneurs could get an entry-level job in some other industry within a matter of weeks if they needed to.

Possession-based safety nets

Many people own a house, a car, or other assets that can be used as an extra safety net, although not a quickly accessible one, in times of need.

Legal insurances

Many individuals have several insurances such as home, car, and medical. The point of these insurances is to cover unexpected negative events, although they are category-specific.

Government safety nets

Though not the most prestigious option, many government programs are available for people who experience a sudden shock. The details vary greatly from country to country, but social programs such as employment insurance, welfare, and subsidized living exist in many high-income countries.

Credit and loans

Forty percent of US households carry credit card debt. Given the high interest rates of 12-15%, spending on credit should only be used as a last resort. Cheaper options for loans include crowdlending online platforms and mortgage providers (if you own a house). In general, debt should be avoided if at all possible. If necessary, look into no- or low-interest loans from family and friends first (see above).

Combine safety nets to get optimal protection

One can imagine **combining these resources in different ways and ending up at 12-24 months of safety net** or more while having nothing in cash savings. Everyone's personal situation will be different, but listing these considerations can generally reduce anxiety around savings buffers and help you feel more confident donating or taking on an ambitious project.

31.4. Setting salaries

When it comes to creating a cost-effective intervention, keeping overhead low is less important than choosing the right intervention and maintaining a well-run organization… but it helps a lot. In addition to leaving more money for other high-impact causes, keeping overhead low is also appealing to many donors.

Salaries are usually the single biggest cost at most starting organizations. So for the most part, keeping overhead low means limiting salaries. Setting them in a way that is fair to your employees, retains talent, and maximizes impact is a challenge. We recommend meeting this challenge by asking employees to put impact first, and to assess their financial need honestly in light of these priorities.

Decouple salaries from management hierarchies and skill

While it is generally understood that nonprofit salaries are lower than for-profit salaries, most nonprofits take their cues from practices in the for-profit world and set salaries as commensurate to experience and skill. While there are some cases where it makes sense to pay for talent, we think this is often a mistake – especially if you are hiring within the effective altruism community or for a role where value alignment is highly important.

EAs are a unique group in that many of them are taking the salary that they feel is ethical, instead of the average amount the market would pay for someone of their skill set. In some cases, this means that they are earning to give and donating a substantial portion of their wages, so they keep much less than they earn. Others are working for nonprofits, taking a much lower salary than they could be making at a for-profit organization. These people are all acting altruistically – they are living more frugally, working more, and taking on more financial risk in order to alleviate the hardship of others. This is a very positive action. In a world where half the population survives on under $5.50 a day,[1] directing a portion of our resources away from ourselves and toward others can move us in the direction of a society where every person is cared for.

Choosing to pay people according to talent, experience, and position in a

---

1 The World Bank, "Nearly Half the World Lives on Less than $5.50 a Day," World Bank Press Release, Oct. 17, 2018, https://www.worldbank.org/en/news/press-release/2018/10/17/nearly-half-the-world-lives-on-less-than-550-a-day.

hierarchy can have a negative effect on work culture. People might start using their salary to appraise the degree to which their contribution is valued. These comparisons can lead to bitterness, especially when combined with the power dynamic inherent between an employee and an employer. What's worse, it ultimately inflates your budget, largely for signaling reasons.

At Charity Entrepreneurship, the co-founders and senior staff tend to have the lowest salaries in the organization.[2] This saves money, but it also communicates a message to every employee that their salary is not an indication of how much they are valued. This invites each individual to consider what salary they need, with full knowledge of the implications in terms of funding counterfactuals and fundraising.

Salaries higher than the "market" undercut your employees' counterfactual impact

The effective altruism community has an abundance of incredibly talented people that would be thrilled to work in an EA position, even for a very low salary. Organizations within effective altruism tend either to have insufficient funding or insufficient management capacity to use the formidable level of talent that the community brings to the table effectively. This means that job applications within the effective altruism community are extremely competitive,[3] and you'll often have plenty of top talent to choose from even if you offer a low salary.

Why is there so much interest from such talented people? It's because the big idea of "effective altruism" is appealing to many smart individuals, and they want to devote their careers to having an impact and helping others. When you hire them, you have a responsibility to guide them toward realizing that impact.

You should, therefore, create a culture where all of you are on the same team, striving together to maximize impact for the world. For example, if you have a really promising candidate or current employee who could do or is doing a lot of good for your organization – but you know of another opportunity where they could do even more good, you should tell them about it and give them

---

2 Joey Savoie, "Setting our salary based on the world's average GDP per capita," Effective Altruism Forum, Aug. 26, 2017, https://forum.effectivealtruism.org/posts/zXLcsEbzurd39Lq5u/setting-our-salary-based-on-the-world-s-average-gdp-per.

3 EA applicant, "After one year of applying for EA jobs: It is really, really hard to get hired by an EA organisation," Effective Altruism Forum, Feb. 25, 2019, https://forum.effectivealtruism.org/posts/jmbP9rwXncfa32seH/after-one-year-of-applying-for-ea-jobs-it-is-really-really.

sincere advice.

Working together to achieve impact also applies to decisions that don't necessarily feel good. If someone who you respect and enjoy working with asks for a raise from $25k to $75k, as a person with an altruistic heart you might be tempted to help them out by saying yes. It will be easy to come up with justifications for this: "Higher salaries lead to less turnover," "This person's work is clearly worth more than $75k anyway so it's still a deal." Sometimes, some of these considerations are true! It is very often worth putting in extra money to retain talent. However, it's easy to create rationalizations to help someone you know personally at the expense of your beneficiaries whom you do not know personally. You should think about whether granting this request will really achieve more impact.

In the context of negotiations,[4] we talk about BATNA – the best alternative to a negotiated agreement. If you take a deal that is worse than your BATNA, your total impact will be lower. While your employee may personally want more money, they care about impact just like you do. They joined your organization because they want to do good. The problem is, if the counterfactual of hiring them is that you would have hired someone else who would've done the job about equally well and for less money, it means that they're not actually achieving any counterfactual impact. In that scenario, they could actually have more impact by switching over to the for-profit sector, taking the salary that is closer to what they prefer, and donating the difference if they manage to make extra on top of that. Raising their salary might feel nice, but you're creating market inefficiencies that ultimately undercut impact. (Take into account as part of your market the existence of highly dedicated EAs who will work for lower salaries. What is relevant is specifically your alternative options as an organization, not the standards in the larger "market" of the industry in general.) Remember, the charity is primarily for your beneficiaries, not for your employees.

When socially appropriate, you should be clear with employees about the (counterfactually informed) value of their work, so that they can choose their careers in such a way as to maximize impact in the manner they feel is best.

Some employees are incredibly high impact – but salaries don't always need to be commensurate with impact

The truth is that top talent for your specific context isn't always that easy to

---

4 See the fundamentals at https://bit.ly/CEnegotiation.

find. So, in many cases, your BATNA will be sufficiently bad that you really can justify fairly high salaries in terms of retention of talent that produces impact. Given that some estimates put the expected value of starting a charity in the $250-500k range (at least in terms of how much we think you would need to donate to GiveWell top charities to achieve an equivalent amount of impact for humans),[5] it is plausible that there will be some positions within your organization that achieve impact in the six-figure range. There will be some situations where finding the right person for the job is a key bottleneck. In those cases, it is worth paying a fairly high salary to retain them. When faced with such a situation, you should ask yourself whether paying a higher salary is likely to address some key bottleneck to impact. If your main bottleneck is funding or management capacity, hiring a staff member who needs a higher salary will probably not be a high-impact choice. On the other hand, if you are struggling to fill a key position with a qualified candidate, it might make sense to raise the salary levels in order to draw more applicants or retain a specific person.

When someone is doing very high-impact work that you cannot replace, your BATNA is unfavorable. Therefore, if it looks like they will stop working or do less work if you don't pay them more, you should increase their wages in order to retain them. This also applies to you – if you feel that you're being tempted to stop working because your salary is too low, consider raising your salary in order to retain yourself.

However, just because you can honestly say that you think someone's work is generating $500k+ of impact that could not happen without them doesn't mean you must pay them a six-figure salary in order to retain them. You don't need to pay people more than the salary they ask for – and since they probably care about impact just as much as you do, it might be easier than you think to get them to ask for less. This is where the culture of your organization makes a huge difference. When people see that salary is not a matter of prestige or the degree to which they are valued, and when people see that you are taking a low salary yourself, then they will remember that, according to their values, the best use of money is to help others.

Remember that the charity sector is not an efficient market. You may find yourself in a position of controlling a very large budget and generating a lot of funding – but just because you have the power to pay very high salaries doesn't mean that doing so is a high-impact choice. On the other hand, you may be

---

5 See again Wildeford, "What is the expected value of creating a GiveWell top charity?"

very high impact and still have trouble raising enough funding to pay all your staff. In the nonprofit world, the relationship between money and value is not straightforward.

Approach salary with compassion and sensitivity – but don't forget the bottom line

Although individuals applying to EA orgs tend to skew toward affluence, people come from diverse backgrounds and contexts. Matters of money carry heavy practical and emotional implications for the majority of people.

Everyone is in a different situation with respect to how much money they need. Some people come from a more affluent background, such that they are in no real danger of being harmed by not having enough money – perhaps due to a variety of safety nets from affluent family and friends. In the event of an emergency, they can easily take out low-interest loans or rely on various social assets such as their parents, romantic partners, or close friends for help. Some people live in countries with stronger social security systems than others, such that their worst-case scenarios are a lot less bad. They will be able to have a more relaxed and flexible attitude about salary.

For others, money is more complicated. Some people are supporting dependents, such as aging relatives who don't work and have medical fees. Some support younger relatives or children. Some people know that they will be responsible for supporting aging relatives in the future, or plan to have children, and therefore need to build up savings. Some people are paying off very large debts. Some people have experienced past deprivation and will generally be more skittish about taking lower salaries due to fear. The unfortunate reality of this world is that if you don't have money, you and the people you care about can be denied basic needs such as shelter and medical care. **The practical repercussions of possibly running out of money can be much more dangerous for people who come from less affluent backgrounds and aren't well connected to social safety nets.**

However, as much as these issues impact you and your coworkers, **they likely impact your beneficiary populations much more severely.** The reality is that things are so bad that it only takes $3k or so to save a person's life. That doesn't mean you need to feel guilty about every dollar or micromanage every penny, but stay honest about the trade-offs you are making and don't forget what is at stake.

Because of these considerations, it is worth having an honest discussion in which you let potential hires know what salaries at your organization tend to be and encourage them to think about their financial needs and goals in light of that. If you maintain a culture of lower salaries among the co-founders and senior staff, it will serve as a gentle implicit reminder of what is at stake and encourage awareness of the counterfactuals that are at play.

Salary is, understandably, a topic where emotions can run high. Remember to have these discussions with the appropriate level of sensitivity and compassion. If you are someone from a more affluent background who is not in any true danger of being harmed by not having enough money, the stress of being in that situation may be hard for you to perceive. Try to be aware of ways in which you may come off as insensitive or out of touch with the realities of most people when talking about salary. Don't forget that controlling the salary of someone who is anxious about their finances puts you in a position of power over them, and this will change how they interact with you. If you are someone from a less privileged background, the pressure of having to lead by example and take a low salary might be a more difficult burden for you. You might struggle with resentment more if other people aren't willing to make the same sacrifices. These are challenging issues in which trade-offs between different priorities must be made, and not everyone will have the same opinion.

Remember that making the right choice for the greater good isn't always easy, but it is worth it because of all the good you can accomplish. **Make a special effort to be accepting and nonjudgmental of other people's choices, while staying extra compassionate about their personal circumstances and doing your best to act in the way that is right and produces the highest impact.**

When does it make sense to splurge on a very high salary?

In our experience, it has not been the case that more talented people demand higher salaries. In fact, we have found that most people who are very dedicated to having an impact and who have thought deeply about what money can buy in terms of helping others have asked for lower salaries, because they are compelled by the cost-effectiveness argument. (Of course, this varies according to each person's financial circumstance, temperament, and guiding philosophy with respect to altruism. There are driven and talented people who do ask for higher salaries.)

However, there are a few situations where the best person for the job is unlikely to be the type of person who is compelled by the idea that taking a lower salary will allow them to do a massive amount of good. The effective altruism community has a lot of very talented people with a diverse array of skills, but sometimes you need to hire someone very specific – for instance, a lobbyist, an auditor, or a lawyer who specializes in a specific issue in a specific country. This issue can also occur when you need to hire someone who lives in a geographic location with fewer effective altruists. The blessing of being able to hire highly talented employees for cheap is only possible when those employees strongly believe in the value of what you are all working on together. This won't always be the case outside of the EA community.

In this scenario, the proverb "you get what you pay for" sometimes applies. You'll have to use market value and your BATNA as your guide, and if necessary offer a higher salary to attract top talent. You should still try to keep this salary low during negotiations, and consider whether getting the work done pro bono is an option – but keep room in your budget for the possibility that you will not be able to hire a specialist cheaply.

There is such a thing as being "too frugal"

We think that most organizations err on the side of being not frugal enough, and that more frugality translates to greater impact. However, there are some people who are overly scrupulous and end up having a lower impact as a result of trying to be frugal and cost-effective.

Author Daniel Pink writes that "the best use of money as a motivator is to pay people enough to take the issue of money off the table."[6] If you or your employees find yourselves spending a lot of time seriously worrying about money in your day-to-day lives, feeling resentful because of money, or starting to burn out on altruism because of it, it is a sign that you may want to increase salary. Even if someone doesn't "need" more money to live, the reality is that none of us are perfectly altruistic, and it's better to be a little "selfish" and put yourself first in some scenarios if the alternative is that you lose your motivation to help. We only suggest that this is done in a mindful fashion – not with guilt, but keeping within certain limitations and being consciously aware of the trade-offs.

---

6 Daniel Pink, *Drive: The Surprising Truth About What Motivates Us* (New York City: River-head Books, 2011). For a quick explanation, see Farnham Street, "Daniel Pink on Incentives and the Two Types of Motivation," Farnham Street Media, accessed Nov. 10, 2021, https://fs.blog/daniel-pink-two-types-of-motivation/.

It's also almost always a good trade to spend money to increase the amount of time and energy you have available – for instance, buying a dishwasher, or avoiding a commute. A good heuristic when making time-money trade-offs is to ask yourself whether your time- and energy-saving expenditure is cheaper per hour than hiring another staff member.

If you find yourself spending $1,000 on something that enables you to work two more hours every week, that is probably a good deal! However, if you find yourself raising your entire salary by $40k because it gives you more time and energy to work, you're probably spending too much. You could hire an entire full-time staff member for that amount. You might still raise a salary by $40k for retention reasons in very rare cases – but that would be because people have drives other than altruism, and it wouldn't be justifiable for time-saving reasons.

Ask about salary expectations during the interview process

People vary widely in terms of what kind of salary they expect. There is no standardized salary in this type of work – you will encounter people asking for $10k and people asking for $100k in the same hiring round. By asking people's expectations during the interview process, you will be able to compare qualified candidates directly against each other and prioritize those more affordable. This also gives you a sense of your next-best option when negotiating salary with the candidate whom you ultimately decide to accept, which, as previously discussed, improves your negotiating power.

Some organizations choose instead to state the salary up front in the job application. Potential employees generally appreciate this because it is more straightforward, but it comes with pros and cons. Listing a high value will likely net you more candidates, but reduce your ability to negotiate salaries downward. Listing a low value will help ensure that whoever does apply will be happy with what they get, but might drive away talented candidates you may have been willing to pay for. Communicating your parameters before hearing the other party's opening bid can put you in a weaker negotiating position, but it can also be beneficial if you are in a high-trust relationship with your negotiating partner. If you want a middle ground, you might say that pay is flexible and that high salaries can be offered under the right circumstances – but mention that you are running a generally frugal organization focused on helping its beneficiaries and that applicants will be encouraged to evaluate their needs honestly. You can also give the range of values that other staff are paid to give applicants a sense of what to expect.

Summary

Salaries are expensive, and it's good to keep them low. We recommend that you and your senior staff especially set yours low in order to remove the "prestige" aspect of a high salary within the organization and create social norms that encourage low salary asks. Paying salaries above the natural "market" rate may have a negative counterfactual impact, which neither you nor your employee wants. For some particularly good employees, the natural "market" rate may be in the six-figure range, but if you maintain a cultural norm of low salary asks and awareness of counterfactuals, they will usually ask for significantly less.

When negotiating salaries, remember that money has different implications for different people. Be compassionate, sensitive, and aware of disparities in circumstance and less visible forms of privilege when discussing salary. However, don't forget that the beneficiaries that you are trying to help are facing much more extreme disparities, on much larger scales, and that their interests ultimately come first.

We're strong proponents of frugality, but there is such a thing as being too frugal, and there are some situations when you should offer a high salary. Discussions about salary typically start right before you make a job offer, and publishing exact salaries up front may limit your scope for negotiation. But, it can be helpful to present hints about salary expectations in your job ads, applications, and interviews – as well as to collect information about the expectations of your prospective employee.

32. Running a charity team

We've talked about the processes that you need to run a charity. But at least as important as your processes are your people. Running a charity team requires all the skills of management and leadership, plus the ability to connect your work to your organization's underlying purpose.

You can visualize your team as concentric circles, starting with your co-founder and gradually moving out to employees, volunteers, and partner organizations. Let's start with the most important and first member of your team: your co-founder.

32.1. Working with your co-founder

Prioritizing your tasks and time requires a multitude of decisions every day. In fact, one could rightly say your main job as co-founders is to make decisions (which is why Part II of this handbook covers this topic in such depth). How should you go about doing so, especially if you have different intuitions about the right path forward?

Nobel Prize winner Daniel Kahneman points out that noise might be even worse for decision-making than biases. While biases are predictable and uniform, noise is random and therefore harder to spot. For instance, Kahneman notes that in one study, radiologists gave the same X-ray a different diagnosis in 20% of cases. This reflects the randomness of noise rather than the uniformity of a bias. One way to counter this is to set up strict processes, ideally algorithms, for your most important decisions.[1] Each co-founder should agree on what tools you want to use for each decision, which will get you on the same page quickly.

Going a step further, it helps if you have outlined a general framework for your decision-making. If you approach a decision with the same values, such as cost-effectiveness, you're off to a good start, already thinking along the same lines. It also helps to have outlined some roles and responsibilities. Many decisions don't necessarily need the approval of all co-founders, which makes for more rapid decision-making and clearer accountability.

If you disagree despite having done all of the above, you still have a variety of options at your disposal. Here are a few specific ways to resolve decision deadlock:

- **What do the data say?** Disagreement usually centers around different intuitions to interpret a specific challenge. This can be resolved if you have data pointing in one direction or the other.

- **Can you test?** Even if you don't have existing data to resolve your controversial question, you can potentially set up a short experiment to get answers. If you target fish farmers as an animal charity and disagree internally about the best messaging, test two or more different versions. You might not always be able to run a statistically significant test, but your experiment can at least give you a better understanding from a qualitative research perspective.

- **Can you reach a compromise?** It does not always have to be only A or B. Maybe both co-founders' concerns can be integrated into a different solution, (A+B)/2.

- **What are the underlying concerns of the dispute?** Dive one level deeper and try to understand the concerns of each co-founder. As outlined in the Robert Fisher classic on negotiation strategy *Getting to Yes*, focus on the interests, not the positions.[2] You might have a disagreement, for example, about the appropriate reimbursement rate for field staff. The person who insists on the upper bound might not necessarily be

---

1 Nathan Matias, "Bias and Noise: Daniel Kahneman on Errors in Decision-Making." *J. Nathan Matias* (Medium blog), Oct. 17, 2017, https://natematias.medium.com/bias-and-noise-daniel-kahneman-onerrors-in-decision-making-6bc844ff5194.

2 Notes on Robert Fisher, *Getting to Yes: Negotiating Agreement Without Giving In* (London: Penguin Publishing Group, 2011), available through https://www.nateliason.com/notes, accessed Nov. 10, 2021.

stuck to a position of higher reimbursement rate. Her underlying interest might be to value the contributions of the field team adequately. This concern could also be solved by other means, e.g., social recognition or performance-based bonuses. Focusing on the interests opens up the field for various out-of-the-box solutions.

- **Can an expert settle the dispute?** You might both agree that your advisor X or your advisory board is best suited to solve a particular conflict. In this sense, you agree to the decision-making method of delegating to someone with more expertise or experience.

- **Can you defer the decision?** While rapid decision-making is a key advantage for start-ups, not every decision needs to be made right at that moment. It might be possible and advisable to wait for a few more days, weeks, or even months. Sometimes, a decision can become irrelevant in the meantime or you both converge on one solution.

- **Can you include the legal board?** This should usually be a last resort, reserved only for strategic high-level decisions or a case of severe co-founder conflict. Legal boards only meet a few times per year, so they are not the best forum in which to take most decisions. It's best to reserve the legal board to weigh in on strategic high-level decisions all co-founders agree on or standard oversight tasks such as auditing.

Strengthening your co-founder relationship

Your co-founder relationship might well be one of the best things in your life and a source of energy for years. Unfortunately, as in the case of marriages, co-founder conflicts and split-ups are more common than people assume. In fact, they are one of the most common reasons that start-ups fail. Need to pivot and change your intervention? Need to work without salary for a few months? That's all doable if the team remains committed. However, if co-founders don't get along, it is often the beginning of the end.

How do you ensure that co-founder issues don't come up in the first place? This might not always come naturally. As a start-up team, you are enmeshed in the daily grind of testing and delivering your intervention. Anything longer-term, such as relationship building, gets forgotten during the most challenging periods if you don't make it a priority.

Thankfully, there are a few ways that you can foster your co-founder relationship without burdening your operational priorities.

Founder nights

All work and no play? Planning for some fun time together can make sense, especially during phases of stress and pressure. This ensures that your interactions are not limited to solving operational issues and making tough decisions. Depending on your interests, you could go for a simple dinner, the movies, sports activities, or a weekend getaway. Avoid the temptation to discuss running your start-up. Focus on being in the moment, sharing stuff from your private life, and discussing broader topics that excite you.

While the key benefit here is bonding, you will notice that these casual meetups can also provide some interesting insights. You might, for instance, discuss the latest trends in technology or findings in psychology and notice that a particular approach could also be applied at your organization. But again, the key benefit is relationship building, so just sit back and enjoy.

As artificial as it might feel, make sure to schedule and prioritize these bonding nights. Otherwise, they will often get forgotten, or canceled due to other pressures.

Happiness & collaboration check-ins

Going out for a movie once in a while is not sufficient for a lasting co-founder relationship. While the founder nights are purely about enjoying companionship, happiness & collaboration check-ins allow you to discuss your satisfaction levels as a co-founder pair and as individuals.

One option is to include these topics in a regular 1:1 meeting that you have scheduled anyhow. However, it might be best to distinguish this type of meeting clearly and schedule it regularly. This prevents you from skipping over the happiness & collaboration questions due to urgent discussion points. Moreover, it sets a different tone and helps you separate this discussion clearly from tough conversations about daily implementation or strategic priorities. A dedicated check-in could, for instance, take place on a monthly basis for two hours.

Below are some of the questions that can guide your happiness & collaboration check-in. As you can see, the list starts with individual satisfaction, including private life, which also affects job satisfaction. It then moves to the interpersonal level, the co-founder collaboration. The questions intentionally include references to common successes, vision, and gratitude. Those are otherwise often neglected, as we are used to focusing on areas for improvement:

- What am I grateful for personally and in our co-founder relationship?
- What has been my personal satisfaction level at the job recently?
- What common successes did we achieve recently?
- What are some aspects that could be improved quickly (low-hanging fruit)?
- What is our vision?

You can decide whether and how to track the progress of these conversations. In general, capturing the outcome of meetings in a Google Doc is a good idea. Yet with these check-ins, it might feel more natural to keep it to a discussion where only a few or no notes are taken. This might also help you open up as a team and tackle the underlying issues of potential conflict.

Founders' Agreement

Intense and legalistic. These are two typical reactions when aspiring entrepreneurs first hear about the idea of a Founders' Agreement (FA). An FA outlines the expectations and preferences of co-founders on the full spectrum of their working relationship and project.

But the idea here is not to draft a static contract that manages every aspect of the relationship in detail. An FA should rather be seen as a dynamic document that triggers the right conversations between founders and prevents misunderstandings and bad feelings. As such, it goes a step further than the happiness & collaboration check-ins and helps manage the relationship on a more strategic level.

What goes into the FA? This depends heavily on the co-founder pair. It usually involves key questions about your collaboration, questions that are often not openly discussed, (wrongly) implicitly assumed, and, in some cases, divisive.

- **Roles and responsibilities:** Your roles and responsibilities might be in flux, especially at an early-stage start-up. However, the more you can define them, the better, as it will help create ownership and prevent misunderstandings ("Oh, I thought you were responsible for this!"). You can define roles and responsibilities top-down or bottom-up.

Top-down would mean starting with core functions of your organization such as fundraising, program development, and recruitment. Bottom-up would be looking at 10 specific tasks that recently came up and seeing whether you agree on who is responsible.

- **Decision-making:** Related to roles and responsibilities are your decision-making procedures. Initially, it makes sense to make all major decisions on a consensus basis. As your responsibilities get defined more clearly and the organization grows, you can hand more of the decision-making to the designated co-founder. Strategic decisions can continue to be taken as a team. Some of the points you could address in an FA: which decisions do we make together, and which do we delegate to a co-founder? How do we deal with lacking consensus? (E.g., include a third party, let an experiment determine the course of action, etc.)

- **Field time:** Being close to your beneficiaries is key in an early-stage organization, as it provides you with critical feedback and allows you to test different iterations of your intervention. For many organizations, this involves spending time in developing countries, which can be draining and challenging for founders who might be separated from their families and friends. From an organizational perspective, you want to optimize for as much leadership team field time as possible. From a personal happiness perspective, however, there are limits, and those should be considered. It is important to make those preferences explicit and find a solution that balances the field presence needs of the organization with the personal preferences of the co-founders, which indirectly affect the organization's success. Specific agreements might include: how often do you spend time in the country? Where exactly are you based (capital vs. regional office)? For how long do you stay at a time?

- **Work/life balance:** Do you work seven days a week for 12 hours a day? Or do you want to enforce email-free weekends? As a start-up, you are likely going to invest more than the regular 40 hours a week. However, personal expectations might differ and should be discussed openly. There is a clear case for not overworking yourselves, as this can result in burnout and negatively affect your decision-making. Specific points to address: do you track co-founders' work time, and if so, how? Are there any work limits? Are weekends intentionally work-free? What is your co-founder vacation policy?

- **Communication**: Strong communication between co-founders is key to your success. In the FA, you may also address topics such as communication preferences. You might, for instance, define that non-urgent topics are generally discussed in Slack while urgent questions are sent on WhatsApp. Or, you might generally want to limit the distracting flow of instant messages and emails and write down all non-urgent questions for your co-founder on your next meeting's agenda. This is especially helpful if you try to adhere to a maker's schedule[3] that avoids distractions. Such rules might seem trivial, but they can improve work happiness and efficiency considerably.

- **Personal happiness and growth**: A team is only as good as its members. Define how each co-founder is committed to taking care of themselves through sports, meditation, or whatever works for them. Outline areas for the personal growth of the founders explicitly. This ensures that the founders grow as the organization grows and longer-term development does not fall victim to daily operational tasks. Founder A might, for example, want to further develop his Google Sheets and statistics skills, while founder B might focus on leadership development and public speaking classes. Growth areas could build on strengths or tackle weaknesses; both strategies have their pros and cons. A lot will depend on the organization's trajectory and the co-founders' personal priorities.

As you can see, an FA is flexible and builds on the preferences of you, the co-founders. Make a copy of our template[4] to get started, and feel free to add or leave out topics. And remember that the FA, while giving some stability and consistency to the co-founder relationship, is not set in stone. Revisit it every three, six, or 12 months to see where you stand and adapt it accordingly.

---

3 See again Graham, "Maker's Schedule, Manager's Schedule."
4 Available at https://bit.ly/CEfounderagree.

A final point: your FA is a great foundation to draft your **Manager User Guide**. This guide defines your preferences as a manager and helps your broader team understand and work with you better.[5]

And remember: a co-founder relationship is often one of the most profound and satisfying relationships in your life, so enjoy and appreciate being on a mission together!

32.2. Leadership & management for start-ups

Your co-founder is the most important person you have to work with, but far from the only one. Management is likely one of those skills for which people overestimate their own abilities, like the famous 1981 experiment that found that 8 out of 10 drivers consider themselves above average.[6] Not all of us fall under the illusion that we are better drivers than average (one friend of our team member Patrick Stadler avoids getting into a car with him after a road trip in Ireland… he'd like to state that in his defense, they drive in the left lane). But, heck, we have definitely all overestimated our management skills in the past and still learn on a daily basis.

Below are some of the lessons on management we've learned at Charity Entrepreneurship; at times naturally, occasionally the hard way.

Not everyone is the same

It might be obvious, but not everybody ticks the same way. So don't manage everyone as you would want to be managed. Or, don't expect that there is one pure form of modern management that applies across the board. Instead, use different leadership styles based on the person. Team member A might appreciate a high degree of autonomy and dislike task assignments that are too up front (e.g., you creating a task in Asana for them). Team member B, on the other hand, may feel in limbo without clear structure and regular check-ins. Adapt the degree of autonomy and your communication style based on your colleague.

---

5 For first steps, see First Round Review, "The Indispensable Document for the Modern Manager," accessed Nov. 10, 2021, https://review.firstround.com/the-indispensable-document-for-the-modern-manager.

6 Ola Svenson, "Are We All Less Risky and More Skillful Than our Fellow Drivers?" *Acta Psychologica* 47 (1981): 143-148, https://doi.org/10.1016/0001-6918(81)90005-6.

Look for verbal and nonverbal cues that indicate what leadership style a person prefers. Just being receptive to those signs can give you a lot of data to work with. Yet even more importantly, ask. Your team members usually have a very good sense of how they prefer to interact with you. This can involve the frequency and style of check-ins, the frequency and channel of your communications, and your common approach to managing tasks (which processes and apps you use). Your weekly 1:1 meeting is a good format in which to bring this up.

An individualized approach also applies to distributing tasks among team members. Ideally, the majority of tasks assigned to someone build on their strengths and interests. Your team members should have the right to grow and expand their skill set, and handing out tasks to someone neither interested nor well qualified to implement them is not sustainable. Consider assigning such activities to another team member, even if it defies the logic of titles or departments (e.g., a research team member helping out the operations person on a complex budgetary spreadsheet model).

Finally, task load calls for a tailored setup. Alex might get easily stressed out with more than a few tasks on his shoulders at any moment. Betty might get bored if she cannot switch between tasks frequently and, therefore, prefers a higher task load. Several techniques can help you figure out the right workload. First, ask about stress levels and progress. It can also help to get a sense of how much more time they need for each task at hand. In this respect, app-based time tracking is a helpful management tool (check out, e.g., Clockify, discussed in Chapter 10.3). The manager gets a sense of how realistic her/his assignments are and can manage priorities better. The team member has a record of time spent, which strengthens his position (to counter a question like, "Does this really take that long?"). The quality of the work might be an even stronger indicator of workload, but should be coupled with the individual's feedback and time spent. Otherwise, you might have employees that produce high-quality work but feel constantly stressed or work around the clock.

Have a plan

Don't mistake a modern management style that gives your staff a lot of autonomy for a free pass to operate without a plan. Even with the most talented and autonomous staff, you as a co-founder are responsible for the overall strategy and implementation. And it is fair to assume that your average staff member needs quite a bit of input in this regard. A frequent mistake is to treat planning as something you do on the side – for instance, only when your busy schedule allows. On the contrary, defining your goals and outlining the path to implement them is one of your key tasks as a manager. You don't want your organization to be the rocket that speeds in the wrong direction. With many options to pursue and the constant uncertainty around their likelihood of success, planning is hard and takes time. Allocate sufficient time and energy for it and delegate seemingly urgent day-to-day tasks to others to free up space. Don't fall into the trap of "I wish I had time for planning but I just need to …"

Don't hesitate, delegate

As the founder, the charity is your baby. You know it inside out, from the high-level strategy down to the Google Sheets script that cleans your database. The temptation, therefore, is to jump right into action as a new task pops up. This proactive attitude serves you well in the earliest days of your org when there is simply nobody to help out. But quickly, you will be able to gather a team of staff, contractors, interns, and volunteers. Instead of carrying out most tasks, take a step back and focus on high-level functions such as strategy, fundraising, recruitment, and planning. The rest can and should be delegated.

Overcommunicate and be available

Knowing every single process at your organization bears another risk: the "Isn't this obvious?" fallacy. As you assign tasks, remain aware that you have a much deeper context than your colleagues. A brief task description without clear examples and goal descriptions might be insufficient. Communicating a strategic change only once or twice is likely not enough to sink into your organization's culture. This simple rule of thumb on "overcommunicating" comes in handy: When you think you have communicated something extensively, add another one or two iterations and you will likely reach an adequate level.

Another way to be a good manager is to remain available for questions and check-ins. This does not mean that you have to respond to Slack messages 24/7 within minutes. Deep work time is important and should be respected by all team members. But don't be that busy manager that never gets back to questions or postpones weekly 1:1 meetings. This is not only demotivating at a personal level but turns you into a bottleneck for the whole organization. One of your key goals as a manager is to enable and support your staff, and being available is the first step in this direction.

Implement coaching-style management

Who likes to feel like a robot that diligently processes tasks fed by a manager? Yes, this is an exaggeration, but traditional management at its worst can be interpreted in such a fashion. Autonomy has always been a key contributor to happiness. This applies even more so to highly skilled and motivated team members. So instead of structuring your relationship with an employee in a traditional way, consider implementing a coaching style. A few differences stand out:

- A coach does not have all the answers. Often they are not an expert in the field of the player. This reflects current working arrangements where you might need to manage someone highly specialized, e.g., a developer helping you implement a database dashboard. It acknowledges that input from the staff member is often, if not always, superior to that of the manager.

- A coach enables and supports someone in implementing their goals. This applies well to modern management. While you might set the general direction as the superior, the staff member should have full ownership of the steps and activities to meet the targets. The manager ensures that there are no roadblocks on the way, provides resources, and helps the other to reflect on progress toward their goals. From this perspective, the team lead works for the team member, not vice versa.

If you would like to explore modern frameworks of leadership further, also take a look at Ray Dalio's *Principles*. His approach, in brief, is famous for a radical (and sometimes uncomfortable) approach to measuring and assessing reality and one's own work outputs.[7] Conscious leadership is another up-and-coming framework, practiced at companies such as Asana, that includes a deeper reflection about one's feelings and a path toward a less self-centered life.[8] Dalio's Principles might come across a bit harsh for some, while conscious leadership may be a touch esoteric, but both are worth checking out.

---

7 Ray Dalio, *Principles: Life and Work* (New York, NY: Simon & Schuster, 2017). See https://www.principles.com/, accessed Nov. 10, 2021.

8 See https://conscious.is/, accessed Nov. 10, 2021.

Help staff grow

At a start-up, there are always fires to extinguish. As a manager, you therefore have a tendency to want your staff to be fully engaged in the critical tasks at hand. That's fair, yet don't forget the mid- to long-term growth of your staff. While you will not be able to match the broad set of training opportunities of a large company, implement a few. These can be modest and include affordable online courses (edX, Coursera, Udemy, etc.), book clubs, and peer-learning among staff.

Even more importantly, understand the direction your team member wants to develop in. Ask about this proactively in 1:1 meetings and ensure that each team member uses at least a few hours per week to develop their skills by, for instance, taking an accounting or coding class. Upskilling staff helps you fill managerial positions later on and makes you an attractive employer. You can also actively contribute to someone's personal development, which is a value in itself. For these reasons, resist the temptation to limit personal development because you fear that they might move on. Losing staff members is not always easy, but is a natural process – and one that strengthens your organization's network.

Build and document processes

"Isn't this what we discussed that one time over Slack?" One of the most frequent mistakes we see co-founders make is not documenting their processes sufficiently. Initially, you are often only two co-founders that communicate frequently. Heck, why would you need to write stuff down? There are, in essence, two main reasons.

- The obvious reason is that your organization will scale and you will need to onboard new staff. Going without written documentation limits your bandwidth, as you are bombarded with the same questions over and over. It also results in the duplication of work – for instance, someone starting a new policy/process on X when it has already been defined in the past. Similarly, if you have documented processes, you can also outsource them beyond your own staff, e.g., to volunteers and contractors on platforms such as Upwork.

- Finally, and most importantly, writing down a process allows you to reflect with greater clarity, get second opinions, and improve it steadily. Even the first time you bring a process to paper, you will immediately spot the potential for improvement: e.g., why does this start with Person A then go to B and then back to A; couldn't Person A complete both tasks together?

Documenting processes and turning them into standard operating procedures (SOPs) improves quality, accountability, and consistency at your org.

The basic elements of SOPs include: the person responsible, the steps necessary to complete a task, and the related deadlines.

In terms of software, you can go from basic to more sophisticated:

- Google Docs works really well to document processes. The key here is not to split up your processes into too many documents, and to combine where possible (e.g., Employee Handbook). Of course, one document alone will also be insufficient, so make sure to have a hub (Google Doc or Spreadsheet) with a constantly updated and easily searchable/sorted list of policies with the related links. Otherwise, be ready to go Easter egg hunting on your Google Drive. You can split policies up according to a departmental (e.g., Operations), thematic (e.g., Finance), or geographic (e.g., India Office) logic.

- Task management software such as Asana works great if you need to set up workflows. There is even specialized workflow software if you need a more tailored solution (e.g., Kissflow or Process.st). There is still value in documenting the bigger picture in a Google Doc and letting the software take care of handling daily process management.

Scale as a leader

The trajectory as a start-up leader is unique. You usually start out with limited management experience and the requirement to take care of everything yourself. And then within one to two years, you might be confronted with a large organization with dramatically different expectations of you at its helm.

There is only one way to go about this: you have to scale as a leader as your organization is scaling around you. Easier said than done, however. Your early qualities as a start-up manager might actually jeopardize the more established organization. The proactive can-do attitude that suited you well in the early days may turn you into a dreaded micromanager. The quick-and-dirty implementation that allowed you to move quickly might at a later stage contribute to compliance risks (e.g., running out of cash due to poor accounting, or getting into trouble with authorities due to a lack of attention).

The table below summarizes how traits that are positive in the early days may turn into liabilities later.

Positive traits in early days	Potential liabilities at later stages
Getting sh… done yourself	Micromanaging
Acting quickly	Compliance and liability issues
No time for management and culture	Poor culture and unhappy staff
Working extremely hard	Burnout of yourself and staff
A plan is overrated	Organization is moving in different directions due to lack of unity
Don't hire a lot and/or don't train a lot	Lack of talent, especially management talent

The mitigation strategy here is not to do everything differently from the beginning. That is impossible, as you would jeopardize your early success. Yet, you have to gradually adapt to your organization's maturity and needs.

You have to move from "do most of it yourself" to "don't do any daily management or implementation." A good framework to think about this is working toward making yourself superfluous. Build an organization that runs well without you.

The final stage of this transition would mean that you (or a new management team) mostly deal with the following high-level matters and leave everything else to others:

- Strategy
- High-level fundraising

- Management of your senior team
- Recruitment and training of senior team
- Culture

Looks pretty different from your starting point, doesn't it? As you steer your start-up forward, plan for the occasional stop to reflect. Have you taken the necessary steps to scale up as a leader (e.g., getting an executive coach or doing psychotherapy)? Have the steps taken been successful? Do you even enjoy working at this level? The latter points to the fact that not everyone is suited for and enjoys working at all stages of an organization's leadership. It is fine to acknowledge that and look into transition plans. At most organizations, some or all members of the co-founding team move on eventually. Your start-up is your baby, but someday it'll grow up and be ready to move forward independently. But right now, you are far, far from this point, so enjoy the ride and continuous learning required as a leader.

32.3. How to excel at remote work

At the time of writing, the COVID-19 pandemic has left many teams across the world fully remote. Lots of team members are keen to go back to an in-person office, missing the jokes and chats, shared lunches, and game nights. At the same time, remote work is feasible and may even be a necessity for many charity entrepreneurs.

Advantages

The two most common immediate reasons for charities to pick a remote setup are **field operations** and **visa issues**. Often, one co-founder needs to set up operations in a developing country while the other takes care of HQ work in a Western city. Visa issues can also necessitate a geographic split. We once had, for instance, several US citizens who were unable to work at a charity's London-based HQ.

Talent and cost are two additional, often underrated, advantages of remote work. For instance, Fish Welfare Initiative is currently working with a Portugal-based fish scientist. The search for unique talent goes beyond geographic borders. Similarly, as a cost-effective nonprofit, lean operations are essential. So, it can help for team members to be based in lower-cost locations. Given today's solid

IT infrastructure in many countries, there are countless destinations that cater to such digital nomads (see, e.g., Nomadlist for ideas).

Remote work done well

One surefire way to ruin a remote org is by applying the same practices as in a non-remote setup and hoping for stellar results. Thankfully, it's not rocket science (or becoming the next GiveWell top charity!) and small tweaks make a big difference.

Quickly walk over to Ed to update him on the latest changes to the fundraising proposal? No longer, in a remote setup. You will rely on writing instead of speech to get your messages across. This has three implications:

- Most of your communication becomes asynchronous. While speech is traditionally associated with synchronous communications, writing works well asynchronously. Your colleague in a different timezone will respond when she starts work. And even your colleague in the same timezone is no longer interrupted by a phone call during deep work, and can instead reply whenever suitable.

- As most communication is written, the art of writing gains importance. Ensure **concise** and **clear** language. This has the additional benefit of forcing you to think through decisions clearly before you communicate them. It's easier to announce something without proper preparation verbally than in writing.

- Misunderstandings occur more easily in writing, as nonverbal cues are missing. So, it becomes even more important to work with empathetic and balanced colleagues. On top, your culture should reinforce the value of always assuming the best intentions in one another, even if a particular message comes across a bit harsh.

Meetings

Meetings, ah, how we love them. As a matter of habit, the temptation is high to organize meetings as in the pre-remote world. Please don't! Meetings can be a huge time suck and will get only worse if they are organized without a clear purpose. Most communications and decisions do not require meetings and can instead be handled through writing. Meetings work especially well if the exchange is highly social, e.g., a 1:1, or if something urgent happened (crisis management). There is also value in meetings for creative brainstorming, although make sure to structure such workshops really well and use the written medium to facilitate the conversation (e.g., Miro whiteboards).

As a basic rule for successful online meetings, opt for discussions instead of presentations or updates. Why?

Presentations and reports can and should be read by participants before the meeting starts. Don't spend half of your meeting repeating content that could have been or was made available to everyone beforehand. If your participants don't have time to prepare, then postpone or cancel the meeting.

Updates by staff, for instance in daily standup meetings, can also be communicated online. You could try, e.g., Slack, tools such as Range.co, or making your calendar transparent to your team. Be creative or use a check-in question generator like checkin.daresay.io.

Even completely dispersed teams meet up in person at some points. A few annual organization-wide meetups are common among many remote companies such as Buffer, which has written a guide on such gatherings.[9]

32.4. Scaling down your team

If you put your employees first, you put impact second.

A cheerful sentiment is that the best way to do good in the world is to make your close contacts happy. Our emotional brains are far more keyed to those closest to us than to lives lived far away. However, like any goal, focusing on those close to you takes away time, resources, and weight from other priorities. This happens all the time in nonprofits that are generally managed by altruistic managers, who take great discomfort in not helping their employees as much as possible.

A stark example of this phenomenon happened to a nonprofit that focused on cleft lip surgery. This nonprofit had historically been run through volunteer surgeons, who would go to lower-income countries and perform free cleft lip surgery en masse for those who could not otherwise afford it. The dilemma

---

9 Nicole Miller, "How to Host a Meetup For Your Community: The Who, What, Where, When, and How," Buffer (blog), Dec. 11, 2014, https://buffer.com/resources/meetups/.

came up when conflicts arose between what was best for the volunteer surgeons and what was best for the patients. Should surgeons be allowed to bring their families to trainings, even though this often impaired the learning of the local doctors and the speed of the process? By putting the happiness of the surgeons first, the charity inadvertently left impact as the second priority. Thankfully, after a restructuring process, the charity realized it needed to put patients first and make decisions based on that principle.

Many charities make the same mistake, prioritizing the welfare of their staff over the welfare of their beneficiaries.

If our surgery charity from the above example was considering what salary to offer a new staff member, they might be faced with two choices. On the one hand, they could offer a lean salary that the employee would take, but not be excited about – say $30k. On the other, they could offer a higher salary that the employee would be happy about – say $50k.

Most altruists will be strongly tempted to help the employee by offering the higher salary, and readily come up with reasoning as to why it's the most altruistic choice for both the employee and the world at large. "Higher salaries lead to less turnover"; "This person is worth more than $50k anyway, so it's still a deal"; "They have a family to support, so it's doing good for them as well." **But these reasons are rarely based on research or consideration of the counterfactuals**. With that $20k extra spent on salary, about seven lives could have been saved – each with their own family who care about them deeply. The decision to pay $20k more than the employee would have accepted might feel good personally, but it's not the trade one of those seven individuals would make.

There will, of course, be times when employee happiness and impact line up, but it's far less common than people think. Often the right decision is the harder one – offering less pay, insisting employees work the full hours they are paid for, letting go of a kind but consistently underperforming employee. None of these choices are easy or fun, but they are the decisions that save the most lives in the end.

Firing

Managing a workplace is hard. On the one hand, your coworkers will often become your friends. You will interact with them within the mostly pleasant modes of behavior that naturally arise in the warm human bonds of friendship and sociability. You'll spend long periods of time together, learn from each other, and work toward a common goal. On the other hand, when you employ someone, there is a whole set of occasionally unpleasant interactions that arise within the dynamics surrounding the purchasing of another person's labor as a commodity. One of these unpleasant dynamics is that you have the power to fire people, and you will occasionally have to use it.

If you are like most people, you're not going to want to do it. You're going to try to find reasons why it may not be necessary. You're going to come up with ways to put off the decision for as long as possible. You'll dread the event and spend a lot of time thinking about how or whether to go through with it.

Procrastinating in this way harms your organization, and your impact. The most important lesson to learn about firing is that you need to do it.

Firing is hard because it goes against many natural human instincts. Most of us are averse to conflict and confrontation in general. We also have a natural instinct to be empathetic, and protect and look out for people we know. Firing someone tends to put them in financial difficulty, and gives them a heavy dose of social rejection. It will never feel good to inflict that upon anyone. Almost all new charities hire too quickly and fire too slowly.

Sounds harsh – doesn't everyone deserve a second chance? Definitely. This is not to promote a hire and fire mentality. Yet, as a greenhorn manager, you tend to let staff go too late. And, unfortunately, you are super busy growing your organization. So you need all the help you can get, right? Let's not lose this person in this critical period of time.

I have been there. We're not talking about cases here where new staff members need some time to get going or might only perform at 90% of what you expected. You usually only consider firing someone when it's really not working out (or you run out of funding): the person has a toxic personality, has a poor work ethic, constantly makes serious mistakes, does not show any signs of improvement, etc. In these cases, consider parting ways earlier than when your intuition tells you.

While difficult, the firing process can still be fair and considerate. Communicate your concerns early, give multiple opportunities to improve, and discuss potential other career avenues for that person. Also, consider a severance package, i.e., continuing to pay a salary for a few additional months. This is a socially correct method, and it also prevents further issues (e.g., the person seeking legal recourse or turning into an "opponent").

Fire people who display abusive behavior immediately

If an employee is engaging in abusive language, intimidation, or harassment, you should fire them immediately. Aside from the fact that these behaviors cause steep morale and productivity drops for the entire team, they are also just inherently harmful to the individuals involved. This may seem obvious from the outside, but it is quite common for people to make excuses for this type of behavior, even when it is directed at them. "It wasn't intentional"; "That's just how they communicate"; "We will put up with this because they're very talented." These justifications end up enabling and even rewarding behavior that ultimately creates massive productivity drops for the rest of the team – not to mention the other harmful consequences of their actions.

While the key advice is "fire immediately," it is always important to understand the situation, hear everyone out, and give warnings and a second chance. Severe forms of abusive language, intimidation, and harassment should directly result in termination – but reality can be more complex than it may seem, so you need time to look at the issue in depth first. You should not prolong an abusive situation for months, but neither should you feel pressured to rush into a decision based on hearsay. Make sure that you have understood what is happening before you act, but don't hesitate to act once you have understood.

If you encounter this situation, it would be a good idea to reconsider your hiring process and talk about what red flags you might have missed that could have alerted you to these issues before you hired this employee.

Fire people for poor performance – but not immediately

While poor performance is less damaging to the organization than abusive behavior, it does hurt your effectiveness. Firing people for poor performance may be more psychologically difficult, because it generally won't feel like the person's "fault" that they are performing poorly.

A poor performer might still be doing enough work that it's worth paying their salary. However, remember that money is not the only cost of an employee. If an average performer is taking up a lot of valuable management time, that is a cost. If the poor performer is making mistakes that end up doing damage or require a lot of time to fix, then that is also a cost. Consider the possibility that you could hire a much more productive employee for the same price.

Poor performance can happen for a variety of reasons, and when dealing with it, it is crucial to identify the problem before firing. (Only up to a point, of course – don't push people to tell you all about their life difficulties unless they volunteer the information. But broadly knowing that the problem falls into the category of a personal issue might help.) If the poor performance seems likely to be a temporary problem, it may be unnecessary to fire them. Try to identify any steps that you might be able to take to fix the issue, such as a performance improvement plan, a different type of work or responsibility, or a different style of management.

If the employee has worked well in the past, the quality of their work is gradually improving, or they seem to have a good attitude and be receptive to feedback and training, it is a sign that things can probably be improved. If the employee doesn't believe the problems can be fixed, the quality of their work is trending downward over time, multiple staff are complaining about them, or they display a consistently negative or difficult attitude toward you or other staff members, it's a sign that things are less likely to get better.

Keep in mind that performance is about the employee's broader effect on the organization. Individual high performance is not enough if they weaken others on the team or make the organization as a whole move less effectively. If they are causing constant conflicts or stopping key decisions from getting made, that is a sign that they might have a broader negative impact. Someone who makes it hard to grow or scale your organization can likewise stall its impact.

Once you have determined that your employee's output is sufficiently low that you could hire someone else who would do it better at equal or lower cost (including the non-financial costs of training a new person), it means that to maximize your impact you will need to fire the underperforming employee.

Mitigating the negative impact of firing people

There are a variety of ways to soften the negative effects of firing a coworker.

- **Handover documents** explain how the job works and link to all the necessary resources. You will need to train a new staff member to replace the one that was fired. Making sure all key employees maintain a handover document is a good way to keep your organization robust to the loss of any staff member. This is also generally a good idea in scenarios where someone stops working for reasons other than getting fired.

- **Organizational slack**, discussed below in 32.5, is the practice of keeping a little extra capacity in your organization. If you and your staff are always racing against time to complete projects, then the loss of a single staff member (or even just any event that impacts productivity) can cause your entire operation to come crashing down. Having extra hands on deck will make your organization more flexible and capable of weathering changes.

- **Team morale** might be affected by firing a coworker. They might not agree with the decision, or they might fear that you will fire them for the same reasons. If people think they can be fired for any reason the moment they slip up, it will create a culture of stress and fear that will harm productivity. This could be mitigated by communicating clearly with the rest of the team about your reasons and reassuring them regarding any concerns they may have. Quash any rumors that may be floating around, and be firm in not sharing any personal information about the employee.

- **Hiring process improvements**: You will need to go through the hiring process all over again. There's no easy way to mitigate this issue, but you can minimize how many times you need to do this by designing your hiring process such that you won't need to fire people as often.

- **Advanced notice and severance pay:** Continuing to pay the employee for a short time after they have been informed that they are fired helps buffer some of the personal inconvenience to them. They might even continue to work during this time but, realistically, you shouldn't expect it. The duration of pay should take into account the traditions in your country of operations and your organization's culture. It will also depend on the notice in the person's contract (which in turn is usually based on the staff member's length at the org and their seniority). It goes without saying that you should always treat people generously before, during, and after firing them. It's the nice thing to do, and it also helps to avoid burning bridges, prevents legal issues, and protects the reputation of your organization. Don't overpromise or do things that require too many resources, though.

What to say, when and how to say it, and other logistics

Before firing

- First, check the local laws regarding firing, as well as the contract you signed with them. In the US, you usually don't have to give a reason for termination. In the EU/UK, you'll need to demonstrate "fair and reasonable procedure." There may be some reasons for which you are not allowed to fire someone (for example, anti-discrimination laws).

- Once you let someone know that you are firing them, there is a chance that they might immediately disappear and become uncontactable. You should account for this – make sure that there are no accounts, passwords, or important documents that you would need the former employee in order to access, and budget for the missing staff time.

- You may wish to lock a terminated employee out of sensitive accounts (for example, bank accounts), internal documents, and email addresses affiliated with the organization. You can use Google's Team Drive feature to streamline some of this.

During firing

- Set the tone immediately with "I have some bad news" – don't try to make small talk or stay upbeat. Clearly state, "Your employment has been terminated" (past tense, because the decision is already made).

- Break the news on a Friday, at the end of the day. This way, they can go home and get some space over the weekend to cool off and calm down before coming in on Monday.

- They will have many questions, such as "When is my last day?" "How long will I be paid?" and "What happens to my visa?" – questions that you should try to anticipate and have answers ready for. Write this out as it allows you to prepare and spot any open questions ahead of the conversation. Avoid getting drawn into extended, emotionally charged discussions – this should not be a debate or a fight.

- Privacy is good, but if there is any risk of legal problems it may help to have at least one other person accompany you as a witness. It will be socially easier if this is a founder or senior staff, and not someone within the same level in the hierarchy.

After firing

- Don't have too many expectations of the employee in the time period after you've broken the news and before their last day at work. This is the time to be friendly and try to part on good terms.

- After the employee stops coming to work, debrief your team about what happened. In the next meeting after the debriefing, make a plan for how the workflow will change.

32.5. Organizational slack

He quit!

It was a tricky decision that Bill had been considering for months. He was an impact-focused EA, and although he thought his job was fairly high impact, he was pretty sure he was very replaceable. In fact, he was unsure he was even needed at the organization, since many of his tasks could have been done by a less experienced employee. And he was one of the five members of the senior team!

There was about 3.5 members' worth of highly difficult work, and Bill figured that if it were reshuffled, they would not even notice his absence. When Bill told his team about it, they were heartbroken. He was a great employee, and they thought his work was not as replaceable as he had determined. But Bill had done the math and he was set on his decision.

The EA organization did not collapse. In fact, for three months everything went totally smoothly. The organization continued its work at a slightly slower rate, with the four remaining senior team members working a bit harder to pull the extra weight. Some tasks were given to more junior employees and were done well; others seemed like junior tasks at first, but required senior staff knowledge to do efficiently and were thus done poorly or slowly. All being said, the organization seemed fine, and Bill was having a strong impact in another organization that needed him so much that work slowed to a crawl on his every day off. Bill felt confident he had made the right choice.

Sadly, in the fourth month after Bill had left, things changed. The organization, which had before been able to work effectively with four senior members, ran into a problem. One of their employees, Sandy, had to leave suddenly since their husband had fallen extremely ill and needed almost full-time attention. The work that had been shouldered by four people now fell onto the shoulders of just three employees, meaning that their organization had no slack; it had already been stretched to its very limits. Sandy loved the organization but had little time. The other employees worked incredible hours and rapidly tried to hire a replacement, but, of course, that was just extra work that they did not have the capacity to handle. The remaining team did what they could: one of them got sloppy, getting everything done, but poorly; another simply could not handle the task load and was always weeks behind, missing important deadlines, including legally mandated ones. The third employee barely slept and worked 12 hours a day, every day, but after a few weeks burned out dramatically and was left only able to perform at 25% of their normal ability.

The organization groaned and limped on for another four months before finally shutting down, eight months after Bill had left. Even more tragically, 12 months later Bill's organization also had to grind to a halt, as their overstretched team could not work without him and he needed to take 2 weeks off to fight a strong cold.

No one blamed Bill. If anything, it was just bad luck, they said – him leaving and Sandy's husband getting sick. But, really, when Bill left he took much of the organizational slack with him, making the organization fragile to shocks and changes. If not Sandy's husband, the crisis would have occurred three months later when one of their largest donors retired and the organization needed to invest much more senior staff time into fundraising than expected. An organization that has been stretched to its limits cannot handle the unexpected, but inevitable shocks that happen.

Many EAs make the same mistake as Bill. Being crucially important to an organization does not mean you are crucially important every day, and an organization that needs every staff member performing at their peak (or even median) to function efficiently will break over time and often. Sometimes, the effects will be apparent soon after; other times, it might take years for the impact to be felt. However, there will always be variance, and times will get tougher than people initially expect. **A better model for an organization to have is that at any time, any single employee could disappear, and your organization should still remain productive and able to stick to its deadlines**. Taking into account organizational robustness when hiring and when changing careers is an important practice that could lead to different choices on both the organization's and the individual's part.

Many EAs are constantly considering their personal impact in an organization. A factor that is often underemphasized is the benefit of organizational slack. For example, **many organizations are set up in such a way that if one employee were unable to work, the entire operation would slow to a crawl.** This obviously makes it very sensitive to large shocks (like an employee falling seriously ill, getting injured, or quitting) and even small changes (e.g., an employee getting sick for a week or needing to take some time off without warning due to a family emergency).

No person can be available 100% of the time, and unpredictable unavailability happens to both senior and junior staff. And if an organization does not have alternative means for getting the work done, it can really do harm. The lack of accounting for this situation happens most often at the higher levels of an operation. For example, **many CEOs make the organization dependent on them to the point where if they left, it would collapse. This is a suboptimal structure,** even if the CEO has no plans to leave: what if they get sick, or their family member falls ill? It only takes one of the hundreds of possible (and some fairly frequently occurring) events to put a single member out of commission.

CEOs are not the only ones who do not take organizational slack and robustness into account. We have seen multiple senior staff members feel as though their impact is unimportant due to the organization having some robustness. No one employee should be so integral to an organization that it would collapse if they left. **A high-impact position could be one where you have three talented staff members and, in theory, the job could be handled by two. This allows you to jump onto new opportunities or have the necessary robustness in the face of hardship.** But often, we have seen employees leave strong, robust teams under the concern that "the organization would survive without them."

32.6. Avoiding burnout: or, the pessimist's guide to self-care

Who do you imagine writes articles about self-care? It's easy to picture a smiling optimist who's really got their life together. They start their day with a smoothie – probably with spinach in it. They rise before the sun to exercise and meditate.

We often feel quite disconnected from this type of person. For instance, some of our team members only recently started running after decades without exercise, and many will probably never willingly eat a salad. Furthermore, our team includes "severely hopeless" pessimists, according to a rather blunt online quiz distributed while researching this chapter. In short, we sometimes represent the opposite of this imaginary self-care-article writer. But in a sense, this perhaps makes us well qualified. If even the grumpiest among us can force down some broccoli and stagger through a jog, you can, too.

As we dive into the intricacies of self-care, remember that **building good habits is tough for everyone.** Insert motivational quote here... ;). And, who knows, maybe someday we too will join the shining ranks of the optimists. In the meantime, we do our best and try to be comfortable with who we are.

Why care about self-care?

It's 2021. The elephant in the room is that you're reading this in the middle of a global pandemic. Taking care of ourselves and each other right now is essential. If you and your loved ones are lucky enough to be safe and healthy, you – like me – have a lot to be profoundly grateful for.

If you haven't already, start with self-care now. And try not to let good habits drop when the pandemic finally lifts, because even in times of normalcy, we need self-care. Positive impact creates happiness; so too does happiness create positive impact. **You can't save the world if you're suffering from burnout.** Taking care of yourself:

- Gives you the energy to help others
- Enhances your creativity and problem-solving
- Helps you bounce back from inevitable setbacks

You want to do the most good you can, but without overstretching yourself and burning out. Deepening your self-awareness (more on this below) will help you strike the balance here. As you explore your limits, working on self-care will help stave off burnout.

Resilience in adversity

Part of why it's so important to make self-care a habit is so that you're equipped to deal with the inevitable bad. If you're normally just about hanging on, obstacles are more likely to trip you flat on your face than if you're generally doing well. (A similar concept applies to your company, too: reflect again on the concept of organizational slack.) Fortunately, a bunch of tools and strategies can help you when the going gets tough. Like everything, they're easier said than done, but worth a try nonetheless:

- **Focus on what you can control.** The rest there's no point in stressing about.

- **Recognize mind traps** (e.g., catastrophizing, projecting your insecurities) and try to avoid them.

- Imagine the **worst-case** scenario and how you might deal with it (negative visualization). Then imagine the **best-case** scenario. Finally, imagine and plan for the **most likely** scenario.

- Having **a plan B** means that even if things don't work out, it's not the end of the world.

- **Reach out** to loved ones, for support as well as distraction.

- Yes, it can be hard to **ask for help**, but imagine if one of your friends were struggling. Just as you'd want to be there for them, so too would they want to be there for you.

- Explore **breathing techniques** (e.g., deliberate breathing or belly breathing).

- Think **long term.** The crisis will pass, and you'll learn from it.

- **Reframe negatives** as positives.
  - For example, stress. Sucks, right? But try naming one achievement you're proud of that involved zero stress. And while you're at it, write down some of your previous achievements to build into a confidence résumé.

- **Find time for self-care.**
  - With a deadline looming, it's hard to hit pause and meditate quietly, for example. But, arguably, the busiest or most stressful times are when self-care is most important.

Sometimes when you're feeling poorly, it's not because of an immediate stressor like a big deadline or sudden crisis, but rather a more nebulous unease. Guilt, imposter syndrome, and feelings of inadequacy aren't fun, but are common. To deal with them, try to:

- Fix what's "enough," e.g., donations or hours of time. Once you've done "enough," don't beat yourself up over not doing more.
- Be cool with imperfection. Perfection does not exist.
- Avoid black-and-white thinking in general – we exist in shades of grey.
- Recognize that if you're smart enough to game the system, you're smart enough to be where you are.
- Be as nice to yourself as you would be to others.

A (free) University of Pennsylvania course on positive psychology and resilience skills covers these and other tips in more detail and is worth exploring.[10]

Finally, **professionals exist for a reason**. Many founders seek help from coaches and psychologists. The CE team is happy to provide recommendations. Remember, you can never be too mentally healthy!

Self-care in the workplace

It's easy to let self-care fall by the wayside, particularly when working in the nonprofit sector. But the mentality of subordinating one's own needs to the broader mission (e.g., "I should work 80 hours a week so I can do as much good as possible") is unsustainable. You won't maximize your impact by burning out. So, in addition to practicing self-care during your free time, it's worth integrating it into your organization to keep yourself and your team motivated.

Here are a couple of practices at CE that promote well-being:

- **Positive management strategies**. (Look back to Chapter 32.2.) Remember that as a leader, you set the example for the team (no pressure!).
- **Team socializing**. For remote work, setting up a regular all-team Zoom social or using Donut (which randomly pairs up team members for socials) can help you connect. For on-site work, grab lunch together or organize social events after work (e.g., board game or movie nights, team dinners or drinks).

---

10 Coursera, "Positive Psychology: Resilience Skills," accessed Nov. 10, 2021, https://www.coursera.org/learn/positive-psychology-resilience.

- **Gratitude**. Be sure to acknowledge your colleagues' hard work. During CE's weekly meeting, each of us talks about what we're grateful for, as well as what we learned and did that week. We also have a channel on Slack for milestones and appreciations.

- **Take a break**. R&R over the weekend and vacation time will help you recharge. During the workweek, it's also worth taking breaks from notifications. This goes for when you're at the office as well as outside it: deep work can lower the stress from interruptions and up your productivity.

Creating a positive workplace atmosphere literally has no downsides. Who wouldn't want to surround themselves with a tight-knit team that shares their ethical outlook? As an added bonus, it can help prevent value drift and ensure your altruism will last.

I haven't really talked about this because it almost goes without saying, but wrapping up is a good moment to emphasize the importance of the people around you. Coworkers, friends, and family form your support network. **Make time for those close to you**; show that you appreciate them. Four hundred years ago, Donne said that no man is an island.[11] Today, as ever, let's recognize and be thankful for this truth.

---

11 From John Donne's famous 1624 poem in opposition to isolationism, "No Man is an Island," Meditation XVII.

33. Summary: Building a charity

33.1. Running a charity legally

Choosing a legal structure: What kind of organization do you want to have, legally? You can opt to enter a fiscal sponsorship relationship with an established organization, which allows you to get up and running quickly, but comes with fees. You could create a nonprofit corporation, which in most jurisdictions is cheap, quick, and easy, but doesn't give the benefits of tax-exempt status. At some point, you may want to register as a charity, which has some great advantages but also a set of responsibilities.

Registering as a charity: Most countries will have a process whereby an organization can register for tax-exempt, charitable status. This usually involves submitting information to the country's charities regulator describing the kinds of activities you intend to do, making clear that they fit into the definition of "charitable" under that country's laws. Your organization will have to define its charitable "purposes" or "objects," which describe the scope of the charity's activities. Gaining approval can be time-consuming, but if you succeed, your organization will be tax-free and can offer tax-deductibility to its donors.

Reporting to the regulator: If you register as a charity, you'll likely owe (at least) an annual report to the charities regulator. The requirements vary from jurisdiction to jurisdiction, but they will commonly want to be assured that (a) your organization is being governed in a responsible way, (b) your finances are being managed according to established standards, and (c) your activities are limited to those defined by your charitable "purposes" or "objects." Your finances may be required to be examined or audited by a professional accountant.

Required and recommended organizational policies: Depending on your jurisdiction, the type of legal structure you choose, and what kind of work you do, you may be legally required to have certain policies in place. For example, if you store any personal information about individuals, you'll likely need to follow a data protection policy. If you have employees, you'll likely need to observe required parental leave, annual leave, sick leave, and other standards. Some types of policies, like anti-harassment policies or equity, diversity, and inclusion policies, might not necessarily be legally required but are so commonplace that not having them can seem egregious to donors or the public.

Receiving grants and donations: You may have legal obligations to fulfill when accepting donations. There may be a minimum of due diligence you need to perform before accepting a large donation or grant from an individual or foundation. If you are able to offer tax-deductibility to your donors, then you'll likely need to provide them with a donation receipt, for which each jurisdiction will have specific requirements.

Giving out grants and moving money: There are rules to follow when money leaves your organization, especially if you are a tax-exempt charity. The charities regulator is concerned that money spent by a charity is allocated to activities that meet the legal definition of charitable. As such, there may be limitations, or procedures to follow when giving out grants (especially to a non-charity or foreign entity) or moving money across borders (even to an affiliated organization based in another country).

Getting help and advice: Fortunately, as a nonprofit, it can be surprisingly easy to find help on many of these issues – even for free! Most big law firms have pro bono programs that can be straightforward to access. Charities organizations, like the National Council of Nonprofits (US) and the Small Charities Coalition (UK), have a wealth of free resources on their websites. Professional organizations like TrustLaw and Charity Finance Group exist to connect nonprofits with professionals and sector-specific resources. The Effective Altruism community has a very vibrant and collaborative forum of operations professionals happy to exchange information, answer questions, and share resources.

33.2. Running a financially sound charity

Any well-run charity needs sound financial management. What does that consist of?

Budgeting

- Your budget defines what you expect to spend to carry out your charity's activities. It tells you (and your prospective donors) how much money you need to raise to get the project off the ground and running.

- Avoid under-budgeting, and always leave contingency amounts for unexpected costs. Avoid over-budgeting, which can send negative signals to donors about your capacity.
- Iterate toward ever-more accurate budgets by checking your budget vs. actual spending.

Banking and moving money

- Choose a bank account that matches the needs of your organization. For currency exchange, use a service like Wise that has better exchange rates than banks.
- Learn about capital controls and restrictions on charity-related cross-border transfers.

Bookkeeping, expenses management, and financial statements

- Simplify by using the same breakdown of categories in your budgeting as you do in your chart of accounts. Simplify further by matching up these categories with those required in reports to tax authorities and donors.
- Import transactions automatically from the bank into your accounting software. If you have lots of expenses, use an app for more advanced expense management.
- Attach transaction records like receipts and invoices in your accounting software.
- Always reconcile the transactions entered into your accounting software with the balances in your bank account statements to make sure the numbers add up.
- Use your accounting software's tags/classes to tie expenditures to specific grants.
- Understand your financial statements, which typically include a Balance Sheet, Income Statement, and Cash Flow Statement. They might be requested by a charity's donors or the tax authorities to understand the charity's financial health and position.

Financial controls

- Implement a set of policies that controls who can spend money, how they can do so, and how the organization's finances are managed and tracked.

- Incorporate accountability measures to protect your organization's finances and staff members, as well as to show regulators and donors its professionalism.

Running a cost-effective organization means keeping costs down

- Spend only on one or two high-impact projects.
- Cut fixed costs.
- Use an activity budget.
- Start with a low salary.
- Watch out for common cost drivers.

33.3. Running a charity team

When managing, remember:

Not everyone is the same – so adjust your management style to the person. Try to accommodate your employees' preferences for task type and load, for example, and for how you communicate with each other. Remember, you can always ask!

Have a plan – don't treat planning as something you do on the side. Defining goals and outlining the path to implementation is one of your key tasks as a manager.

Don't hesitate, delegate – focus on high-level tasks (e.g., strategy, fundraising, recruitment, planning) and delegate the rest. Delegation is often possible earlier in an org's trajectory than generally assumed (e.g., through contractors).

Overcommunicate and be available – to keep your team on the same page on everything from individual tasks to overarching strategy. Communicate and then communicate again, and maybe a bit more after that. And make sure you're available to your employees (within reason, of course!).

Create a positive culture – by giving positive feedback and leading by example.

Implement coaching-style management – support your team without the need to have all the answers yourself. Also look into newer management trends including self-organization, conscious leadership, and the principles methodology.

Hire late, fire early – because your employees influence your whole org. Make sure you're certain about hires. And, hard as it is, as soon as you realize an employee isn't working out, let them go in a fair and socially adequate way.

Help staff grow – through training opportunities, online courses, and peer learning. Upskilling your employees benefits you both. And don't fear talented employees leaving: think of it as expanding your network.

Build and document processes – writing out standard operating procedures, for example, will ease onboarding and allow you space to reflect on how to improve your workflow.

Scale as a leader – different stages of your organization require different leadership styles. Starting from doing everything yourself as an early-stage start-up, you'll eventually end up delegating all but high-level tasks.

And so the learning begins...

You've read this thick book covering some of the most important content for founding a charity. But if charity entrepreneurship is the path you choose, this is just the start. You will read dozens of books and, more importantly, learn lessons through experimentation, experience, and wise advisors.

When you run a project that aims to do the most good, there's always something to improve. You won't find all the answers in this book, or anywhere else. But as you build your new organization, you will gain tools, support, and structures to get better and better at making a difference.

The challenges are great, but so are the rewards – altruistically, professionally, and personally. If you are motivated to save a stadium full of lives, there are few better ways than founding a highly effective NGO. There are so many problems still unsolved and so much good still to be done. We have an incredible opportunity to help others in ways that would have been impossible in the past.

The next step? Get connected! Effective charity entrepreneurship is a small but growing community. The CE community is here to help you launch the next generation of charities, with higher impact than those that came before. There are countless ways to contribute, from being a key volunteer, to a trusted mentor, to a co-founder of the next great charity.

charityentrepreneurship.com

What books next?

With so many great books on these subjects, you're probably wondering where to start. Here are a few of our favorites.

The Lean Startup

If I could recommend one book to help your charity progress well, it would be this. Running lean and effective is key for any new entrepreneur.

How to Measure Anything

The best book on measuring the seemingly unmeasurable. A great resource to train up your ability to gather information and make the best call.

The Life You Can Save

The book that started the journey toward charity for many on our team, it highlights both the size and importance of the difference you can make.

Principles

The structures in life and work that help you learn from mistakes, build effective teams, and accomplish your goals.

Doing Good Better

An introduction to effective altruism, the movements dedicated to making the greatest possible difference in the world.

Epic Measures

Chronicles a true entrepreneurial journey in the public health space – and shows how a small co-founding team can make a huge difference.

Getting Things Done

The canonical book on productivity and task management, it describes one of the most used productivity systems in the world today.

Worked your way through these top recommendations? Find a longer list at charityentrepreneurship.com/recommended-resources.html.

Bibliography

Aaron. "Graphology as a Personnel Selection Method." EffortlessHR. May 5, 2017. https://www.effortlesshr.com/blog/graphology-as-a-personnel-selection-method/.

Adegbuyi, Fadeke. "The Complete Guide to Deep Work." Doist. Accessed Nov. 10, 2021. https://blog.doist.com/deep-work/.

AdvisoryCloud. "The #1 Platform for Board Membership." Accessed Nov. 10, 2021. https://www.advisorycloud.com/.

Against Malaria Foundation. "Net distributions – World." Accessed Nov. 10, 2021. https://www.againstmalaria.com/Distributions.aspx.

Against Malaria Foundation. "Net Distributions." Accessed Nov. 10, 2021. https://www.againstmalaria.com/Nets.aspx.

AI Impacts. "Evidence on good forecasting practices from the Good Judgment Project: an accompanying blog post." Accessed Nov. 10, 2021. https://aiimpacts.org/evidence-on-good-forecasting-practices-from-the-good-judgment-project-an-accompanying-blog-post/.

Alexander, Scott. "Nash Equilibria and Schelling Points." LessWrong. June 28, 2012. https://www.lesswrong.com/posts/yJfBzcDL9fBHJfZ6P/nash-equilibria-and-schelling-points.

Allen, David. "gtd." Accessed Nov. 10, 2021. https://gettingthingsdone.com/.

Altman, Sam. "Startup Playbook." Accessed Nov. 10, 2021. https://playbook.samaltman.com/#execution.

Altman, Sam. Twitter Post. Jan. 23, 2018. https://twitter.com/sama/status/955900505875558400.

Anderson, David. "Guest post: Proven programs are the exception, not the rule." The GiveWell Blog. Last modified March 21, 2019. https://blog.givewell.org/2008/12/18/guest-post-proven-programs-are-the-exception-not-the-rule/.

Animal Advocacy Careers. "Effective animal advocacy nonprofit roles spot-check." Oct. 19, 2020. https://www.animaladvocacycareers.org/post/effective-animal-advocacy-nonprofit-roles-spot-check.

Berger, Alexander. "Errors in DCP2 cost-effectiveness estimate for deworming." The GiveWell Blog. Feb. 3, 2014. https://blog.givewell.org/2011/09/29/errors-in-dcp2-cost-effectiveness-estimate-for-deworming/.

Bill & Melinda Gates Foundation. "Open Access Policy FAQ." Accessed Dec. 8, 2021. https://www.gatesfoundation.org/about/policies-and-resources/open-access-policy-faq.

Bill & Melinda Gates Foundation. "Our story." Accessed Nov. 10, 2021. https://www.gatesfoundation.org/about/our-story.

BlitzResults. "Meat-Calculator to Evaluate the Environmental Impact of Meat Consumption." March 23, 2021. https://www.blitzresults.com/en/meat/.

BoardnetUSA. "Home." Accessed Nov. 10, 2021. http://www.boardnetusa.org/public/home.asp.

BoardSource. "Board Posting & Matching Programs by Region." Accessed Nov. 10, 2021. https://boardsource.org/fundamental-topics-of-nonprofit-board-service/composition-recruitment/board-recruitment/board-posting-matching/.

BoardSource. "Executive Evaluation and Compensation." Accessed Nov. 10, 2021. https://boardsource.org/fundamental-topics-of-nonprofit-board-service/executive-evaluation-compensation/.

Bock, Laszlo. "Here's Google's Secret to Hiring the Best People." Wired. April 7, 2015. https://www.wired.com/2015/04/hire-like-google/.

CAGI. "TrustLaw." International Geneva Welcome Centre. Accessed Nov. 10, 2021. https://www.cagi.ch/en/ngo/pro-bono-legal-assistance/trustlaw.php.

Calderari, Caio. "Design Resources - Growing List." Caio Calderari Medium. Aug. 3, 2018. https://calderaricaio.medium.com/growing-list-of-design-resources-67c72a5d4f56.

Callaway, Ewen. "'Randomistas' who used controlled trials to fight poverty win economics Nobel." Nature News. Oct. 14, 2019. https://www.nature.com/articles/d41586-019-03125-y.

Canva. "Canva's ultimate guide to font pairing." Accessed Nov. 10, 2021. https://www.canva.com/learn/the-ultimate-guide-to-font-pairing/.

Carey, Ryan. "How much do Y Combinator founders earn?" 80,000 Hours (blog). May 27, 2014. https://80000hours.org/2014/05/how-much-do-y-combinator-founders-earn/.

Carey, Ryan. "The payoff and probability of obtaining venture capital." 80,000 Hours (blog). June 25, 2014. https://80000hours.org/2014/06/the-payoff-and-probability-of-obtaining-venture-capital/.

CE Team. Internal "Early 2021 CEA." Google Sheets. Accessed Nov. 10, 2021.

CFCF. "Research design and evidence.svg." Sept. 2, 2015. https://commons.wikimedia.org/wiki/File:Research_design_and_evidence.svg.

Charity Entrepreneurship. "Charity Ideas." Accessed Dec. 10, 2021. https://www.charityentrepreneurship.com/charity-ideas.html

Charity Entrepreneurship. "Expert View." Accessed Nov. 10, 2021. https://www.charityentrepreneurship.com/expert-view.html.

Charity Entrepreneurship. "How Logistics Will Influence Which Intervention You Pick." April 17, 2017. https://www.charityentrepreneurship.com/blog/how-logistics-will-influence-which-intervention-you-pick.

Charity Entrepreneurship. "Is it Better to Be a Wild Rat or a Factory Farmed Cow? A Systematic Method for Comparing Animal Welfare." Sept. 17, 2018. https://www.charityentrepreneurship.com/blog/is-it-better-to-be-a-wild-rat-or-a-factory-farmed-cow-a-systematic-method-for-comparing-animal-welfare.

Charity Entrepreneurship. "Summaries on Areas we are No Longer Researching." March 14, 2016. https://www.charityentrepreneurship.com/blog/summaries-on-areas-we-are-no-longer-researching.

Charity Entrepreneurship. "The Value of Being Flexible." June 22, 2016. https://www.charityentrepreneurship.com/blog/the-value-of-being-flexible.

Charity Entrepreneurship. "What People Overvalue When Hiring." Sept. 25, 2014. https://www.charityentrepreneurship.com/blog/what-people-over-value-when-hiring.

Charity Entrepreneurship. "Why We Look at the Limiting Factor Instead of the Problem Scale." Jan. 28, 2019. https://www.charityentrepreneurship.com/blog/why-we-look-at-the-limiting-factor-instead-of-the-problem-scale.

Charity Entrepreneurship. Internal "Intervention level research questions and process poverty." Google Document. Accessed Nov. 10, 2021.

Charity Science Foundation. "Scaling Down Charity Science Outreach." Aug. 12, 2016. https://www.charityscience.com/operations-details.

Cheung, Adora. "How to Prioritize Your Time." Jotengine. Sept. 2019. https://jotengine.com/transcriptions/ZaUOX0RT9hYxYLR0K3whsQ.

Citizens Advice. "How to run focus groups." Dec. 18, 2015. https://www.citizensadvice.org.uk/Global/CitizensAdvice/Equalities/How%20to%20run%20focus%20groups%20guide.pdf.

Clark, D. "Charities in the UK - Statistics & Facts." Sept. 13, 2021. https://www.statista.com/topics/3781/charities-in-the-uk/.

Clear, James. "How to be More Productive and Eliminate Time Wasting Activities by using the 'Eisenhower Box.'" James Clear. Accessed Nov. 10, 2021. https://jamesclear.com/eisenhower-box.

Clear, James. Atomic Habits: An Easy & Proven Way to Build Good Habits & Break Bad Ones. New York City: Avery Publishing, 2018.

Conscious Leadership Group. "Ready to say no to drama? We'll show you how." Accessed Nov. 10, 2021. https://conscious.is/.

Coursera. "Positive Psychology: Resilience Skills." Accessed Nov. 10, 2021. https://www.coursera.org/learn/positive-psychology-resilience.

Dalio, Ray. *Principles: Life and Work*. New York City: Simon & Schuster, 2017.

Darwin, Charles, Frederick Burkhardt, and Sydney Smith. *The Correspondence of Charles Darwin 2*. 1st ed. Cambridge: Cambridge University Press, 1986, 1837–43.

DCP3. "Economic Evaluation Methods." Accessed Nov. 10, 2021. http://dcp-3.org/economic-evaluations.

de Maine, Bridget. "How Many Good Experiences Finally Outweigh a Bad One?" Collective Hub (blog). May 15, 2017. https://collectivehub.com/2017/05/how-many-good-experiences-finally-outweigh-a-bad-one/.

Donald, Sam. "Why We (Still) Don't Recommend Microfinance." Giving What We Can. Last modified April 15, 2018. https://www.givingwhatwecan.org/post/2014/03/why-we-still-dont-recommend-microfinance/.

Donne, John. "No Man is an Island." Meditation XVII, 1624.

Dribbble. "Discover the world's top designers and creatives." Accessed Nov. 10, 2021. https://dribbble.com/.

Duckworth, Angela. "Grit: The power of passion and perseverance." TED. May 19, 2013. https://www.ted.com/talks/angela_lee_duckworth_grit_the_power_of_passion_and_perseverance?language=en.

Duffy, Jill. "The Best To-Do List Apps for 2021." PC Mag. June 4, 2021. https://www.pcmag.com/picks/the-best-to-do-list-apps.

EA applicant. "After one year of applying for EA jobs: It is really, really hard to get hired by an EA organisation." Effective Altruism Forum. Feb. 25, 2019. https://forum.effectivealtruism.org/posts/jmbP9rwXncfa32seH/after-one-year-of-applying-for-ea-jobs-it-is-really-really.

EA Hub. "Connect and Keep Up to Date." Last updated June 8, 2021. https://resources.eahub.org/learn/connect/.

Effective Altruism Forum. "Indirect Long-Term Effects." Accessed Dec. 8, 2021. https://forum.effectivealtruism.org/tag/indirect-long-term-effects.

Effective Altruism. "The EA Newsletter." Accessed Nov. 10, 2021. https://www.effectivealtruism.org/ea-newsletter-archives/.

80,000 Hours. "Board Posting & Matching Programs by Region." Accessed Nov. 10, 2021. https://80000hours.org/job-board/.

80,000 Hours. "Our list of high-impact careers." Accessed Nov. 10, 2021. https://80000hours.org/career-reviews/#government-and-policy.

Eliason, Nathaniel. "Atomic Habits by James Clear." Accessed Nov. 10, 2021. https://www.nateliason.com/notes/atomic-habits-james-clear.

Eliason, Nathaniel. "Getting to Yes by Robert Fisher." Accessed Nov. 10, 2021. https://www.nateliason.com/notes.

Ethics Unwrapped. "Veil of Ignorance." Ethics Unwrapped Glossary, McCombs School of Business. Accessed Nov. 10, 2021. https://ethicsunwrapped.utexas.edu/glossary/veil-of-ignorance.

Farnam Street. "First Principles: The Building Blocks of True Knowledge." Farnam Street Media Inc. Accessed Nov. 10, 2021. https://fs.blog/first-principles/.

Farnam Street. "Future Babble: Why expert predictions fail and why we believe them anyway." Farnam Street Media Inc. Accessed Nov. 10, 2021. https://fs.blog/future-babble-why-expert-predictions-fail-and-why-we-believe-them-anyway/.

Farnham Street. "Daniel Pink on Incentives and the Two Types of Motivation." Farnham Street Media. Accessed Nov. 10, 2021. https://fs.blog/daniel-pink-two-types-of-motivation/.

Faye, Michael. "Metal Roofs - A Lesson from the True Poverty Experts." GiveDirectly (blog). Aug. 6, 2013. https://www.givedirectly.org/metal-roofs-a-lesson-from-the-true-poverty-experts/.

Feloni, Richard. "Google HR boss says asking these questions will instantly improve your job interviews." Business Insider. April 15, 2015. https://www.businessinsider.com/google-laszlo-bock-interview-questions-2015-4.

First Round Review. "The Indispensable Document for the Modern Manager." Accessed Nov. 10, 2021. https://review.firstround.com/the-indispensable-document-for-the-modern-manager.

Fisher, Robert. *Getting to Yes: Negotiating Agreement Without Giving In.* London: Penguin Publishing Group, 2011.

Fontjoy. "Font pairing made simple." Accessed Nov. 10, 2021. https://fontjoy.com/.

Frost, Jim. "What is the Relationship Between the Reproducibility of Experimental Results and P Values?" *Statistics By Jim.* Accessed Nov. 10, 2021. https://statisticsbyjim.com/hypothesis-testing/reproducibility-p-values/.

Galef, Julia. *The Scout Mindset: Why Some People See Things Clearly and Others Don't.* New York, NY: Portfolio, 2021.

Gallo, Carmine. "How The first 15 Minutes of Amazon's Leadership Meetings Spark Great Ideas And Better Conversations." Forbes. June 18, 2019. https://www.forbes.com/sites/carminegallo/2019/06/18/how-the-first-15-minutes-of-amazons-leadership-meetings-sparks-great-ideas-and-better-conversations/?sh=238001e54ca9.

GiveDirectly. "Financials." Last modified Sept. 20, 2021. https://www.givedirectly.org/financials/.

GiveDirectly. "Research at GiveDirectly." Accessed Nov. 10, 2021. https://www.givedirectly.org/research-at-give-directly/.

GiveWell. "Charity Science Health - Exit Grant." Dec. 2019. https://www.givewell.org/research/incubation-grants/charity-science-exit-grant-july-2019.

GiveWell. "Cost-Effectiveness." Last modified Nov. 2017. https://www.givewell.org/how-we-work/our-criteria/cost-effectiveness.

GiveWell. "Developing-world corrective surgery." 2010. https://www.givewell.org/international/health/surgery#What_is_the_bottleneck_to_more_surgeries_money_or_skilled_labor.

GiveWell. "Fortify Health - General Support (2019)." Jan. 2020. https://www.givewell.org/research/incubation-grants/fortify-health/august-2019-grant.

GiveWell. "GiveWell's Cost-Effectiveness Analyses." Last updated Sept. 2021. https://www.givewell.org/how-we-work/our-criteria/cost-effectiveness/cost-effectiveness-models.

GiveWell. "Most Charities' Evidence." Accessed Nov. 10, 2021. https://www.givewell.org/giving101/Most-Charities-Evidence.

GiveWell. "Notes from Research Conversations." Last updated Oct. 2021. givewell.org/research/conversations.

GiveWell. "Our Top Charities." Last modified Nov. 2020. https://www.givewell.org/charities/top-charities.

GiveWell. "Research on Moral Weights – 2019." 2019. https://www.givewell.org/how-we-work/our-criteria/cost-effectiveness/2019-moral-weights-research.

GiveWell. "Standard of Living in the Developing World." Accessed Nov. 10, 2021. https://www.givewell.org/international/technical/additional/Standard-of-Living.

GiveWell. "Your Dollar Goes Further Overseas." Accessed Nov. 10, 2021. https://www.givewell.org/giving101/Your-dollar-goes-further-overseas.

Giving What We Can. "What are the best charities to donate to in 2021?" Accessed Nov. 10, 2021. https://www.givingwhatwecan.org/best-charities-to-donate-to-2021/.

Glennerster, Rachel. "Module 8.3, Pre-analysis plans, Plain." Accessed Nov. 10, 2021. https://rachel-glennerster.squarespace.com/lecture-notes.

Golden, Lonnie. "The Effects of Working Time on Productivity and Firm Performance, Research Synthesis Paper." *International Labor Organization (ILO) Conditions of Work and Employment Series*, no. 33, Conditions of Work and Employment Branch (Aug. 2012). SSRN: https://ssrn.com/abstract=2149325.

Gollin, Maxwell. "How the Latest Facebook Algorithm Changes Affect Marketers." Falcon.io. May 7, 2021. https://www.falcon.io/insights-hub/industry-updates/social-media-updates/facebook-algorithm-change/.

Gooen, Ozzie. "Visual Sensitivity Analysis in Guesstimate." The Guesstimate Blog. May 17, 2016. https://medium.com/guesstimate-blog/analysis-view-with-guess-timate-4afadd87f72c.

Gordon, Kelley. "5 Principles of Visual Design in UX." Nielsen Norman Group. March 1, 2020. https://www.nngroup.com/articles/principles-visual-design/.

Graham, Paul. "Maker's Schedule, Manager's Schedule." July 2009. http://www.paulgraham.com/makersschedule.html.

Greenberg, Jason, and Ethan R. Mollick. "Sole Survivors: Solo Ventures Versus Founding Teams." Jan. 23, 2018. http://dx.doi.org/10.2139/ssrn.3107898.

Gugelev, Alice, and Andrew Stern. "What's Your Endgame?" *Stanford Social Innovation Review* (2015), https://www.philanthropy.org.au/images/site/misc/Tools__Resources/Publications/2015/Winter_2015_Whats_Your_Endgame.pdf.

Gugerty, Mary Kay, and Dean Karlan. *The Goldilocks Challenge: Right-Fit Evidence for the Social Sector.* California: OUP USA, 2018.

Happier Lives Institute. "Career Advice." Accessed Nov. 10, 2021. https://www.happierlivesinstitute.org/career-advice.html.

Happier Lives Institute. "HLI Has Hatched: Strategy Update after the Charity Entrepreneurship Incubation Program." Oct. 29, 2019. https://www.happierlives-institute.org/blog/hli-has-hatched-strategy-update-after-the-charity-entrepre-neurship-incubation-program.

Harris, Jamie. "Pre-registration: The Effects of Career Advising Calls on Expected Impact for Animals." OSF Registries. June 29, 2020. https://osf.io/pwufc.

Hassenfeld, Elie. "New Incentives update." The GiveWell Blog. Feb. 12, 2021. https://blog.givewell.org/2016/10/06/new-incentives-update/.

Heath, Dan. *Upstream: The Quest to Solve Problems Before They Happen.* New York: Avid Reader Press / Simon & Schuster, 2020.

Hemeon, Marc. "How to not suck at design, a 5 minute guide for the non-designer." Startupgrind. April 30, 2017. https://medium.com/startup-grind/how-to-not-suck-at-design-a-5-minute-guide-for-the-non-designer-291efac43037.

Hopper, Elizabeth. "Can Helping Others Help You Find Meaning in Life?" The Greater Good Science Center at UC Berkeley. Feb. 16, 2016. https://greatergood.berkeley.edu/article/item/can_helping_others_help_you_find_meaning_in_life.

Hubbard, Douglas W. *How to Measure Anything.* Hoboken, New Jersey: John Wiley & Sons, Inc., 2010.

Hubbard, Douglas. *The Failure of Risk Management.* Hoboken, NJ: Wiley, 2009.

Huff, Darrell. *How to Lie with Statistics.* California: Penguin Group, 2009.

Hunter, J.E., F.L. Schmidt, & M.K. Judiesch. "Individual differences in output variability as a function of job complexity." *Journal of Applied Psychology,* 75(1), (1990): 28-42.

Impact Opportunity. "Search Jobs." Accessed Nov. 10, 2021. https://impactopportunity.org/jobs/.

Jaffe, Andrew. "Knightian Uncertainty." *Andrew Jaffe: Leaves on the Line.* May 3, 2017. https://www.andrewjaffe.net/blog/2017/05/knightian-uncer.html.

Janzer, Cinnamon. "7 Employee Handbook Examples You Should Steal From." Workest by Zenefits. Nov. 25, 2019. https://www.zenefits.com/workest/employee-handbook-examples/.

J-PAL/CLEAR South Asia Evaluating Social Programs 2017. "Theory of Change." Course lecture, J-PAL/CLEAR South Asia at IFMR, Delhi. July 2017. https://www.povertyactionlab.org/sites/default/files/Lecture%202-THEORY%20OF%20CHANGE.pdf.

Karnofsky, Holden. "Cash transfers vs. microloans." The GiveWell Blog. Last modified April 17, 2013. https://blog.givewell.org/2013/01/04/cash-transfers-vs-microloans/.

Karnofsky, Holden. "How we evaluate a study." The GiveWell Blog. Last modified Sept. 2, 2016. https://blog.givewell.org/2012/08/23/how-we-evaluate-a-study/.

Karnofsky, Holden. "Why we can't take expected value estimates literally (even when they're unbiased)." The GiveWell Blog. July 25, 2016. https://blog.givewell.org/2011/08/18/why-we-cant-take-expected-value-estimates-literally-even-when-theyre-unbiased/.

Kestenholz, Daniel. "Minimalist Productivity System." July 12, 2019. https://danielkestenholz.org/minimalist-productivity-system/.

Kuhn, Ben. "Why and how to start a for-profit company serving emerging markets." Effective Altruism Forum. Nov. 5, 2019. https://forum.effectivealtruism.org/posts/M44rw22o5dbrRaA8F/why-and-how-to-start-a-for-profit-company-serving-emerging.

Kyd, Charley. "How to Create Monte Carlo Models and Forecasts Using Excel Data Tables." ExcelUser, Inc. Accessed Nov. 10, 2021. https://exceluser.com/1157/how-to-create-monte-carlo-models-and-forecasts-using-excel-data-tables/, for an in-depth explanation.

Lighthouse. "One on One Meeting Questions Great Managers Ask Their Teams." Accessed Nov. 10, 2021. https://getlighthouse.com/blog/one-on-one-meeting-questions-great-managers-ask/.

Ling, Dana Lee. "Introduction to Statistics using Google Sheets." Accessed Nov. 10, 2021. http://www.comfsm.fm/~dleeling/statistics/text6.html.

Lozan, Teodora. "[Study]: 101,421,493 Posts Show How To Write The Best Content On Facebook vs. Instagram vs. Twitter In 2020." Socialinsider. Nov. 14, 2019. https://www.socialinsider.io/blog/social-media-content-research/.

Masaoka, Jan. "A Board Member 'Contract.'" Blue Avocado. Oct. 9, 2009. https://blueavocado.org/board-of-directors/a-board-member-contract/.

Matias, Nathan. "Bias and Noise: Daniel Kahneman on Errors in Decision-Making." *J. Nathan Matias (Medium blog)*. Oct. 17, 2017. https://natematias.medium.com/bias-and-noise-daniel-kahneman-onerrors-in-decision-making-6bc844ff5194.

McGregor, Jena. "Companies turn to quirky interview questions - even after Google says they don't work." The Washington Post. March 29, 2016. https://www.washingtonpost.com/news/on-leadership/wp/2016/03/29/companies-turn-to-quirky-interview-questions-even-after-google-says-they-dont-work/.

Miller, Nicole. "How to Host a Meetup For Your Community: The Who, What, Where, When, and How." Buffer (blog). Dec. 11, 2014. https://buffer.com/resources/meetups/.

MITx MicroMasters Programs. "About the Program." Accessed Nov. 10, 2021. https://micromasters.mit.edu/dedp/.

Muecke, Simeon, and Anja Iseke. "How Does Job Autonomy Influence Job Performance? A Meta-Analytic Test of Theoretical Mechanisms." *Academy of Management Proceedings*, no. 1 (2019). https://doi.org/10.5465/ambpp.2019.145.

National Council of Nonprofits. "Conflicts of Interest." Accessed Nov. 10, 2021. https://www.councilofnonprofits.org/tools-resources/conflicts-of-interest.

National Council of Nonprofits. "Nonprofit Impact Matters: How America's Charitable Nonprofits Strengthen Communities and Improve Lives." Accessed Dec. 9, 2021. https://www.nonprofitimpactmatters.org/site/assets/files/1015/nonprofit-impact-matters-infographic-sept-2019.pdf.

New Incentives. "Home." Accessed Nov. 10, 2021. https://www.newincentives.org/.

Newport, Cal. *Deep Work: Rules for Focused Success in a Distracted World.* New York City: Grand Central Publishing, 2016.

NHMRC. "Homeopathy." Last modified Oct. 14, 2021. https://www.nhmrc.gov.au/about-us/resources/homeopathy.

Open Philanthropy. "History of Philanthropy." Accessed Nov. 10, 2021. https://www.openphilanthropy.org/research/history-of-philanthropy.

Open Philanthropy. "Open Philanthropy farm animal welfare research newsletter." Accessed Nov. 10, 2021. https://us14.campaign-archive.com/home/?u=66df-320da8400b581cbc1b539&id=de632a3c62.

Pink, Daniel. *Drive: The Surprising Truth About What Motivates Us.* New York City: Riverhead Books, 2011.

Putter, Bretton. "Startup due diligence begins with your cofounder(s)." Forbes. Feb. 25, 2019. https://www.forbes.com/sites/brettonputter/2019/02/25/co-foundd-startup-due-diligence-begins-with-your-cofounder/.

Ratcliffe, Susan. *Oxford Essential Quotations*. 4 ed. Oxford University Press, 2016. eISBN: 9780191826719.

Rosenberg, Marshall. *Nonviolent Communication*. California: Puddledancer Press, 2015.

S., Jonah. "Many Weak Arguments vs. One Relatively Strong Argument." Less-Wrong. June 3, 2013. https://www.lesswrong.com/posts/9W9P2snxu5Px746LD/many-weak-arguments-vs-one-relatively-strong-argument.

Sarek, Karolina. "Are you working on a research agenda? A guide to increasing the impact of your research by involving decision-makers." Effective Altruism Forum. Sept. 24, 2019. https://forum.effectivealtruism.org/posts/RZjGBH-veK7rK8GLm3/are-you-working-on-a-research-agenda-a-guide-to-increasing.

Savoie, Joey. "Empirical data on value drift." Effective Altruism Forum. April 22, 2018. https://forum.effectivealtruism.org/posts/mZWFEFpyDs3R6hD3r/empirical-data-on-value-drift.

Savoie, Joey. "How to make an impact in animal advocacy, a survey." Effective Altruism Forum. Aug. 26, 2018. https://forum.effectivealtruism.org/posts/jR2LKoXoL4Aq9T2MQ/how-to-make-an-impact-in-animal-advocacy-a-survey.

Savoie, Joey. "Setting our salary based on the world's average GDP per capita." Effective Altruism Forum. Aug. 26, 2017. https://forum.effectivealtruism.org/posts/zXLcsEbzurd39Lq5u/setting-our-salary-based-on-the-world-s-average-gdp-per.

Savoie, Joey. "The Importance of Time Capping." Charity Entrepreneurship. Dec. 16, 2018. https://www.charityentrepreneurship.com/blog/the-importance-of-time-capping.

Savoie, Joey. "Triple Counting Impact in EA." Effective Altruism Forum. May 26, 2018. https://forum.effectivealtruism.org/posts/fnBnEiwged7y5vQFf/triple-counting-impact-in-ea.

Schmidt, F., and J. Hunter. "The validity and utility of selection methods in personnel psychology: Practical and theoretical implications of 85 years of research findings." *Psychological Bulletin* 124 (1998): 262-274. https://doi.org/10.1037/0033-2909.124.2.262.

Schmidt, Frank. "The Validity and Utility of Selection Methods in Personnel Psychology: Practical and Theoretical Implications of 100 Years of Research Findings." (2016). https://www.researchgate.net/publication/309203898_The_Validity_and_Utility_of_Selection_Methods_in_Personnel_Psychology_Practical_and_Theoretical_Implications_of_100_Years_of_Research_Findings.

Schulz, Kathryn. "On being wrong." TED talk. 2011. https://www.ted.com/talks/kathryn_schulz_on_being_wrong/transcript?language=en.

Shuteyev, Paul. "Top 15 Digital Marketing Experts To Follow In 2021." Snov.io Labs (blog). Last updated Aug. 18, 2021. https://snov.io/blog/digital-marketing-gurus/.

Šimčikas, Saulius. "List of ways in which cost-effectiveness estimates can be misleading." Effective Altruism Forum. Aug. 20, 2019. https://forum.effectivealtruism.org/posts/zdAst6ezi45cChRi6/list-of-ways-in-which-cost-effectiveness-estimates-can-be.

Singal, Jesse. "Want To Know Whether A Psychology Study Will Replicate? Just Ask A Bunch Of People." Research Digest. Oct. 16, 2019. https://digest.bps.org.uk/2019/10/16/want-to-know-whether-a-psychology-study-will-replicate-just-ask-a-bunch-of-people/.

Singer, Peter. *The Life You Can Save: Acting Now to End World Poverty.* New York: Random House, 2009.

Smith, J.E., and R.L. Winkler. "The optimizer's curse: skepticism and postdecision surprise in decision analysis." *Management Science* 52, no. 3 (2006): 311-22.

Smith, Jeremy N. *Epic Measures: One Doctor. Seven Billion Patients.* New York, NY: Harper Wave, an imprint of HarperCollins Publishers, 2015.

Spector, Paul E. "Perceived Control by Employees: A Meta-Analysis of Studies Concerning Autonomy and Participation at Work." *Human Relations* 39, no. 11 (1986): 1005-1016. doi:10.1177/001872678603901104.

Stafforini, Pablo. "'Crucial Considerations and Wise Philanthropy', by Nick Bostrom." *Pablo's Miscellany.* Last updated Feb. 2, 2020. http://www.stafforini.com/blog/bostrom/.

Sunstein, C.R., and R.H. Thaler. *Nudge: Improving Decisions About Health, Wealth, and Happiness.* London: Penguin Books, Feb. 24, 2009.

Svenson, Ola. "Are We All Less Risky and More Skillful Than our Fellow Drivers?" *Acta Psychologica* 47 (1981): 143-148, https://doi.org/10.1016/0001-6918(81)90005-6.

TemplateLAB. "50 Best Model Release Forms (Free Templates)." Accessed Nov. 10, 2021. https://templatelab.com/model-release-forms/.

TermsFeed. "Setting Up Newsletters for GDPR Compliance." Dec. 23, 2020. https://www.termsfeed.com/blog/gdpr-email-newsletters/.

The Cash Learning Partnership. "The State of the World's Cash 2020." Accessed Nov. 10, 2021. https://www.calpnetwork.org/resources/collections/state-of-the-worlds-cash-2020/.

The Life You Can Save. "Newsletter Archive." Accessed Nov. 10, 2021. https://us3.campaign-archive.com/home/?u=30da440b4264260fc5f00ebc3&id=d8f0721547.

The World Bank. "Nearly Half the World Lives on Less than $5.50 a Day." World Bank Press Release. Oct. 17, 2018. https://www.worldbank.org/en/news/press-release/2018/10/17/nearly-half-the-world-lives-on-less-than-550-a-day.

Todd, Benjamin. "Career reviews: Tech startup founder." 80,000 hours. Aug. 2014. https://80000hours.org/career-reviews/tech-entrepreneurship/.

Todd, Benjamin. "Which industry has the highest paying jobs?" 80,000 Hours (blog). May 2017. https://80000hours.org/articles/highest-paying-jobs/.

Utilitarianism. "What Is Utilitarianism?" Accessed Nov. 10, 2021, https://www.utilitarianism.net/.

Vistaprint. "How to come up with a business name." Accessed Nov. 10, 2021. https://www.vistaprint.com/hub/business-name-ideas.

Whetstone, Lauren. "EA Survey 2018: Community Demographics & Characteristics." Rethink Priorities. Sept. 20, 2018. https://rethinkpriorities.org/publications/eas2018-community-demographics-and-characteristics.

Wiblin, Robert. "Most people report believing it's incredibly cheap to save lives in the developing world." 8000 Hours (blog). May 9, 2017. https://80000hours.org/2017/05/most-people-report-believing-its-incredibly-cheap-to-save-lives-in-the-developing-world/.

Wigmore, Ivy. "Inbox Zero." TechTarget. June 2014. https://whatis.techtarget.com/definition/inbox-zero.

Wikipedia. "Groupthink." Last modified Nov. 2, 2021. https://en.wikipedia.org/wiki/Groupthink.

Wikipedia. "Illusion of Control." Last modified March 20, 2021. https://en.wikipedia.org/wiki/Illusion_of_control.

Wikipedia. "Publication of Darwin's theory." Last modified June 18, 2021. https://en.wikipedia.org/wiki/Publication_of_Darwin%27s_theory.

Wikipedia. "Scope neglect." Last modified July 28, 2021. https://en.wikipedia.org/wiki/Scope_neglect.

Wildeford, Peter. "How I Am Productive." Lesswrong. Aug. 27, 2013. https://www.lesswrong.com/posts/JTHe5oGvdj6T73o4o/how-i-am-productive.

Wildeford, Peter. "Using a Spreadsheet to Make Good Decisions: Five Examples." Effective Altruism Forum. Nov. 25, 2016. https://forum.effectivealtruism.org/posts/q7s8v7LjAdcYXAyAs/using-a-spreadsheet-to-make-good-decisions-five-examples.

Wildeford, Peter. "What is the Expected Value of Creating a GiveWell Top Charity?" Effective Altruism Forum. Dec. 17, 2016. https://forum.effectivealtruism.org/posts/drRsWTctSqNRveK56/what-is-the-expected-value-of-creating-a-givewell-top.

Wix. "Pick the Website Template You Love." Accessed Nov. 10, 2021. https://www.wix.com/website/templates.

Wolfram MathWorld. "Bonferroni Correction." Accessed Nov. 10, 2021. https://mathworld.wolfram.com/BonferroniCorrection.html for a more detailed explanation of the mechanics and further resources.

Wong, May. "Stanford study finds walking improves creativity." Stanford News. April 24, 2014. https://news.stanford.edu/news/2014/april/walking-vs-sitting-042414.html.

Yakubchik, Boris. "It is Effectiveness, not Overhead that Matters." 80000 Hours (blog). Nov. 4, 2011. https://80000hours.org/2011/11/it-is-effectiveness-not-overhead-that-matters/.

Yong, Ed. "Online Bettors Can Sniff Out Weak Psychology Studies." The Atlantic. Aug. 27, 2018. https://www.theatlantic.com/science/archive/2018/08/scientists-can-collectively-sense-which-psychology-studies-are-weak/568630/.

Yutang, Lin. *The Importance of Living*. London: Duckworth, 2020.

Notes on your charity

Made in the USA
Middletown, DE
19 July 2023

34858701R00262